FEMALE CRIMINALITY

GARLAND LIBRARY OF SOCIOLOGY
(VOL. 22)

GARLAND REFERENCE LIBRARY
OF SOCIAL SCIENCE
(VOL. 796)

GARLAND LIBRARY OF SOCIOLOGY

Race and Ethnic Relations: An Annotated Bibliography, by Graham C. Kinlock

The Clinical Sociology Handbook, by Jan M. Fritz

Jewish Family Issues: A Resource Guide, by Benjamin Schlesinger

Social Support and Health: An Annotated Bibliography, by John G. Bruhn, Billy U. Philips, Paula L. Levine, and Carlos F. Mendes de Leon

The Sociology of Mental Illness: An Annotated Bibliography, by Richard K. Thomas

Dimensions of Communities: A Research Handbook, by Dan A. Chekki

The Sociology of Work: A Critical Annotated Bibliography, by Parvin Ghorayshi

The Sociology of Religion: An Organizational Bibliography, by Anthony J. Blasi and Michael W. Cuneo

The Political Economy of the Social Sciences, by Frederick H. Gareau

Substance Abuse Among American Minorities: An Annotated Bibliography, by Howard M. Rebach

Labor Market Segmentation and Its Implications: Inequity, Deprivation, and Entitlement, by Dahlia Moore

Female Criminality: The State of the Art, by Concetta C. Culliver

The Religious Roots of American Sociology, by Cecil E. Greek

American Society in the Buddhist Mirror, by Joseph B. Tamney

Organizational and Interorganizational Dynamics, by Jacob Peters and Doreen L. Smith

The Black Family in a Changing Black Community, by Richard A. Davis

FEMALE CRIMINALITY
The State of the Art

edited by
Concetta C. Culliver

GARLAND PUBLISHING, INC. • NEW YORK & LONDON
1993

Library of Congress Cataloging-in-Publication Data

Female criminality : the state of the art / Concetta C. Culliver, editor.
p. cm. — (Garland library of sociology ; v. 22) (Garland reference library of social science : v. 796)
ISBN 0–8153–0484–6
1. Female offenders—United States. 2. Women prisoners—United States. 3. Criminal justice, Administration of—United States. I. Culliver, Concetta C., 1935– . II. Series. III. Series: Garland reference library of social science ; v. 796.
HV6046.F363 1993 92-27490
364.3'74'0973—dc20 CIP

Printed on acid-free, 250-year-life paper
Manufactured in the United States of America

Contents

Preface

Writing About Female Offenders

After completing my essay "Female Criminality: The State of the Art" (for purpose of this publication, the title has been changed to "Women and Crime: An Overview") to be presented at the Mid-South Sociological Conference, I had no idea that it would culminate in this collection of essays on women and crime authored by various criminologists, sociologists, and psychologists, some renowned, and some just beginning to share their knowledge, research, and expertise regarding women offenders. It all happened when I submitted the manuscript to Dr. Dan Chekki, Sociologist and Editor, University of Winnipeg.

Feeling a sense of captivation about the manuscript, he indicated that in its present form it was suitable for journal article publication. However, he took it a step further and suggested that I consider editing a book of manuscripts concerning female offenders to be published by Garland Publishing, Inc. With his encouragement and the advice and encouragement of Dr. Freda Adler, Criminologist and pioneer writer about women offenders, I took Dr. Chekki's suggestion; hence, *Female Criminality: The State of the Art.*

Since the 1960s, much has changed about the female offender in American society, to the extent that many believe we have a new "female criminal," considering the types of crimes now committed by women offenders. However, one must be somewhat circumspect when alluding to the "new female criminal" phenomenon only in terms of crime typology; other factors need to be considered to substantiate the "new" female criminal. In years gone by, female offenders committed more crimes of a sexual nature or crimes involving shoplifting. However, for the female offender of today, it is not only prostitution and shoplifting, it is also embezzlement, fraud, forgery, larceny-theft, illegal drug involvement, assault, murder, and child abuse, among other crimes. Female offenders, in fact, have moved to center stage with their male offender counterparts, and criminologists, sociologists, psychologists, political scientists, and economists are hard pressed to study the factors that lead women to commit crime, to understand how the criminal justice system (law enforcement, courts, corrections) responds to female offenders, and to remain current about critical issues and research pertinent to the study of female criminality.

Lois West, writing for the *New York Times* about the study of women, contends that numerous theoretical and ideological schools exist to explain gender-related matters; yet, there is no consensual agreement concerning the various schools of thought explaining issues relevant to female criminality. Despite this, West concurs that matters of this nature are best discussed in university settings.

An Overview of the Book

This book or compilation of materials is designed for use in a variety of courses in criminology, criminal justice, sociology, psychology, and women's studies. Moreover, it has been created to keep researchers abreast of key issues and problems regarding the female offender. Of the three major sections into which the book is divided, Part I contains a general overview of women and crime dating back to the days of Cesare Lombroso, pioneer criminologist, who wrote about women and crime in the late nineteenth and early twentieth centuries. Subsequent paragraphs emphasize contemporary facts and information explaining the female offender in terms of prevalence and crime topology. Also considered in Part I is the apparent increase in female crime and what the trend may portend.

As the decades roll by, more researchers are joining the ranks in an effort not only to account for the types of crimes in which women are now engaging, but also to explain the reasons for their criminal behavior. Consequently, in Part II, I deemed it important to emphasize some of these newer developments.

While Joan McCord, Criminologist, Temple University, documents some issues and problems pertaining to women in general—those which could lead women to crime—Sociologist Jack Levin and Criminologist James A. Fox explore yet a newer development of female criminality—the female serial killer, an aspect of criminality that has always been perceived as a male's domain.

How the criminal justice system (police, courts, corrections) responds to female criminals is the essence of Part III. Selections include excerpts about plea bargaining, sentencing, and incarceration. Attempts are made to explain gender differences concerning arrest, sentencing, and treatment services for female offenders. Of particular interest is the essay by Renée Kasinsky, which focuses on the criminal justice system response to pregnant women drug users, now a major problem for the criminal justice system.

The Epilogue provides some projections about women and crime, as well as research and programmatic needs of the female offender by the year 2000, less than a decade away.

The book concludes with an author's corner. Here, the Biographical Sketches provide information about each contributing author.

Acknowledgments

I would like to thank all contributing authors for making this publication a reality. In addition, their willingness to contribute confirms the need for more attention to be directed toward female offenders.

A special acknowledgment and thanks are extended to Dan Chekki of the University of Winnipeg, School of Sociology, Winnipeg, Canada, who through reading my manuscript "Female Criminality: The State of the Art" saw the need for me to edit and publish a collection of essays authored by some of the best criminologists, sociologists, and psychologists researching and writing about female criminals today.

A final word of thanks goes to the Chairman of my department, Gene Garfield, who, in his own inestimable way, contributes to everything that goes on in my department. In addition, a note of appreciation is extended to the Dean of my college, Dr. John Thompson, for the encouragement rendered with regard to faculty research and publication in the College of Business and Public Affairs. Expressions of appreciation are extended to Dr. Andy Batts, Chairman of the Computer Science Department, and his assistant, Mike Jett, Murray State University, for their technical assistance; to the Garland Publishing staff for assistance and support; and to my student aide, Alene Tinsley, for her never-ending support.

PART I

An Overview and General Problems and Trends

Women and Crime: An Overview

Concetta C. Culliver
Murray State University

Introduction

Generally speaking, when we hear the words "crime" or "criminal," immediately there is a stereotypical image of a "young male offender." Crime in America has often been perceived as a young man's domain with women as victims of crime. The picture, nevertheless, has changed: women are not only victims of crime, but they are also perpetrators of crime, and criminologists, researchers, and others concerned about crime in our nation are obliged to examine the role of women in the crime process.

Female criminality is not a new phenomenon; rudiments about women's involvement in crime have historical dimensions. In the fourteenth century, for example, females were convicted of petty theft (stealing), pickpocketing, and prostitution. Also, revealing facts about female criminality were illustrated in Jones' (1980) book, *Women Who Kill.* In this case, Jones talked about female criminals who murdered their lovers or husbands in defiance of the male patriarchal society.

In the past, the crime rate among women was miniscule; consequently, the focus of criminology became the crime patterns of male offenders. Any attention directed toward female offenders, even though scant, portrayed them to be physical, emotional, or psychological aberrations. In Cesare Lombroso's 1894 book *The Female Offender*, it was shown that while women were generally passive and less criminal than men, there still existed a small group of females that was devoid of certain characteristics associated with femininity: piety, weakness, passiveness, and low intellectual status; these women were more prone to criminal behavior. Lombroso, in fact, saw these women as possessing a demeanor that resembled the male criminal or even the noncriminal man, and thus created a theory termed "the masculinity hypothesis," which assumed that females with masculine behavior accounted for the few crimes committed by women. Nevertheless, excessive body hair, wrinkles, crow's-feet, and an abnormal cranium were all characteristics that distinguished the criminal woman from the noncriminal woman. Later, the female criminal was depicted as a sexually controlling deviant who relished manipulating men for profit or even being manipulated by them. Some 50 years after Lombroso, Pollak (1950) described the female offender as a deviant creature whose criminal behavior was concealed because criminal justice officials were reluctant to arrest, convict, and punish her for crimes committed. Pollak called this the "chivalry hypothesis."

During the 1950s and 1960s, criminologists concluded that juvenile female offenders were troubled, disturbed individuals who had poor self-esteem and had experienced alienation in the home. Criminal behavior, usually sexual promiscuity, became the "escape hatch" for them to compensate for a problematic home life plagued with absent fathers, domineering and overly protective mothers, or poor parenting in general. Females (adolescent, adult) were labeled as sexual deviants if they engaged in premarital sex, and this was a prevailing theme during this period.

With the 1970s came a "changed" female criminal—one who was no longer viewed as a "sexual deviant" or as some "petty shoplifter," but one whose criminal offenses almost paralleled those of her male counterpart. Female offenders, for example, engaged in different kinds of criminal behavior that involved larceny, fraud (including welfare fraud), forgery, vagrancy, and embezzlement (Rothman & Simon 1975; Steffensmeier 1985), and even crimes of a violent nature (Mannie & Hirschel 1982). More female delinquency was noted, especially for status offending (sexual misconduct, incorrigibility, and running away from home) (Chesney-Lind 1973, 1977), or even criminal offenses that were similar to male juvenile delinquency (Hindelang 1971). Some felt that the women's movement had triggered a female crime wave (Adler 1975; Rothman & Simon, 1975). Adler (1975) and Simon (1975) argued that as women's social roles changed, so would their lifestyles change to become more like those of males, including criminal activity.

As for the 1980s, women continued to fill the ranks among the criminal offender population in American society. Although the female offender population is not as enormous as that of the male offender population, women are now committing more serious property offenses: larceny, forgery, fraud, embezzlement, and drug offenses (Allen & Simonsen 1986; U.S. Department of Justice 1988). Advocates holding a sociopolitical view suggest that the rise in female crime came as a result of the women's liberation movement of the 1960s. Some criminologists believe that the increase in female arrests can be attributed to angry police of the 1960s and 1970s who were disgruntled about affirmative action programs, thus causing an erosion of the chivalry hypothesis (Chesney-Lind 1986). Chesney-Lind further contended that differences in socialization and life experiences can lead to female criminality. Young women, for example, become truant, run away from home, and engage in petty thievery because of physical and sexual abuse experienced in the home. Barak (1986) pointed out that the courts have done very little to curtail the violence directed against young females in the home.

Using their "power-control theory" to explain female criminality, Hagan, Gillis, and Simpson (1985) stated that female crime is induced by economic factors, social class status, and family structure. Elaborating further on family structure, the researchers concluded that girls reared in families that are "father-dominated" or "paternalistic" are socialized into domesticity, causing stifled freedom and a proneness to criminal behavior. Contrary to this, the researchers found that the behavior of young girls reared in middle-class "egalitarian" families in which the power was shared equally between husband and wife, or even reared in single-family households, resembled the law-violating behavior of their brothers (Hagan, Simpson, & Gillis 1987).

In spite of the reasons or concerns about female criminality, this area lacks the necessary research to understand fully the interaction of female offenders within the criminal justice system as a whole. This essay attempts to accomplish four goals: to report facts and statistics germane to the amount and types of crime committed by female offenders; to review available literature concerning the management of female offenders by the police, the courts, and corrections; to make recommendations for future research concerning female offenders; and to suggest treatment programs for the incarcerated female offender.

Female Criminality: Prevalence and Crime Typology

Allen and Simonsen (1986) studied female crime statistics over a 5-year period (1978–1982) and indicated that the crime rate for female offenders increased by 16.2%, while the arrest rate for male offenders grew by only 12.4%. Aggravated assault was the most commonly reported offense for the female juvenile offender. In this case, there was a 5.4% increase for the juvenile female offender, whereas this same offense showed a 6.2% decrease for the juvenile male offender. As for violent crime arrests for female offenders, Allen and Simonsen reported a 20% increase, tripling the decrease shown for male violent offenders.

According to *Uniform Crime Reports* (U.S. Department of Justice 1988b), female juvenile offenders under the age of 18 are most often arrested for prostitution and the status offense of running away from home. Running away from home, a common recourse for females facing severe problems at home, reflected rates and percentages that remained constant from year to year.

Further examination of *Uniform Crime Reports* revealed significant increases for larceny-theft and motor vehicle theft for juvenile female offenders. When comparisons were made between male and female juvenile offenders for drug and liquor violations and curfew violations, significant increases were reported for female offenders.

Prostitution, an age-old crime involving the female offender, was assessed by Allen and Simonsen (1986) for the period 1978–1982. Prostitution among the juvenile female offender decreased by 5% and increased by 14% for the adult female offender.

When reviewing arrest statistics relevant to female prostitution, one must keep in mind that this is merely skimming the surface, since prostitution is a victimless crime. However, when a female is arrested for prostitution, most often it is because of flagrant solicitation, rampant disease, or a local prostitute roundup campaign by the police. Yet, female prostitution in America still centers on organized vice operating with the pimp, the madam, the landlord, the crooked vice cop, etc., all taking their cut.

Moreover, prostitution continues to be a way for women to support drug addiction (Blumstein, et al. 1986; Speekhart & Sangin 1985). In a study by Anglin and Hser (1987), criminal behavior among Anglo and Hispanic female narcotics users was examined. Results indicated that, once addicted, crimes such as burglary, robbery, forgery, theft, and prostitution became a means by which these women were able to supply themselves with heroin or cocaine. Also, repetition of the crime was contingent upon the need for narcotics. Similarly, Inciardi and Pottieger (1986) conducted a study of two groups of female heroin and cocaine addicts.

Results revealed that the heavy-user group had committed more crimes than the group of females who had used less cocaine or heroin. When File (1976) studied black and white female narcotics users, she found that these women had been arrested for a multiplicity of crimes: larceny, forgery, robbery, assault, weapons offenses, homicide, gambling, and court-related offenses. White female offenders, however, were most often arrested for drug possession and drug and liquor sales. In a similar vein, Goetting and Howser (1983) found that more women had been incarcerated for drug offenses (cocaine, heroin) and suggested that female drug involvement appears to be greater than that of male offenders.

Some researchers studied crime statistics of black women. For example, Von Hentig (1942), the first to study black female criminality, noted that black females were more apt to commit homicide and aggravated assault than white females. Other researchers reported more violent criminal behavior for the black female juvenile offender (Ageton 1983; Cernkovich & Giordano 1979; Laub & McDermott 1985; Lewis 1981).

Meanwhile, Glick and Neto (1977) examined the criminal records of female offenders (misdemeanants, felons) and found that female offenders serving 1 year or less had been convicted in the following proportions: 41% for property crimes (shoplifting, forgery, fraud); 20% for drug offenses; and 11% for violent crimes (assault, battery, armed robbery). Female felony offenders with 1 or more years were convicted as follows: 43% for violent crimes (murder, armed robbery); 29% for property crimes (forgery, fraud, larceny); and 22% for drug offenses. Female property offenders were the recidivists committing such crimes as larceny, prostitution, and drug offenses. Women who murdered were most often first-time offenders. Habitual offenders were the prostitutes, the drug offenders, and the petty thieves.

The Female Offender and the Police

A female offender's first contact with the criminal justice system is the point of arrest. However, when examining arrest data, some researchers and criminologists are reluctant to accept that arrest data are indicative of proportionate involvement in crime with respect to an offender's sex, race, or class. Quetlet (1842) was the first to argue that arrest data, by their very nature, are prone to biases that could interfere with a police officer's decision to make an arrest.

Pollak (1950), a sociologist, claimed that arrest differentials do exist within the American system of justice, and that these differentials stem from a systematic bias favoring women. He also lamented that the crimes committed by women are the least likely to be reported and the least likely to result in arrest because of systematic bias in policing. Moreover, police officers display a sense of benevolence toward female offenders; if children are at home without caretakers, then officers are even more reluctant to arrest female offenders (Chesney-Lind 1977; Frazier, Bock, & Henretta 1983). The fact that police officers tend to identify female offenders with their mothers, sisters, or daughters is another reason why police officers are reluctant to arrest female offenders, especially when the offenses are not serious (Allen & Simonsen 1986).

Police bias in favor of female offenders for all offense categories was found in the Krohn, Curry, and Nelson-Kilger (1983) study. In this case, when compared to their male counterparts, female offenders were the least likely to be referred for prosecution for felony and misdemeanor offenses. Adler (1975) remarked that "females are less likely to be arrested and, when arrested, are less likely to be convicted than males involved in exactly the same sort of crime" (p. 49).

While it has been shown that female offenders are not as likely to be arrested by the police and referred for prosecution, Simon (1975) claimed that more female offenders were being arrested by the police for property offenses. She further stated that this increase may have resulted from police officers' becoming less benevolent and chivalrous toward female offenders. Haskell and Yablonsky (1973) supported this belief and added that police officers have developed a rigid attitude toward female offenders because of women asking for equality. Status offense violations continue to be a major problem found with juvenile offenders. However, when one examines the arrest data pertaining to juveniles and status offending, it is clearly noted that more girls than boys are arrested for status offense violations such as running away from home, curfew violations, and incorrigibility (Chesney-Lind 1989). As for criminal offenses, girls are arrested most often for shoplifting (Shelden & Horvath 1986).

Commenting on the reasons for girls receiving harsher treatment from the police, Visher (1983) asserted that police officers use a harsher style of behavior with young girls as a means to deter them from committing further offenses—status or criminal. Moreover, a girl's demeanor appears to be a strong determinant when deciding to make an arrest, especially those who violate middle-class standards.

Female Criminality and the Courts

While it appears that crime patterns among women in American society are changing, the question remains: How are female offenders handled at the adjudicatory level? Some researchers believe that the female offender is accorded more leniency than male criminal offenders

(Armstrong 1977; Nagel 1969; Pollak 1950; Rothman & Simon, 1975; Steffensmeier & Kramer 1982). Others feel that female offenders are treated more harshly by the courts, especially when prior criminal history is considered or when the female offender has committed a more serious type of offense (Allen & Simonsen 1986; Foley & Rasche 1976). The preferential treatment directed toward female offenders when facing prosecution evolves from the paternalistic attitudes of prosecutors and judges who strongly believe that women are the weaker sex and should be afforded protection. With this view, prosecutors and judges tend to liken female offenders to their wives, mothers, sisters, and daughters; and if the offender is a housewife or especially a mother, the chances for incarceration are extremely slim, particularly where no serious offense has been committed.

Krohn, Curry, and Nelson-Kilger (1983) believed that the paternalistic attitudes of judges will diminish rapidly as women continue to commit more crime. Nonetheless, criminal behavior is still perceived as a male domain; so when a female commits an offense, especially a violent one, she receives a double dose of punishment. She is punished for committing the offense and punished for stepping out of her role as a woman (Bishop & Frazier 1984). In situations where male and female offenders face conviction for a similar offense, most likely the prosecutor will drop charges against the male offender and convict the female offender.

More specifically, studies have been done to assess the extent to which the female offender is dealt with at the moment of adjudication. These studies have focused primarily on how judges respond to male and female offenders during the sentencing phase. In the Foley and Rasche (1976) study, for example, it was revealed that female offenders were treated more harshly than their male counterparts. This study, however, did not control for seriousness of offense or for prior record. When these factors were used, the impact of gender on sentencing no longer was significant (Green 1961; Hagan 1974). Yet, when Nagel (1969) used "seriousness of offense" as a controlling variable, still more leniency was directed toward female offenders at the time of sentencing.

A study conducted in Los Angeles with 10,500 male and female felony offenders found judges to be more lenient with female offenders than with male offenders, especially where the female offender was nonwhite ("Judicial Leniency Toward Women Found" 1984). From this study, it also was confirmed that punishment for female offenders was not as severe in cases where women were the sole providers or caretakers of young children, for sending them to jail or prison would leave the children homeless. When certain controls were considered (seriousness of offense, prior criminal record), lenient sentencing strategies were no longer used. Even with relaxed sentencing strategies, rarely are females given the death penalty (Hagan 1987). Over 1,400 offenders have been sentenced to death; of these, only 14 were women (Allen & Simonsen, 1986). While the majority of research studies involving female offenders have entailed arrest and sentencing decisions with regard to gender differences, research on the female offender and plea negotiations appears to be a neglected arena. However, plea bargaining plays an important role in the disposition of criminal offenses. It is estimated that approximately 80% of all felony cases and 95% of all misdemeanor cases are disposed of through plea bargaining (Flanagan & McLeod 1983; Newman 1966). One study by Bernstein et al. (1977) examined the impact of gender on plea bargaining using proportionate reduction with offense severity of conviction charge, independent of the severity of the initial charge. Results of the study revealed that female offenders were dealt with more harshly because of violations concerning traditional sex-role expectations and expectations regarding normal law-abiding behavior. Another study scrutinized presentence reports of male and female offenders and found no evidence to say that female offenders were disadvantaged during plea negotiations (Bishop & Frazier 1984).

Kruttschnitt (1982) was interested in the role of probation officers and sentencing dispositions of female offenders. Her study found that female offenders received more lenient sentences when they had no previous psychiatric record, had never used drugs or alcohol, were in good standing with their employers, were economically dependent on another person, and were respectable individuals. Meanwhile, much of the gender effect pertaining to male and female offenders emerges during the presentence investigation. It is here that court probation officers' attitudes concerning female offenders, in general, are influenced by paternalism and chivalry on the basis of gender role.

Findings from a study conducted by Frazier, Brock, and Henretta (1983) contended that probation officers' presentence recommendations can have a major impact on sentencing, even to the extent of keeping a female offender from being incarcerated. More female offenders continue to receive probation, fines, and suspended sentences than male offenders. The few women who are sentenced to prison are more likely to receive consideration for early parole or other alternative dispositions. But as women continue to commit more crime, sentencing strategies will not be as lenient; women, in fact, will be sentenced more harshly since the paternalistic attitudes of judges will continue to diminish.

Upon an examination of female offenders among juvenile court populations, it appears more often than not that girls are adjudicated and incarcerated for status offenses, which include running away from home, sexual promiscuity, and incorrigibility (Black & Smith 1981; Chesney-Lind 1989; Kratcoski 1974). This action, according to Chesney-Lind (1989), is no different from the days when the juvenile court system was first established in 1899 in America: between the years 1899 and 1909, a higher percentage of girls, than boys, were committed to reformatories for immorality or waywardness.

Even with the enactment of the Juvenile Justice and the Delinquency Prevention Act of 1974 for deinstitutionalization of status offenders, juvenile court officials continue to charge and incarcerate more female status offenders. Meanwhile, officials who oppose components of the act strongly feel that it gave girls the freedom to run away from home (Office of Juvenile Justice and Delinquency Prevention 1985) and that efforts to relocate them have been seriously hampered by this legislation. In the streets, runaway girls fall prey to more serious criminal behavior—prostitution, drugs, and pornography.

In the courts, the treatment of juvenile female status offenders is of a different nature, and some researchers have explained this differential treatment in terms of "sexuality," assuming that females are sexual beings who resort to crime for sexual reasons and the offense itself does not have to be sexually related (Chesney-Lind 1989; Klein 1973; Milkman 1975). Lerner (1986) remarked that even though the conduct of female juvenile offenders is viewed in terms of a girl's sexuality, the primary emphasis is on maintaining and preserving paternalism in juvenile courts mainly for social control.

Finally, Tielmann and Landry (1981), studying gender bias in the juvenile justice system, agreed that female status offenders are disproportionally represented among the court population, and this representation has resulted from societal expectations of girls. However, when the type of offense and prior record were observed, the researchers found no gender bias on the part of the system and concluded that the role of parents in initiating the status offense arrest could have accounted for the treatment received by female status offenders in the juvenile court system.

Female Criminality and the Correctional System

Today, more than ever, female offenders are under heavy lock and key and serving time in local jails and state and federal prisons. While the precentage rate of incarcerated women is lower than that of the male incarcerated population, higher percentages of women are being committed to jails and state and federal institutions; the majority are serving time for such crimes as larceny, theft, embezzlement, forgery, fraud, drug dealing, and crimes of violence—abusing their children or murdering their husbands or boyfriends.

More specifically, according to the Bureau of Justice Statistics (cited in Newman & Anderson 1989), as of 1983, there was a total of 223,551 offenders assigned to local jails. Of these, 15,769 were adult female offenders, and 117 were female juvenile offenders. A large number of female offenders (adult, juvenile) committed to local jails are from the South. Florida and Texas incarcerate the most adult female offenders. A high percentage of female juvenile offenders are incarcerated in the state of Florida.

When Bresler and Leonard (1978) analyzed the characteristics of women jailed in San Francisco, they found the majority of these women to be white, unemployed, unskilled, mothers of young children at home, unmarried, and repeat offenders. Drugs and/or alcohol were the contributing factors to their arrests. There are fewer numbers of women jailed in rural areas. At times, one would find from two to three women jailed annually in rural jails (Minnesota Governor's Commission on Crime Prevention and Control 1977).

In 1976, according to Sullivan and Victor (1988/1989), there were about 11,000 females in state and federal prisons. By 1986, the number had risen to 26,000—a rise of 138%. The percentage of men assigned to prison had increased by 94%.

Applebome (1989) also indicated that the female prison population has increased at a faster rate than that of the male prison population. More women are serving time in prison for writing bad checks, child abuse, drug offenses, larceny, and domestic violence. Applebome found that California, Connecticut, and New York are the states showing the highest percentages of women in prison.

Glick and Neto (1977) described the typical female prison offender to be young, poor, nonwhite, unmarried, a mother, and a high school dropout. Moreover, female incarcerated offenders were shown to have a history of drug problems and were victims of physical and sexual abuse. Any work experience for these women was of short duration and involved unskilled labor employment.

Cole (1989) mentioned that female prisoners are like male prisoners: they are the "disadvantaged losers" in the American society—a society that is complicated and highly competitive. McDonough et al. (1981) characterized female offenders imprisoned in Michigan from 1968 to 1978. They found that almost 70% of the women were high school dropouts, approximately 50% of the women had been unemployed or had held unskilled jobs, 90% were from poor families, and approximately 73% of the women were nonwhite. Most of the women were caring for dependent children at the time they were admitted to prison; practically all of the women were without male companions. A few of the women had alcohol problems, and half of them used drugs. In this study, larceny and forgery were the predominant offenses for which the women were incarcerated. Regardless of the reason incarcerated, female prisoners tend to be very dependent, and this dependence is escalated by exposure to prison life.

Currently, there are 47 state correctional institutions and 13 federal prisons that house female offenders in the United States. These institutions are smaller than those for males and are classified as minimum security facilities. In these prisons, the social relationships among female prisoners has been widely researched. As in other types of prison institutions, homosexual relationships are common. However, for females in prisons, these relationships appear not to be coerced as in male correctional institutions. Female offenders, with needs similar to nonincarcerated women, want to nurture and to be nurtured. Consequently, they tend to form pseudo family relationships, adopting various roles such as father, mother, daughter, and sister. "Playing family" for these women could result from the desire to create family ties that never even existed in their lives before being incarcerated, or perhaps, it could be a woman's way of dealing with the tensions brought on by prison life. However, many incarcerated women had ties to their children that were severed by imprisonment; thus, attaching oneself to a pseudo family relationship could be a way of substituting for this loss.

Women in prison were described by Heffernan (1972) to be of three basic types: "the square," basically a noncriminal who, in a fit of anger, may have shot or stabbed her husband or boyfriend; "the life," a repeat offender who has committed such crimes as shoplifting, prostitution, drug abuse, and drug sales; and "the cool," the aloof individual who does not participate in prison activities and who is highly manipulative. The "square" presents very few problems for the correctional staff; they follow conventional values and adhere to the rules of prison life. The "life" is rebellious and rejects prison authority; these women present major problems for the prison staff.

Contemporary programs for female prisoners continue to be a missing element. The few existing programs for female prisoners tend to build on sexual stereotypes or on the aspect of "feminine role." Such programs include cosmetology, food service, housekeeping, and sewing. Educational programs for women stop at the secondary level, whereas for male offenders, it can stop with the college degree. A study conducted by editors of the *Yale Law Journal* found the following programs available in at least one of the 15 female prisons surveyed: clerical, cosmetology, dental technology, floral design, food service, garment design, housekeeping, keypunch, and nurses' aide.

Medical, nutritional, and recreational services in women's prisons are scarce. Of particular concern is the need for adequate medical care. Today, most female prisons share physicians and hospital facilities with male prisons. The use of psychotropic drugs is 10 times higher in women's prisons.

Female prisoners found support through the courts for their need for improved programs and services. In the 1979 case of *Glover* v. *Johnson*, for example, female offenders of the Detroit House of Corrections claimed that the educational and vocational programs were inferior when compared to those offered male prisoners. In this instance, the courts ruled that prison officials were obligated to improve educational and vocational services for female offenders. This decision links with a prior court case, *Barefield* v. *Leach* (1974), with regard to equal treatment for male and female offenders concerning rehabilitation opportunities.

More concern for the female offender and her children is being shown by correctional officials. Increasingly, programs are being effectuated to allow interaction between incarcerated mothers and children. In some cases, children are allowed to meet with their mothers for extended periods in playrooms and nurseries.

In summary, female criminality is an issue that can no longer be disregarded. Though still in its infancy, the study of women and crime has moved center stage, and criminologists, though baffled about the extent to which the female criminal has moved beyond sexual deviancy to criminal behavior of a more serious nature, have made it a research priority to collect in-depth information in an effort to understand more about female offenders—who are they and what led them to criminal behavior.

Furthermore, it is essential to remain current as to how the criminal justice system (police, courts, corrections) responds to female criminals. Consequently, researchers have focused attention in the areas of differential sentencing practices, the police response to women offenders, and the treatment of incarcerated women.

References

Abadinsky, H. (1987). *Crime & justice.* Chicago: Nelson-Hall.

Adler, F. (1975). *Sisters in crime: The rise of the new female criminal.* New York: McGraw-Hill.

Ageton, S.S. (1983). The dynamics of female delinquency, 1976–1980. *Criminology* 21: 555–584.

Allen, H., & Simonsen, C. (1986). *Corrections in America.* New York: Macmillan.

Anglin, M., & Hser, Y. (1987). Addicted women and crime. *Criminology* 25: 359–397.

Applebome, P. (1989). Women in U.S. prisons: Fast-rising populations. In J. Sullivan & J. Victor (eds.), *Criminal justice annual editions* (pp. 223–224). Guilford, CT: Dushkin.

Arditi, R., Goldberg, F., Jr., Hartle M., Peters, J., & Phelps, W. (1973). The sexual segregation of American prisons. *Yale Law Journal* 82: 1243–1271.

Armstrong, G. (1977). Females under the law—protected but unequal. *Crime and Delinquency* 23: 109–120.

Barak, G. (1986). Feminist connections and movement against domestic violence. *Criminal Justice Reform Journal of Crime & Justice* 9: 139–162.

Barefield v. *Leach.*, Civ. No. 10282 (D.C.N.Y. 1974).

Barnes, H., Teeter, E., & Teeter, N. (1959). *New horizons in criminology.* Englewood Cliffs, NJ: Prentice-Hall.

Bernstein, I., Kick, E., Leung, J., & Schultz, B. (1977). Charge reduction: An intermediary stage in the process of labeling criminal defendants. *Social Forces* 56: 362–384.

Bishop, D., & Frazier, C. (1984). The effects of gender in charge reduction. *Sociological Quarterly* 25(3): 385–396.

Black, T., & Smith, C. (1981). *A preliminary national assessment of the number and characteristics of juveniles processed in the juvenile court system.* Washington, DC: U.S. Government Printing Office.

Blumstein, A., Cohen, J., Roth, J., & Visher, C. (1986). *Criminal careers and career criminals* (Vols. 1 and 2). Washington, DC: National Academy Press.

Bresler, L., & Leonard, D. (1978). *Women's jail: Pretrial and post-conviction alternatives.* San Francisco: Unitarian Universalist Service Committee.

Cernkovich, S.A., & Giordano, P.C. (1979). A comparative analysis of male and female delinquency. *Sociological Quarterly* 20: 131–145.

Chesney-Lind, M. (1971). Female juvenile delinquency in Hawaii. Master's thesis, University of Hawaii. 1973 Judicial enforcement of the female sex role. *Issues in Criminology* 3: 51–71.

——— (1973). Judicial enforcement of the female sex role: The family court and the female delinquent. *Issues in Criminology* 8: 51–59.

——— (1977). Judicial paternalism and the female offender: Training women to know their place. *Crime and Delinquency* 23: 121–130.

——— (1986). Women and crime: The female offender. *Sigma: Journal of Women in Culture and Society* 12: 78–96.

——— (1989). Girl's crime and woman's place: Toward a feminist mode of female delinquency. *Crime and Delinquency* 35: 5–29.

Cole, G. (1989). *The American system of criminal justice.* Pacific Grove, CA: Brooks/Cole.

File, K. (1976). Sex roles and street roles. *International Journal of the Addictions* 11: 263–268.

Flanagan, T., & McLeod, M. (eds.) (1983). *Sourcebook of criminal justice statistics, 1982* (U.S. Department of Justice, Bureau of Justice Statistics). Washington, DC: U.S. Government Printing Office.

Foley, L., & Rasche, C. (1976). A longitudinal study of sentencing patterns for female offenders. Presented at the American Society of Criminology annual meeting, Chicago.

Frazier, C., Bock, E., & Henretta, J. (1983). The role of probation officers in determining gender differences in sentencing severity. *Sociological Quarterly* 24: 305–318.

Glick, R., & Neto, V. (1977). *National study of women's correctional programs.* Washington, DC: U.S. Department of Justice.

Glover v. *Johnson*, 478 F. Supp. 1075 (E.D. Mich. 1979).

Goetting, A., & Howser, M. (1983). Women in prison: A profile. *Prison Journal* 63: 27–46.

Green, E. (1961). *Judicial attitudes in sentencing.* New York: Macmillan.

Hagan, J. (1974). Extra-legal attributes and criminal sentencing: An assessment of a sociological viewpoint. *Law and Society Review* 8: 357–383.

Hagan, J. (1987). *Introduction to criminology.* Chicago: Nelson-Hall.

Hagan, J., Gillis, A.R., & Simpson, J. (1985). The class structure and delinquency: Toward a power control theory of common delinquent behavior. *American Journal of Sociology* 90: 1151–1178.

Hagan, J., Simpson, J., & Gillis, A.R. (1987). Class in the household: A power-control theory of gender and delinquency. *American Journal of Sociology* 92: 788–816.

Haskell, M., & Yablonsky, L. (1973). *Crime and delinquency.* Chicago: Rand-McNally.

Heffernan, E. (1972). *Making it in prison. The square, the cool, and the life.* New York: Wiley.

Henry, S. (1988). Women in prison. In J. Sullivan & J. Victor (eds.), *Criminal justice annual editions* (pp. 228–230). Guilford, CT: Dushkin.

Hindelang, M.J. (1971). Age, sex, and the versatility of delinquent involvements. *Social Problems* 18: 522–535.

Inciardi, J., & Pottieger, A. (1986). Drug use and crime among two cohorts of women narcotics users: An empirical assessment. *Journal of Drug Issues*, 14: 91–106.

Jones, A. (1980). *Women who kill.* New York: Fawcett Book Group.

Judicial leniency toward women found (1984, November 23). *Kansas City Times*, A15.

Klein, D. (1973). The etiology of female crime: A review of the literature. *Issues in Criminology* 8: 3–30.

Kratcoski, P. (1974). Differential treatment of delinquent boys and girls in juvenile court. *Child Welfare* 53: 16–22.

Krohn, M.D., Curry, J.P., & Nelson-Kilger, S. (1983). Is chivalry dead? An analysis of changes in police disposition of males and females. *Criminology* 21: 417–438.

Kruttschnitt, C. (1982). Respectable women and the law. *Sociological Quarterly* 23: 221–234.

Laub, J.H., & McDermott, M.J. (1985). An analysis of serious crime by young black women. *Criminology*, 23: 81–97.

Lerner, G. (1986). *The creation of patriarchy.* New York: Oxford.

Levine, J., Musheno, M., & Palumbo, D. (1986). *Criminal justice in America.* New York: Wiley.

Lewis, D. (1981). Black women offenders and criminal justice: Some theoretical considerations. In M. Warren (ed.), *Comparing female and male offenders* (p. 94+). Beverly Hills, CA: Sage.

Lombroso, C. (1894). *The female offender.* New York: Appleton.

McDonough, J., Iglehart, A., Sarri, R., & Williams, T. (1981). *Females in prison in Michigan, 1968–1978.* Ann Arbor: University of Michigan, Institute of Social Research.

Mannie, H., & Hirschel, J. (1982). *Fundamentals of criminology*. Albany, NY: Delmar.

Mannie, H., Hirschel, J., & Simon, R. (1975). *The contemporary women and crime*. Washington, DC: U.S. Government Printing Office.

Milkman, M. (1975). She did it all for love: A feminist view of the sociology of deviance. In M. Milkman and R.M. Kanter (eds.), *Another voice* (p. 216+). New York: Anchor Books.

Minnesota Governor's Commission on Crime, Prevention and Control (1977). A study of the local secure facilities in Minnesota. St. Paul: Author.

Nagel, S. (1969). *The legal process from a behavioral perspective*. Homewood, IL: Dorsey.

Nelson, J. (1979). Implication for the icological study of crime: A research note. In W.K. Parsonage (ed.), *Victomology*. Beverly Hills: Sage.

Newman, C. (1966). *Conviction: The determination of guilt or innocence without trial*. Boston: Little, Brown.

Newman, D., & Anderson, P. (1989). *Introduction to criminal justice*. New York: Random House.

Office of Juvenile Justice and Delinquency Prevention. (1985). *Runaway children and the juvenile justice and delinquency prevention act: What is the impact?* Washington, DC: U.S. Government Printing Office.

Pollak, O. (1950). *The criminality of women.* Philadelphia: University of Pennsylvania Press.

Quetlet, L. (1969). *A treatise on man and the development of his faculties*. (A facsmile reproduction of the English translation of 1842.) Gainesville, FL: Scholars Facsmile and Reprints.

Rothman, D., & Simon, R. (1975). Women in the courts. *Chitty's Law Journal* 23: 171–181.

Shelden, R. (1981). *Sex discrimination in the juvenile justice system. Memphis, Tennessee, 1900–1917.* In M.Q. Warren (ed.), *Comparing female and male offenders* (p. 70). Beverly Hills, CA: Sage.

Shelden, R., & Horvath, J. (1986). Processing offenders in a juvenile court: A comparison of males and females. Paper presented at the Western Society of Criminology, Newport Beach, CA.

Simon, R.J. (1975). *Women and crime.* Lexington, MA: D.C. Heath/Lexington Books.

Speekhart, G., & Sangin, M. (1985). Narcotics use and crime: An analysis of existing evidence for a causal relationship. *Behavior Science and the Law* 3: 259–283.

Spohn, C., Gruhl, J., & Welch, S. (1987). The impact on the ethnicity and gender of defendants on the decision to reject or dismiss felony charges. *Criminology* 25(1): 175–191.

Steffensmeier, D., & Kramer, J. (1982). Sex-based differences in the sentencing of adult criminal defendants. *Sociology & Social Research* 66: 289–304.

Steffensmeier, D.J., & Steffensmeier, R.H. (1980). Trends in female delinquency: An examination of arrest, juvenile court, self-report, and field data. *Criminology* 18(1): 62–85.

Sullivan, J., & Victor, J. (1988/1989). *Criminal justice annual editions.* Guilford, CT: Dushkin.

Tielmann, K., & Landry, P. (1981). Gender bias in juvenile justice. *Journal of Research in Crime and Delinquency* 18: 47–88.

U.S. Department of Justice. (1987). *Crime in the United States: Uniform crime reports—1986.* Washington, DC: U.S. Government Printing Office.

U.S. Department of Justice. (1988a). *Report to the nation on crime and justice.* Washington, DC: U.S. Government Printing Office.

U.S. Department of Justice. (1988b). *Uniform crime reports.* Washington, DC: U.S. Government Printing Office.

Visher, C.A. (1983). Gender, police arrest decisions, and notions of chivalry. *Criminology* 21: 5–28.

Von Hentig, H. (1942). *The criminality of the colored woman* (Studies Series C1). Boulder: University of Colorado, 231–260.

The Putative Problem of Female Crime

Craig J. Forsyth
Shelley B. Roberts
Robert Gramling
The University of Southwestern Louisiana

Abstract

This research analyzes the debate on female crime, both violent crimes and property crimes, from 1943 to 1989 from theoretical perspectives associated with the sociology of social problems. The data reveal a gradual increase in both violent and property crimes by females, although the increase in property crime is much more dramatic and is accounted for almost entirely by the increase in larceny. Crime data are also compared with regard to the attention being paid to female crime (as measured by scholarly publications).

Introduction

One of the more evident trends in the criminological/deviance literature in recent years has been the increased attention being devoted to female crime (Adler 1975; Adler & Simon 1979; Ageton 1983; Austin 1982; Baunach 1977; Bowker 1981; Box & Hale 1984; Bruck 1975; Cullen, Golden, & Cullen 1979; Datesman, Scarpitti & Stephenson 1975; Fox & Hartnagel 1979; Giordano, Kerbel, & Dudley 1981; Hindelang 1979; Hoffman-Bustamante 1973; James & Thornton 1980; Krohn, Curry, & Nelson-Kilger 1983; Loy & Norland 1981;

Mann 1984; Norland & Shover 1977; Pollak 1950; Rosenblatt & Greenland 1974; Shannon 1975; Shover et al. 1979; Simon 1975; Simon & Benson 1980; Smart 1977; Smith & Visher 1980; Steffensmeier 1978, 1980, 1981, 1983; Steffensmeier & Cobb 1981; Steffensmeier & Steffensmeier 1980; Visher 1983; Weis 1976).

The major debate within this literature revolves around the issue of the "new female criminal." This research examines the rhetoric surrounding that debate and then locates it within the sociology of social problems. Finally, we examine the statistics on female crime from 1943 to 1989 as compared to the attention given to it (measured by the number of publications on the topic).

The Support

In the 1970s many predicted that we were in the midst of the initial phase of a movement, proclaiming the emergence of the "new female criminal" (Adler 1975:248). It was Adler's contention that there was a criminogenic side to the liberation/emancipation of females.

> A post–World War II population explosion had discredited the once sacrosanct status of motherhood. Technology altered the necessity and social and political developments challenged the desirability of a total female commitment to homemaking. Freed by medical advances from the burden of unwanted pregnancies, encouraged by opportunities, and goaded by economic obligations, women in droves left their kitchens and carriages to take their chances in the wide world. They became soldiers, sailors, sky marshals, stevedores, doctors, lawyers, and executives. From such advantageous platforms many of them also launched careers in burglary, larceny, auto theft, forgery, counterfeiting, and embezzling. There were few activities, criminal or noncriminal, which they did not embrace with avid interest and ample ability.

Adler goes on to say what has become perhaps the most quoted statement regarding the female criminal.

> The forces behind equal employment opportunity, women's liberation movements, and even public-health problems like lung cancer and heart disease have been causing and reflecting a steady erosion of the social and psychological differences which have traditionally

> separated men and women. It would be natural to expect parallel developments in female criminality . . . [;] as the position of women approximates the position of men, so does the frequency and type of their criminal activity. It would, therefore, seem justified to predict that if present social trends continue women will be sharing with men not only ulcers, coronaries, hypertension, and lung cancer (until recently considered almost exclusively masculine diseases) but will also compete increasingly in such traditionally male criminal activities as crimes against the person, more aggressive property offenses, and especially white collar crime. As women invade the business world, there is no reason to expect them to be any more honest than men, and to the extent that crime is related to motivation and opportunity, the incidence of such white-collar offenses as embezzlement and fraud should achieve par[ity] with men. (251–252)

However, Simon (1975), another major voice in the analysis of trends in female crime, qualified Adler's blanket statement by stating that

> the increase in the proportion of arrests of women for serious crimes is due almost wholly to the fact that women seem to be committing more property offenses than they have in the past. . . . This last finding is most congruent with our major hypothesis: that women's participation in selective crimes will increase as employment opportunities expand and as [their] interests, desires, and definitions of self shift from a more traditional to a more liberated view. The crimes that are considered most salient for this hypothesis are various types of property, financial, and white-collar offenses. (39–40)

More recently, Fox and Hartnagel (1979) and Austin (1982) have given support to the general assertions of Adler and Simon.

This thesis resulted in an abundance of research on women and crime that continues to the present. The cornucopia of research has not substantiated the presence of a female crime wave or a new female criminal, but neither has it extinguished the debate.

The Opposition

While it is clear that some change has occurred in female crime, most previous research has indicated that the traditional patterns of feminine crime have remained relatively stable (Steffensmeier 1978, 1980, 1981, 1983; Steffensmeier & Cobb 1981; Steffensmeier & Steffensmeier 1980; Weis 1976). Weis (1976) calls the new female criminal an invention.

> Contrary to mass media, pop-criminological, and system agent impressions, . . . both "official" and "unofficial" data on crime among women show that the relationship between the women's movement and changes in female criminal behavior is tenuous. The tenuous nature of the relationship can be traced to theoretical progenitors, reliance on official crime statistics, logical errors of inference, and questionable interpretations of data, especially regarding the proposed causal relationship between "liberation" and crime. . . . National arrest data and self-reports of delinquent behavior show that the "new female criminal" is an invention, that the women's movement cannot be held responsible for changes in female criminal behavior which data indicate simply have not happened. (17)

Steffensmeier (1978, 1980) reached the same conclusion.

> Female arrest patterns have changed very little over the past decade. . . . [W]hatever changes have occurred appear to be due to changing law enforcement practices, market consumption trends, and the worsening economic position of many females in the U.S. rather than changing sex-roles or the improved occupational, educational, and economic position of women. (1980:1087)

> The new female criminal is more a social invention than an empirical reality. . . . [T]he proposed relationship between the women's movement and crime is, indeed, tenuous and even vacuous. Women are still typically non-violent, petty property offenders. (1978: 580)

Box and Hale (1984:484) found little in their research to support the belief that "female emancipation is generally criminogenic," and locate the stimulus for the continued debate on the putative problem of female crime with a "cozy silence of agreement rare in sociology."

This occurrence of the new female criminal is similar to the debate asserting the emergence of the new elderly criminal (Cullen, Wozniak, & Frank 1985; Forsyth & Gramling 1988; Forsyth & Shover 1986). In order to understand the debate of the issue of female criminals and other putative social problems, it is first necessary to examine the two most basic theoretical positions within the literature of social problems.

The Sociology of a Social Problem

The focus for a theory of social problems is to account for the emergence and maintenance of claims-making and responding activities. Such a theory should address the process by which a putative condition becomes a social problem (Spector & Kitsuse 1977:76). The social problem of female crime has produced two scenarios of claims-making activity to account for its emergence: the traditionalist and the constructionist accounts.

The Constructionist Argument

Basically the constructionist argument is that there has been no significant change in the activity in question, but that activities which were not previously defined as problematic, or rates of activity which were not previously defined as problematic, have been defined as a problem (*cf.* Blumer 1971; Hazelrigg 1986; Lopata 1984; Spector & Kitsuse 1977; Woolgar & Pawluch 1985).

The reasons for this redefinition are myriad and range from needs for the criminal justice bureaucracy to maintain clients (Cicourel 1976; Rains 1984), and vested interest (*cf.* Belknap 1977; Currie 1972; Dickson 1969; Embree 1977; Forsyth & Gramling 1988; Forsyth & Shover 1986; Szasz 1970) through sensationalism (Best & Horiuchi 1985), to new information (Forsyth & Olivier 1990). Whatever the reason, from the constructionist approach, the primary issue is the definition process itself, not the activity. In order to argue the constructionist approach one must show that female crime has remained relatively constant while interest and concern have increased.

Forsyth and Shover (1986) argue this approach with respect to elderly crime. They contend that the current focus on elderly crime is a product of three basic factors. The first of these factors is the vested interest of the criminal justice bureaucracy. As the baby boom cohort moved through the high-crime-committing ages (15–24), this caused an increase in the crime rate and a corresponding growth in the criminal justice bureaucracy. Once this large cohort passed the high-crime-committing years the crime rate began to fall. Bureaucracies justify their existence by the number of clients they process. Therefore, the criminal justice bureaucracy, because it was faced with a declining number of clients, began to cast about for new ones, and elderly crime was a previously untapped resource.

A second factor is the fashion by which scholarship is evaluated in most academic disciplines. The summa of academic activity has always been the scholarly publication. Thus, academics are always looking for "hot new areas" of research, where the competition is less fierce and the probability of publication greater. The criminal justice interest in elderly crime provided such an area, and scholars were quick to respond.

These two factors were exacerbated by the media. Always hungry for news, the media was all too happy to provide coverage of this new "crime wave" (Fishman 1978; Humphries 1981; Sheley & Ashkins 1981). Huge percentage increases were reported. These increases were accurate but misleading, since the numerical base was originally so low. For example, a numeric increase from two crimes to four leads to an accurate but misleading 100% increase.

The third factor, which has affected both media and scholarly attention, is the uniqueness of the juxtaposition of old age and crime, which appear almost antithetical (*cf.* Goetting 1983; Morton 1976). This is not unlike the idea that brought female criminology to our attention (*cf.* Adler 1975; Cullen, Wozniak, & Frank 1985:159–160; Morton 1976; Weis 1976). Thus Forsyth and Shover (1986) argue that elderly crime has remained relatively stable, while the increased focus has stemmed from three sources: criminal justice agencies, the mass media, and scholars.

Best and Horiuchi (1985) present another such case. Although the actual incidence of Halloween sadism (putting dangerous objects or substances in children's Halloween candy) has been so consistently low over the last 25 years that the probability of a child getting altered candy is virtually zero, the hue and cry fanned by media attention has virtually eliminated "trick or treating."

The Traditionalist Argument

The distinctive feature of the social problem argument of the traditionalist is objective conditions and causes (Woolgar & Pawluch 1985). Again using the example of elderly crime, the traditionalist argument would be that this increased attention being paid to crimes by the elderly is a reflection of significant increases in crimes committed by that group.

Documentation usually involves the significant percentage increases in elderly crime, as opposed to the constructionist argument which uses small numerical increases. Sunderland (1982:42) examined arrest data for the state of Virginia, and pointed to the problem in such reports:

> Depending upon how statistics are reported startling increases can be estracted from arrest reports. For example in my review of 32 categories in recent years in Virginia it was found that in 1975 two robbery arrests were reported of persons over 65 years of age. This increased to three in 1980.

The traditionalist argument would cite a 50% increase, the constructionist would use an undramatic numerical increase of one (Forsyth & Shover 1986).

Comparing Theoretical Approaches

Few social phenomena present themselves in pure black or white terms, and the social scientist is generally quite accustomed to working somewhere within the gray spectrum. It is quite unrealistic to expect data on crime to support totally one of the two conceptualizations presented here. Probably the most fruitful way to view the two theoretical positions is as extremes of a continuum. If the rise in attention to female crime closely parallels the rise in female crime, then our analysis would lend support to the traditionalist model. If the rise in attention to female crime greatly exceeds the increase in female crime then, our analysis would tend to support the constructionist model. It is in this gray area that most researchers locate emergent social problems. This is where Forsyth and Olivier (1990) locate the putative problem of satanic activity, and Forsyth and Gramling (1988) explain similar considerations with regard to elderly crime.

Methodology

As stated previously, our purpose here is to investigate the relationship between female crime and the attention it is receiving. The crime statistics used in this research were obtained from the Federal Bureau of Investigation's *Uniform Crime Reports* (1943–1989).[1]

To supplement and check the references on female crime that we were already familiar with, we also obtained data on the number of publications concerning female crime from a search of the Social Science Citation Index for articles on the subject of female crime (including crime, criminality, criminals). Using new references obtained, we then searched the reference section of these individual articles. We ended our search when we were no longer finding new articles to add to our list, in a computerized version of the "snowball" sample (Glaser & Strauss 1967). A problem in this method, of course, is that it is perhaps impossible to obtain a complete list of all publications on a subject. But we felt that any omissions would be distributed randomly and therefore would not bias our findings in any significant way.

Findings

Examining Figure 1, it is quite obvious that since World War II the proportion of total crimes committed by females is on the increase. In 1943, 9.7% of total crimes (9.38% of violent crimes and 9.87% of nonviolent crimes) were committed by females. By 1989, this had risen to 19.7% of total crimes (13.92% of violent crimes and 23.86% of nonviolent crimes).

Figure 1 also includes the annual percentage of total published articles and books (1943–1989) found in the procedure described above.[2] The trends appear to be similar, with "scholarly interest" paralleling incidence of crime until the early 1980s when publications began to taper off while female crime continued to rise. On the surface then the findings would seem to support the traditionalist argument. However, remember that proportions are subject to radical change with small numerical increases. Thus, the increase from the 10% range to the 20% range, while impressive on a graph with a 20+% range bounds, misses the point that over 50% of the population have increased from less than 10% of the crimes to less than 20% of the crimes. Figure 2 presents the raw data for female crime. Examining Figure 2, the fact that female crimes are still a fraction of total crimes becomes much more obvious.

Finally, the type of crime is also of importance if we are to understand the phenomenon in question. It is obvious from both Figures 1 and 2 that property crimes constitute the primary increases in female crime. Figure 3 breaks down female property crime by FBI categories (burglary, larceny, arson, and motor vehicle theft). Figure 4 breaks down female violent crime by FBI categories (murder, rape, robbery and assault). Here it is very obvious that the primary increases in female property crime are due to increases in the larceny-theft category.

The conclusions that can be drawn from these data follow:

1. Female crime is increasing, both numerically and as a percentage of total crime.
2. The primary increase in female crime is in the "property crime" category.
3. Within property crimes most of the increase can be accounted for by increases in one category; larceny-theft (larceny accounts for 88.5% of nonviolent female crime and 62.2% of all female crime).
4. Within violent crimes most of the increase is in one category, assault, which accounts for 92.3% of all violent female crime.

Figure 1
Female Crime Violent and Nonviolent

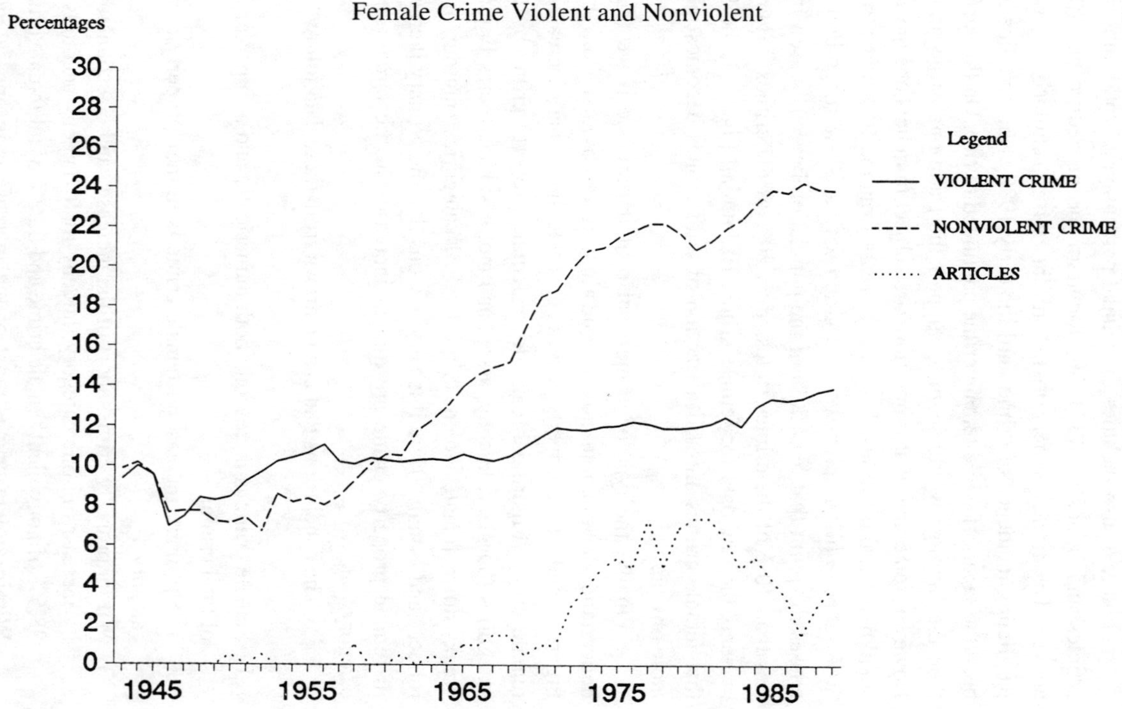

Figure 2
Female Crime and All Crimes

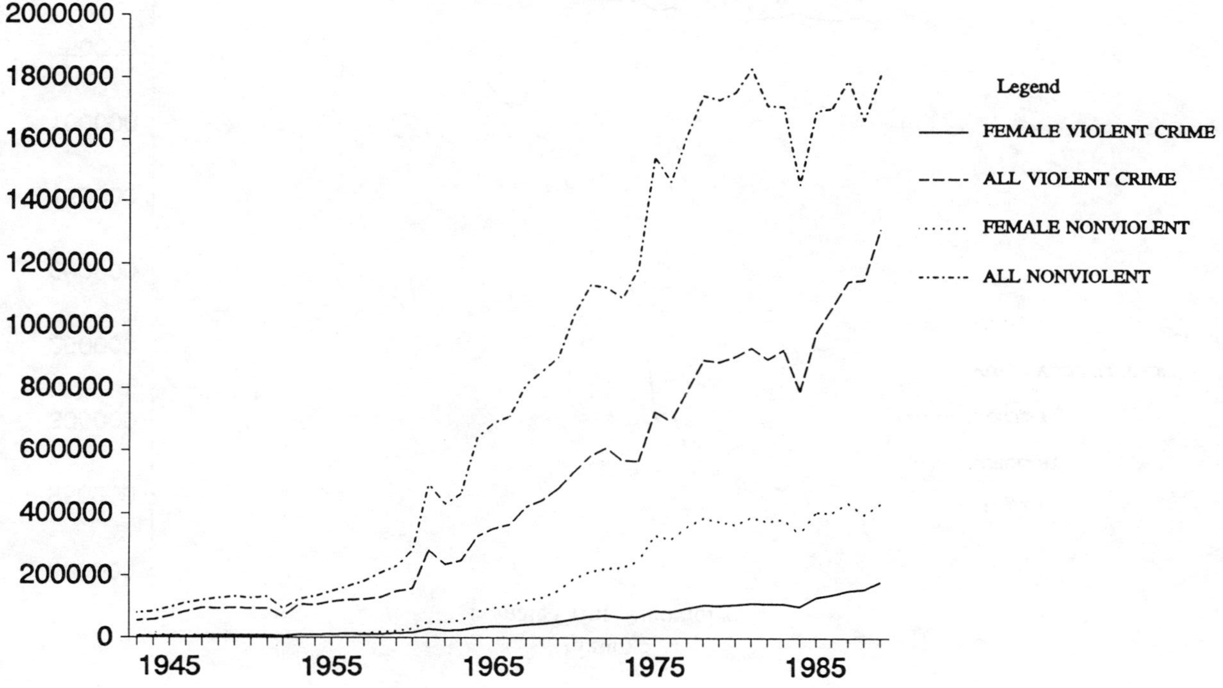

Figure 3
Female Crime Nonviolent

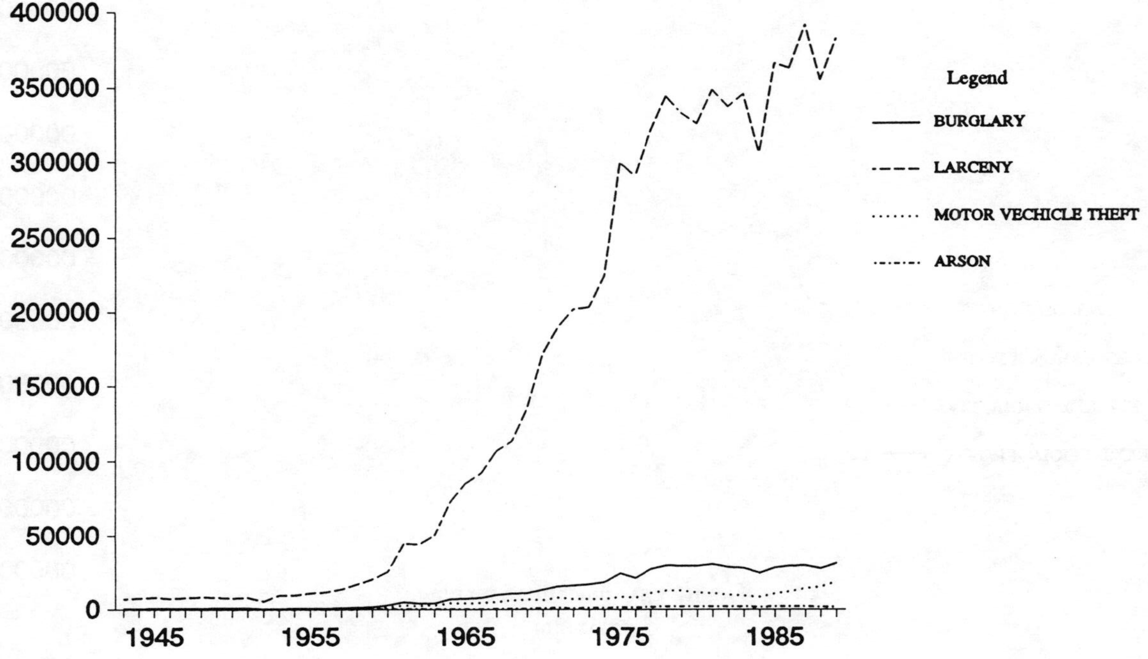

Figure 4
Female Crime Violent

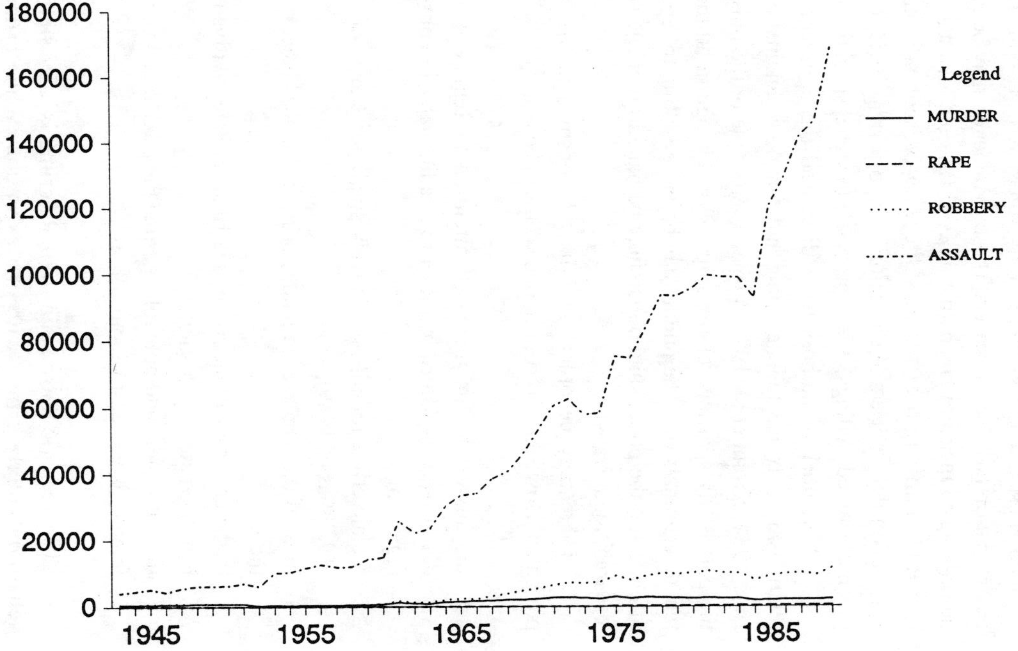

Discussion

Since World War II, the portion of total crimes committed by females has gradually increased. Since World War II, female emancipation has also increased. These two factors may be related, but attempting to measure emancipation is always tenuous and subject to question. Furthermore, there is the ever-present admonition that correlation does not equal causation. While perhaps trite, in this case given the mixed findings, it is appropriate to signal special caution.

A number of authors have discussed the apparent statistical relationship between female crime and female emancipation (Box & Hale 1984; Krohn et al. 1983; Visher 1983). One of the most noted of the potentially spurious relationships is the change in attitude toward female criminals (i.e., the public may be more willing to report female offenders to the police, and police may be handling female suspects in less traditional ways).

There may be other spurious relationships in the basic data presented. However, the bottom line seems to be that

1. the answer to the increased attention to female crime is not definitively explained by either the traditionalist or constructionist argument;
2. female crime remains a relatively small percentage of total crime (19.7% as of 1989);
3. most of the increases in female crime lie in one category (larceny-theft);
4. in the case of violent crime, nearly all female involvement again is in one category, assault;
5. in both violent and nonviolent crime the predominant category for females is the least serious offense.

The scenario surrounding female crime is very similar to the debate on elderly crime, with one exception. While crimes by the elderly represent less than 1% of total crime, crimes by females represent a larger and an increasing portion of total crime. So, while the attention to elderly crime has waned, the focus on female crime continues and has at least ambiguous support. The relationship between emancipation and crime certainly is not clear and even very questionable, but that does not mean problems related to female crime are not deserving of attention. Careful monitoring in the ensuing decades is justified.

Notes

1. The limitations of this data are that crimes cleared by arrest are the reported data. Thus, differential arrest rates due either to factors associated with being male or female or to the disproportionate types of crimes committed are potentially biasing factors. Researchers who use FBI statistics have been mindful of validity problems. Regardless of these shortcomings the FBI Uniform Crime Reports are the best official data with offender characteristics.

2. It must be noted, that *no direct comparison* can be made between the percentage of *total* articles published on the subject of female crime in a given year, and the percentage of crimes committed by females in *each* year. The data are presented on the same graph only so that some "feel" can be obtained for the relationship, and for the sake of parsimony.

References

Adler, F. (1975). *Sisters in crime: The rise of the new female criminal.* New York: McGraw-Hill.

———, & Simon, R. (1979). *The criminology of deviant women.* Boston: Houghton Mifflin.

Ageton, S.S. (1983). The dynamics of female delinquency, 1976–1980. *Criminology* 21: 555–584.

Austin, R.L. (1982). Women's liberation and increases in minor, major, and occupational offenses. *Criminology* 20: 407– 430.

Baunach, P.J. (1977). Women offenders: A commentary on current conceptions of women and crime. *Quarterly Journal of Corrections* 1: 14–18.

Belknap, M. (1977). The merchants of repression. *Crime and Social Justice* 7: 49–58.

Best, J., & Horiuchi, G.T. (1985). The razor blade in the apple: The social construction of urban legends. *Social Problems* 32: 488–499.

Blumer, H. (1971). Social problems as collective behavior. *Social Problems* 18: 298–306.

Bowker, L.H. (1981). *Women and crime in America.* New York: Macmillan.

Box, S., & Hale, C. (1984). Liberation/emancipation, economic marginalization, or less chivalry: The relevance of the three theoretical arguments to female crime patterns in England and Wales, 1951–1980. *Criminology* 22: 473–497.

Bruck, C. (1975). Women against the law. *Human Behavior* 4: 24–33.

Cicourel, A. (1976). *The social organization of juvenile justice*. New York: Wiley.

Cullen, F.T., Golden, K.M., & Cullen, J.B. (1979). Sex and delinquency: A partial test of the masculinity hypothesis. *Criminology* 17: 301–310.

———, Wozniak, J.F. & Frank, J. (1985). The rise of the elderly offender, will a "new" criminal be invented? *Crime and Social Justice* 15: 151–165.

Currie, E.P. (1972). Crimes without criminals: Witchcraft and its control in Renaissance Europe. *Law and Society Review* 6: 7–32.

Datesman, S.K., Scarpitti, F.R., & Stephenson, R. 1975. Female delinquency: An application of self and opportunity theories. *Journal of Research In Crime and Delinquency*. 12: 107–123.

Dickson, D. (1969). Bureaucracy and morality: an organizational perspective on a moral crusade. *Social Problems* 16: 143–156.

Embree, S. (1977). The state department as moral entrepreneur: Racism and imperialism as factors in the passage of the Harrison Narcotics Act. In D.F. Greenberg (ed.), *Corrections and punishment* (pp. 193–204). Beverly Hills: Sage.

Fishman, M. (1978). Crime waves as ideology. *Social Problems* 25: 531–543.

Forsyth, C., & Gramling, R. (1988). Elderly crime: Fact and artifact. In B.R. McCarthy & R. Langworthy (eds.), *Older offenders: Perspectives in criminology and criminal justice* (pp. 1–13). New York: Praeger.

Forsyth, C., & Olivier, M.D. (1990). The theoretical framing of a social problem: Some conceptual notes on satanic cults. *Deviant Behavior* 11: 281–292.

Forsyth, C., & Shover, N. (1986). No rest for the weary . . . Constructing a problem of elderly crime. *Sociological Focus* 19: 375–386.

Fox, J., & Hartnagel., T.F. (1979). Changing social roles and female crime in Canada: A time-series analysis. *Canadian Review of Sociology and Anthropology* 16: 96–104.

Giordano, P. & Cernkovich, S.A. (1979). On complicating the relationship between liberation and delinquency. *Social Problems* 26: 467–481.

Giordano, P.C., Kerbel, S. & Dudley S. (1981). The economics of female criminality: An analysis of police blotters, 1890–1975. In H. Bowker (ed.), *Women and crime in America* (pp. 65–82). New York: Macmillan.

Glaser, B.G., & Strauss, A.L. (1967). *The discovery of grounded theory: Strategies for qualitative research.* Chicago: Aldine.

Goetting, A. (1983). The elderly in prison: Issues and perspectives. *Journal of Research in Crime and Delinquency* 20: 291–309.

Hazelrigg, L.E. (1986). Is there a choice between constructionism and objectivism? *Social Problems* 33: 1–13.

Hindelang, M.J. (1979). Sex differences in criminal activity. *Social Problems* 27(2): 143–156.

Hoffman-Bustamante, D. (1973). The nature of female criminality. *Issues in Criminology* 8: 117–136.

Humphries, D. (1981). Serious crime, news coverage, and ideology: A content analysis of crime coverage in a metropolitan paper. *Crime and Delinquency* 27: 191–205.

James, J., & Thornton, W. (1980). Women's liberation and the female delinquent. *Journal of Research in Crime and Delinquency* 17: 230–244.

Krohn, M.D., Curry, J.P., & Nelson-Kilger, S. (1983). Is chivalry dead? An analysis of changes in police dispositions of males and females. *Criminology* 21: 417–438.

Lopata, H.Z. (1984). Social construction of social problems over time. *Social Problems* 31: 249–72.

Loy, P., & Norland, S. (1981). Gender convergence and delinquency. *Sociological Quarterly* 22: 275–283.

Mann, C.R. (1984). *Female crime and delinquency.* Tuscaloosa: University of Alabama Press.

Morton, J. (1976). Women offenders: Fictions and facts. *American Journal of Correction* 38: 36–37.

Norland, S., & Shover, N. (1977). Gender roles and female criminality: some critical comments. *Criminology* 15: 87–101.

Pollak, O. (1950). *The criminality of women.* Philadelphia: University of Pennsylvania Press.

Rains, P. (1984). Juvenile justice and the boys' farm: surviving a court-created population crisis, 1909–1948. *Social Problems* 31: 500–513.

Rosenblatt, E., & Greenland, C. (1974). Female crimes of violence. *Canadian Journal of Criminology and Corrections* 16: 173–180.

Shannon, R. (1975). Women in Crime: Equality on the wanted list. *Oui Magazine* 4: 50, 118, 121–122.

Sheley, J.F., & Ashkins, C.D. (1981). Crime, crime news, and crime views. *Public Opinion Quarterly* 45: 492–506.

Shover, N., Norland, S., James, J., and Thornton, W.E. (1979). Gender roles and delinquency. *Social Forces* 58: 162–175.

Simon, R.J. (1975). *Women and crime.* Lexington, MA: D.C. Heath./Lexington Books

Simon, R.J., & Benson, M. (1980). Evaluating changes in female criminality. In M.W. Klein & K.S. Leilmann (eds.) *Handbook of criminal justice evaluation* (pp. 549–571). Beverly Hills: Sage.

Smart, C. (1976). *Women, crime, and criminology: A feminist critique.* London: Routledge and Kegan Paul.

Smith, D.A., & Visher, C.A. (1980). Sex and involvement in deviance/crime: A quantitative review of the empirical literature. *American Sociological Review* 45: 691–701.

Spector, M. & Kitsuse, J. (1977). *Constructing social problems.* Menlo Park, CA: Cummings.

Steffensmeier, D.J. (1978). Crime and the contemporary woman: An analysis of changing levels of female property crime, 1960–75. *Social Forces* 57(2): 566–584.

——— (1980). Sex differences in patterns of adult crime, 1965–77: A review and assessment. *Social Forces* 58(4): 1080–1108.

——— (1981). *Patterns of female property crime, 1960–1978: A postscript.* In Lee H. Bowker (ed.), *Women and crime in America* (pp. 59–65). New York: Macmillan.

——— (1983). Organizational properties of sex-segregation in the underworld: Building a sociological theory of sex difference in crime. *Social Forces* 61: 1010–1032.

Steffensmeier, D., & Cobb, M.J. (1981). Sex differences in urban arrest patterns, 1934–79. *Social Problems* 29: 37–50.

Steffensmeier, D.H. & Steffensmeier, R.H. (1980). Trends in female delinquency: An examination of arrest, juvenile court, self-report, and field data. *Criminology* 18(1): 62–85.

Sunderland, G. (1982). Geriatric crime wave: The great debate. *The Police Chief* 49: 40, 42, 44.

Szasz, T. (1970). *The manufacture of madness.* New York: Delta.

Visher, C.A. (1983). Gender, police arrest decisions, and notions of chivalry. *Criminology* 21: 5–28.

Weis, J.G. (1976). Liberation and crime: the invention of the new female criminal. *Crime and Social Justice* 6: 17–27.

Woolgar S., & Pawluch, D. (1985). Ontological gerrymandering: The anatomy of social problems explanations. *Social Problems* 32: 214–227.

The Changing Complexion of Female Crimes: A Sex and Race Comparison, 1960–1990

Thomas J. Durant, Jr.
Louisiana State University

Introduction

This essay focuses on trends in female crimes over a three-decade period: 1960 to 1989, using arrest data obtained from the *Uniform Crime Reports* (*UCR*). National crime trends reveal a sharp rise in the overall rate of crime during the 1960s and 1970s, followed by a leveling off of the rate of crime in the 1980s. With the aim of capturing the period effects of these trends, particular attention is given to comparing female criminality of the most recent period, 1980 to 1989, with the earlier periods, 1960 to 1969 and 1970 to 1979. In order to provide a comparative frame of reference, trends in female crimes will be compared with trends in male crimes. In this way, a more complete picture of gender differences and similarities in crime trends can be obtained. In addition, this essay includes a comparison of crimes between black females and white females, based on Louisiana conviction data for 1985 and 1990. This comparison is viewed as important because very few studies have disaggregated female crimes by race.

Before going directly into the analysis, a word of caution should be made concerning limitations in the measurement of female criminality. Although these limitations are widely known among criminologists, they are briefly mentioned here because of their relevance to this analysis. First, many crimes are not reported or known by the police and are not included in the *UCR* crime statistics. Second, many property crimes, such as white-collar crimes, organized crimes, and political crimes, are not included in the *UCR*. Third, and of particular relevance to this analysis, is the fact that the *UCR* data do not record race and social class of female criminals nor do they provide the racial breakdown of female offenders. Also, the *UCR* computes crime and arrest rates on the basis of census-enumerated aggregated population figures that do not take into account intradecennial population changes that consistently undercount ethnic groups, particularly blacks (Mann 1984). A more complete review of limitations of official crime statistics in the measurement of female criminality is provided by Flowers (1987:81–83).

Sex Differences in Arrests: 1960–1989

Sex differences in criminal behavior have been well established. In general, males have historically and persistently committed the vast majority of the crimes in the United States (Christiansen & Jensen 1972; Farrington 1981; Hindelang 1971; U.S. Department of Justice 1989). Although a number of sociological, psychological, and biological theories have attempted to explain gender differences in criminal behavior, sociological explanations have received relatively more emphasis. These theories have been presented in other chapters in this book and will not be repeated here. The aim here is to determine differences in female crime trends from 1960 to 1989, especially how the latter decade in this period compares with earlier decades.

The data in Table 1 show that the percentage of females arrested of all reported arrests increased continuously from 10.8% in 1960 to 19.2% in 1989. The greatest increases occurred between 1980 and 1989 and between 1960 and 1969. These data reveal a trend toward a growing proportion of female arrests of total arrests for crimes in the United States.

Table 1
Percentage of Total Arrests by Males and females
United States 1960 to 1989

Year	Total Arrests	Percent Males	Percent Females
1960	3,323,741	89.2	10.8
1969	4,126,216	86.4	13.6
1970	5,184,125	85.6	14.4
1979	5,513,617	83.2	16.8
1980	6,652,448	84.3	15.7
1989	8,495,179	81.8	19.2

Source: Adapted from *Uniform Crime Reports*, Washington, DC: Federal Bureau of Investigation, U.S. Dept. of Justice 1960, 1969, 1970, 1979, 1980, 1989.

The data in Table 2 show that the percentage of females arrested for violent crimes increased only slightly from 10.7% in 1960 to 11.3% in 1989. These data support the conclusion that female violent crimes have remained relatively low and stable in comparison to male violent crimes. Persistently, males have been arrested for the vast majority of the violent crimes in the United States: 89.3% in 1960, and 88.7% in 1989.

The data for property crime, however, reveal quite a different trend. As shown in Table 3, thepercentage of females arrested of total arrests for property crimes increased significantly from 10.3% in 1960 to 26.9% in 1989. Thus, female arrests have accounted for an increasing share of the total arrests for property crimes over the past three decades while their arrests for violent crimes have remained relatively constant. This finding also suggests that the increase in overall female arrests can be attributed largely to the increase in female arrests for property crimes. But even with the increase in female arrests for property crimes, females continue to commit a very small proportion of the total crimes in the United States when compared to males.

Table 2
Percentage of Total Arrests for Violent Crimes by Males and Females, United States, 1960 to 1969

Year	Total/Violent	Percent Males	Percent Females
1960	99,102	89.3	10.7
1969	167,681	90.1	9.1
1970	175,886	90.3	9.7
1979	260,773	89.7	10.3
1980	316,072	90.1	9.1
1989	427,620	88.7	11.3

Source: Adapted from *Uniform Crime Reports*, Washington, DC: Federal Bureau of Investigation, U.S. Dept. of Justice 1960, 1969, 1970, 1979, 1980, 1989.

Table 3
Percentage of Total Arrests for Property Crimes by Males and Females, United States, 1960 to 1989

Year	Total/Property	Percent Males	Percent Females
1960	364,178	89.7	10.3
1969	626,560	82.9	17.1
1970	820,478	81.0	19.0
1979	1,103,276	77.1	22.9
1980	1,213,280	78.7	21.3
1989	1,439,426	73.1	26.9

Source: Adapted from *Uniform Crime Reports*, Washington, DC: Federal Bureau of Investigation, U.S. Dept. of Justice 1960, 1969, 1970, 1979, 1980, 1989.

Another method of analyzing trends in female crimes is to assess the number of females arrested for serious crimes as apercentage of all females arrested. Simon's (1975) analysis of *Uniform Crime Reports* data revealed that the percentage of females arrested for serious crimes (i.e., Type I offenses: homicide, forcible rape, aggravated assault, robbery, burglary, larceny, auto theft, and arson) increased more rapidly for females than for males between 1955 and 1970. These increases ranged from 8.5% to 23.8% for females and from 10.4% to 18.4% for males. Simon (1975) found that the increasing proportion of women arrested for serious crimes was due almost entirely to increases in their rate of property offenses. However, recent data adapted from the *UCR* reveal that the proportion of females arrested for serious crimes decreased from 30.3% in 1979 to 25.1% in 1989 (U.S. Department of Justice 1979, 1989).

In order to obtain a closer look at trends in female crimes, more detailed data on specific types of violent and property crimes are included in Tables 4, 5, and 6. These data showpercentage change in female arrests compared to male arrests for specific crimes over a three-decade period. The data in Table 4 show that the percent increase in arrests for violent crimes was higher for males than females from 1960 to 1969 but was higher for females between 1970 and 1979 and between 1980 and 1989. For each of the three periods, the percent increase in arrests of females for property crimes was over twice that for males.

From 1960 to 1969, females arrested for robbery experienced the greatest increase (+155.8%), followed by homicides (+55.5%) and aggravated assault (+37.3%). However, in the next two decades, aggravated assault increased by 59% and 64.3%, respectively; robbery increased by 74.3% and 29.4%, respectively; and homicides decreased by 1.8% from 1970 to 1979, then increased slightly by only 5.5% from 1980 to 1989 (Tables 5 and 6). During the periods 1970 to 1979 and 1980 to 1989, the percent increases in arrests for violent crimes were higher for females than males (Tables 5 and 6).

Turning to trends in females arrested for property crimes, the following rank ordering in percent change occurred from 1960 to 1969: stolen property (+263%); larceny-theft (+196%); embezzlement and fraud (+156%); auto theft (+155%); burglary (+105%); and forgery (+84%) (Table 4). From 1970 to 1979, the following rank ordering in percent change occurred for females arrested for property crimes: embezzlement and fraud (+184%); arson (+102%); stolen property

(+91%); burglary (+72%); larceny-theft (+62%); forgery (+62%); and auto theft (+54%) (Table 5). And for the period 1980 to 1989, the following rank ordering in percent change occurred for females arrested for property crimes: auto theft (+73%); stolen property (+51%); embezzlement and fraud (+34%); forgery (+32%); larceny-theft (+31%); and burglary (+19%) (Table 6). Over the period from 1969 to 1989, the rank ordering in percent change in females arrested for property crimes was as follows: embezzlement and fraud (+280%); burglary (80.9%); stolen property (+57%); larceny-theft (+36.2%); forgery (+23.2%); and auto theft (–84%).

In addition to the above trends in female arrests for violent crimes and property crimes, there are several other crimes that deserve to be mentioned. The data in Tables 4, 5, and 6 reveal substantial increases inpercentages of females arrested for narcotics and drug-related offenses, which increased by an alarming 517% between 1960 and 1969, increased by 6% between 1970 and 1979, then substantially increased by 176% between 1980 and 1989. Prostitution and driving while intoxicated also experienced sizable increases during the same three periods. The substantial increase in such offenses reflect widespread changes in social behavior, and lifestyles of young people, of which increasing numbers are females. These data also show that over the three-decade period under study, gender equity in criminal arrests increased for drug-related and property crimes. Simon (1975:42) predicts that, if present trends continue, "approximately equal numbers of men and women will be arrested for larceny and for fraud and embezzlement by the 1990's; and for forgery and counterfeiting the proportions should be equal by the 2010's." Whether this prediction will come true or not is dependent upon a number of interrelated social and behavioral changes and the rate in which these changes occur in our society. However, current trends do point in the predicted direction.

Table 4
Percentage of Total Arrests for Specific Crimes by Males and Females, United States, 1960 to 1969

	Number (1960)		Percentage Change (1960–1969)	
Crime	Males	Females	Males	Females
Total	2,963,364	360,177	20.3	56.0
Homicide	5,722	1,018	61.8	55.5
For. rape	6,862	—	56.6	—
Robbery	30,953	1,585	92.2	155.8
Agg. assault	46,698	8,195	57.0	37.3
Burglary	113,559	3,800	50.2	104.7
Larceny-theft	160,696	31,754	61.7	196.3
Auto theft	52,381	1,988	70.4	154.9
Violent crime	88,499	10,603	70.6	57.2
Property crime	326,636	37,542	59.1	184.9
Other assaults	109,336	11,843	50.3	94.6
Forgery/count.	17,187	3,342	120.8	83.9
Embezz/fraud	28,088	5,026	30.5	156.2
Stolen property	8,664	812	263.1	262.7
Weapons	29,033	1,703	114.7	159.8
Prostitution	7,452	18,181	14.2	80.1
Sex offenses	36,904	8,342	−12.2	−39.4
Narcotics	26,384	4,520	487.6	516.7
Gambling	107,640	10,659	−42.3	−48.6
Against family	33,963	3,047	−05.1	13.3
DWI	130,288	8,102	72.4	86.5
Liquor laws	68,967	12,062	65.2	41.1
Drunkenness	1,110,400	94,268	−12.8	−23.9
Disord. conduct	343,189	52,966	6.1	17.8
Vagrancy	117,840	9,479	36.9	1.6
Others	371,358	67,485	45.5	104.6

Source: Adapted from *Uniform Crime Reports,* Washington, DC: Federal Bureau of Investigation, U.S. Dept. of Justice 1960, 1969.

Table 5
Percentage of Total Arrests for Specific Crimes by Males and Females, United States, 1970 to 1979

	Number (1970)		Percent Change (1970–79)	
Crime	Males	Females	Males	Females
Total	4,440,899	743,226	3.4	24.2
Homicide	8,247	1,524	15.6	–1.8
For. rape	11,754	3	52.3	4,433.3
Robbery	56,651	3,580	36.0	74.3
Agg. assault	82,221	11,906	57.5	59.0
Burglary	212,245	10,737	25.9	71.6
Larceny-theft	350,992	138,826	40.7	61.9
Auto theft	95,284	5,329	–15.9	54.0
Arson	6,454	611	47.1	101.6
Violent crime	158,873	17,013	47.3	57.6
Property crime	664,975	155,503	27.9	62.5
Other assaults	196,384	29,220	22.4	34.9
Forgery/count.	25,077	8,366	15.5	62.4
Embezz/fraud	49,033	18,377	55.3	184.0
Stolen property	34,794	3,600	63.2	90.7
Vandalism	79,543	6,759	68.6	86.7
Weapons	73,520	5,321	22.7	41.0
Prostitution	7,662	26,771	151.7	37.6
Sex offenses	34,707	5,427	10.9	–32.8
Narcotics	211,824	42,329	28.9	5.8
Gambling	56,992	4,981	–42.3	–29.8
Against family	39,108	4,095	–45.3	–24.1
DWI	337,786	24,558	60.1	124.9
Liquor laws	151,899	22,408	23.5	48.7
Drunkenness	1,195,079	91,143	–46.3	–43.2
Disord. conduct	428,046	73,481	–6.3	6.7
Vagrancy	46,452	6,847	–66.1	–63.7
Loitering	7,169	43,649	–37.8	–36.6
Runaways	70.,434	40,880	–42.0	–21.5
Other	508,542	103,245	22.5	23.9

Source: Adapted from *Uniform Crime Reports,* Washington, DC: Federal Bureau of Investigation, U.S. Dept. of Justice 1970, 1979.

Table 6
Percent Change in Arrests for Specific Crimes by Males and Females, United States, 1980 to 1989

	Number (1980)		Percent Change (1970–89)	
Crime	Males	Females	Males	Females
Total	5,608,028	1,044,420	23.9	47.9
Homicide	11,148	1,588	11.5	5.5
For. rape	19,966	166	17.0	53.0
Robbery	95,427	7,394	6.2	29.4
Agg. assault	158,131	22,252	53.3	64.3
Burglary	313,108	21,704	–19.3	18.6
Larceny-theft	542,147	227,248	21.8	30.8
Auto theft	87,859	8,327	47.4	73.2
Arson	11,337	1,550	–13.1	2.5
Violent crime	284,672	31,400	33.3	53.0
Property crime	954,451	258,829	10.3	31.0
Other assaults	271,329	44,009	71.9	98.0
Forgery/count.	35,701	16,063	16.2	31.8
Embezz/fraud	114,441	79,706	14.7	34.0
Stolen property	77,936	9,056	32.5	50.5
Vandalism	151,996	14,391	9.6	42.0
Weapons	98,828	7,329	23.9	37.6
Prostitution	18,916	38,366	12.5	23.3
Sex offenses	41,879	2,867	40.2	69.3
Narcotics	326,050	51,125	118.0	176.4
Gambling	26,913	3,077	–59.8	–32.4
Against family	29,182	3,383	9.2	98.3
DWI	811,636	87,624	8.1	37.9
Liquor laws	244,801	44,136	25.6	63.8
Drunkenness	698,853	58,334	–33.7	–14.0
Disord. conduct	346,652	61,597	8.0	46.1
Vagrancy	19,216	2,714	3.7	1.1
Loitering	37,349	11,057	3.5	17.2
Runaways	37,811	52,703	12.6	3.3
Others	979,416	166,654	56.3	75.3

Source: Adapted from *Uniform Crime Reports,* Washington, DC: Federal Bureau of Investigation, U.S. Dept. of Justice 1980, 1989.

Black Female vs. White Female Criminality

Sex of the offender is used as a major category for the classification of crimes by the *Uniform Crime Reports*. However, the *UCR* does not provide a breakdown of female crimes by race. Likewise, very few studies on female crime provide a breakdown of their data by race. One of the results of this omission is a serious scarcity of information on black female criminality, compared to white female criminality (Laub & McDermott 1985; Lewis 1981). Thus, this area is given special attention in this section.

A number of hypotheses correlating race and sex with criminal behavior are found in the literature. One thesis is that black females are more inclined to violent crimes than white females. One of the earliest studies conducted by Von Hentig (1942) revealed that black females exhibited high rates of homicide and aggravated assault when compared to white females. This finding was also supported by Laub and McDermott (1985), Ageton (1983), Lewis (1981), and Cernkovich and Giordano (1979).

The social status inequality thesis posits that type, frequency, and pattern of criminal behavior vary with social class. In other words, lower-class black females would be expected to exhibit criminal patterns similar to those exhibited by lower-class white females (Gora 1982:60; Mulvihill, Tumin, and Curtis 1969:425; Sutherland & Cressey 1966:139–140). Others postulate differential interaction between race and sex in relationship to criminal behavior. For example, Adler (1975:138–139) postulates that "black women do exhibit behavior that is significantly different from that of white women, and criminal patterns which show more affinity for white-male than white-female deviancy." Adler also contends that "black female criminality parallels the criminality of black males more closely than the criminality of white women does that of white men," and that "the criminality of the black female . . . exceeds that of the white female by a greater margin than black males over white males." The convergence thesis, also posited by Adler (1975:134), contends that patterns of criminal behavior for black and white females are growing more similar due to decreasing social differences, the impact of common social forces upon females as a group, and females' converging paths toward liberation. This thesis was supported by Smith and Visher's (1980:698) study.

Lewis (1981:95–102) delineates a series of explanatory models which could account for differential patterns of black female criminality, including age distribution of the female population, economic deprivation, status/role equality, distinctive socialization, gender-role expectations, racism, and sexism. Laub and McDermott (1985) conducted a study with National Crime Survey victimization data on juvenile offenders, covering the period from 1973 to 1981. A number of Adler's hypotheses were tested. Their study found limited support for Adler's proposition that differences by sex in criminal behavior are greater among whites than among blacks and that differences by race are greater among females than among males. Both of the propositions were supported for violent crimes but not for property crimes or total crimes. However, the black-white female crime convergence thesis did receive support, reportedly due to substantial declines in black female offending over time while white female offending remained constant. The "masculinization hypothesis," which focuses on the convergence of crime rates between the sexes for both races, was not supported by Laub and McDermott's (1985) study.

Laub and McDermott (1985) and Lewis (1981) identified many theoretical and methodological limitations of past studies on female criminality, in general, and black female criminality, in particular. These limitations range from inadequate data and unsound theories to methodological flaws. The data used in this analysis certainly do not remove all of these limitations and can only be considered as a specific case analysis based on conviction data from the state of Louisiana. Nonetheless, the data do disaggregate female criminal convictions by race for the most recent period for which data are available, 1985 to 1990.

The Louisiana Data

The data in Table 7 show criminal convictions for black females compared to white females. The objective here is to determine if past differences in crimes between black females and white females can be supported with the use of recent Louisiana conviction data. Although most studies have used arrest data in making sex and race comparisons, their data do not provide a racial breakdown of female crimes.

As shown in Table 7, from 1985 to 1990, convictions for violent crimes for black females increased by 49.4%, compared to a decrease of 36.1% for white females. Greater increases occurred for robbery and aggravated assault among black females, while aggravated assault ranked first and robbery second for white females. Although the differences in convictions for violent crimes for black females and white females were not as great as anticipated, the volume and percent increase were much higher for black females. This is consistent with past findings based on arrest data. Although our data point to a narrowing of the gap between violent crimes between black females and white females, a more definitive conclusion must await further research based on national data.

The data in Table 7 also show that convictions for property offenses for black females increased by 36.4% compared to only 0.6% for white females. It is important to note, however, that the volume of convictions for property crimes did not differ greatly between black females and white females in 1985, but the difference was much greater in 1990. Black females experienced a greater increase in property crimes, including burglary and larency-theft than white females. Increases in convictions for white females were higher for forgery/counterfeiting and DWI. These findings support earlier results which showed that violent crimes represent only a small proportion of the total crimes committed by females.

The data in Table 7 also reflect substantial increases in convictions of females for alcohol- and drug-related crimes. However, the percent increase in narcotics convictions was higher among black females while the percent increase in convictions for DWI was higher for white females.

Table 7
Total Criminal Convictions of Black and White Females in the State of Louisiana, 1985–1990

	Black Females			White Females		
Crime	1985	1990	PC*	1985	1990	PC*
Homicide	20	24	20.0	12	10	16.7
Robbery	16	26	62.5	16	10	37.5
Agg. assault	41	65	58.5	33	19	42.4
Burglary	14	35	150.0	35	45	28.6
Larceny-theft	222	315	41.9	206	166	19.4
Violent crime	77	115	49.4	61	39	–36.1
Property crime	352	480	36.4	338	340	0.6
Forgery/count.	101	109	7.9	82	115	40.2
Stolen prop.	15	21	40.0	15	14	6.7
Prostitution	10	2	–80.0	7	5	–28.6
Against nature	9	40	–344.4	9	12	33.3
Narcotics	88	291	230.7	179	289	61.5
DWI	26	27	3.9	204	135	33.8

Source: Adapted from Louisiana Department of Corrections, Information Services, Baton Rogue, Louisiana 1991.

* PC = Percent change.

Table 8 shows the tabulations of convictions for all crimes, respectively, for black females and white females for 1985 and 1990. The data show that total convictions for black females increased from 635 to 1,058, or by 67%, compared to an increase from 894 to 899, or only a 0.6% increase, for white females. Convictions for all property crimes increased by 33% for black females, compared to a decrease by 4% for white females. Convictions for all violent crimes increased by 41% for black females, but decreased by 32% for white females. Thus, the data reveal that from 1985 to 1990, convictions for both violent crimes and property crimes increased much more among black females than among white females.

In 1990, convictions for property crimes comprised 46% of the total convictions for black females, compared to 39% for white females (Table 8). Also, convictions for violent crimes comprised 11% of the total convictions for black females, compared to 5% for white females. For both black females and white females, convictions for both property crimes and violent crimes, respectively, comprised a smallerpercentage of the total convictions in 1990 than five years earlier. This finding suggests that females were convicted for a wider variety of crimes in 1990 than in 1985.

It should be noted that these results are based on conviction data from a southern state where the arrest and conviction rates for blacks are much higher than those for whites. This is true for females as well as males. Thus, one might expect higher conviction rates for black females in part because of higher conviction rates of black females by the criminal justice system compared to white females. To the extent that racial discrimination and inequities in the administration of criminal justice account for these differences, black females would have a greater probability of arrest and conviction than white females. In addition, criminal convictions are frequently the results of plea bargaining, which is used in over 90% of all criminal convictions.

Table 8

Criminal Convictions: Total and Percent of Total For Property Crimes, Violent Crimes, and Other Crimes, for Black and White Females, State of Louisiana, 1985 and 1990

	Black Females					White Females				
	1985		1990			1985		1990		
Type	No.	%	No.	%	PC*	No.	%	No.	%	PC*
Property crimes	369	58	491	46	33	368	41	354	39	–4
Violent crimes	83	13	117	11	41	65	7	44	5	–32
Other crimes	183	28	450	43	146	461	51	501	56	9
Total	635	100	1,058	100	67	894	100	899	100	.6

Source: Adapted from Louisiana Department of Corrections, Information Services, Baton Rouge, Louisiana 1985 and 1990.

* PC = Percent change

Summary

When the larger picture of crime is viewed, the findings of this study support the findings of past studies—that is, females still commit a very smallpercentage of the total crimes; males continue to commit the vast majority of the total crimes in the United States; although the proportion of crimes committed by females has increased substantially over the past three decades, this increase can largely be attributed to the increase in female property crimes; over the past three decades, thepercentage of violent crimes committed by females has remained relatively stable; moreover, the percent increases in both property and violent crimes over the past three decades have been greater for females than for males.

Serious crimes (Type I offenses) increased substantially among females between 1960 and 1979 but thereafter began to decline as a proportion of all serious crimes. This finding suggests that the proportion of females arrested for serious crimes is leveling off as we move into the 1990s. Also, any significant changes in serious crimes committed by females will likely be affected by a disproportionate increase in female property crimes.

Violent crimes that increased the most among females include robbery and aggravated assault. Female homicides showed the greatest decrease, especially between 1970 and 1989. During the most recent period, however, the percent increase in total female arrests for violent crimes was greater than that for males. Property crimes that increased the most among females over the three-decade period include embezzlement/fraud, forgery, larceny-theft, and receiving stolen property. From 1960 to 1969, receiving stolen property, larceny-theft, embezzlement/fraud, auto theft, burglary, and forgery all experienced higher percent increases among females during the latter period, 1980 to 1989.

The findings based on Louisiana conviction data reveal that, from 1985 to 1990, both violent crimes and property crimes increased at a higher rate for black females than for white females. Greater increases occurred for robbery and aggravated assault among black females, white aggravated assault increased the most for white females, followed by robbery. Black females experienced a greater increase in convictions for burglary and larceny than white females. However, white females experienced a greater increase in convictions for forgery/counterfeiting and driving while intoxicated than black females. In 1985 and 1990 convictions for violent crimes represented a smaller proportion among white females than among black females, but declined among both groups during this period.

Both black and white females experienced substantial increases in convictions for narcotics and drug-related violations. However, the increase in narcotics convictions was higher among black females while the increase in driving while intoxicated was higher among white females. Both black females and white females experienced a smallerpercentage increase in total convictions in 1990 than in 1985. This finding suggests that both black and white females were convicted for a wider variety of crimes in 1990 than in 1985.

Although the above findings generally support the findings of past studies, it should be noted that the above findings are based on arrest data obtained from the *Uniform Crime Reports* and Louisiana conviction data. The *UCR* data are based only on arrests and do not provide a breakdown of female crimes by race. The Louisiana conviction data use only convictions and include only one state, which make generalizations risky. There is a dire need for better data for conducting research in this important area.

References

Adler, F. (1975). *Sisters in crime: The rise of the new female criminal.* New York: McGraw-Hill.

Ageton, S.S. (1983). The dynamics of female delinquency, 1976–1980. *Criminology* 21: 555–584.

Cernkovich, S.A., & Giordano, P.C. (1979). A comparative analysis of male and female delinquency. *Sociological Quarterly* 20: 131–145.

Christiansen, K., & Jensen, S. (1972). Crime in Denmark—a statistical history. *Journal of Criminal Law, Criminology and Political Science* 63: 82.

Farrington, D. (1981). The prevalence of convictions. *British Journal of Criminology* 21: 173.

Flowers, R.B. (1987). *Women and criminality: The woman as victim, offender, and practitioner*. New York: Greenwood Press.

Gora, J.G. (1982). *The new female criminal: Empirical reality or social myth?* New York: Praeger.

Hindelang, M. (1971). Age, sex, and the versatility of delinquent involvements. *Social Problems* 18: 522–535.

Laub, J.H., & McDermott, M.J. (1985). An analysis of serious crime by young black women. *Criminology* 23: 81–97.

Lewis, D.K. (1981). Black women offenders and criminal justice: Some theoretical considerations. In M. Warren (ed.), *Comparing female and male offenders*. (p. 94+). Beverly Hills, CA: Sage.

Louisiana Department of Corrections. (1991). *Criminal Convictions 1985; 1990.* Baton Rouge, LA. Division of Information Services.

Mann, C.R. (1984). *Female crime and delinquency*. Tuscaloosa: University of Alabama Press.

Mulvihill, D., Tumin, J.M., & Curtis, L. (1969). *Crimes of violence* (Vol. 12). A staff report submitted to the National Commission on the Causes and Prevention of Violence. Washington, DC: U.S. Government Printing Office.

Simon, R.J. (1975). *Women and crime*. Lexington, MA: D.C. Heath/Lexington Books.

Smith, D.A., & Visher, C.A. (1980). Sex and involvement in deviance/crime: A quantitative review of the empirical literature. *American Sociological Review* 45: 691–701.

Sutherland, E.H., & Cressey, D.R. (1966). Principles of criminology (7th ed.). Philadelphia: Lippincott.

U.S. Department of Justice. Federal Bureau of Investigation (1960). *Uniform crime reports*. Washington, DC: U.S. Government Printing Office.

——— (1969). *Uniform crime reports*. Washington, DC: U.S. Government Printing Office.

——— (1970). *Uniform crime reports*. Washington, DC: U.S. Government Printing Office.

——— (1979). *Uniform crime reports*. Washington, DC: U.S. Government Printing Office.

——— (1980). *Uniform crime reports*. Washington, DC: U.S. Government Printing Office.

——— (1989). *Uniform crime reports*. Washington, DC: U.S. Government Printing Office.

Von Hentig, H. (1942). *The criminality of the colored woman.* Studies (Series C1). Boulder: University of Colorado, 231–260.

Trends in Female Crime, 1960–1990

Darrell Steffensmeier
The Pennsylvania State University

Cathy Streifel
Purdue University

Introduction

The issue of trends in female crime continues to be the subject of a lively debate in both the popular and the scientific press. That debate has centered around two questions in particular: Has female crime been changing in recent decades and, if so, in what ways? What accounts for the changes that have occurred?[1]

There are a number of information sources on trends in female crime. We concentrate on FBI arrest statistics, the largest source of data on crime in contemporary America and the one that has been available for the longest period of time. To understand better the meaning of arrest patterns for particular crimes and the dynamics of women's roles in crime, however, we make frequent comparison to findings from other sources and from more detailed studies.

Table 1 uses FBI statistics to illustrate female/male crime differences in several ways. To simplify matters, the 27 crimes for which the FBI provides arrest data are grouped into 7 categories. The first columns in Table 1 show the female percentage (or share) of all arrests for a particular offense. The remaining columns provide profiles of male and female arrest patterns by showing the percentage of male and female arrests represented by each crime category. Those percentages are given for the two end years of 1960 and 1990. The

Table 1
Female Percentage of Arrests, and Male and Female Arrest Profiles

	Female % of Arrests			Profiles (in percentages)			
				Females		Males	
Offense	1960/62	1974/76	1988/90	1960/62	1988/90	1960/62	1988/90
Against persons							
Homicide	17	14	12	0.2	0.1	0.1	0.2
Aggravated assault	14	13	13	1.9	2.1	1.4	3.0
Weapons	4	8	7	0.5	0.7	1.0	1.7
Simple assault	10	13	15	3.5	5.1	3.8	6.1
Major Property							
Robbery	5	7	8	0.4	0.5	0.9	1.3
Burglary	3	5	8	1.1	1.6	3.9	3.9
Stolen property	8	10	11	0.2	0.7	0.3	1.2
Minor property							
Larceny-theft	17	30	30	9.4	20.2	5.6	9.6
Fraud	15	34	43	1.5	6.6	1.0	1.8
Forgery	16	28	34	1.0	1.4	0.6	0.6
Embezzlement	—	28	37	—	0.1	—	0.2
Malicious mischief							
Auto theft	4	7	9	0.6	0.7	1.8	1.4
Vandalism	—	8	10	—	1.3	—	2.3

Arson	—	11	14	—	0.1	—	0.3
Drinking/drugs							
Public Drunkenness	8	7	9	25.1	3.6	35.9	7.7
DWI	6	5	11	2.6	9.0	4.9	14.6
Liquor laws	13	14	17	3.4	4.7	2.6	4.7
Drug abuse	15	13	14	1.0	6.0	0.7	7.4
Sex/sex related							
Prostitution	73	73	65	4.3	3.4	0.2	0.4
Runaway/curfew	—	54	59				
Sex offenses	17	8	8	2.0	0.3	1.2	0.9
Disorderly conduct	13	17	18	13.7	5.8	10.7	5.4
Vagrancy	8	14	12	2.7	0.2	3.6	0.3
Suspicion	11	13	15	3.2	0.1	3.0	0.1
Miscellaneous							
Against family	8	10	16	1.0	0.4	1.3	0.5
Gambling	8	9	15	2.0	0.2	2.8	0.2
Other/nontraffic	15	15	15	18.6	19.6	12.5	22.8

embezzlement figures of 0.1 for males in 1990 and 0.2 for females mean, respectively, that only one-tenth of 1% of male arrests were for embezzlement, and only two-tenths of 1% of all female arrests were for embezzlement.

Table 2 displays female arrest rates per 100,000 and male arrest rates per 100,000 for selected crimes across the three time periods. These rates help to show the shifts in arrest patterns during the past three decades and the similarities between these shifts for both sexes. Note, for example, how both male and female arrest rates for public drunkenness have declined very sharply, while the rates for driving while intoxicated (DWI) have risen sharply.

There are considerable similarities between the male and the female profiles and in their arrest trends. For both males and females, the three most common arrest categories are DWI, larceny-theft, and other/nontraffic—a residual category that includes mostly criminal mischief, public disorder, or other minor types of crime. Together, these three offenses account for 47% of all male arrests and approximately 49% of all female arrests. Similarly, arrests for murder, arson, and embezzlement are relatively rare for males and females alike, while arrest categories such as liquor law violations (mostly underage drinking), simple assault, and disorderly conduct represent middling ranks for both sexes.

The most important gender differences in arrest profiles involve the proportionately greater involvement of women in minor property crimes (approximately 28% of all female arrests versus 12% of male arrests) and in prostitution-type offenses and the relatively greater involvement of males in crimes against persons and major property crimes (17% for males versus 11% for females). The relatively high involvement of females in minor property crimes, coupled with their low involvement in the more masculine or serious kinds of violent and property crime, is a pattern that shows in most comparisons of gender differences in crime.

Looking first at the 1990 data, except for prostitution and runaway/curfew violations (the only offenses for which female arrest rates exceed those for males), the female percentage of arrests is highest for the minor property crimes (averaging about 35%) and lowest for masculine crimes like robbery and burglary (7% to 8%).

Table 2
Male and Female Arrest Rates per 100,000
for 1960/61, 1975/76, and 1989/90

	Male Arrest Rates			Female Arrest Rates		
	1960/61	1975/76	1989/90	1960/61	1975/76	1989/90
Homicide	9	16	16	2	2	2
Ag. assault	102	200	317	16	28	50
Robbery	65	131	124	3	10	12
Burglary	274	477	320	9	27	31
Larceny	291	749	859	74	321	403
Fraud	70	114	157	12	58	132
Pub. drunkness	2,573	1,201	624	212	87	71
DWI	344	971	1,193	21	80	176
Drug violations	50	522	815	8	79	166
Gambling	202	60	14	19	6	2
Other/non traffic	871	1,140	2,109	150	197	430
Total	70,60	7,850	9,211	831	1,384	2,122

Regarding trends in the female share of offending over the previous three decades, the female percentage of arrests has increased substantially for minor property crimes—from an average of 16% in the early 1960s to 29% for the mid-1970s to 35% for 1990. Meanwhile, the percentages for most other crimes have increased much more slowly (by 1% to 3% for each period). For a number of categories, the female percentage of arrests has held steady or declined slightly, including arrests for homicide, aggravated assault, public drunkenness, and drug law violations. For all three periods, the female percentage of arrests has been high for minor property and sex-related or public order offenses that, as discussed later, involve behavior consistent with traditional female gender roles.

Other Sources of Evidence

The patterns reported for the *Uniform Crime Report* (*UCR*) data are generally consistent with data from victimization surveys like the National Crime Survey (NCS). In NCS interviews, victims are asked whether their assailants were male or female and whether they reported the crime to the police. The comparison of the NCS and *UCR* data substantiates the low female involvement in masculine types of crime. For example, according to NCS data collected in the early 1970s (when the survey was first initiated), women offenders accounted for about 7% of robberies, 8% of aggravated assaults, 15% of simple assaults, and 5% of all motor vehicle thefts reported by victims. More recent statistics from the late 1980s show almost identical percentages across these offenses.

Self-report studies of delinquency that concentrate mainly on nonserious classes of behavior often show patterns that differ somewhat from those of the *UCR*, such as higher percentages of female offending overall but lower percentages for sexual misconduct. However, when data are collected on a wide variety of both serious and nonserious law violations, and on frequency as well as prevalence of offending, self-report studies confirm the *UCR* patterns of comparatively low female involvement in serious offenses, particularly at higher frequencies, and greater involvement in the less serious categories (Elliott, Ageton, & Huzinga unpublished).

The National Youth Survey, generally recognized as the best of the self-report studies, also provides information on delinquency trends for male and female adolescents from the late 1960s to the early 1980s. The survey indicates increases in certain delinquent behaviors (e.g., alcohol and drug use) among both male and female adolescents and decreases in other delinquent behaviors (e.g., theft, assault) but stable gender differences in delinquency. After reviewing the data, Elliott, Ageton, and Huzinga (unpublished) conclude that during this time frame, the self-report data "show no significant decline in the [male-to-female] sex ratios on eight specific offenses."

The evidence also shows that female gang activity is neither much different nor more violent now in comparison to the past. Whatever change has occurred is largely a byproduct of recent immigration patterns into the United States, especially the large influx of Hispanics. As compared to other ethnic groupings, Hispanic youth gangs and drug-traffic groups more often include female co-offenders and associates. In urban areas where Hispanic migration has been heaviest (e.g., Los Angeles, New York), some observers have interpreted the Hispanic female involvement as evidence of an upsurge in female gang activity brought on by changing gender roles. This sort of confused reasoning—in this case, casting a demographic trend into an overall societal trend in female delinquency or female roles—is a fairly common practice among commentators.

Statistics on males and females incarcerated in state and federal prisons provide additional information on female crime trends. From roughly the mid-1920s to the present, the female percentage of the total prison population has held between 3 and 5 percent. The female percentage was about 5% in the 1920s, about 3% in the 1960s, and is about 5% today. As with male incarceration rates, female rates rose very sharply—more than doubled—during the 1980s. Most women in prison today are there for homicide or aggravated assault (mostly domestically related) and for drug-related offenses. Although the difference may partly reflect more lenient sentencing of female offenders, the fact that the female percentage of prisoners is considerably smaller than the female percentage of arrestees reflects the less serious nature of female crime relative to male crime. Many female arrestees have committed minor offenses that are less likely to result in imprisonment.

Finally, female involvement in professional and organized crime has not been rising and continues to lag far behind male involvement. Women continue to be hugely underrepresented in traditionally male-dominated associations that involve safecracking, fencing operations, gambling operations, and racketeering. The state of Pennsylvania's decade report on organized crime identified only a handful of women who were major players in large-scale gambling and racketeering activities (Pennsylvania Crime Commission 1991), and their involvement was a direct spinoff of association with a major male figure (i.e., daughter, spouse, or sister). The extent and nature of women's involvement in the 1980s, moreover, was comparable to that of the 1970s.

Some Cautions in Using *UCR* Arrest Statistics for Trend Comparisons

Three major problems are associated with using *UCR* data to assess trends in female crime. First, the rate of arrests, like any official measure of crime, is a function of behavior defined as criminal and the control measures established to deal with it. Because of changes in reporting practices and policing, the ability of law enforcement agencies to gather and record arrest statistics has improved greatly over time—especially since 1960. However, gauging the effect of these changes on the reporting of female crime is difficult. It is generally recognized that comparing sex differences in arrest rates over a given period of time (intersex comparison as in Table 1) is safer than using the rates either as a measure of the incidence of female crime for a specific year, or to assess changes in the levels of female crime over time, for example, to compare arrest rates of females today with those of a decade or so ago (intrasex comparison as in Table 2).

A glance at Table 2—where female arrest rates in the 1960s are compared to female rates today—certifies the considerable reliability problem that exists in within-sex comparisons. Note, for example, that female arrest rates are smaller today for offenses like public drunkenness (female rate per 100,000 dropped from 212 in 1960 to 71 in 1990) and gambling (female rate per 100,000 dropped from 19 to 2). Should we conclude from these rates that substantially less drinking and gambling are occurring among women today? Observed arrest patterns such as these help explain why we (and most researchers) focus on *gender differences* in arrest rates. Nonetheless, using the *UCR* arrest data to make between-sex comparisons over time has some risks that are described later.

A second problem with the *UCR* data is that the offense categories are *broad* and are derived from a heterogeneous collection of criminal acts. For example, the offense category of larceny-theft includes shoplifting a $10.00 item, theft of a radio from a parked auto, theft of merchandise by an employee, and cargo theft amounting to thousands of dollars. The broad offense category of fraud includes passing bad checks of small amounts to stock frauds involving large sums of money. Burglary includes unlawful entry into a neighbor's apartment to steal a television to safecracking. Arrests are not distinguished in terms of whether the suspect is the sole or major perpetrator, an accomplice, or a bystander. In sum, offenses representing dissimilar events and covering a range of seriousness are included in the same category. The *UCR* arrest data do not permit an assessment of variation *within* offense categories. We will be returning to this crucial point frequently throughout our discussion.

A third problem concerns the label "serious crime" that is used in the *UCR* to refer to the Index or Type I offenses—homicide, forcible rape, aggravated assault, robbery, burglary, larceny-theft, auto theft, and arson. It sometimes is claimed that the proportion of women arrested for serious crimes has been increasing dramatically and that the increase has been greater among females than males. On closer inspection, however, we find that the increased arrest of women for serious or index crimes is almost entirely due to more women being arrested for larceny, especially for shoplifting. However, neither law enforcement nor the citizenry view larceny as a comparably serious crime.

Social and Legal Forces Shape Both Male Criminality and Female Criminality

An important point about the movement of female arrest rates over the past several decades is its parallel of the movement of male arrest rates (see Table 2). For both males and females, arrest rates increased for some offense categories, decreased for others, and held stable for still others. This suggests that the rates of both sexes are influenced by similar social and legal forces, independent of any condition unique to women.

That the factors contributing to criminality are generally the same for females as for males is supported by other evidence. Societies and subgroups within a society that have high male rates also have high female rates, whereas groups or societies that have low male rates also have low female rates. Also, research on arrest and prisoner populations establishes that female offenders tend to be of low socioeconomic status, poorly educated, under- or unemployed, and disproportionately from minority groups, and they often have dependents who rely on them for economic support. Female offenders have a social profile similar to that of their male counterparts, with one exception—the much greater presence of dependent children among female offenders. As is true for male crime and delinquency, female offending is attributable to normal learning processes, desire for peer acceptance, search for excitement, economic pressures, lack of sufficient stakes in conformity, and availability of illicit opportunities.

However, because their social situations typically include greater constraints on delinquent behavior, women may need a higher level of provocation before turning to crime, especially serious crime. Crime is more stigmatizing for females, both in terms of self-labeling and audience-labeling, so that females who choose criminality must traverse a greater moral and psychological distance than similarly situated males.

Factors Contributing to Gender Differences in Crime

The greater taboos against female crime and deviance that have pervaded all societies throughout history seem rooted in two powerful focal concerns: (a) female beauty/sexual virtue and (b) nurturant role obligations. These very different goals in life demand more consistent conformity than do male goals, and the gender norms and opportunities attendant upon them do much to explain gender differences in crime.

Reasons for the less extensive involvement of women in crime include their socialization for domestic roles, the masculine image of most criminal enterprises, familial responsibilities, and societal norms about the proper role of the female. Women are linked more intimately into networks of interpersonal ties, and their moral decisions are more influenced by an ethic of caring that inhibits criminal activities that hurt others and/or that may lead to separation from loved ones. Women find that the characteristics of criminals and criminal behavior are more at variance with the values of womanhood and of being female than do males whose traits often seem compatible with criminal activity. Crime is almost always stigmatizing for females. There are no acceptable deviant roles for women comparable to those for romanticized "rogue" or "macho" males. In contrast, for males—especially young males—crime may serve to enhance and verify their masculinity.

Female access to crime opportunities is also restricted. Familial and other nurturant responsibilities restrict women's time and mobility, making it difficult to pursue a criminal career. Concerns about female sexuality (e.g, virtue) result in greater surveillance of females; the threat of sexual victimization constrains women's mobility, keeping them away from nighttime streets, bars, and other crime-likely locations. Additionally, their lesser physical strength and aggressiveness, whether real or perceived, limits the ability of women to engage in certain types of criminal behavior and to function effectively in the criminal community in general. Physical prowess, strength, and speed are useful for committing crimes such as burglary and robbery. These physical traits are also instrumental for protection, for enforcing contracts, and for recruiting and managing reliable associates. Although some crimes are more physically demanding than others, persistent involvement in crime, regardless of crime type, is likely to entail a lifestyle that is physically demanding and dangerous.

The masculine-type demands of the criminal environment and the gender norms described above place potential female offenders at a clear disadvantage in selection and recruitment into criminal groups, in the range of criminal career paths open to them, and in opportunities for tutelage and rewards. When females do gain entry into crime groups, they often act as subordinate partners or accomplices, and they are placed in roles organized around female attributes, particularly sexual ones that limit their range of opportunities.

As the arrest patterns in Table 1 display, female criminal involvement is highest for those crimes most consistent with traditional gender norms and for which females have the most opportunity and lowest for those crimes that diverge the most from traditional gender norms and for which females have little opportunity. The only offense categories for which female arrest rates exceed those of males are prostitution and runaway/curfew. The large share of female arrests for these offenses reflects, on the one hand, gender differences in the marketability of sexual services and a sexual double standard on the other. Although the number of male customers patronizing prostitutes exceeds the number of prostitutes, customers are rarely sanctioned. Similarly, although self-report studies show male runaway rates to be as high as female rates, female runaways are more likely to be arrested.

The lowest percentage of female arrests occurs for the serious property crimes of robbery and burglary, which require behavior very much at odds with traditional female gender norms and with their skills and contacts. When females do engage in such crimes, it is generally in peripheral and/or subordinate roles that exploit women's relational concerns or their sexuality and reinforce their subordination to men (Steffensmeier 1983). Moreover, female offenders (e.g., a teenage female group) typically rob female victims or male victims who are intoxicated.

However, the female share of arrests is high for the minor property crimes of larceny-theft, forgery, and fraud—activities compatible with roles traditionally fulfilled by females. For example, women can (and often do) commit shoplifting offenses while carrying out the traditional female role of making family purchases. Similarly, check forgery and welfare and credit card fraud also may be seen as an extension of traditional female consumer/domestic roles. Females also commit a large share of embezzlement offenses, ostensibly a white-collar crime. However, females arrested for embezzlement are typically lower-level bookkeepers or bank tellers, occupations in which females hold over 90% of the jobs. Female involvement in the more serious and lucrative occupational and/or business crimes (e.g., insider trading, price fixing, toxic waste dumping) is almost nonexistent.

Female involvement is quite high in various kinds of substance abuse, especially the popular substances such as alcohol and marijuana. Female participation in drug use is much lower for drugs tied to drug subcultures and to the criminal underworld in general. In addition, women involved in hard drug use (e.g., heroin, cocaine) are frequently introduced to it by a lover, boyfriend, or spouse.

Even female violence, an activity incompatible with female gender norms, is tied closely to the female role and to domestically related conflicts. Relative to males, females rarely kill or assault strangers or acquaintances. Rather, victims of female violence tend to be intimates such as spouses, lovers, and children. Also, the offenses usually take place within the home, and self-defense is often a motive.

As noted, recent decades have witnessed an increase in the female share of offending for some kinds of crime, especially property crime. Criminologists disagree about whether the trends in female arrests better reflect traditional gender-role expectations or new role patterns. The latter are examined next.

Untangling the Causes of Recent Trends in the Female Share of Offending

Four basic explanations have been offered for recent trends in female arrests/crime. These include the following:

1. The **more formal policing** thesis, which argues that changes in female arrest trends are not due to changes in levels of female offending per se but to less biased or more effective official responses to female criminality (i.e., arrests are a poor indicator of female crime).
2. The **liberation** or **greater female employment** thesis, which proposes that the improved status of women (especially their advances in the paid work force) is the social trend most relevant to the increase in female criminality.
3. The **economic adversity** or **feminization of poverty** thesis, which argues that higher levels of poverty and economic

insecurity faced by large subgroups of women in American society is the social trend most relevant to female crime trends.

4. The **expanded opportunities for female-type crimes** thesis which claims that shifts in dimensions of crime favoring female involvement is the social trend most relevant to female crime trends. Technological, monetary, governmental, and market consumption trends since World War II have expanded the opportunities for female-type crimes more rapidly than for male-type crimes. This perspective holds that the female share of offending is influenced more by the nature of crime characterizing a specific society than by changes in female motivations or in the social and economic positions of women.

This list of possible explanations of female crime trends is not exhaustive. Other trends such as greater drug use or addiction among females, subtle shifts in the underworld (e.g., less professionalism), and greater social disorganization at the societal level also may affect the crime patterns of men and women differentially.

More Formal Policing

Since the arrest rate is a function of definitions of criminality and formal social control mechanisms designed to deal with crime, trends in the female share of arrests may reflect changes either in criminal statutes or in law enforcement practices. The fact that self-report and victimization surveys fail to show any real increase in the female share of offending over the past 15 to 20 years (see earlier discussion) supports the view that the increase in the female percentage of arrests is at least partly a function of law enforcement trends that have contributed to more official counting of female offending.

Changes in criminal statutes that broaden the definition of a crime to include less serious forms of an activity may serve to increase the level of female involvement since females, when involved in a particular crime, are more likely to commit its less serious forms. For example, recent changes in DWI statutes have broadened the definition of DWI by lowering the blood alcohol content (BAC) that constitutes the legal definition of DWI. The revised DWI statutes authorize the police to arrest the less serious drunk driver, which in turn leads to a higher proportion of female offenders. In other areas of crime, the growth in the number of police per capita has enhanced their ability to dip more deeply into the pool of offenders, thus picking up more female offenders.

Changes in law enforcement practices and in statistical coverage may account for some of the increase in female arrest rates relative to male arrest rates. The trend in policing over the last three decades has been toward greater professionalism and more routine bureaucratic procedures. These changes can be hypothesized to have increased the arrests of females in a number of ways.

First, less chivalrous attitudes toward women and increased sociolegal pressures to administer the law in a nondiscriminatory way may have caused gender to become a less potent factor in determining arrest probability. Second, an increased awareness of female crime may have led to greater suspicion and surveillance of women. Third, because of their expanding use of informants, police are more likely to arrest females to gather evidence against male offenders with whom the females are associated. For instance, with respect to burglary and robbery, a number of police officers have commented to the senior author as follows:

> This printout shows more female burglars and robbers than it should. A lot of them are being "squeezed." Say a couple of guys do a burglary. Maybe the one guy's girlfriend drops them off or, more common yet, they take the stuff (e.g., jewelry) back to her apartment. We bust her, charge her with burglary or receiving [stolen property] figuring she will talk. Especially if she has kids, she don't want to spend time in jail.

Fourth, improvements in police recording practices that include greater accuracy in recording a suspect's sex have resulted in less "hidden" female crime (e.g., when sex is unknown at end-of-year tabulating, the arrestee is recorded as "male").

Fifth, changes in sanctioning policies on the part of welfare agencies and department stores may affect trends in arrests and prosecution of crimes such as fraud and larceny-theft, that is, those crimes likely to be committed by women. The rise in female arrests for larceny-theft/shoplifting in the 1960s and early 1970s corresponds to the growth in self-service shopping and to stricter enforcement practices directed at shoplifting. Both trends leveled off by the late 1970s and 1980s. During the 1980s in particular, the formal charging of shoplifters (i.e., place of business reporting the shoplifter to the police) was deemphasized in favor of more informal handling. In fact, many states now have civil recovery laws whereby store police have the option to recovering a civil penalty from apprehended shoplifters in place of arrest (Davis, Lundman, & Martinez 1991). The civil penalty includes the retail value of the merchandise and other "compensatory damages." These civil recovery laws have expanded across states during the past decade, as has their use overall. The comment by a longtime store security official of a large department store chain, as told to the senior author, captures the gist of this trend:

> Back in the sixties we overhauled the whole security system—more cameras, more store police, more recordkeeping, you name it. The mood was nab 'em and turn 'em over to the police. A lot of that has changed. It is still there to nab them [shoplifters] but we release a bigger percentage now. It's cheaper and less hassle. These shoplifting recovery laws have been a big help here.

Finally, in recent years white-collar crime units have been added in many urban police departments. So far, the volume of arrests by these units has been relatively small, and they have had minimal impact on overall arrest trends. This could change in the 1990s, however, with the expansion of more manpower and resources. Should this occur, the female percentage of larceny or fraud arrests is likely to rise somewhat if attention is paid primarily to thefts or frauds perpetrated by low-level employees in highly monitored positions. Otherwise (e.g., if upper-level and lucrative white-collar crimes are targeted), the female percentage of arrests for these offenses will be affected only minimally.

Female Liberation: Effects of Female Employment on Female Crime

> A Bellefonte [Pennsylvania] woman was charged with stealing items—about $200 in merchandise—from the Wal-Mart store while she was an employee. Jane Doe [alias] was arrested by Patton Township police on charges of theft and receiving stolen property. (*Centre Daily Times*, November 23, 1991, 3B)

> I was selling real estate and [when] showing this one house, I noticed what turned out to be $800 in a wallet on a chair in the living room. At the time I was helping to support my mother and my funds were low. I had the key to the house, so I went back later and took the money. I served three years in the state penitentiary [even though it was my first conviction]. The prosecutor gave the case a lot of play. I was publicized as the "real-estate-lady-burglar." (Personal communication, Anonymous, September 9, 1991)

The view that greater female participation in the public sphere, especially in the paid labor market, will lead to a rise in female crime is longstanding in criminology. Clarence Darrow wrote in 1922:

> No doubt as women enter the field of industry formerly occupied by men, and as she takes her part in politics and sits on juries, the percentage of female criminals will rise rapidly. As she takes her place with men she will be more and more judged as men are judged, and will commit the crimes that men commit, and furnish her fair quotas of the penitentiaries and jails. (78)

In contemporary times, a similar argument has been set forth (Simon 1975; Simon & Landis 1991). Simon writes that "As women acquire more education, enter the labor force full-time, and assume positions of greater authority, prestige, and technical skills, they will use the opportunities available to them to commit white-collar property offenses in the same proportions as do their male counterparts" (Simon & Landis 1991:4). Also, as a corollary to the property crime hypothesis, Simon predicts opposite effects for violent crimes: "Also as a function of an improved socioeconomic status, they [women] will move away from the role of victim and extricate themselves from situations that are likely to result in violent acts" (p. 4).

There is some correspondence between the female arrest trends and female occupational and educational trends. Women made up approximately 34% of the work force in 1960; that percentage climbed to 40% in 1975 and to 46% in 1990. Female educational levels also rose sharply over this time. Women made up 35% of all college graduates in 1960; that percentage climbed to 43% in 1975 and to 52% in 1990.

We agree with Simon that female involvement in employee theft and white-collar crime is (probably) greater today than a decade or two ago. It is reasonable to assume that at least some proportion of the increasing number of working women have capitalized on their opportunities for work-related thefts and frauds, as indicated by the two examples above. In this regard, the similarity is considerable between the current situation and that of the late nineteenth century when female involvement in domestic theft (also an occupational crime) was unusually high due to the kinds of work roles then available to women.

We disagree, however, with the view that female employment trends have had much of an impact on female *arrest* trends. That view (a) overlooks the fact that the crime categories of larceny and fraud are poor indicators of white-collar offenses, (b) neglects arrest trends that are incongruent with the employment trends, and (c) rests on shaky theoretical reasoning.

UCR *Arrest Data a Poor Indicator of White-Collar/Occupation-Related Crime*

Simon's (1975) "reading" of the *UCR* arrest data mistakenly construes arrest statistics on larceny, fraud, and forgery as white-collar and/or occupational crimes. She wrongly uses the statistics as supporting evidence linking economic opportunity for females to trends in female crime. The available evidence shows that the typical arrestee in these offense categories committed a nonoccupational crime such as shoplifting or passing bad checks. One recent analysis (Steffensmeier 1987) of 1981 police files in a Standard Statistical Metropolitan Area (SMSA) county in Pennsylvania found that less than 2% of all arrests for larceny, fraud and forgery were for an occupational crime.

Moreover, while the embezzler is usually a trusted employee (an exception is the club treasurer who embezzles), so few persons are arrested for embezzlement (fewer than for any other crime) that the crime is relatively insignificant in terms of overall crime patterns.

Thus, while in fact there may be more employee theft by women today than a decade or two ago (e.g., because there are more women in the paid labor force), that *cannot* be extrapolated or determined by the *UCR* arrest statistics. One police official in a mid-sized eastern city—whose "job is to go over all the [arrest] reports to make sure everything is tagged right"—told the senior author:

> We do have some finer breakdowns for fraud and larceny. Fraud is broken out into checks, credit cards, theft of services, and theft of leased property. Those are the big ones [in terms of arrests]. There are other breakdowns, like impersonating a public servant or fortune telling, but you seldom get an arrest on that. Deceptive business practices is another one—but no arrests in 1990. But, no, we don't have a distinct category for a theft or a fraud that is executed by an employee. There are very few arrests for that—to my thinking, it would be less than one percent of the [theft and fraud] total.

Statistical Inconsistencies

The hypothesized effects of female employment on female crime trends are at odds with selective arrest patterns.

Larceny trends. The relevant legal charge and *UCR* classification for employee or occupation-related theft is larceny-theft. However, the female percentage of arrests for larceny peaked in the early 1970s and has declined slightly since, even though the percentage of women in the labor force continued to rise sharply. That percentage rose from 46% in 1975 to 58% in 1990, an increase that is larger than for the previous decade. (The percentage of the total labor force that is female also increased, from 40% in 1975 to 46% in 1990.) The increase, moreover, was especially large in managerial and professional positions that, in particular, are expected to lead to white collar arrests.

Violent crimes. The female percentage of violent offending has not declined as predicted by the employment hypothesis but has remained generally stable (see Table 1). The female percentage was unchanged for aggravated assault, rose for other assaults, and declined for homicide. The decline for homicide, moreover, appears to be a byproduct of higher rates of felony-murders committed by males, as discussed later.

Age by sex trends. The trends in female employment (and in women's status in general) should have more of an impact on the arrest patterns of young adult and middle-aged women than on arrest levels of adolescent and elderly women. Younger women have been most affected by changing gender role attitudes and employment trends. However, changes in the female share of arrests are comparable across age groups whether the entire period (1960–1990) is considered or the individual decades (e.g., 1960–1970) are examined (Steffensmeier & Streifel 1991). For instance, the change in the female percentage of arrests for larceny is as large among juvenile females and older females (ages 50 and over) who for the most part are not in the labor force or have been affected only minimally by the employment trends.

Shaky Theoretical Reasoning

The view that greater labor force participation, higher educational levels, and greater occupational mobility for women will increase their involvement in property crime, especially white-collar crime, is at odds with major theories of male crime that link crime to such things as lack of legitimate opportunities, economic hardship, and diminished ties to conventional society. For example, employment may reduce the temptation to commit crime by assuring a steady income and/or by creating an attitude of upward mobility that itself is conducive to conformity. In addition, a steady income lessens women's dependency on males, who may initiate their involvement in crime. Taken together, some of the effects of greater employment opportunity may produce crime while other effects reduce it; employment may increase the prospect for committing some kinds of property crime (e.g., employee theft, bad checks) but diminish it for other kinds (e.g., shoplifting).

Second, the emphasis in the "employment-causes-female-crime" thesis is on the effects of upward mobility and the movement of women into managerial or administrative positions that provide them with opportunities to steal, defraud, or embezzle. However, this approach ignores the increasing numbers of downwardly mobile, or poor, women who commit petty thefts and frauds. The approach also ignores the characteristics of those (few) female offenders arrested for white-collar offenses. Daly's (1989) study of a group of federal offenders incarcerated for embezzlement, fraud, and forgery reached the following conclusion:

> Men's white-collar crimes were both petty and major, but almost all the women's were petty. Although half or more of the employed men were managerial or professional workers, most employed women were clerical workers. Higher proportions of women were black and had no ties to the paid labor force; fewer women had a four-year college degree. The women's socioeconomic profile, coupled with the nature of their crimes, makes one wonder if "white-collar" aptly describes them or their illegalities. . . . These data suggest that if women's share of white-collar arrests increases, it will stem from (1) increasing numbers of women in highly monitored, money-changing types of clerical, sales, or service jobs, and (2) increasing numbers of poor or unemployed women attempting to defraud state and federal governments or banks by securing loans, credit cards, or benefits to which they are not legally entitled. (790)

Third, it may be that the path is circuitous by which female employment gains contribute to selective property crimes like fraud and forgery. It is reasonable to assume that female employment enhances the prospects for women to acquire credit and secure loans, so that working women may have greater opportunities to commit credit-based frauds such as bad checks. Increasing numbers of employed but poor women further encourages a drift toward those kinds of frauds and forgeries, as we discuss next.

Finally, although attitudes apparently have shifted somewhat toward greater acceptance of women working and combining career and family, other areas of gender roles have changed very little: in gender-typing in children's play activities and play groups, in the kinds of personality characteristics that both men and women associate with each gender, in the expectation that women will be the gatekeepers of male sexuality, in the importance placed on physical attractiveness of women and their pressures to conform to an ideal of beauty and/or femininity, and in female responsibilities for child-rearing and nurturing activities more broadly such as caring for the sick and the elderly.

Female Economic Adversity

Statistics on the current economic status of American women show that changes have occurred in some areas but not in others and that the economic situation is better today for some women but worse for others. More women are in the labor force full-time, more have completed college and obtained professional degrees, and more hold managerial and professional positions. At the same time, however, a larger segment of the female population faces poverty and economic insecurity today than 25 years ago. Women continue to be segregated into the low-paying, low-status, traditionally female occupations (e.g., clerical, sales), while they are still virtually excluded from top management positions and those industrial and service occupations requiring the highest levels of technical and mechanical skills. Furthermore, from 1960 to the mid-1980s, the ratio of female-to-male median incomes has remained essentially unchanged. In addition, rising rates of divorce, illegitimacy, and female-headed households have increased the economic hardships of many women, thereby increasing the pressure to commit crime—especially in the context of a soaring consumerism that has raised expectations and demands for material goods or products.

The view that feminization of poverty, not women's liberation, is the social trend most relevant to female criminality is consistent with some of the arrest patterns already observed. First, female arrest gains are not limited to larceny and fraud but extend to other property crimes as well. For example, the female percentage of burglary and robbery arrests has risen in small but consistent fashion, suggesting that worsening economic conditions for many women may be having a diffuse effect on female property crime as a whole. Second, the movement in the female percentage of arrests for property crimes is similar across age groups, implying that economic insecurity is both widespread and spread fairly evenly among women of differing ages. Third, studies of the characteristics of female offenders are very consistent. Typical female offenders bear little resemblance to the liberated "female crook" described by some commentators; instead, they are unemployed women or women working at low-paying occupations, or are minority women drawn from backgrounds of profound poverty.

Expanded Opportunities for Female-Type Crimes

Not only do some societies offer greater opportunities for illegal conduct than other societies (e.g., industrialized societies are "target rich" for property crimes because of the mass production of goods), societies also differ in the proportion of crime opportunities that favor female involvement. Because female offenders (like male offenders) gravitate toward activities that are easily available and within their skills, the level of female crime in a given society will be strongly swayed by the availability of crime opportunities that are suited to female interests and abilities.

Changes in American society since World War II have caused crime to assume new dimensions and forms that provide greater crime opportunities for one sex relative to the other. Female gains in property crime offending, in particular, can be seen as a byproduct of opportunities created by the evolution of patterns of productive activity in American society (transportation, merchandising, currency, etc.), rather than to changes in female motivation or in their social and economic positions. The changes in productive activity are especially important because of their impact on the routine activities and lifestyle adaptations of women as compared to men.

The opportunities for traditional types of female crime have been expanding at a faster pace than have traditional male crimes. The increased supply of goods and their self-service marketing, a credit-based currency, consumerism, and a social welfare type of government have resulted in more opportunities for traditionally female types of theft and fraud. These expanded opportunities for female-based consumer crimes have occurred in an economic context that (increasingly) has required many women to support themselves in traditionally low-paying jobs. Historically, a high proportion of female property crime in American society has involved minor thefts (e.g., shoplifting, domestic theft), fraudulent exchange transactions (e.g., bad checks, con games), and contraband smuggling (e.g., transporting drugs, food, or other commodities), crimes that are an extension of traditional consumer and domestic roles. Males also engage in such crimes in even larger numbers, but the representation of such crimes among all male crime is proportionately lower than for females.

Incidentally, the impact of changing patterns of productive activity that have drawn more women into the "white-collar" workplace also can help to explain the likelihood of more female occupational crime today (even though that trend cannot be construed from the arrest data but is consistent with anecdotal evidence). Women today are greatly overrepresented in occupations in which employee thefts and frauds are possible—that is, women outnumber men in many white-collar occupations, such as sales personnel, clerical workers, and bank tellers.

Thus, recent shifts in the form or dimension of crime offer females greater access to some kinds of crime-likely situations *because* they are playing traditional roles, particularly in their roles as primary consumers. There are many sides to performing traditional gender roles, so that the type of criminal opportunity (and the changes therein) is likely to be a critical factor in determining female involvement. Later on, we examine how the opportunity-for-female-type crime thesis helps to explain female arrest trends for selective crimes such as fraud and homicide.

Drugs and Other Factors

The four explanations of female crime trends we just described do not exhaust the possibilities. For example, some observers believe that the rate of female crime is more affected by social disorganization (e.g., family disruption and societal conflict) than is the male rate; it may be that American society is more socially disorganized than in the past.

Another possibility has to do with the strain and weakened constraints experienced by males and females from failure to attain *sex-specific* goals (economic goals for males versus domestic goals for females). Recent trends in rates of marriage (downward trend) and divorce (upward trend) may contribute to higher levels of female crime by increasing the probability of females failing to attain domestic goals. Obviously, this view offers a very different causal path from that suggested by the liberation thesis.

A third possibility is that the greater numbers of working women cause a crime-producing effect by contributing to a sense of relative deprivation or entitlement among women who are not working outside the home or among those who are being paid less than their male colleagues for the same work. Viewed this way, the female employment thesis may converge in some ways with the economic adversity hypothesis. Economic need, as well as opportunity, may contribute to the increased female involvement in property crimes.

A fourth possibility has to do with subtle shifts in the underworld that may raise or dampen the prospects for female involvement. Given the male dominance of the underworld and the sexism characterizing it, female crime opportunities are partly dependent on whether male criminals find females to be useful. For example, in recent years women have become useful for successful drug trafficking because they are likely to have clean records, create less suspicion, and can conceal drugs more easily. At the same time, the underworld appears to be younger, more amateurish, and less professional today. It is generally observed that professional crime groups are less likely to admit women into their groups and allow them to play fairly active roles. A dealer in stolen goods told the senior author, "The better thief will seldom involve a woman. Kids and shitass thieves, yes. Lotta times they will involve their girlfriend all the way. Dope and shitass thieves have paved the way [for greater female involvement]" (Personal communication, Anonymous, April 4, 1990).

Last, trends in drug usage and addiction may help account for female crime trends. It is commonly observed that drug addiction amplifies income-generating crime for both sexes but more so for female than male crime. Females face greater constraints against crime and thus need a greater motivational push. Female involvement in burglary and robbery, in particular, typically occurs after addiction and is likely to be abandoned when drug use ceases. Drug use is also more likely to initiate females into the underworld and criminal subcultures, especially by connecting them to drug-dependent males who utilize them as crime accomplices or exploit them as "old ladies" who support the man's addiction. In these ways, the rise in drug dependency among both males and females would impact more strongly on female criminality.

Statistical Time-Series Analyses

To date, only two studies (Box & Hale 1984; Steffensmeier & Streifel 1992) have sought to assess the factors influencing female property crime trends through a statistical time-series analysis. Because of difficulties in finding suitable indicators for the differing theoretical perspectives on female arrest trends, both are limited somewhat in their generalizability

Box and Hale (1984) analyzed conviction data from England and Wales for the years 1951 to 1980. Their results gave little support to the liberation-causes-crime thesis but provided limited support for the economic-marginalization thesis. They found no clear relationship between their measures of emancipation (fertility, female college enrollments, female labor force participation, number of unmarried women) and trends in female offending. However, female unemployment levels—their measure of marginalization—had a significant positive effect on female levels of crime. The variable with the strongest effect on levels of female offending was changing patterns in policing, measured by the gender composition of the police force.

Steffensmeier and Streifel (1992) found similar results, based on a time-series analysis of U.S. arrest data for the years 1960 to 1985. The results were at odds with the liberation thesis but instead contended that trends in the female share of property offending were largely a by product of trends toward more formal policing and greater opportunities for consumer-related thefts (e.g., shoplifting) and to a lesser extent to trends in the economic marginality of women. The authors found that female-to-male labor force participation was *negatively* associated with the FP/A for larceny, not of other factors. Nor was female employment related to other property crimes such as burglary or robbery as might be expected if female employment masculinizes the attitudes of women who work or creates feelings of relative deprivation among women more generally. Also, the female percentage of embezzlement—the only *UCR* offense category that mainly includes arrests for occupationally based crimes—was negatively related to female employment trends.

However, Steffensmeier and Streifel did find that female employment trends were positively related to female arrest trends for fraud (i.e., the higher the rate of female employment, the higher their arrest rate for fraud). They interpreted this finding as consistent with the argument, noted above, that female employment gains have resulted in an increase in opportunities for credit-linked frauds (e.g., passing bad checks, credit card fraud).

Cross-sectional results that compare the female percentage of offending from one locality to another in the United States support the time-series data. A recent study by Streifel (1990) found that gender differences in rates of property offending across SMSAs could not be explained by variations in gender equality in legitimate spheres (e.g., paid employment family roles). However, the other factors examined—female economic marginality, formalization of social control, and opportunities for female consumer-based crimes—were fairly good predictors of gender differences in arrest rates for property crimes. The summary on the next page is a profile of urban localities with a higher as compared to a lower female share of arrests for property crimes.

This profile holds regardless of offense type examined—robbery, burglary, larceny-theft, forgery, fraud, embezzlement, or drug law violations. None of the indicators of female liberation (paid employment, educational levels, salary levels) was related to the FP/A at a statistically significant level for any of the offense categories. Rather, higher female-to-male arrest levels are linked to structural conditions in which women face adverse rather than favorable economic circumstances.

High FP/A	*Low FP/A*
More formal policing	Less formal policing
More opportunities for female-based consumer crime	Fewer opportunities for female-based consumer crime
More occupational segregation	Less occupational segregation
More female-headed households	Fewer female-headed households
Higher rates of illegitimacy	Lower rates of illegitimacy
Higher rates of female unemployment	Lower rates of female unemployment
Lower educational levels	Higher educational levels

Close-up Look at Trends for Selective Crimes

The explanations of female crime trends described above are better viewed as intertwined rather than mutually exclusive, as the discussion below indicates. Female arrest gains or losses in selective crimes in several crime categories are highlighted. We focus in particular on how changes in productive activity shape the crime opportunities for women as compared to those for men.

Larceny-theft. The female percentage of arrests for larceny-theft almost doubled between 1960 and 1975 (increasing from 17% to 30%) but held steady after this time. This pattern reflects a combination of factors, some of which are offsetting. First, it reflects increased opportunities for shoplifting—a female-type crime—across the three decades but especially in the 1960s, which saw a rapid growth in shopping malls, self-service marketing, and small, portable products that outpaced protection-against-theft measures. Second, that trend has been countered somewhat by increased opportunities for male-type crimes, such as bicycle theft and theft from parked automobiles, across the three decades but especially in the 1980s when the availability of bicycles and motor vehicles expanded rapidly. At the same time, changes in store security policies toward less formal handling of shoplifters has enabled male arrests for larceny to keep pace with female arrests in the 1980s.

Fraud. The female percentage of fraud arrests has risen continuously over the years, from about 15% in the early 1960s to about 43% today. This increase can be attributed to several factors, including the growing numbers of poor women, the increased efficiency in detecting fraud offenders, as well as the growth in a credit-based currency in American society that has contributed to greater opportunities for check and/or other kinds of credit-related frauds. A cross-national comparison helps to show the significance of this factor. The FP/A for fraud and forgery is much higher in the United States (roughly 40%) than in the European nations (about 15%), even though the percentage of women working is as high or higher in those countries. The apparent reason for this difference is that the European nations lag behind the United States in a monetary system that is credit-based; they, therefore, provide fewer opportunities for bad checks, credit card fraud, and so forth. Note, also, that many of the European countries are moving toward a monetary system that is credit-driven, so that we would expect the percentage of female arrests for fraud or forgery to rise during the 1990s in the European nations.

Burglary. A small but steady rise has occurred in the female percentage of burglary arrests, especially during the 1980s. A principal reason for this rise is that female burglary rates have been holding steady over the past decade and a half, as compared to male burglary rates which have dropped considerably. It appears that prospective male burglars are selecting drug trafficking as a preferred profit-making crime. The rise also reflects a growth in burglary targets that are more suitable for female involvement (e.g., houses or apartments that are unoccupied during the daytime). There are different forms of burglary, ranging from unlawful daytime entry of an unoccupied house to breaking into a commercial establishment for purposes of stealing merchandise or robbing a safe. The most common form of female participation in burglary is as an accomplice of a male burglar, where the target is an unoccupied house or apartment dwelling, and when it is daytime.

Several trends in productive activity have increased the number of dwellings that are unoccupied and lack effective guardianship, especially during the day. The growth in suburban housing, greater frequency of leisure activity outside the home, and greater numbers of women at work have exposed households to greater risk because family members are away or because there are fewer intimate neighbors to look after property while residents are away from home. These conditions also create targets that are more suitable for female involvement, such as (a) solo offenders or with female co-offenders who unlawfully enter and take property or cash from unoccupied homes or apartments nearby to where they live and (b) accomplices to male burglars for purposes of checking a dwelling's occupancy by posing as a saleslady or as someone who is in need of directions or use of the telephone.

Several other factors have a bearing on female arrest trends for burglary (and the other property crimes):

1. Increase in drug-related burglaries and robberies that involve women as solo perpetrators or women as accomplices of male burglars and robbers.
2. Increase in "hard times" faced by women, especially young women who are single parents (who are heads of single-parent households).
3. The expanding role of the informant system within law enforcement has contributed to more arrests of females who are targeted for information or testimony against male offenders with whom the females are associated.

Homicide. The FP/A for homicide has decreased over the past three decades, declining from 17% in 1960 to 10% in 1990. One interpretation of this trend links it to greater female autonomy and the option of women today—through divorce, abuse shelters, and so forth—to escape abusive males who victim-precipitate their own deaths at the hands of anguished female spouses or lovers (Simon & Landis 1991).

Instead, the downward trend in the female share of arrests for homicide reflects a shift in homicide patterns since the 1960s toward a proportionate increase in the incidence of felony-murder and stranger killings. The percentage of all homicides committed in the course of a felony (e.g., robbery, burglary, drug dealing, "hit" killing) have nearly tripled since 1960 (from about 7% to about 20%). Males are overwhelmingly the participants in incidences of felony-murder or contract killings, whereas homicides involving female perpetrators almost always occur during non criminal activity (e.g., domestic quarrels). This shift in homicide patterns toward more male-type killings explains the gradual rise in the male share of homicide arrests.

The increase in felony-related murders appears to be due to several factors: (a) the growth in convenience stores and the like that have led to more suitable targets for robbery, (b) the greater availability of firearms, and (c) the strong consumer appetite for hard drugs that has fostered a violent drug trade (especially in large urban areas) whose victims range from drug rivals to innocent bystanders. The slayers in these drug-related homicides are overwhelmingly male. Should this trend toward a more instrumental or materialistic use of violence persist, we would expect the female percentage of homicides to continue its downward trend. However, if drug-related killings and other felony-murders subside, then the female percentage of homicide offenders may rise somewhat.

Driving while intoxicated. The female percentage of arrests for DWI increased gradually from 5% in 1975 to 11% in 1990. The increase is due to a combination of factors. First, DWI statutes have been changed toward a broader or less strict definition of DWI (see earlier discussion). Second, the proportion of drivers who are female has increased. This reflects the growing necessity of the automobile in modern American society, especially in the lives of women as they carry out their work roles, fulfill their family responsibilities, and pursue their leisure activities. Third, women have greater freedom of movement today and there is greater acceptance of females who drink in public places. Fourth, the number of single and divorced females who drink socially at bars and other social gatherings has increased; these are at risk of driving while intoxicated and at night when enforcement accelerates.

The significance of these trends in affecting female trends in DWI arrests is reflected in responses drawn from recent interviews conducted by the senior author of lower-court judges in Pennsylvania (who are responsible for processing DWI arrests). When asked about DWI arrests, for example, one judge responded:

> It's still mostly male but we steadily keep seeing more women [charged for DWI]. Mostly, they're in their twenties and early thirties and [they] get arrested around midnight or later. The reasons are not that complex, really. There are more women who drive nowadays and the law's a lot stricter. You can get hammered [arrested] for just a couple of drinks now. Another thing, a lot of the gals I see for drunk-driving have been out hitting a bar or a party on a Friday or Saturday night to socialize or to meet guys. A lot of these gals are divorced and they want to meet guys. The guys buy them drinks or whatever. They [the women] end up driving home having had a drink or two too many. If they're unlucky, they get caught (Interview, June 8, 1991).

Implications and Conclusions

Four general conclusions can be drawn about recent trends in female crime. First, the principal change in the female share of offending involves the overall rise in property crime (especially minor thefts and frauds). Second, that increase appears due largely to the convergence of market consumption trends and the worsening economic conditions of large subgroups of women. Other factors, such as greater female drug addiction and greater female participation in the public sphere, may have exacerbated those trends. In this sense, need and opportunity may account for some of the increased female involvement in property crime. Third, when arrests are used as the indicator of female-to-male crime levels, changing enforcement practices toward more formal policing is a major contributing factor. Fourth, the significance of these factors will vary across specific offenses.

For example, the rise in the female percentage for burglary arrests can be attributed to the *interplay* of rising levels of female poverty, increased drug-dependency among women, more opportunities for female types of burglary, greater police targeting of female co-offenders to inform on male offenders, declining professionalism within the ranks of burglary and the underworld more generally and a move away from burglary to drug trafficking on the part of prospective male offenders (thus causing a drop in male burglary rates).

If we combine the *UCR* arrest data with other sources of evidence on female crime, we find female involvement today is greatest in sex-related offenses like prostitution (legal euphemisms sometimes include vagrancy, disorderly conduct, and runaways), in popular forms of substance abuse, and in petty thefts and hustles (shoplifting, theft of services, falsification of identification, passing bad checks, credit card forgery, welfare fraud, employee theft, and street-level drug dealing). Volumes of arrests for larceny (less so, fraud) have become so great in recent decades as to have an impact upon total arrest rates, including the index offenses of the *Uniform Crime Reports*.

In comparison to male offenders, females are far less likely to be involved in serious offenses, and the monetary value of thefts, property damage, drugs, injuries, and so forth of female offenses is typically smaller than that of male offenses. Females are also more likely than males to be solo perpetrators or to be part of small, relatively nonpermanent crime groups or partnerships. When female offenders are involved with others, particularly in more lucrative thefts or other criminal enterprises, they typically act as accomplices to males who both organize the crime and are the central figures in its execution (see Steffensmeier, 1983, for a review). Perhaps the most significant gender difference is the overwhelming dominance of males in more organized and highly lucrative crimes, whether based in the underworld or the upperworld.

These basic gender differences in quantity and quality of crime are consistent with traditional gender-role expectations, behaviors, and opportunities. Moreover, the differences can be traced at least as far back as the sixteenth century, perhaps even earlier. Premodern crime records document the lesser female involvement in crime, especially in its more serious and more violent forms. But the historical record also shows that, as in contemporary times, there always have been cases of women initiating robberies and thefts against strangers in the evening, in undesirable locations, and of using weapons in the course of the act. There also is evidence of women playing active and independent roles in large-scale organizations of crime, with some women even achieving leadership positions in vice operations, fencing networks and so forth.

For example, based on her analysis of female crime in the fourteenth century, Hanawalt writes, "Perhaps the most surprising of the property crimes in which to find a heavy concentration of women is in burglary. Women committed 12% of all burglaries—a considerably higher percentage than in modern burglary" (1976:132).

Note also this conclusion from McMullan's (1984) study of female crime in sixteenth-century London:

> Women were well represented in the criminal underworld, operating especially as thieves, confidence cheats, receivers of stolen property, and prostitutes. They were also important as accomplices. They teamed up with men and children. They acted as lookouts, and as transporters of incriminating evidence, stolen goods, and criminal technology. Some, like Moll Cutpurse, were directors of thieving gangs. . . . Some women formed associations of their own. There existed female gangs of shoplifters and house burglars, and counterfeiting seems to have attracted female apprentices. Pickpocket teams were often composed of two or three women fronting as prostitutes. . . . Other [prostitutes] robbed their victims while servicing them. (118)

Then, Beattie's (1975) description of female crime in eighteenth-century England:

> Far fewer women were indicted for the most serious offenses [such as] robbery, burglary, and horse theft [female proportion was 11%]. . . . At the same time, theft by servants, stealing from shops,

> and picking pockets occupied a more prominent place among women's crimes than men's. . . . Though some women entered houses to steal, women robbers were much less common. If they engaged in street crime, it was more often as an associate or decoy, or they picked on children, for a number of women were indicted for enticing a child into an alley or house in order to take its clothes to sell or pawn. (95)

Finally, note Ellington's (1869) description of female offenders in mid-nineteenth-century New York:

> The female criminals of New York seldom, if ever, reform—but go from bad to worse. After pocket-picking, shoplifting; after shoplifting, an accomplice of burglars; then drugging men and robbing them of their money . . . after that it may be murder. (449)

These descriptions of female crime in premodern times are consistent with other anecdotal and statistical evidence and help to place in context the sometimes conflicting interpretations about the extent and quality of female crime today.

Conclusion

Whether the female share of offending will rise or fall during the next decade or two depends on the interplay of the explanatory factors described earlier. For example, in recent years an increase has occurred in special white-collar units in many police departments. That trend may push up the rate of arrests for occupation-related thefts and frauds within the relevant *UCR* categories, particularly for women. Second, the increasing numbers of women who drive and more stringent law enforcement directed at DWI offenders will sustain the upward trend in the female share of persons arrested for DWI. Third, trends in female poverty and drug dependency, especially within minority populations, will shape female crime trends during the 1990s. If the trends of the past two decades persist (toward greater female drug use and greater female economic adversity), we can expect small increases in the female percentage of arrests for property crime, especially for burglary and robbery. On the other hand, should the drug trend be reversed and poverty among minority males reduced, then we can expect a drop in felony-murders that, in turn, will lead to small increases in the female percentage of homicide (since felony-murders are committed overwhelmingly by minority males). Finally, changes in the nation's ethnic composition due to immigration may affect female offending for selective crimes, including gang delinquency. Since Hispanic groups are prone to include female co-offenders in their crime networks, we can expect the continued influx of Hispanics into the large urban areas to increase somewhat the overall involvement of females in delinquent gangs and drug distribution groups.

Given the available data, we are unable to answer with certainty whether female crime is changing and how these changes are to be explained. Answers to these questions will require research along several fronts. First, there is a need to examine closely the kinds of crimes women commit within the broad categories as defined by penal statute and/or by official collection agencies such as the *Uniform Crime Reports*. At present, we have no systematic evidence regarding the qualitative nature of contemporary female offending, especially as it compares to contemporary male offending or to female offending in the past. Local studies of police files are needed that would provide a detailed breakdown of the kinds of crime committed by women (and men) and the nature of their criminal roles. Such studies would also provide a baseline for evaluating future trends in female crime. Unfortunately, because of concerns about privacy and police impropriety, police departments have become reluctant to provide such access.

Second, research is needed that examines whether the reasons motivating men and women offenders are similar when they commit the same types of crime and whether those reasons have changed over time. Both historical and contemporary research suggests that women differ somewhat in their motivations to commit crimes and the vocabularies they use to justify their crimes. More so than for men, the law violations of women are often tied to an emotional relationship to others and the fulfillment of role expectations within that relationship. Women may use the money gained for personal excesses, but more often it is considered necessary to fulfill a caretaking role or to maintain a love relationship.

Third, explanatory factors must be found that are simple yet robust in interpreting female crime trends. For example, the argument seems meandering that the drop in the female percentage of homicides is due to the greater ability of women to extricate themselves from domestic situations that are likely to lead to violence because of their improved economic status. A simpler and more robust explanation has to do with the shift in homicide patterns toward instrumental-type murders that are overwhelmingly committed by males (thus lowering the female percentage of total homicide arrests).

Finally, both theory and research on female crime needs to employ a multivariate approach that incorporates a variety of explanatory factors to account for trends in the female percentage of offending. Any approach that emphasizes only one factor or theory at the expense of others is likely to be misleading.

Note

1. For reasons of space and to avoid clutter, we have constrained the literature citations. Readers wanting a more complete enumeration should consult prior writings by Steffensmeier and colleagues, including Steffensmeier (1980a, b; 1983; 1989); Steffensmeier & Allan (1990); Steffensmeier & Streifel (1991; 1992); Steffensmeier, Allan, & Streifel (1989).

References

Beattie, J. (1975). The criminality of women in eighteenth-century England. *Journal of Social History* 8: 80–117.

Box, S., & Hale, C. (1984). Liberation/emancipation, economic marginalization, or less chivalry: The relevance of three theoretical arguments to female crime patterns in England and Wales, 1951–1980. *Criminology* 22: 473–497.

Daly, K. (1989). Gender and varieties of white collar crime. *Criminology* 27: 769–794.

Darrow, C. (1922). *Crime: its causes and treatment.* Montclair, NJ: Patterson-Smith.

Davis, M., Lundman, R., & Martinez, R., Jr. (1991). Private corporate justice: Store police, shoplifters, and civil recovery. *Social Problems* 38: 395–411.

Ellington, G. (1869). *Women of New York.* New York: Arno Press.

Elliott, D., Ageton, S., & Huzinga, D. (1987). Social correlates of delinquent behavior. Unpublished paper.

Hanawalt, B. (1976). The female felon in fourteenth-century England. In S. Stuart (ed.), *Women in medieval society.* Philadelphia: University of Pennsylvania Press.

McMullan, J. (1984). *The canting crew: London's criminal underworld, 1550–1700.* New Brunswick, NJ: Rutgers University Press.

Pennsylvania Crime Commission (1991). *1990 report—organized crime in Pennsylvania: A decade of change* (Darrell Steffensmeier, Project Director/Principal Writer). Harrisburg: Commonwealth of Pennsylvania.

Simon, R. (1975). *The contemporary woman and crime.* Washington, DC: National Institute of Mental Health.

Simon, R., and Landis, J. (1991). *The crimes women commit, the punishments they receive.* Lexington, MA: D.C. Heath.

Steffensmeier, D. (1980a). Assessing the impact of the women's movement on sex-based differences in the handling of adult criminal defendants. *Crime and Delinquency* 26: 344–357.

——— (1980b). Sex differences in patterns of adult crimes, 1965–77: A review and assessment. *Social Forces* 58(4): 1080–1108.

——— (1983). Organizational properties and sex-segregation in the underworld: Building a sociological theory of sex differences in crime. *Social Forces* 61: 1010–132.

——— (1987). The kinds of property crimes women commit. Paper presented at annual meeting of American Society of Criminology.

——— (1989). On the causes of white-collar crime: An assessment of Hirschi and Hindelang's claims. *Criminology* 27: 345–358.

Steffensmeier, D., & Allan, E.A. (1988). Sex disparities in arrests by residence, race, and age: An assessment of the gender convergence/crime hypothesis. *Justice Quarterly* 5: 53–80.

——— (1990). Gender, age, and crime. In J. Sheley (ed.), *Handbook of contemporary criminology.* New York: Macmillan.

Steffensmeier, D.J., Allan, E., & Streifel, C. (1989). Development and female crime: A cross-national test of alternative explanations. *Social Forces* 68: 262–283.

Steffensmeier, D.J., & Streifel, C. (1991). Age, gender, and crime across three historical periods: 1935, 1960, and 1985. *Social Forces* 69: 869–894.

——— (1992). Trends in female-to-male arrests for property crimes: A test of alternative explanations. *Justice Quarterly* 9:77–103.

Streifel, C. (1990). *Correlates of the female percentage of arrests across U.S. SMSAs*. Unpublished doctoral dissertation. The Pennsylvania State University.

Women charged with shoplifting. (1991, November 23). *Centre Daily Times*, 3B.

PART II

New Developments in Female Criminal Behavior

Gender Issues

Joan McCord
Temple University

As Estes (1957) noted, sound theory rests on undermining a "mountain of stereotypes deposited by centuries of prescientific attempts to comprehend behavior" (p. 617). The work of this chapter rests in attempting to do that undermining around three topics of criminological research: (a) causes of crime, (b) fear of crime, and (c) domestic violence.

Causes of Crime

Crime, it has been said, arises from a perceived lack of opportunities to achieve success through legitimate means (e.g., Cloward & Ohlin 1960; Glaser 1978) and through association with people whose values are antisocial (e.g., Elliott, Huizinga, & Ageton 1985; Matsueda & Heimer 1987; Snyder, Dishion, & Patterson 1986). Each of these theories appears to be on shaky ground when the domain of inquiry includes females as well as males.

There should be little doubt regarding the fact that women have fewer opportunities for occupational success than men, whether they have chosen art (e.g., Higonnet 1990) or more conventional occupations (see, e.g., Davis & Robinson 1991; Rosenfeld & Kalleberg 1990; Treiman & Roos 1983). Were it the case that a perceived lack of opportunities to achieve success through legitimate means produces criminals, one would expect to find crime rates particularly high among Caucasian women; they are not (Cernkovich & Giordano 1979;

Farnworth, McDermott, & Zimmerman 1988; Feyerherm 1981; Jensen & Eve 1976; Steffensmeier & Steffensmeier 1980).

Serious criminal behavior has been largely the province of males. Adolescence, the period when girls and boys increase their activities with one another, should therefore result in particularly marked increases in the association of girls with people whose values are antisocial. Were it the case that association with people whose values are antisocial gives rise to crime, one would expect to find sharp increases in crime rates for females as they enter adolescence. Yet, sharp increases in serious crimes by females do not appear during early adolescence.

Various theorists have argued that male delinquents play out masculine roles through their delinquency (e.g., Bacon, Child, & Barry 1963; Lamb 1976; Miller 1958; Whiting, Kluckhohn, & Anthony 1958). Theories about sex-role behavior ought to be considered in relation to how females and males interact to create the roles that male delinquents may assume to be masculine. The potential importance of gathering such evidence for understanding delinquency was suggested by a longitudinal study of girls in Sweden (Stattin & Magnusson 1990). Girls who became physically mature in advance of their classmates tended to have older friends and, if they did, to become delinquents.

Evidence that delinquency among girls tends to be less serious than delinquency among boys depends upon taking a short-term view. Girls become mothers, and mothers influence the behaviors of their offspring—so that the net effects of antisocial behaviors may be greater for females than for males. Although a good deal is known about how mothers affect their offspring (Liska & Reed 1985; McCord 1991; Wells & Rankin 1988), far too little is known about the forces that affect maternal behavior.

On the one hand, there is some evidence that girls who associate with gangs compete for the best criminal boys, thus providing encouragement for criminality and rewarding it (Campbell 1984). On the other hand, some evidence suggests that sisters suppress antisocial behavior (Jones, Offord, & Abrams 1980), even as brothers tend to protect their sisters from predatory males (Anderson 1989).

Serious consideration of the etiology of crime ought to include an examination of the role that females play in relation to male criminality. Girls may encourage boys to steal in order to receive presents; they may enjoy the prowess of males and admire them for what could be considered courageous acts. Just as women have inspired art and poetry among those for whom these types of behavior seem appropriate, they may inspire crime among those whose natural activities include antisocial acts.

Too narrow a view of criminal behavior has led to the acceptance of theories about the etiology of crime that overlooks possibilities that women participate without being on the front lines, so to speak. One gender issue, then, is to insist that criminal behavior be considered from a broader perspective than that defined by male activities.

Fear of Crime

Women, especially elderly women, are reported to exhibit a greater fear of crime than men, especially young men (Akers et al. 1987; Clemente & Kleiman 1977; Skogan & Maxfield 1981; Stafford & Galle 1984; Warr 1984, 1990). This has been described as an apparent anomaly because victimization rates are higher among men than among women and are lowest among elderly women as compared with the other demographic groups classified by age and sex.

Corrections have been made in terms of vulnerability and exposure time. For example, Skogan and Maxfield (1981) show that the vulnerability of women leads to their defensive behavior, which, in turn, results in low rates of victimization. Stafford and Galle (1984) note that the conventional measure of victimization rates assumes equal levels of exposure. Corrected for exposure time, elevation of fear among women in relation to victimization rates tends to be reduced.

Although the effects of isolation, vulnerability, and experiences of victimization seem to have a cumulative effect on fear of crime—an effect that "did not multiply to the special disadvantage of particular groups" (Skogan 1987:151), evidence also suggests that females report greater fear than do males for standardized situations. Warr (1990), for example, presented males and females with vignettes. Respondents were asked to report how likely they would be to fear becoming a victim of a crime under the circumstances described. Warr suggests that crime-relevant cues may have different meanings for males and females, with only the latter interpreting presence of a young male as a cue for possible rape.

It has been assumed that the fears of females require a special explanation that can account for failure to find a strong correlation between victimization experiences and fear of crime. Measures of victimization, however, have been androgenic. Respondents have typically been asked about their experiences as victims during the prior year. But why should one assume that effects of all victimizations disappear after a couple of years merely because effects of modal crimes do so?

The effects of rape can be enduring (Atkeson et al. 1982; Kilpatrick et al. 1989; Nadelson et al. 1982). These often include traumatic investigations and, sometimes, abortions.

Measures of fear have typically asked about going out alone in the neighborhood at night. There is reason to doubt that such a question measures the same thing among males as among females. At very young ages, girls are taught not to go out alone (Maccoby & Jacklin 1974). The proscription against going out alone is reinforced through advertising that rarely depicts females outside alone. Furthermore, women are told that if they go out alone or if they are found in certain areas, they are inviting their own victimization. Social desirability contributes to a response set that would elevate reporting of fear even in the absence of learning.

A second gender issue consists in developing measures of fear and of victimization that are neutral with regard to the types of events they purport to measure. This requires greater sensitivity to differences in socialization between men and women.

Domestic Violence

The relatively new crime of domestic violence has a special position among gender issues. Because women are considered to be primary targets of domestic violence, crime reduction in this arena is a feminist issue. A look at what has been done, however, raises doubts about the adequacy of research aimed to protect women in their homes.

Reporting on an early randomization study of intervention, Sherman and Berk (1984) seemed to show that arresting husbands would reduce domestic violence. Cautionary voices suggested taking a second look. In that second look, projects were designed to test whether arrest was more effective than alternatives.

Dunford, Huizinga, and Elliott (1990), for example, report results of their attempt to replicate in Omaha the results found by Sherman and Berk for Minneapolis. For the Omaha study, Dunford, Huizinga, and Elliott randomly assigned cases of domestic violence to one of three responses. The eligible cases involved probable cause for misdemeanor assault among couples who had spent part of the prior year living together, provided neither had a prior arrest warrant on file. Comparisons showed that arrest was no more effective than was separation or counseling. Similar results have been shown by Ford (1990) from his study in Indianapolis.

In Minneapolis as in Omaha and Indianapolis, evaluation of impact involved looking for incidents in which a victim was revictimized by the same person. The searches for recidivism as measured by official records were restricted to the original jurisdictions. And, to qualify as recidivism, the assault must have occurred within a period of six months.

Studies of crime outside the home show that specialization, as defined by sequential committing of similar offenses, is a relatively rare occurrence (Petersilia 1980; Wolfgang, Figlio, & Sellin 1972; Wolfgang, Thornberry, & Figlio 1987). Further, Berk and Newton (1985) found that among 783 cases of wife battery in southern California, less than 2% had any previous conviction for wife battery. Yet, in cases of domestic violence, researchers have narrowed perception of recidivism not only to committing a similar offense within six months—but also to doing it against the same target.

Evidence suggests that batterers and battered have been exposed to violence during childhood (e.g., Hotaling & Sugarman 1986; Walker 1988). It seems likely that a pattern learned from years of exposure would be unaltered by a brief encounter with a police officer. To test the contrary hypothesis, one would expect careful measures. Yet, little attention has been given to evaluating the validity of the types of evidence being used to formulate policy (Weis 1989). Despite the amount of time and effort spent on studies designed to identify ways to reduce domestic violence, the results have failed to address the fundamental question of whether victims are better off after the intervention than they were before.

Surprisingly, studies of domestic violence have not systematically gathered information about the prior records of offenders. Just as foot patrols seem to displace crime without preventing it (Pate, Wilson, & Kelling 1981), arrests may merely be spreading victimization.

Of course it is more difficult to trace criminal behavior of the assaulters than it is to check victimization of a single victim. But why should that difficult task not be undertaken, especially if one is serious about trying to find a solution to domestic violence?

Prior studies show that multiple victimization is common (Aromaa 1984; Baril 1984; Fishman 1984; Gottfredson 1989; Manzanera 1984). Other studies also show that those who use violence in one relationship are inclined to be violent in others (Fagan 1989; Fagan, Stewart, & Hansen 1983; Hotaling & Straus 1989; Walker 1984). Theories attributing crime targets to lifestyle or to routine activities would suggest that unless victims of domestic abuse change their ordinary habits, they would be at risk for further victimization (Cohen & Felson 1979; Garofalo 1987; Miethe, Stafford, & Long 1987). There is, therefore, reason to believe that checking only for same victim-assailant pairs provides a poor measure for the effects of preventive programs.

Fagan et al. (1984) and Grau, Fagan, and Wexler (1985) reported that the severity of injury increased for women who obtained restraining orders when compared with those who used alternative interventions. They concluded that nonpunitive interventions without teeth may be counterproductive.

A serious attempt to test the effectiveness of intervention strategies would require follow-up for at least two years and would include checking for evidence of domestic violence in alternative places or checking for evidence of the victim being worse off as a consequence of the intervention. The victim might be worse off because of more severe beatings by the same or a different person. Women could also be worse off after interventions because they lost financial support.

One ought to wonder whether the attempts to study reduction of domestic violence look half-hearted to the official agents carrying out those projects. If they do, and if the official agents are also only half-heartedly indicating that violence against women is wrong, the interventions may be exacerbating the problem.

More than three decades ago, Bandura and Walters (1959) interviewed fathers of delinquents. They learned that these fathers conveyed their own favorable attitudes toward aggressive behavior by the way they scolded their sons for aggression. The fathers' favorable attitudes in turn appeared to encourage further antisocial behavior. Nevertheless, there seems to be no evidence that officers on domestic routines are required to oppose the use of violence against women.

Until recently, acts of violence against women were only occasionally considered to be criminal (Breines & Gordon 1983; Dobash & Dobash 1981; Pleck 1989). Although the official view has changed, at least in the United States, there is reason to believe that the incidence of domestic violence has continued to be high.

In part, the failure to reduce domestic violence appears to be a consequence of a naive approach to prevention, an approach which could be considered akin to an attack on spotolism. Spotolism, as one might have guessed, is a disease for which the symptoms are spots. Sometimes spotolism seems to be reduced with calamine lotion, sometimes with quinine and sometimes with antibiotics. Overall, however, the various techniques appear to be equally good and equally bad in combatting spotolism. Treatment against spotolism would not have occurred had it not been recognized that the symptoms represented more than one malady. An attempt to reduce spotolism would have resulted in seeking a single preventive technique for flea bites, measles, chicken pox, and scarlet fever, an all but impossible task.

To reduce domestic violence, researchers should develop a taxonomy of domestic violence. Such a taxonomy would go beyond noting whether offending symptoms can be considered felonies or misdemeanors, first offenses or repetitions.

One taxonomy might focus on background beliefs about the legitimacy of violence. Langan and Innes (1986) found that half the women they interviewed, all of whom were victims of domestic violence, did not report their victimization to the police. Approximately half of those who did not report to the police said that their most important reason was that the *abuse was a private or personal matter.* Some of these women may have believed the use of violence against them was a legitimate act. In such cases, interference by the law might lead to rejection of the law rather than to conformity. Furthermore, with such a background culture, women might find it difficult to prosecute or to leave men who abuse them.

In a culture that excuses violence against women while opposing it in principle, one could expect occurrences of violence against women to be most frequent under conditions that free men from responsibility (e.g., when they are drinking). Domestic violence would be sporadic under these conditions. Its prevention might well require a different approach from that required under the first set of conditions. In some such cases, for example, actions that emphasize responsibility (which could include arrest) might reduce violence.

In a culture that clearly opposes violence against women, there might be effective psychological treatments. Abusive behavior would be viewed as intolerable by both the aggressor and the victim; it would then make sense to attempt to develop techniques for control of undesired behavior.

Prior experiments have assigned abusers to untested counseling programs. Before such programs are considered treatments for domestic violence, they ought to be evaluated in terms of their effects on violent behavior.

It is possible that some so-called treatment programs increase the use of violence. In a study some years ago, the Joseph J. Peters Institute (1980) discovered that treating rapists in groups with only other rapists tended to increase recidivism. The researchers reasoned that these results occurred because the men lacked incentives for questioning the legitimacy of their actions. Some treatment programs for violence against women expose the men to similar normalization and reinforcement processes (Ptacek 1988).

Another category system of domestic violence might consider prior reporting experiences of the abused women. Are women less likely to report violence and more likely to be victims if they have had the experience that nothing much happens if they report the violence? Providing networks for assistance to the victimized women could be an effective intervention.

Adequate research on domestic violence ought to take account of the alternatives available to women exposed to violence. Does a woman's employment alter the effects of arrest? Domestic violence might be reduced through providing alternative living arrangements to victims.

Research about domestic violence has largely ignored the topic of rewards. Rewards, however, are likely to be more relevant to choices than are threats of punishments. Carroll (1982) provides some evidence: In his study, offenders and nonoffenders were asked to evaluate a series of "crime opportunities" that varied along dimensions of possible punishment, potential gain, probability of punishment, and probability of gain. For both offenders and nonoffenders, the amount and probability of gains had more than twice the influence of punishment.

What rewards follow violence? Some wives are more compliant after the use of violence (Dobash & Dobash 1979). Are there ceremonies of reconciliation? Do the men win praise from their social groups? Coming to understand and to reduce domestic violence will require some breaks with tradition and a broad perspective on gender issues.

References

Akers, R.L., LaGreca, A.J., Sellers. C., & Cochrane, J. (1987). Fear of crime and victimization among the elderly in different types of communities. *Criminology 25*(3): 487–505.

Anderson, E. (1989). Sex codes and family life among poor inner-city youths. *Annals of the American Academy of Political and Social Science* 501: 59–78.

Aromaa, K. (1984). Three surveys of violence in Finland. In R. Block (ed.), *Victimization and fear of crime* (pp. 11–21). Washington, DC: U.S. Government Printing Office.

Atkeson, B.M., Calhoun, K.S., Resick, P.A., & Ellis, E.M. (1982). Victims of rape: Repeated assessment of depressive symptoms. *Journal of Consulting and Clinical Psychology* 50: 96–102.

Bacon, M.K., Child, I.L., & Barry, H., Jr. (1963). A cross-cultural study of correlates of crime. *Journal of Abnormal and Social Psychology* 66: 291–300.

Bandura, A., & Walters, R.H. (1959). *Adolescent aggression*. New York: Ronald.

Baril, M. (1984). The victims' perceptions of crime and the criminal justice system: A pilot study of small shopkeepers in Montreal. In R. Block (ed.), *Victimization and fear of crime* (pp. 75–86). Washington, DC: U.S. Government Printing Office.

Berk, R.A., & Newton, P.J. (1985). Does arrest really deter wife battery? An effort to replicate the findings of the Minneapolis spouse abuse experiment. *American Sociological Review* 50: 253–262.

Breines, W., & Gordon, L. (1983). The new scholarship on family violence. *Signs: Journal of Women in Culture and Society* 8(3): 490–531.

Campbell, A. (1984). *The girls in the gang*. New Brunswick, NJ: Rutgers University Press.

Carroll, J.S. (1982). The decision to commit the crime. In J. Konecni & E.B. Ebbesen (eds.), *The criminal justice system* (pp. 49–67). San Francisco: W.H. Freeman.

Cernkovich, S.A., & Giordano, P.C. (1979). A comparative analysis of male and female delinquency. *Sociological Quarterly* 20: 131–145.

Clemente, F., & Kleiman, M.B. (1977). Fear of crime in the United States: A multivariate analysis. *Social Forces* 56: 519–531.

Cloward, R.A., & Ohlin, L.E. (1960). *Delinquency and opportunity*. New York: Free Press.

Cohen, L.E., & Felson, M. (1979). Social change and crime rate trends: A routine activity approach. *American Sociological Review* 44: 588–608.

Davis, N.J., & Robinson, R.V. (1991). Men's and women's consciousness of gender inequality: Austria, West Germany, Great Britain, and the United States. *American Sociological Review* 56: 72–84

Dobash, R.E., & Dobash, R.P. (1979). *Violence against wives*. New York: Free Press.

——— (1981). Community response to violence against wives: Charivari, abstract justice and patriarchy. *Social Problems* 28(5): 563–581.

Dunford, F.W., Huizinga, D., & Elliott, D.S. (1990). The role of arrest in domestic assault: The Omaha police experiment. *Criminology* 28: 183–206.

Elliott, D.S., Huizinga, D., & Ageton, S.S. (1985). *Explaining delinquency and drug use*. Beverly Hills, CA: Sage.

Estes, W.K. (1957). Of models and men. *American Psychologist* 12: 609–617.

Fagan, J. (1989). Cessation of family violence: Deterrence and dissuasion. In L. Ohlin & M. Tonry (eds.), *Family violence,* Volume 11: *Crime and justice: A review of research* (pp. 377–425). Chicago: University of Chicago Press.

Fagan, J., Friedman, E., Wexler, S., & Lewis, V.S. (1984). *National family violence evaluation: Final report*. San Francisco: URSA Institute.

Fagan, J., Stewart, D.K., & Hansen, K.V. (1983). Violent men or violent husbands? Background factors and situational correlates. In D. Finkelhor, R.J. Gelles, G.T. Hotaling, & M. Straus (eds.), *The dark side of families* (pp. 49–67). Beverly Hills, CA: Sage.

Farnworth, M., McDermott, M.J., & Zimmerman, S.E. (1988). Aggregation effects on male-to-female arrest rate ratios in New York State 1972 to 1884. *Journal of Quantitative Criminology* 4(2): 121–135.

Feyerherm, W. (1981). Measuring gender differences in delinquency. In M.Q. Warren (ed.), *Comparing male and female offenders* (pp. 46–54). Beverly Hills, CA: Sage.

Fishman, G. (1984). Differential victimization patterns: An analysis of crime victims in polar neighborhoods in Haifa. In R. Block (ed.), *Victimization and fear of crime* (pp. 45–49). Washington, DC: U.S. Government Printing Office.

Ford, D.A. (1990). The deterrent effect of prosecution. Paper presented at the 40th annual meeting of The Society for the Study of Social Problems, Washington, DC.

Garofalo, J. (1987). Reassessing the lifestyle model of criminal victimization. In M.R. Gottfredson & T. Hirschi (eds.), *Positive criminology* (pp. 23–42). Newbury Park, CA: Sage.

Glaser, D. (1978). *Crime in our changing society*. New York: Holt, Rinehart & Winston.

Gottfredson, G.D. (1989). The experience of violent and serious victimization. In N.A. Weiner & M.E. Wolfgang (eds.), *Pathways to criminal violence* (pp. 202–234). Newbury Park, CA: Sage.

Grau, J., Fagan, J., & Wexler, S. (1985). Restraining orders for battered women: Issues of access and efficacy. *Women and Politics* 4(3): 13–28.

Higonnet, A. (1990). *Berthe Morisot*. New York: Harper & Row.

Hotaling, G.T., & Straus, M.A. (1989). Intrafamily violence and crime and violence outside the family. In L. Ohlin & M. Tonry (eds.), *Family ciolence,* Volume 11: *Crime and justice: A review of research* (pp. 315–375). Chicago: University of Chicago Press.

Hotaling, G.T., & Sugarman, D.B. (1986). An analysis of risk markers in husband to wife violence: The current state of knowledge. *Violence and Victims* 1: 101–124.

Jensen, G.F., & Eve, R. (1976). Sex differences in delinquency: An examination of popular sociological explanations. *Criminology* 13(4): 427–448.

Jones, M.B., Offord, D.R., & Abrams, N. (1980). Brothers, sisters, and antisocial behaviour. *British Journal of Psychiatry* 136: 139–145.

Joseph J. Peters Institute (1980). A ten year follow-up of sex offender recidivism (final report). Philadelphia, PA: Joseph J. Peters Institute.

Kilpatrick, D.G., Saunders, B.E., Amick-McMullan, A., Best, C.L., Veronen, L.J., & Resnick, H.S. (1989). Victim and crime factors associated with the development of crime-related post-traumatic stress disorder. *Behavior Therapy* 20: 199–214.

Lamb, M.E. (1976). The role of the father: An overview. In M.E. Lamb (ed.), *The role of the father in child development*. New York: Wiley.

Langan, P.A., & Innes, C.A. (1986). *Preventing domestic violence against women* (Bureau of Justice Statistics Special Report). Washington, DC: U.S. Department of Justice.

Liska, A.E., & Reed, M.D. (1985). Ties to conventional institutions and delinquency: Estimating reciprocal effects. *American Sociological Review* 50: 547–560.

Maccoby, E.E., & Jacklin, C.N. (1974). *The psychology of sex differences*. Stanford, CA: Stanford University Press.

McCord, J. (1991). The cycle of crime and socialization practices. *Journal of Criminal Law and Criminology* 82(1): 211–228.

Manzanera, L.R. (1984). Victimization in a Mexican city. In R. Block (ed.), *Victimization and fear of crime* (pp. 51–56). Washington, DC: U.S. Government Printing Office.

Matsueda, R.L., & Heimer, K. (1987). Race, family structure, and delinquency: A test of differential association and social control theories. *American Sociological Review* 52: 826–840.

Miethe, T.D., Stafford, M.C., & Long, J.S. (1987). Social differentiation in criminal victimization: A test of routine activities/lifestyle theories. *American Sociological Review* 52: 184–194.

Miller, W.B. (1958). Lower class culture as a generating milieu of gang delinquency. *Journal of Social Issues* 14: 5–19.

Nadelson, C.C., Notman, M.T., Zackson, H., & Gornick, J. (1982). A follow-up study of rape victims. *American Journal of Psychiatry* 139(10): 1266–1270.

Pate, A., Wilson, V., & Kelling, G.L. (1981). Reported crime in Newark and Elizabeth and arrests in Newark. *The Newark Foot Patrol Experiment.* Washington DC: The Police Foundation.

Petersilia, J. (1980). Criminal career research. In N. Morris & M. Tonry (eds.), *Crime and justice* (vol. 2) (pp. 321–379). Chicago: University of Chicago Press.

Pleck, E. (1989). Criminal approaches to family violence, 1640–1980. In L. Ohlin & M. Tonry (eds.), *Family violence,* Volume 11: *Crime and justice: A review of research* (pp. 19–57). Chicago: University of Chicago Press.

Ptacek, J. (1988). The clinical literature on men who batter: A review and critique. In G.T. Hotaling, D. Finkelhor, J.T. Kirkpatrick, & M.A. Straus (eds.), *Family abuse and its consequences: New directions in research* (pp. 149–162). Newbury Park, CA: Sage.

Rosenfeld, R.A., & Kalleberg, A.L. (1990). A cross-national comparison of the gender gap in income. *American Journal of Sociology* 96(1): 69–106.

Sherman, L.W., & Berk, R.A. (1984). The specific deterrent effects of arrest for domestic assault. *American Sociological Review* 49: 261–272.

Skogan, W. (1987). The impact of victimization on fear. *Crime and Delinquency* 33: 135–154.

Skogan, W.G., & Maxfield, M.G. (1981). *Coping with crime: Individual and neighborhood reactions.* Beverly Hills, CA: Sage.

Snyder, J., Dishion, T.J., & Patterson, G.R. (1986). Determinants and consequences of associating with deviant peers during preadolescence and adolescence. *Journal of Early Adolescence* 6(1): 29–43.

Stafford, M.C., & Galle, O.R. (1984). Victimization rates, exposure to risk, and fear of crime. *Criminology* 22(2): 173–185.

Stattin, H., & Magnusson, D. (1990). *Pubertal maturation in female development*. Hillsdale, NJ: Lawrence Erlbaum.

Steffensmeier, D.J. & Steffensmeier, R.H. (1980). Trends in female delinquency: An examination of arrest, juvenile court, self-report, and field data. *Criminology* 18(1): 62–85.

Treiman, D.J., & Roos, P.A. (1983). Sex and earnings in industrial society: A nine-nation comparison. *American Journal of Sociology* 89(3): 612–650.

Walker, L.E. (1984). *The battered woman syndrome*. New York: Springer.

——— (1988). The battered woman syndrome. In G.T. Hotaling, D. Finkelhor, J.T. Kirkpatrick, & M. Straus (eds.), *Family abuse and its consequences* (pp. 139–148). Newbury Park, CA: Sage.

Warr, M. (1984). Fear of victimization: Why are women and the elderly more afraid? *Social Science Quarterly* 65(3) 681–702.

——— (1990). Dangerous situations: Social context and fear of victimization. *Social Forces* 68(3): 891–908.

Weis, J.G. (1989). Family violence research methodology and design. In L. Ohlin & M. Tonry (eds.), *Family violence,* Volume 11: *Crime and justice: A review of research* (pp. 117–162). Chicago: University of Chicago Press.

Wells, L.E., & Rankin, J.H. (1988). Direct parental controls and delinquency. *Criminology* 26(2): 263–285.

Whiting, J.W.M., Kluckhohn, R., & Anthony, A. (1958). The function of male initiation ceremonies at puberty. In E.E. Maccoby, T.M. Newcomb, & E.L. Hartley (eds.), *Readings in social psychology* (pp. 359–370). New York: Holt, Rinehart and Winston.

Wolfgang, M.E., Figlio, R.M., & Sellin, T. (1972). *Delinquency in a birth cohort*. Chicago: University of Chicago Press.

Wolfgang, M.E., Thornberry, T.P., & Figlio, R.M. (1987). *From boy to man, from delinquency to crime*. Chicago: University of Chicago Press.

Women and the Newest Profession: Females as White-Collar Criminals

Jay Albanese
Niagara University

Abstract

This essay employs data from both the United States and Canada to show how opportunity factors have played a dramatic role in the rise of white-collar crimes by females. Economic, technological, and demographic changes are shown to have resulted in a dramatic increase in the proportion of females in the white-collar work force and a corresponding increase in their arrests for white-collar crimes. Similarities and differences between the seriousness of male versus female white-collar crimes and what level of "equity" may be expected in the future are also assessed. The potential impact of changes in economic conditions, the importance of sex differences, and the glass ceiling phenomenon are each considered.

Women and the Newest Profession

The invention of the term "white-collar crime" is now 50 years old. As such, it is one of the "newest" forms of crime, compared to more traditional forms of criminal behavior. Its inventor, sociologist Edwin Sutherland (1949), focused primarily on a survey of crimes committed by corporations in his pioneering book *White Collar Crime*. The issue of the offender's sex, therefore, did not figure in his writing. In recent years, however, white-collar crimes committed by individuals have received a great deal of attention, due to a number of large and highly publicized frauds. It will be shown here that changes in the economy, technology, and demographics have resulted in a dramatic escalation of female involvement in this form of criminal behavior, compared to males, during the last two decades in both the United States and Canada.

What is White-Collar Crime?

Much of the confusion over precisely what constitutes white-collar crime can be attributed to Sutherland's original definition. He refers to crimes by "persons of high social status" that are committed "in the course of" an occupation. Clearly, the acts of *individuals* are included in this definition. The second part of the definition, however, appears to *omit* individual crimes, such as income tax evasion or credit card fraud, which are usually unconnected with one's occupation. Likewise, occupational thefts committed by *working-class* individuals, such as embezzlement or bribe-taking, also seem to fall outside Sutherland's definition (Sparks 1979). Sociologist Edwin Lemert (1972) claims to have once asked Sutherland whether he meant a specific type of crime, or crime committed by a specific type of person, in his definition of white-collar crime. Sutherland said he was not sure.

Ironically, the debate continues today. Hirschi and Gottfredson (1987) argue that white-collar crimes are those that occur "in an occupational setting" (p. 961), but two years later, in response to a critique, they claimed that the definition is *not* limited to "crimes committed by employees" (Hirsch & Gottfredson 1989:362). But others continue to hold that white-collar crimes are limited to those that are occupationally related (Steffensmeier 1989). Indeed, as Steffensmeier has suggested, "the meaning of the term white collar crime is notoriously uncertain" (p. 347).

Much of this current definitional debate is unnecessary, as it was 50 years ago. It seems arbitrary to distinguish white-collar crime from other forms of crime solely by the kind of person engaging in it. No such distinctions are made about the social position of the mugger, burglar, or rapist because it is simply not relevant. From Beccaria (1764) forward, the offense, not the offender, has been the unit of analysis for defining any kind of crime. The primary problem with offender-based conceptions of white-collar crime is that they can be misleading in focusing on often spurious offender attributes. As Sutherland declared in 1949, the historical bias in studies that focused exclusively on the crimes of the poor (i.e., street crimes) is as significant "as it would be if the scholars selected only red-haired criminals for study and reached the conclusion that redness of hair was the cause of crime" (p. 9).

Likewise, most white-collar crime occurs during the course of one's occupation, but it does not appear to be a *necessary* element in defining white-collar crime. Another important factor in distinguishing white-collar crime from other forms of criminal behavior is that it requires *planning and organization* (unlike most street crimes) and also involves trickery. That is to say, white-collar crime usually can be distinguished from conventional crimes by its use of advance preparation of some kind, as well as fraud, rather than randomness in its commission and the use of force or stealth (Albanese 1987). Therefore, taking the best parts of Sutherland's definition, and adding the dimensions noted here, a general definition of white-collar crime would read:

> Planned or organized illegal acts of fraud, usually accomplished during the course of legitimate occupational activity, committed by an individual or corporate entity.

Opportunity Factors: Economy, Technology, Demography

The best predictor of crime, especially white-collar crime, is opportunity. One cannot engage in certain criminal behaviors if denied the opportunity to do so. While a trash collector can engage in income tax fraud, he or she generally lacks the opportunity to engage in securities fraud. It can be expected, therefore, that white-collar crime will increase as the opportunities for it expand.

Opportunities for white-collar crime increase primarily as the result of three influences: changes in the economy, technology, and demographics. Computerized transactions of all sorts, 24-hour stock trading, and purchases on credit are examples of increased opportunities for fraud due to advances in both the economy and technology (Albanese 1988; McIntosh 1975). Demographics play a role inasmuch as young people are generally denied the opportunity to commit white-collar crime. Embezzlement, forgery, and fraud generally require bank accounts, credit ratings, and, oftentimes, occupational access. This is supported by the fact that most offenders arrested for crimes of fraud are older (over 25 years old) and better educated than the "typical" criminal. Therefore, an aging population would likely affect the opportunities for white-collar crime, and clearly, this is now occurring. In 1970, the median age in both the United States and Canada was approximately 27. More recently the median age has been 33 in both countries, and it is expected to continue rising past the age of 40 by the year 2020, as life expectancy increases and birth and immigration rates remain low (Dumas 1987; Spencer 1989).

Sex is another demographic factor that contributes to the incidence of white-collar crime. If the proportion of female white-collar workers is increasing (compared to males), it can be expected that they will engage in white-collar crime at an increasing rate (as compared to males).

This suggests four hypotheses:

1. Female white-collar workers are increasing at a faster rate than males, resulting in proportionally increasing new opportunities for white-collar crime by females.
2. The rate at which females engage in white-collar crime is increasing faster than it is for males, due to the higher rate of female infiltration into the white-collar work force.
3. The types of white-collar crimes committed by women are generally less serious than those committed by men, because men still occupy a higher proportion of higher-level positions of financial trust and control.

4. The comparative seriousness of male versus female white-collar crime will equalize, as female infiltration of the white-collar work force slows, and women are promoted to positions of financial trust and control in similar proportions to men.

Hypothesis 1: Females in the White-Collar Work Force

Census data and data gathered from the Departments of Labor in both the United States and Canada indicate that the infiltration of female workers into the white-collar work force is increasing at a dramatic pace.

Table 1
Women in Managerial Positions

Year	United States	Canada
	%	%
1970	31.7	15.4
1980	36.8	N/A
1988	44.7	42.5

Source: Connelly and MacDonald (1990), U.S. Bureau of the Census (1975, 1980), and U.S. Department of Labor (1989).

As Table 1 illustrates, in 1988 approximately 45% of all managerial positions in the United States, and 43% in Canada, were held by women. This contrasts with 32% and 15% respectively, 20 years earlier. These employment gains are significant and include positions such as public officials, public administrators, business managers, accountants, architects, engineers, natural scientists, health professionals, teachers, counselors, social scientists, lawyers, writers, artists, and designers. Therefore, Hypothesis 1 appears to be supported, inasmuch as female infiltration into the white-collar work force has grown by 176% in Canada and 41% in the United States during the last two decades. This also implies, of course, that the number of males holding managerial positions has declined proportionally during this period.

Hypothesis 2: The Female White-Collar Crime Rate

Men still hold the majority of management and professional positions in the United States and Canada, although Table 1 makes it clear that they now hold approximately 55% to 57% of these positions, versus 68% (in the United States) and 85% (in Canada) in 1970, a huge decline in only 20 years. A consequence of this trend is many new female employees in the white-collar work force in North America. The rapidly rising rate of female employment gains would suggest that the rate at which females are committing white-collar crimes would be increasing faster than the male rate. This assumes, of course, that increased opportunities are a reliable predictor of increased crimes.

Table 2 presents the female rate of participation in white-collar crimes in the United States as measured by arrests.

Table 2

Female Participation in White-Collar Crime in the United States

	(Total arrests/ percentage female)			
	1970	1980	1989	% Change
Fraud	66,465	259,330	257,618	
	27%	41%	45%	+67%
Forgery and counterfeiting	39,811	71,496	72,042	
	24%	31%	34%	+42%
Embezzlement	7,531	7,790	11,687	
	25%	28%	40%	+60%

Source: Federal Bureau of Investigation (1980, 1989).

It can be seen that the total number of arrests for the crimes of fraud, forgery and counterfeiting, and embezzlement have increased significantly over the last 20 years. The rate at which females are arrested for these crimes has increased significantly as well. In 1970, females accounted for approximately 25% of all these white-collar arrests overall, but two decades later the proportion has increased by 67% for fraud, 42% for forgery and counterfeiting, and 60% for embezzlement. Although males still comprise the majority of arrests for these white-collar crimes, their arrest rate has dropped as the female rate has climbed.

The situation in Canada is similar. As Table 3 indicates, the rate at which females are arrested for fraud has increased 33% since 1974.

Table 3
Female Participation in White-Collar Crime in Canada

	Total arrests/percentage female			
	1974*	1980	1989	% Change
Fraud (total)	18,452	30,681	35,782	
	21%	24%	28%	+33 %
Bank check	11,834	18,420	20,104	
	22%	26%	30%	+36%
Credit card	1,163	2,252	3,263	
	22%	23%	23%	+5%
Other frauds	5,415	10,009	12,415	
	18%	21%	26%	+44%
Counterfeiting	333	112	188	
	18%	21%	13%	–28%
Bankruptcy act	246	107	134	
	15%	14%	9%	–40%
Securities act	251	108	152	
	24%	6%	14%	–42%

Source: Centre for Justice Statistics (1974, 1989).

* 1974 was the first year fraud arrest breakdowns by type were tabulated.

The only exceptions to the rise in female arrests rates is for counterfeiting Canadian currency and bankruptcy and securities act violations. These will be discussed later.

It should be noted that arrest rate is not the most reliable indicator of crime, as arrest rates can change independent of crime rates, due to changes in police practices, personnel, and the reporting behavior of victims. Likewise, more white-collar crimes exist than are included in these short lists, but the American and Canadian governments have not seen these as frequent or serious enough to count. Examples of omitted offenses include conspiracy, extortion, bribery, perjury, obstruction of justice, official misconduct, and regulatory offenses (for a complete listing, see Albanese 1987). Nevertheless, these data on national arrest trends are the most comprehensive available.

Given the information presented in Tables 2 and 3, it appears that Hypothesis 2 is supported. The rate at which females participate in white-collar crime (as measured by arrests) appears to have increased significantly in the United States during the last 20 years, matched by a substantial increase in female arrests for fraud in Canada.

Hypothesis 3: The Seriousness of Female White-Collar Crime

The precipitous rise of females in the white-collar work force is a relatively recent phenomenon, due to a host of economic, social, technological, and political influences (Adler 1975; Simon 1975). Alhtough it is difficult to measure precisely, it is probably true that many more females than males hold lower management and professional positions, due to their shorter tenure in these jobs. As a result, it might be expected as a consequence that men would commit more serious white-collar crimes than females, due to their greater access to higher positions of financial trust and control.

Neither Canada nor the United States distinguishes among the relative severity of the white-collar crimes they count in national arrest statistics. Unlike the United States however, Canada includes violations of the bankruptcy and securities act in its arrest figures. These are offenses which, presumably, require a greater degree of occupational access than would a credit card or check fraud. Although arrests for these offenses are few (less than 153 for each offense each year), the proportion of females arrested for these offenses has dropped by approximately 100 arrests per offense since 1974 (see Table 3). These data may offer an indirect indication that the seriousness of white-collar crimes by females is lower than that for males, perhaps due to their more limited access to higher management positions. More information is needed, however, about other types and larger numbers of white-collar crimes and their characteristics before firm conclusions can be drawn regarding the relative seriousness of male versus female white-collar crime suggested by Hypothesis 3.

Hypothesis 4: An Equitable Future?

The rationalizations provided by female white-collar criminals in certain limited studies appear to differ somewhat from those of males. Perhaps the best of these were conducted by Cressey (1953), Zietz (1981), and Daly (1989). Cressey and Zietz examined the motives of imprisoned male and female bank embezzlers, respectively, while Daly analyzed white-collar convictions for several different offenses involving both males and females. Cressey found that males justified their embezzling as "borrowing" resulting largely from personal financial problems, such as business debts, gambling, and over-spending in general. Zietz, however, found female offenders more often rationalized their embezzlement as a means to preserve family integrity. Daly found that both men and women employed the same justifications, although women more often cited family financial need versus personal problems. Regardless of the rationalization, however, there are no inherent biological differences that make one sex more susceptible to the temptations of white-collar crime than the other.

The infiltration of females into the work force undoubtedly will slow as they achieve greater "parity" with male white-collar workers (however "parity" may be defined). It would be reasonable to expect that the rate at which females commit white-collar crimes will slow correspondingly.

Nevertheless, it should also be expected that women will continue to commit crimes in proportion to their opportunities, as men do. Whether or not the rate at which men and women white-collar workers commit crimes will equalize cannot be determined until females hit their saturation point in the white-collar work force. This is impossible to know in advance, although data presented in Tables 1, 2, and 3 are suggestive. For all three white-collar crimes counted in the United States, women account for approximately 40% of all arrests. They also constitute 45% of the white-collar work force. Two decades earlier, women accounted for approximately 25% of all arrests and 32% of the white-collar work force. There appears to be a remarkable correspondence between female white-collar crime arrests and the presence of women in white-collar positions of employment.

In Canada, the results are similar, although not as dramatic. In 1974, females constituted approximately 20% of white-collar arrests and 15% of the work force. Now, they comprise 25% of white-collar arrests and 42% of the work force. The direction of these results follow those in the United States. The slight lag in arrest rates behind white-collar work force participation may be attributable to a greater proportion of lower-level positions held by females. Other, yet unmeasured, factors may also account for this difference. The proportion of women in closely monitored "pink-collar" positions, those who commit white-collar crimes that are not occupationally related, and knowledge of the arrest preferences of employers and police would also help to explain the inexact association between arrests and work force participation (Chapman 1980; Daly 1989; Howe 1977).

Implications

The implications of these hypotheses and data are significant. The proportion of women female white-collar workers in both the United States and Canada has increased dramatically during the last two decades. This has been matched by an increase in the proportion of females arrested for white-collar crimes during this period, suggesting an association between opportunity (white-collar work force participation) and arrests of women for white-collar crimes, a relationship that has held for men for many years.

Whether or not females ultimately will reach "parity" with men in both white-collar work force infiltration and in crime commission will depend on three factors: the economy, sex differences, and the "glass ceiling" phenomenon. With regard to the first, the economies of the United States or Canada experience a significant recession in the coming years, then female participation in the white-collar work force could drop substantially, due to their lack of seniority in many management and professional positions. If the opportunity-crime relation holds up, female white-collar arrests also could be expected to drop.

Second, female white-collar arrests tend to lag behind their relative numbers in the white-collar work force (i.e., men commit more crimes than their relative presence in the work force would suggest). It remains to be seen whether this is due to the differential opportunity of females in the white-collar occupations, employer complaints and their relation to police arrest practices, female participation in nonoccupational white-collar crimes, or to sex differences, such as in the case of violent crime where men consistently commit approximately nine times more homicides, rapes, robberies, and serious assaults than do women (Federal Bureau of Investigation 1990).

Finally, it has been reported that a number of female management workers experience a "glass ceiling," where employers promote women to supervisory positions that never quite reach the levels of their male counterparts (Garland & Driscoll 1991). As Sparks (1979) observes, the nonparticipation of women in sophisticated white-collar crimes may be "a clear indication of the continued exclusion of women from the social and economic roles that would make that participation possible" (p. 178). If this phenomenon continues, opportunities for women to commit white-collar crimes on the scale that men do will never be reached.

References

Adler, F. (1975). *Sisters in crime: The rise of the new female criminal.* New York: McGraw-Hill.

Albanese, J.S. (1987). *Organizational offenders* (2nd ed.). Niagara Falls, NY: Apocalypse Publishing.

——— (1988). Tomorrow's thieves. *The Futurist* 22(5): 25–28.

Beccaria, C. (1764). *Essay on crimes and punishments.* New York: Bobbs-Merrill.

Centre for Justice Statistics (1974). *Canadian crime statistics.* Ottawa: Statistics Canada.

——— (1989). *Canadian crime statistics.* Ottawa: Statistics Canada.

Chapman, J.R. (1980). *Economic realities and the female offender.* Lexington, MA: Lexington Books.

Connelly, M., MacDonald, P., & MacDonald, M. (1990). *Women and the labour force.* Ottawa: Canadian Government Publishing Centre.

Cressey, D.R. (1953). *Other people's money: A study in the social psychology of embezzlement.* Montclair, NJ: Patterson Smith.

Daly, K. (1989). Gender and varieties of white collar crime. *Criminology 27*(4): 769–794.

Dumas, J. (1987). Report on the current demographic situation in Canada. *Current Demographic Analysis*: 2(1): 20–27.

Federal Bureau of Investigation (1980). *Crime in the United States.* Washington, DC: U.S. Government Printing Office.

——— (1989). *Crime in the United States.* Washington, DC: U.S. Government Printing Office.

——— (1990). *Crime in the United States.* Washington, DC: U.S. Government Printing Office.

Garland, S.B., & Driscoll, L. (1991, April 29). Can the FEDs bust through the "glass ceiling"? *Business Week*, 33.

Hirschi, T., & Gottfredson, M. (1987). Causes of white-collar crime. *Criminology* 25: 949–974.

——— (1989). The significance of white-collar crime for a general theory of crime. *Criminology* 27: 359–371.

Howe, L.K. (1977). *Pink collar workers.* New York: Avon.

Lemert, E. (1972). *Human deviance, social problems, and social control* (2nd ed.). Englewood Cliffs, NJ: Prentice-Hall.

McIntosh, M. (1975). *The organization of crime.* London: Macmillan.

Simon, R.J. (1975). *Women and crime.* Lexington, MA: D.C. Heath/Lexington Books.

Sparks, R.F. (1979). "Crime as business" and the female offender. In F. Adler & R.J. Simon (eds.), *The criminology of deviant women* (pp. 171–179). Boston: Houghton Mifflin.

Spencer, G. (1989). *Projections of the population of the United States by age, sex, and race: 1988 to 2080* (U.S. Bureau of Census Current Population Reports, Series P-25, No. 1018). Washington, DC: U.S. Government Printing Office.

Steffensmeier, D.J. (1989). On the causes of "white collar" crime: An assessment of Hirschi and Gottfredson's claims. *Criminology 27*: 345–358.

Sutherland, E.H. (1949). *White collar crime.* New York: Dryden Press.

U.S. Bureau of Census (1975). *Statistical abstracts of the United States.* Washington, DC: U.S. Government Printing Office.

——— (1980). *Statistical abstracts of the United States.* Washington, DC: U.S. Government Printing Office.

U.S. Department of Labor (1989). *Handbook of labor statistics.* Washington, DC: U.S. Government Printing Office.

Zietz, D. (1981). *Women who embezzle or defraud: A study of convicted felons.* New York: Praeger.

Compared to What? Delinquent Girls and the Similarity or Differences Issue*

Ruth Seydlitz
University of New Orleans

Research on female delinquency has been characterized by a search for the best comparison group. That group could not be boys, according to theorists from 1895 (the date of Lombroso's book on females) through the 1960s, because girls are utterly different. That group *must* be boys, according to feminists of the 1970s, because the sexes are equal. In this study, I attempt to clarify and extend this long-standing debate by rephrasing the key issue: If our aim is to learn more about female delinquency in particular, then the best approach is to compare girls with girls, examining differences among them.

To set the present study in context, I begin with a historical review of theories about female crime and delinquency. Next, I describe my own theoretical framework, which merges Nye's (1958) social control theory with feminist work on adolescent socialization. A section on the data and methods used for this study is followed by a discussion of my results. I find important intragender differences in rates of delinquency, with early adolescent girls rebelling more strongly against a combination of weak parental affection and strong parental controls. Males do not show so marked an intragender variation by age.

* This study utilizes the data of the National Survey of Youth, 1972, originally collected by Martin Gold and made available by the Inter-University Consortium for Political and Social Research. Neither the original collector nor the Consortium bear responsibility for the analyses or interpretations presented here.

I thank Nicole Hahn Rafter for her comments on an earlier version of the paper.

Contrary to what we might conclude from Chodorow's (1978) key work on adolescent socialization, the delinquent behavior of early adolescent girls is affected just as strongly by the quality of their relationships with their fathers as their mothers. I conclude with recommendations for researchers who aim, as I do, at a more complete understanding of female crime and delinquency.

Crime and Delinquency: An Overview

The Focus on Gender Differences

Crime and delinquency researchers have focused mainly on males, and for many decades theorists used separate theories to explain male and female deviance (Cernkovich & Giordano 1987; Figueira-McDonough & Selo 1980). Theories of male delinquency stressed social, political, and economic factors such as educational and occupational opportunities and the influence of peers (Canter 1982a; Chilton & Datesman 1987). Theories of female delinquency, in contrast, emphasized psychological factors and family variables or interpreted sociological factors in psychological terms (Chilton & Datesman 1987; Giordano 1978).

In fact, until the 1970s, theorists treated females as if they were entirely different creatures from males (Jones 1981; Klein 1973). Cesare Lombroso, W.I. Thomas, Sigmund Freud, Kingsley Davis, and Otto Pollak explained female crime in terms of females' bodies. Gisela Konopka; Clyde Vedder and Dora Somerville; John Cowie, Valerie Cowie, and Eliot Slater; and others perpetuated this tradition through the 1960s by discussing female offenders in terms of their sexuality. These gender-essentialist theorists assumed that women are by nature passive, emotional, narcissistic, and deceitful (Jones 1981; Klein 1973). Those who wrote in this differences tradition created a good woman–bad woman dichotomy that presented bad women (i.e., criminal females) as rebels against femininity and the true nature of women. Many of them suggested that the best treatment for deviant females was to help them to adjust to their true nature and their domestic role.

The Focus on Similarities Across Gender

In the early 1970s, feminists began criticizing the differences tradition as sexist (e.g., Jones 1981; Klein 1973). Perhaps in reaction, some theorists attempted to link the feminist movement itself to female crime (e.g., Adler 1975; Simon 1975). But the only contribution of work associating the women's movement with female crime was to stimulate researchers to compare crime and delinquency across gender in order to demonstrate the fallacy of theories linking the women's movement with female crime (Chesney-Lind 1986). These comparisons of crime and delinquency across gender showed that although females commit less frequent and less serious acts, the pattern of offenses for males and females is similar (Canter 1982b; Cernkovich & Giordano 1979; Cullen, Golden, & Cullen 1979; Eve 1982; Hindelang 1971; Jensen & Eve 1976; Norland & Shover 1977). Males' incidence and prevalence of involvement in delinquency is significantly greater for many acts, but rank order correlations for the similarity in incidence and prevalence of offending across gender are quite high (0.82 to 0.93) and significant (Canter 1982b; Hindelang 1971). These scholars, in short, introduced a new tradition in which the emphasis fell on gender similarity, not differences.

The finding that the pattern of delinquency involvement is similar for males and females led some researchers and theorists to argue that the same theoretical factors can be used to explain male and female delinquency (Canter 1982a; Figueira-McDonough & Selo 1980; Giordano 1978; Hagan, Gillis, & Simpson 1985; Jensen & Eve 1976; LaGrange & White 1985:20; Shover & Norland 1978). Studies have shown that some concepts originally used in theories of male delinquency—family relationships, belief in the law, peer involvement, and attitudes toward school—are also important in understanding female delinquency (Canter 1982a; Cernkovich & Giordano 1987; Giordano 1978; Norland et al. 1979; Rankin 1980). These researchers suggested that females are less delinquent than males because they have lower levels on variables that increase delinquency and higher levels on variables that inhibit it.

Figueira-McDonough and Selo's (1980) reformulation of the equal opportunity thesis, which states that increased opportunities for females will increase female crime, is a good example of work arguing that if males and females have the same level on theoretical variables, they will act similarly. In their reformulation, Figueira-McDonough and Selo hypothesize, first, that "the illegal activities engaged in by girls with high success aspirations and low access to material and legitimate opportunities will be similar to the misbehavior of boys" (p. 338), due to strain. They hypothesize, next, that "similar levels of frustration will lead to similar behavior by the two sexes if they have equal knowledge of and comparable access to illegitimate means" (p. 339). Third, they argue that "low levels of control, under conditions of strain, will result in similar delinquent behavior among males and females" (p. 340). Thus, the older assumptions about gender differences were rejected in favor of assumptions about gender similarity.

There were problems with these attempts to use theories originally developed for males to explain females' criminality, problems that Chesney-Lind (1986) criticizes as the "'add women and stir' approach" (p. 84). In her 1989 article, Chesney-Lind points out the androcentric bias in many of the established theories of delinquency that researchers attempted to apply to females. Clifford Shaw and Henry McKay's cultural transmission theory, Frederick Thrasher's and Albert Cohen's writings on delinquent gangs, Walter Miller's analysis of lower-class focal concerns, Richard Cloward and Lloyd Ohlin's opportunity theory, Edwin Sutherland's differential association theory, and Travis Hirschi's social control theory were all formulated mainly with reference to males. Harris (1977) examined the possibility of incorporating gender into supposedly general theories of criminal deviance but found that, when gender was included, the theories of structured strain, differential opportunity, and subcultural differences developed logical fallacies. He also found the inclusion of gender to be problematic for two other theories—those of differential association and control. Beyond the logical difficulties, the gender differences in levels on theoretical variables failed to account for the gender gap in crime and delinquency. Moreover, theories originally developed to explain male offending fail to account for females' victimization and economic deprivation, which may be factors in female crime (Chesney-Lind 1986, 1989; Chilton & Datesman, 1987; Hill & Crawford 1990;

Rosenbaum 1989; Simpson 1991; Steffensmeier & Allan 1988). The questions raised by such writers began to shift interest back toward the issue of gender differences, although they did not return to the assumption of Lombroso et al. of inherent differences between the sexes.

The Focus on the Gender Gap in Offending

Because attempts to understand the gender differences in crime and delinquency using variables from theories originally created for males have been unsuccessful thus far, theorists are now trying to explain directly the gender gap in crime and delinquency (Box & Hale 1984; Chesney-Lind 1986, 1989; Hagan & Kay 1990; Hagan, Gillis, & Simpson 1985; Hagan, Simpson, & Gillis 1979, 1987, 1988; Harris 1977; Hoffman-Bustamante 1973; Steffensmeier & Allan 1988; Steffensmeier, Allan, & Streifel 1989; Thompson 1989). Hoffman-Bustamante (1973), for example, suggests that the gender difference in commission of crime is due to "differential role expectations for men and women, sex differences in socialization patterns and application of social control, structurally determined differences in opportunities to commit particular offenses, differential access or pressures toward criminally oriented subcultures and careers, and sex differences built into the crime categories themselves." (p. 117)

Alternatively, Harris (1977) revises labeling theory to create a theory of deviant type-scripts. He suggests that females are less deviant than males because there are fewer deviant type-scripts for females, who are already out of the competition for jobs (also see Best & Luckenbill 1990). Further, assigning females deviant typescripts and labeling them deviant is dysfunctional insofar as it removes females from the home, disrupting the family and reducing men's labor force participation. Harris (1977) predicts that greater male dominance is associated with lower rates of female crime. However, Best and Luckenbill (1990) found that states with higher male dominance have higher, not lower, female to male ratios of homicides. So far, deviant type-scripts theory has not produced results that can explain the gender gap in offending.

Power-control theory attempts to explain the gender difference in common delinquency in terms of women's relative lack of power in the work force and the home (Hagan, Gillis, & Simpson 1985; Hagan, Simpson, & Gillis 1979, 1987, 1988; Hagan & Kay 1990; Hill & Atkinson 1988; Singer & Levine 1988). Delinquency is the result of the presence of power and the absence of control (Hagan, Gillis, & Simpson 1985:1174). Power-control theorists suggest that sons have more power vis-à-vis the mother than daughters do because fathers have more authority in the workplace. Mothers are the primary instrument of familial control, and daughters are its primary objects. Due to their greater power and the resulting absence of controls, sons are more delinquent than daughters.

Contrary to power-control theory, which predicts greater gender differences in offending in the upper classes, Thompson (1989) predicts greater gender differences in drinking problems in the unemployed class because (a) parental controls are weaker in the unemployed class, especially for males, (b) males reject closeness to and display indifference toward others to avoid seeming traditionally feminine, and (c) women are less hurt by unemployment than males. He found that gender differences in drinking problems were greater in the unemployed class. Thus, locating the gender gap in the occupational structure is problematic.

According to Steffensmeier and Allan (1988), gender equality theory cannot explain age, race, and rural-urban residential differences in the arrest rates of males and females. Those differences can be explained by three other factors: females' greater opportunities to commit certain consumer crimes, formal social control, and economic marginality of women. Box and Hale (1984) also found no support for the liberation/emancipation theory of female crime, except for one offense—theft from employers—but economic marginalization and formal social control theories were supported. Steffensmeier, Allan, and Streifel (1989) tested four explanations of the percentage of females arrested in various countries for homicide and major property and minor property offenses. They found that gender equality theory and women's economic marginality could not explain cross-cultural differences in the percentage of females arrested, but opportunities for female-based consumer crimes and formalization of social control could account for these differences. They suggest that national economic development increases opportunities to commit consumer crimes, which increases female crime, and that development causes greater formalization of social control, which results in more arrests of females for crimes and better record-keeping.

Chesney-Lind (1986, 1989) recommends directions for further work to develop a theory that can explain both female crime and delinquency and the gender gap in offending. In 1986, she suggests three factors that might be useful in explaining the lower criminality of females: (a) greater control of females, (b) greater disapproval of female crime, and (c) sexism in the criminal world. Chesney-Lind (1989) stresses that an adequate theory of female crime and delinquency must be aware of the patriarchal context of society and must examine the manner in which the juvenile and criminal justice systems enforce the patriarchal ideal of women's place. It needs to account for the abuse of females, how their victimization and responses are shaped by their status, and how their victimizers are able to use the juvenile justice system to keep females at home and vulnerable.

Although the research reviewed above attempts to explain the gender gap in offending, only some of these investigators expect the same factors to explain offending by both males and females (Boritch & Hagan 1990; Box & Hale 1984; Hagan, Gillis, & Simpson 1985; Hagan, Simpson, & Gillis 1988; Steffensmeier & Allan 1988). These researchers suggest that the gender gap is due to females having higher levels on variables that inhibit offending while males have higher levels on factors conducive to offending. They use results showing similarities in male and female offending to support their argument. For example, Boritch and Hagan (1990) demonstrate the similarity in the long-term patterns of arrest rates for males and females, and Steffensmeier and Streifel (1991) show that the distribution of crime by age across offenses is essentially the same for males and females. Others, such as Chesney-Lind (1986, 1989) expect that female-specific factors may help to explain at least some of female crime and delinquency.

The Focus on Intragender Differences

A more recent direction in the study of female crime and delinquency is being set by new research on intragender differences. The need to examine differences among females in offending is demonstrated by Hill and Crawford (1990), who point to the significant differences in types of offenses committed by black and white adult females. Moreover, according to Hill and Crawford, social-psychological factors explain white females' offenses, while structural/deprivation variables are more useful for understanding black females' acts. Ageton (1983) reported significant race and social class differences in the prevalence of females' assaultive crimes. White females are the race-gender group least likely to be arrested, while black males are most likely to be arrested and white males and black females have similar arrest rates (Chilton & Datesman 1987; Tillman 1987). Chilton and Datesman (1987) argue that studies of gender differences in offending take race and age into account in order to produce a more complete picture of gender differences and avoid misleading interpretations. In fact, they state that "theories based on gender differences alone will be incomplete—if not misleading. . . . A general explanation for men's and women's crime rates must incorporate gender, race, age, and economic status" (p. 168). Simpson (1991) uses three theories—neo-Marxian, power-control, and socialist-feminist—to improve an understanding of intragender differences in crime due to race and class. The importance of race and class in female delinquency is demonstrated by Campbell's (1987) study of Puerto Rican gangs in New York City. Daly (1989) illustrates that gender differences in court are the result of differences in family circumstances, especially for blacks.

To extend research in this new area of intragender differences in delinquency, I examined how the effect of parental controls on delinquency varies by age and gender. I chose to concentrate on parental controls for several reasons. First, the family has long been considered central to an understanding of delinquency, thus it plays a key role in many theories, especially those of social control (Dembo et al. 1986; Hirschi 1969; Nye 1958) and power-control (Hagan, Gillis, & Simpson 1985; Hagan, Simpson, & Gillis 1979, 1987, 1988). Second, recently there has been renewed interest in the effect of the family on delinquency (Gove & Crutchfield 1982; Hagan, Simpson, & Gillis 1987; Hirschi 1983; Laub & Sampson 1988; Wilkinson 1974). Third, theorists who focus on gender differences in delinquency raise an intriguing issue with implications that reach well beyond the field of crime: Do family-related variables affect daughters more than sons? Many theorists hold that females *are* more influenced by family dynamics (Gibbons 1976; Gold 1970; Haskell & Yablonsky 1974; Monahan 1957; Nye 1958; Toby 1957; Wattenberg & Sanders 1954), and this belief affects practices in the juvenile justice system, but some argue that males and females are equally influenced (e.g., Canter 1982a; Norland, Thornton, & James 1979). Thus, this new research direction continues to deal with the old question of gender similarities and differences.

We need to consider age as well as class and race if we are to understand fully intragender differences in delinquency. Age, although often omitted, is a crucial variable. Rates of crime and delinquency vary by age (Empey 1982; Greenberg 1977; Hirschi 1969; LaGrange & White 1985; Steffensmeier & Streifel 1991). In addition, adolescents' particular age affects parental assessments of behavior and the intensity of child-parent conflicts (Gottlieb & Chafetz 1977; Gottlieb & Heinsohn 1973). Further, the relationship between children's attachment to their parents and parental controls on delinquency may vary by the child's age (Hirschi 1969; LaGrange & White 1985; Nye 1958).

Affection for Parents, Parental Control, and Delinquency

A number of theories deal with parental effects on delinquency, including Hirschi's (1969) social control and Hagan, Gillis, and Simpson's (1985) and Hagan, Simpson, and Gillis' (1979, 1987) power-control. For this study, I use the framework provided by Nye's (1958) social-control theory as it presents two important advantages. First, it has no androcentric bias and, second, it hypothesizes considerable complexity in the effect of parents on delinquency. Nye suggests curvilinear relationships between some parental controls and delinquency, specifies interactions between different types of controls and delinquent behavior, shows gender differences in the effects of various kinds of controls on delinquency, and implies that age affects the relationship between parental controls and delinquent acts.

Nye's Social-Control Theory

Nye's theory specifies four different kinds of controls: indirect control, direct control, internalized control, and need satisfaction (Nye 1958; Wells & Rankin 1988:265). *Indirect control* is the attachment the adolescent has to parents and other noncriminal people due to his or her affection for these people. When adolescents feel affection for others, they refrain from delinquency to avoid embarrassing, disappointing, or hurting these people. *Direct controls* are external to the adolescent and imposed by restriction and punishment. According to Nye, parents reduce delinquency when they control their children's time away from home, choice of companions, and activities. *Internalized control*, the socialized conscience, is formed in part through the parent-child relationship and the child's acceptance of the parents. *Need satisfaction* refers to the adolescent's ability to fulfill his or her needs legitimately. According to Nye, the family affects the adolescent's ability to satisfy his or her needs through legitimate means.

These four types of controls are interrelated. In fact, Nye specifies that the level of affectional identification with the parents influences the effect of direct controls on delinquency; direct controls are better inhibitors of delinquency when adolescents are more attached to their parents. Nye claims that "evasion of and actual rebellion against direct controls might be expected to be less frequent . . . in cases in which there is an accepting relationship toward parents" (p. 71).

Nye specifies that the effect of controls will vary by gender and implies that parental control will differ by age. He explicitly states that parents have a greater effect on females' behavior. Direct controls are more important for females; moreover, indirect and internal controls have more impact for males. Nye does not delineate age differences in the influence of parents on delinquency, but he implies that parental control decreases as adolescents become older and make the normal change from dependency on the parents to greater independence.

Because Nye does not specify age and gender differences in the interaction of indirect controls, direct controls, and delinquency, we need to supplement his theory by drawing on the literature concerning adolescent socialization.

The Adolescent Socialization Literature

The literature on adolescent socialization suggests that commission of delinquency will be greatest when adolescents are less attached to their parents but are nonetheless expected to obey their parents. Ellis (1986) states that rebellion against parental control is more likely in families in which low affection is combined with coercive control. Conflict between parents and adolescents increases when internalization of parents' values is low and parental control is high. Internalization is reduced when there is less affection between parents and adolescents because affection is required for internalization to occur (Kagan 1984; Nye 1958). Further, the adolescent's view of the legitimacy of parental control effects the degree of conflict with parents. Rebellion is less likely when parental control is viewed as legitimate, and this control is carried out in the context of warmth and love (Ellis 1986). When mutual attachment and trust are absent, adolescents are more likely to feel that parental rules are illegitimately imposed; there is less reason to internalize.

In addition, the combination of rigid parental control and low affection for parents may be an indication of a dysfunctional family. Families with this combination may be rigidly disengaged, with low cohesion (emotional bonding) and low adaptability (ability to change power structures, rules, and roles in response to new situations) (Olson, Sprenkle, & Russell 1979). Families with overly harsh controls, interactions fraught with intimidation, low cohesion, and low expressions of warmth are more likely to produce individuals with behavior problems (Beavers 1982; Laub & Sampson 1988).

The timing of parental control may contribute to rebellion (Ellis 1986). Early on, parent-adolescent conflict may worsen (Floyd & South 1972) because some adolescents seek to develop a separate sense of self, largely by defying and irritating their parents (Josselson 1980). As Ellis (1986) claims, "Permissive parents may crack down as their children enter their teen years and seek a differentiation of self—a sudden and mistimed use of control that may literally be too much, too late" (p. 174). Thus, based on this literature, commission of delinquency should be greatest when younger adolescents are expected to obey rules established by parents for whom they feel little affection.

Other literature suggests that this interaction of delinquency, affection for parents, and parental rules is more likely to occur for females and is especially likely to happen for affection for the mother and the rules set by the mother. Females separate from their mothers and develop an individual sense of self during adolescence, whereas males complete this process earlier (Bardwick 1971; Chodorow 1978). Separation is portrayed as a time of conflict and ambivalence in the mother-daughter relationship (Chodorow 1978; Douvan & Adelson 1966). Mothers want to be close to their daughters but also wish to push their daughters away so that the daughters will develop independence. Daughters tend to have great affection for their parents but desire to be independent.

Problems in the separation process are exacerbated by the characteristics of the early childhood relationship. The mother-son relationship differs from that of the mother-daughter in that the former relationship emphasizes uniqueness while the latter one stresses similarity (Chodorow 1978). Further, the mother-daughter relationship is unilateral: the mother treats the daughter as an extension of herself (Kagan & Moss 1962). Thus, mother-daughter relationships have more problems with fusion (Chodorow 1978) and daughters have more trouble developing a separate identity (Cross 1975). Males' identification with others, moreover, is less personal: they identify with the position while females identify with the person (Chodorow 1978; Lynn 1967).

Thus, females separating from their mothers during early adolescence may have more conflicts with their parents, particularly their mothers. These conflicts may be more likely to occur if females are less attached to their parents since they may have a stronger desire for independence, especially from parents' rules. Therefore, they may want more freedom from parents' rules than parents are willing to give and may be more likely to evade and rebel against the rules. In general, females are more likely than males to drift toward independence and to internalize parents' rules (Douvan & Adelson 1966; Hoffman 1980); however, females who feel less affection for their parents may be less likely to internalize parents' rules (Kagan 1984; Nye 1958) and more likely to break the rules.

Based on the literature presented from Nye's social-control theory and adolescent socialization, it is expected that commission of delinquency is more likely when adolescents have less affection for their parents yet are expected to obey parents' rules. This relationship among delinquency, affection for parents, and the need to obey parents' rules is expected to occur more often for females in early adolescence and is anticipated to involve affection for the mother and the mother's rules more often than attachment to the father and obedience of the father's rules.

This delinquency-parental affection-rules interaction has several significant implications. By drawing on Nye's theory, I have been able to distinguish between indirect and direct parental controls and thus can use both types in my empirical analysis. While Hagan, Simpson, and Gillis (1988), in their important power-control theory, also distinguish between indirect and direct controls (which they call relational and instrumental controls, respectively), they do not consider the possibility that the two may interact with each other in relationship to delinquency. Nor do they investigate the effect of age on the relationship between parental controls and delinquency. Some studies have investigated the effects of both indirect and direct controls for males (Rankin & Wells 1990; Wells & Rankin 1988); I will be examining their effects on both males and females. My examination, moreover, will provide a test of Chodorow's (1978) influential theory about adolescent development as it relates to the differential effects of parental supervision on males and females.

Data

For this study, I drew a subsample from the National Survey of Youth data consisting of 872 white adolescents (402 females and 470 males) who lived with both biological parents. I restricted my analyses to this subgroup to control for racial and home status differences in delinquency (Johnson 1986; Rosen 1985) and in the influence of parents on delinquency (Cernkovich & Giordano 1987; Nye 1958). (For more details on the data set, see Seydlitz, forthcoming.)

Variables

I used two measures of delinquency. The *delinquent acts* measure consists of the commission of incidents of vandalism, deliberate physical injury, theft of an item worth less than $5, trespassing, group fighting, carrying a concealed weapon, and threatening personal harm. *Status-substance abuse acts* included commission of incidents of unexcused absence from school, lying about one's age or identity, drinking alcohol without parents' permission, and smoking marijuana. (For more details on the methods used by the National Survey of Youth, see Gold & Reimer 1975.)

I omitted eight acts from the analyses because they were rarely performed, especially by females or adolescents in particular age groups: running away, hitting parents, lying about what one will do, entering a building without permission, taking a car, using drugs other than marijuana, and medium and major theft.[1] To analyze the remaining behaviors, I used factor analysis with oblique rotation to determine the number of dimensions represented. The two factors, *delinquent acts* and *status-substance abuse acts*, emerged.[2] Scores on *delinquent acts* were the number of the seven types of acts committed and ranged from zero to six. The scores on *status-substance abuse acts* were the number of the four acts committed and ranged from zero to four. The factor loadings and index reliabilities are shown in Appendix A.

A factor analysis with oblique rotation was conducted to determine the number of dimensions represented by the 30 parent-related items.[3] Ten factors emerged. The first five factors—affectional attachment to the father, affectional attachment to the mother, consideration for parents, identification with parents' lifestyle, and agreement with parents' ideas and opinions—all measure affection for the parents, thus fitting Nye's (1958) definition of indirect controls. Scores on each factor were the sum of the adolescent's score on each item that loaded on the factor. (The items, factor loadings, index reliabilities, and range of scores are shown in Appendix B.)

The other five factors—control of leisure time, control of clothing, the need to obey parents' rules, supervision, and spankings—fit Nye's definition of direct controls, for they measure restriction, supervision, and punishment. However, since the adolescent socialization literature focuses on how lack of affection for parents is related to rebellion against parents' rules, in what follows I will use only the need to obey parents' rules. Scores on this factor were calculated by summing the adolescent's score on each item that loaded on this factor. (The items, factor loadings, index reliability, and range of scores for the need to obey parents' rules are shown in Appendix B.)

I hypothesized that the interaction of affection for parents, the need to obey parents' rules, and delinquency should occur most often for early adolescent females. Therefore, I analyzed the interaction separately for each age-gender group. Because age was curvilinearly related to some parental controls and to status-substance abuse acts, I categorized age into four groups, thus ensuring a linear association of age with each parental control and with each measure of delinquency within each age category. The four age groups were 11 and 12, 13 and 14, 15 and 16, and 17 and 18; eight age-gender groups were examined.

Methods and Results

To test the hypothesis that delinquency is greatest when adolescents who have low affection for their parents are nonetheless expected to obey, I used two-way ANOVA. For each measure of delinquency for each age-gender group, I analyzed five interactions: the need to obey parental rules with each indirect parental control—affectional attachment with the mother, affectional attachment with the

Table 1

Conditional Means and ANOVA Statistics for the Significant Interactions for Females Ages 13 and 14*

A. Interactions with Delinquent Acts

	Attachment to the Father: Low	Attachment to the Father: High		Attachment to the Mother: Low	Attachment to the Mother: High
Parents' Rules			Parents' Rules		
Low	0.593 (27)	0.789 (19)	Low	0.692 (26)	0.650 (20)
High	1.900 (10)	0.667 (21)	High	1.714 (14)	0.529 (17)
	Interaction: $F(1, 73) = 7.38$ ($p < .01$)			Interaction: $F\ (1, 73) = 5.12$ ($p < .05$)	
	Model: $R^2\ (3, 73) = 0.137$ ($p < .05$)			Model: $R^2\ (3, 73) = 0.138$ ($p < .05$)	

	Identification with Parents' Life: Low	Identification with Parents' Life: High		Consideration for Parents: Low	Consideration for Parents: High
Parents' Rules			Parents' Rules		
Low	0.600 (20)	0.727 (22)	Low	0.591 (22)	0.750 (24)
High	1.923 (13)	0.231 (13)	High	1.909 (11)	0.600 (20)
	Interaction: $F(1, 64) = 13.62$ ($p< .001$)			Interaction: $F\ (1, 73) = 8.26$ ($p < .01$)	
	Model: $R^2\ (3, 64) = 0.256$ ($p < .001$)			Model: $R^2\ (3, 73) = 0.155$ ($p < .01$)	

	Agreement with Parents: Low	Agreement with Parents: High
Parents' Rules		
Low	0.667 (24)	0.682 (22)
High	1.524 (21)	0.100 (10)
	Interaction: $F(1, 73) = 7.83$ ($p < .01$)	
	Model: $R^2\ (3, 73) = 0.168$ ($p < .01$)	

B. Interactions with Status-Substance Abuse Acts

Parents' Rules	Attachment to the Father: Low	Attachment to the Father: High
Low	0.346 (26)	0.571 (21)
High	1.429 (14)	0.211 (19)

Interaction: $F(1, 76) = 15.82$ ($p < .001$)
Model: R^2 $(3, 76) = 0.228$ ($p < .001$)

Parents' Rules	Attachment to the Mother: Low	Attachment to the Mother: High
Low	0.333 (21)	0.500 (20)
High	1.200 (15)	0.308 (13)

Interaction: F $(1, 65) = 6.74$ ($p < .05$)
Model: R^2 $(3, 65) = 0.153$ ($p < .05$)

Parents' Rules	Consideration for Parents: Low	Consideration for Parents: High
Low	0.400 (20)	0.481 (27)
High	1.462 (13)	0.250 (20)

Interaction: $F(1, 76) = 12.24$ ($p < .001$)
Model: R^2 $(3, 76) = 0.213$ ($p < .001$)

* Numbers in parentheses are the number of adolescents in the group.

father, identification with parents' lifestyle, consideration for parents, and agreement with parents' ideas and opinions. To categorize the parental-control variables, I divided the respondents into two groups, low or high, based on their level on each of the six parental-control measures. Although it would be preferable to split the adolescents into more categories on each parental control, the small number of adolescents in each age-gender group rendered further divisions impossible.

My analyses supported the hypothesis that, for females in early adolescence, delinquency is greatest when adolescents are expected to obey parents for whom they have a low degree of affection. Eight of the 10 possible interactions of indirect parental controls and the need to obey parents' rules with delinquency were significant for females ages 13 and 14 and only one was significant for any other age group (males ages 15 and 16). For females ages 13 and 14, there were five significant interactions with delinquent acts and three with status-substance abuse acts (see Table 1). Further, one additional interaction, status-substance abuse acts with agreement with parents' ideas and opinions and the need to obey parents' rules, approached significance ($p < 0.10$) for this age-gender group. The interaction that was significant for males ages 15 and 16 was that of status-substance abuse acts with affectional attachment to the father and the need to obey parents. However, due to the total number of interactions tested and the number examined for each age-gender group, the interaction for males ages 15 and 16 was probably significant by chance; therefore, it is not discussed here nor shown in Table 1.

All interactions for females ages 13 and 14 showed the anticipated pattern of means: delinquency was highest when the indirect parental control was low and the need to obey parents' rules was high. This pattern supported the expectation derived from Nye (1958), and the adolescent socialization literature that rebellion against parental rules is more likely when the adolescent feels less affection for the parents. The configuration of means suggested that adolescents who are more distant from their parents are less willing to accept parents' rules and more likely to resent parents' attempts to control adolescents' behaviors by making rules that adolescents are supposed to obey. The finding that this interaction occurred overwhelmingly for females ages 13 and 14 supported the expectation derived from the adolescent socialization literature that early adolescent females are more susceptible to the increase in delinquency that occurs from being expected to obey rules created by people for whom they feel little affection.[4]

The significant interactions for females ages 13 and 14 were further examined to determine the importance of each parent.[5] The results showed that it does not matter which parent makes the rules (see Table 2). Just one interaction—consideration for parents and delinquent acts with the need to obey parents' rules—was significant for only one parent's rules, those of the father (see Table 2, panel A). For the other eight original interactions that were significant for females ages 13 and 14, the interactions were either significant for both parents' or neither parent's rules (see Table 2, panels B through E). Moreover, the proportion of variance explained is similar for mothers' and fathers' rules.

Further, there was no evidence that attachment to the mother is more important than attachment to the father. For the interactions of delinquent acts and parents' rules with attachment, the proportion of variance explained when attachment to the father wass virtually identical to that explained when attachment is to the mother. However, agreement with the mother may be more important than agreement with the father. The models for the interaction of agreement with the mother, each parent's rules, and delinquent acts were significant (at the 0.05 level), while the ones for agreement with the father were not and the models for the interactions including agreement with the mother explained a greater proportion of the variance than those for the father, regardless of which parent made the rules (see Table 2, panels F and G).

It was possible that attachment to the mother and the mother's rules were not more important than those for the father because the daughters were equally attached to each parent and felt that they had to obey each parent's rules equally. Thirty-four percent of the females were strongly attached to both parents, 34 percent were weakly attached

Table 2

Conditional Means and ANOVA Statistics for the Interactions that Are Part of the Significant Interactions for Females Ages 13 and 14*

A. Interactions among Consideration for Parents, Parents' Rules, and Delinquent Acts

	Consideration for Parents: Low	Consideration for Parents: High
Father's rules		
Low	0.696 (23)	0.814 (27)
High	1.800 (10)	0.471 (17)

Interaction: $F(1, 73) = 7.38$ ($p < .01$)
Model: R^2 (3, 73) = 0.122 ($p < .05$)

B. Interactions among Attachment to the Mother, Parents' Rules, and Delinquent Acts

	Attachment to the Mother: Low	Attachment to the Mother: High
Father's Rules		
Low	0.778 (27)	0.739 (23)
High	1.615 (13)	0.357 (14)

Interaction: $F(1, 73) = 5.43$ ($p < .05$)
Model: R^2 (3, 73) = 0.116 ($p < .05$)

	Attachment to the Mother: Low	Attachment to the Mother: High
Mother's Rules		
Low	0.720 (25)	0.727 (22)
High	1.600 (15)	0.400 (15)

Interaction: F (1, 73) = 5.62 ($p < .05$)
Model: R^2 (3, 73) = 0.123 ($p < .05$)

C. Interactions among Identification with Parents' Lifestyle, Parents' Rules, and Delinquent Acts

	Identification with Parents' Lifestyle: Low	Identification with Parents' Lifestyle: High
Fathers' Rules		
Low	0.826 (23)	0.727 (22)
High	1.800 (10)	0.231 (13)

Interaction: $F(1, 64) = 7.48$ ($p < .01$)
Model: R^2 (3, 64) = 0.171 ($p < .01$)

	Identification with Parents' Lifestyle: Low	Identification with Parents' Lifestyle: High
Mothers' Rules		
Low	0.700 (20)	0.762 (21)
High	1.769 (13)	0.214 (14)

Interaction: F (1, 64) = 10.20 ($p < .01$)
Model R^2 (3, 64) = 0.205($p < .01$)

D. Interactions among Agreement with Parents, Parents' Rules, and Delinquent Acts

	Agreement with Parents			Agreement with Parents	
	Low	High		Low	High
Fathers' Rules			Mothers' Rules		
Low	0.815 (27)	0.696 (23)	Low	0.769 (26)	0.667 (21)
High	1.444 (18)	0.000 (9)	High	1.474 (19)	0.182 (11)
	Interaction: F (1, 73) = 6.07 ($p < .05$)		Interaction: F (1, 73) = 5.25 ($p < .05$)		
	Model: R^2 (3, 73) = 0.136 ($p < .05$)		Model R^2 (3, 73) = 0.133 ($p < .05$)		

E. Interactions among Attachment to the Mother, Parents' Rules, and Status-Substance Abuse Acts

	Attachment to the Mother			Attachment to the Mother	
	Low	High		Low	High
Fathers' Rules			Mothers' Rules		
Low	0.393 (28)	0.500 (24)	Low	0.423 (26)	0.609 (23)
High	1.500 (12)	0.250 (16)	High	1.286 (14)	0.118 (17)
	Interaction: F(1, 76) = 12.88 ($p < .001$)		Interaction: F (1, 76) = 13.01 ($p < .001$)		
	Model: R^2 (3, 76) = 0.211 ($p < .001$)		Model R^2 (3, 76) = 0.182 ($p < .01$)		

F. Interactions among Agreement with the Mother, Parents' Rules, and Delinquent Acts

	Agreement with the Mother			Agreement with the Mother	
	Low	High		Low	High
Fathers' Rules			Mothers' Rules		
Low	0.800 (30)	0.700 (20)	Low	0.759 (29)	0.667 (18)
High	1.444 (18)	0.000 (9)	High	1.474 (19)	0.182 (11)
	Interaction: $F(1, 73) = 6.18$ ($p < .05$)			Interaction: F (1, 73) = 5.25 ($p < .05$)	
	Model: R^2 (3, 73) = 0.135 ($p < .05$)			Model R^2 (3, 73) = 0.133($p < .05$)	

G. Interactions among Agreement with the Father, Parents' Rules, and Delinquent Acts

	Agreement with the Father			Agreement with the Father	
	Low	High		Low	High
Fathers' Rules			Mothers' Rules		
Low	0.714 (35)	0.867 (15)	Low	0.667 (33)	0.857 (14)
High	1.238 (21)	0.000 (6)	High	1.261 (23)	0.143 (7)
	Interaction: $F(1, 73) = 5.03$ ($p < .05$)			Interaction: F (1, 73) = 4.80 ($p < .05$)	
	Model: R^2 (3, 73) = 0.082 ($p < .10$)			Model R^2 (3, 73) = 0.086 ($p < .09$)	

* Numbers in parentheses are the number of adolescents in the group.

to both parents, and 32 percent were strongly attached to only one parent. The original, continuous variables of attachment to the mother and attachment to the father were significantly correlated ($r = 0.461$). Most females (54%) were low on the need to obey both parents' rules, while 25% were high on the need to obey both parents, and 21% were high on the need to obey only one parent. The original five-point items for the need to obey the mother and the father were significantly correlated ($r = 0.560$). Thus, daughters may be equally attached or unattached to both parents and equally likely to obey or disregard each parent's rules.

All interactions had the same pattern of means. Delinquency was greatest when indirect parental control was low and the need to obey the particular parent's rules was high. This configuration of means again supported the expectations derived from Nye (1958) and the adolescent socialization literature that rebellion against parental rules is greatest when young females are less attached to their parents.

Discussion

The hypothesis is supported: the delinquency of early adolescent females is greater when they are expected to obey parents for whom they feel little affection, while the delinquency of other age-gender groups is not sensitive to this particular combination of affection for parents and parental rules. Daughters, ages 13 and 14, who are expected to obey rules created by parents that the daughters do not care for are more delinquent than females who are not expected to obey their parents' rules or daughters who are highly attached to their parents. Further, attachment to the mother is not more important than attachment to the father, and it is irrelevant which parent makes the rules, although agreement with the mother's ideas and opinions may be more important than agreement with those of the father.

The results show that Nye's (1958) social-control theory is useful in understanding female delinquency. As Nye expected, rebellion against parents' direct control is greater when adolescents are less attached to their parents. However, the theory is not adequate to comprehend completely the findings since Nye did not anticipate that the delinquency-enhancing effect of low attachment and coercive control would occur only for early adolescent females. The results demonstrate that the modifications of Nye's theory suggested by the adolescent socialization literature were necessary because parent-adolescent conflicts and rebellion against parental rules are more likely for early adolescent females.

The findings support the expectation derived from Chodorow's (1978) work that adolescents' relationships with their parents differ by gender. The combination of low affection for parents and high need to obey them was conducive to delinquency only for females. Further, the specificity of the interaction among delinquency, indirect parental controls, and the need to obey parents' rules suggests that there is something different about females ages 13 and 14. It is possible that early adolescent females are in a particular stage of the maturation process which makes them more susceptible to the delinquency-enhancing effects of the combination of low affection for parents and coercive direct controls. It could be that early adolescent females are going through the separation process presented earlier (Bardwick 1971; Chodorow 1978; Douvan & Adelson 1966).

However, the findings do not support Chodorow's hypothesis that there are more conflicts in the mother-daughter relationship than in that of the father-daughter. There was no greater conflict with the mother and no greater disobedience of the mothers' rules. Low attachment to the father, as well as to the mother, when combined with the need to obey either parent, increases females' deviant behaviors. Thus, if early adolescent females are completing the separation process discussed earlier, then they are separating from both parents, not just the mother, with the resultant increases in conflicts with both parents and rebellion against both parents' rules. Daughters may want freedom from both parents if they are relatively unattached to their parents.

As Simpson (1991) claims, there is indeed a need to examine intragender differences in delinquency. The importance of race and class in understanding female crime and delinquency has been acknowledged and demonstrated in the literature (Ageton 1983;

Campbell 1987; Chilton & Datesman 1987; Hill & Crawford 1990; Simpson 1989, 1991).

However, the importance of age in studying intragender differences in crime and delinquency has rarely been mentioned (Chilton & Datesman 1987). The necessity of including age in studies of female delinquency is illustrated by the finding that, even with race and home status controlled, early adolescent females differ from other females in their reactions to the combination of low affection and high direct controls. In contrast, there are no age variations for males. Thus, in the study of intragender differences in the effects of parents on delinquency, age may be more important for females than males.

Conclusion

The search for the best comparison group for understanding female crime and delinquency is not over, probably because there is no perfect comparison group. Contrary to the implications of the differences tradition, examining the similarity in male and female crime and delinquency is useful. However, contrary to work in the similarity or equality tradition, males are not the perfect comparison group. The problem with both the differences and the similarity traditions is that both treated females as a homogeneous group, thus ignoring differences among women. Recent studies, including the current one, demonstrate the importance of examining intragender differences to obtain a more complete understanding of female crime and delinquency (Ageton 1983; Campbell 1987; Chilton & Datesman 1987; Hill & Crawford 1990; Tillman 1987). Women vary along many dimensions—race, age, economic status, relationship to their families, marital status, history of abuse—and these differences affect the commission of deviant behavior.

As this study indicates, we probably need to draw information from several fields if we are to understand female crime and delinquency. For this study, I had to integrate Nye's (1958) social-control theory of delinquency with literature on adolescent socialization, especially that of the Chodorow (1978) tradition. To meet fully Chesney-Lind's (1986, 1989) requirements for a complete theory of female delinquency, future researchers should consider drawing on other potentially useful literature. Works on dysfunctional families and feminist writings would help us understand abuse and females' reactions to abuse (e.g., Chesney-Lind 1989; Rosenbaum 1989). As Hagan, Simpson, and Gillis (1988) have clearly shown, adolescent socialization literature and feminists' work concerning socialization, such as that of Chodorow (1978) and Gilligan (1982), could assist in comprehending the maturation and socialization processes and may explain both how greater control of females is possible and why female crime receives greater disapproval. In addition, legal writings on the development of law and the courts, particularly the juvenile court, and feminists' work on law and juvenile court practices may provide understanding on why females' coping strategies have been criminalized (e.g., Chesney-Lind 1989; Rafter 1990; Rosenbaum 1989; Schlossman & Wallach 1978). Feminists' studies of law are particularly important because these investigations show the power of law to define and disqualify women due to the androcentric standard of law (Eisenstein 1988; Simpson 1989; Smart 1989). Further, examinations of the history of attitudes toward and treatment of female offenders and the social movements that affected attitudes and treatment, such as the eugenics and social purity movements of the Progressive era, are necessary to understand current attitudes and practices (e.g., Rafter 1990; Schlossman & Wallach 1978). To understand more completely female crime and delinquency, social-control theory must be combined with work on how systems of social control, those of the family and those external to it, react differently to females.

Notes

1. Adolescents were questioned about their commission, within the last 3 years, of 17 acts ranging from minor acts such as lying about their ages to serious behaviors such as gang fighting and carrying a concealed weapon. When the respondents admitted commission of an act, they were questioned further concerning the circumstances of the three most recent incidents. If the interviewer determined that the incident was not trivial, he or she asked more questions, including when the incident occurred and, when appropriate, the value of the stolen or damaged property. The information concerning when the

value of the stolen or damaged property. The information concerning when the incident occurred was used to determine if the behavior occurred within the last year and the details about the value of the stolen property was used to create three theft categories: minor theft (less than $5), medium theft ($5-$50) and major theft (more than $50). Thus, there was information on the adolescent's commission of 19 acts committed within the year prior to the interview.

2. The delinquency factors are similar to those found in other studies (Krohn & Massey 1980; Regan & Vogt 1983). The clustering of the items that were used in both the current study and Regan and Vogt's study is identical and the delinquent acts factor in the current study is similar to the factor Krohn and Massey called serious delinquent behavior.

3. Most of the parent-related items were five-answer, Likert format items, and a factor loading of .5 was required for inclusion on the index.

4. The percentage of variance explained by the models is not impressive, ranging from 14% to 26% but the models include only two dimensions of one theoretical variable, parental control. This percentage of explained variance is similar to percentages from other studies that examined the effect of parents on delinquency (e.g., Hirschi 1969; LaGrange & White 1985; Wiatrowski, Griswold, & Roberts 1981).

5. For delinquent acts, ten interactions were tested, the interaction of the five indirect parental controls with the need to obey the father's rules and the interaction of the five indirect controls with the need to obey the mother's rules. Because agreement with parents could be separated into agreement with each parent, four other interactions were investigated for delinquent acts, agreement with the mother with each parent's rules and agreement with the father with each parent's rules. For status-substance abuse acts, six interactions were examined: attachment to the mother, identification with parents' life-styles, and consideration for parents with the need to obey the father's rules and with the need to obey the mother's rules. In these analyses, the need to obey each parent's rules and agreement with each parent were categorized into two groups; low and high.

References

Adler, F. (1975). *Sisters in crime: The rise of the new female criminal.* New York: McGraw-Hill.

Ageton, S.S. (1983). The dynamics of female delinquency, 1976–1980. *Criminology* 21: 555–584.

Bardwick, J.M. (1971). *Psychology of women: A study of bio-cultural conflicts.* New York: Harper & Row.

Beavers, W.R. (1982). Healthy, midrange, and severely dysfunctional families. In F. Walsh (ed.), *Normal family processes* (pp. 45–66). New York: Guilford Press.

Best, J., & Luckenbill, D.F. (1990). Male dominance and female criminality: A test of Harris's theory of deviant type-scripts. *Sociological Inquiry* 60: 71–86.

Boritch, H., & Hagan, J. (1990). A century of crime in Toronto: Gender, class, and patterns of social control, 1859 to 1955. *Criminology* 28: 567–599.

Box, S., & Hale, C. (1984). Liberation/emancipation, economic marginalization, or less chivalry: The relevance of three theoretical arguments to female crime patterns in England and Wales, 1951–1980. *Criminology* 22: 473–498.

Campbell, A. (1987). Self-definition by rejection: The case of gang girls. *Social Problems* 34: 451–466.

Canter, R.J. (1982a). Family correlates of male and female delinquency. *Criminology* 20: 149–167.

——— (1982b). Sex differences in self-report delinquency. *Criminology* 20: 373–393.

Cernkovich, S.A., & Giordano, P.C. (1979). Delinquency, opportunity, and gender. *Journal of Criminal Law and Criminology* 70: 145–151.

——— (1987). Family relationships and delinquency. *Criminology* 25: 295–321.

Chesney-Lind, M. (1986). Women and crime: The female offender. *Signs: Journal of Women and Culture in Society* 12: 78–96.

——— (1989). Girls' crime and woman's place: Toward and feminist model of female delinquency. *Crime and Delinquency* 35: 5–29.

Chilton, R., & Datesman, S.K. (1987). Gender, race, and crime: An analysis of urban arrest trends, 1960–1980. *Gender and Society* 1: 152–171.

Chodorow, N. (1978). *The reproduction of mothering: Psychoanalysis and the sociology of gender.* Berkeley: University of California Press.

Cross, K.P. (1975). Women as new students. In M. Mednick, S. Tangri, & L. Hoffman (Eds.), *Women and achievement: Social and motivational analyses* (pp. 339–353). New York: Wiley.

Cullen, F.T., Golden, K.M., & Cullen, J.B. (1979). Sex and delinquency: A partial test of the masculinity hypothesis. *Criminology* 17: 301–310.

Daly, K. (1989). Neither conflict nor labeling nor paternalism will suffice: Intersections of race, ethnicity, gender, and family in criminal court decisions. *Crime and Delinquency*, 35(1): 136–168.

Dembo, R., Grandon, G., La Voie, L., Schmeidler, J., & Burgos, W. (1986). Parents and drugs revisited: Some further evidence in support of social learning theory. *Criminology* 24: 85–104.

Douvan, E., & Adelson, J. (1966). *The adolescent experience.* New York: Wiley .

Eisenstein, Z.R. (1988). *The female body and the law.* Berkeley: University of California Press.

Ellis, G.J. (1986). Societal and parental predictors of parent-adolescent conflict. In G.K. Leigh & G.W. Peterson (Eds.), *Adolescents in families* (pp. 155–178). Cincinnati: South-Western Publishing.

Empey, L.T. (1982). American delinquency: Its meaning and construction. Homewood, IL: The Dorsey Press.

Eve, R.A. (1982). Untangling the sex difference in delinquency: Social bonds, peers, gender roles and body images. Paper presented at the American Sociological Association Annual Meeting, San Francisco.

Figueira-McDonough, J., & Selo, E. (1980). A reformulation of the "equal opportunity" explanation of female delinquency. *Crime and Delinquency*, 26: 333–343.

Floyd, H., & South, D. (1972). Dilemma of youth: The choice of parents or peers as a frame of reference for behavior. *Journal of Marriage and the Family* 34: 627–634.

Gibbons, D.C. (1976). *Delinquent behavior.* Englewood Cliffs, NJ: Prentice-Hall.

Gilligan, C. (1982). *In a different voice: Psychological theory and women's development.* Cambridge, MA: Harvard University Press.

Giordano, P.C. (1978). Girls, guys, and gangs: The changing social context of female delinquency. *Journal of Criminal Law and Criminology* 69: 126–132.

Gold, M. (1970). *Delinquent behavior in an American city.* Belmont, CA: Brooks/Cole.

Gold, M., & Reimer, D.J. (1975). Changing patterns of delinquent behavior among Americans 13 through 16 years old. *Crime and Delinquency Literature* 7: 483–517.

Gottlieb, D., & Chafetz, J.S. (1977). Dynamics of familial, generational conflict and reconciliation: A research note. *Youth and Society* 9: 213–224.

Gottlieb, D., & Heinsohn, A.L. (1973). Sociology and youth. *Sociological Quarterly* 14: 249–270.

Gove, W.R., & Crutchfield, R.J. (1982). The family and juvenile delinquency. *Sociological Quarterly* 23: 301–319.

Greenberg, D.F. (1977). Delinquency and the age structure of society. *Contemporary Crises* 1: 189–223.

Hagan, J., Gillis, A.R., & Simpson, J. (1985). The class structure of gender and delinquency: Toward a power-control theory of common delinquent behavior. *American Journal of Sociology* 90: 1151–1178.

Hagan, J., & Kay, F. (1990). Gender and delinquency in white-collar families: A power-control perspective. *Crime and Delinquency* 36: 391–407.

Hagan, J., Simpson, J., & Gillis, A.R. (1979). The sexual stratification of social control: A gender-based perspective on crime and delinquency. *British Journal of Sociology* 30: 25–38.

——— (1987). Class in the household: A power-control theory of gender and delinquency. *American Journal of Sociology* 92: 788–816.

——— (1988). Feminist scholarship, relational and instrumental control, and a power-control theory of gender and delinquency. *British Journal of Sociology* 39: 301–336.

Harris, A.R. (1977). Sex and theories of deviance: Toward a functional theory of deviant type-scripts. *American Sociological Review* 42: 3–16.

Haskell, M.R., & Yablonsky, L. (1974). *Juvenile delinquency.* Chicago: Rand McNally.

Hill, G.D., & Atkinson, M.P. (1988). Gender, familial control, and delinquency. *Criminology* 26: 127–147.

Hill, G.D., & Crawford, E.M. (1990). Women, race, and crime. *Criminology* 28: 601–623.

Hindelang, M.J. (1971). Age, sex, and the versatility of delinquent involvements. *Social Problems* 18: 522–535.

Hirschi, T. (1969). *Causes of delinquency.* Berkeley: University of California Press.

——— (1983). Crime and the family. In J.Q. Wilson (ed.), *Crime and public policy* (pp. 53–68). San Francisco: ICS Press.

Hoffman, M.L. (1980). Moral development in adolescence. In J. Adelson (Ed.), *Handbook of adolescent psychology* (pp. 295–343). New York: Wiley.

Hoffman-Bustamante, D. (1973). The nature of female criminality. *Issues in Criminology* 8: 117–136.

Jensen, G.F., & Eve, R. (1976). Sex differences in delinquency: An examination of popular sociological explanations. *Criminology* 13(4): 427–448.

Johnson, R.E. (1986). Family structure and delinquency: General patterns and gender differences. *Criminology* 24: 65–84.

Jones, A. (1981). *Women who kill.* New York: Fawcett Crest.

Josselson, R. (1980). Ego development in adolescence. In J. Adelson (Ed.), *Handbook of adolescent psychology* (pp. 188–210). New York: Wiley.

Kagan, J. (1984). *The nature of the child.* New York: Basic Books.

Kagan, J., & Moss, H.A. (1962). *Birth to maturity: A study in psychological development.* New York: Wiley.

Klein, D. (1973). The etiology of female crime: A review of the literature. *Issues in Criminology* 8: 3–31.

Krohn, M.D., & Massey, J.L. (1980). Social control and delinquent behavior: An examination of the elements of the social bond. *Sociological Quarterly* 21: 529–543.

LaGrange, R.L., & White, H.R. (1985). Age differences in delinquency: A test of theory. *Criminology* 23: 19–45.

Lambroso, C. (1895). *The Female Offender.* New York: D. Appleton.

Laub, J.H., & Sampson, R.J. (1988). Unraveling families and delinquency: A reanalysis of the Gluecks' data. *Criminology* 26: 355–380.

Lynn, D.B. (1967). Sex-role and parental identification. In G.R. Medinnus (Ed.), *Readings in the psychology of parent-child relations* (pp. 273–285). New York: Wiley.

Monahan, T.P. (1957). Family status and the delinquent child: A reappraisal and some new findings. *Social Forces* 35: 251–258.

Norland, S., & Shover, N. (1977). Gender roles and female criminality: Some critical comments. *Criminology* 15: 87–101.

Norland, S., Thornton, W.E., & James, J. (1979). Intrafamily conflict and delinquency. *Pacific Sociological Review* 22: 223–240.

Nye, F.I. (1958). *Family relationships and delinquent behavior.* New York: Wiley.

Olson, D.H., Sprenkle, D.H., & Russell, C.S. (1979). Circumplex model of marital and family systems: I. Cohesion and adaptability dimensions, family types, and clinical applications. *Family Process* 18: 3–28.

Rafter, N.H. (1990). *Partial justice: Women, prisons, and social control* (2nd ed.). New Brunswick, NJ: Transaction Publishers.

Rankin, J.H. (1980). School factors and delinquency: Interactions by age and sex. *Sociology and Social Research* 64: 420–435.

Rankin, J.H., & Wells, L.E. (1990). The effect of parental attachments and direct controls on delinquency. *Journal of Research in Crime and Delinquency* 27: 140–165.

Regan, L., & Vogt, V. (1983). Critical analysis of male and female delinquency. Paper presented at the Midwest Sociological Annual Meeting, Kansas City, MO.

Rosen, L. (1985). Family and delinquency: Structure or function? *Criminology* 23: 553–573.

Rosenbaum, J.L. (1989). Family dysfunction and female delinquency. *Crime and Delinquency* 35: 31–44.

Schlossman, S., & Wallach, S. (1978). The crime of precocious sexuality: Female juvenile delinquency in the Progressive era. *Harvard Educational Review* 48: 65–94.

Seydlitz, R. (forthcoming). The effects of age and gender on parental control and delinquency. *Youth and Society*.

Shover, N., & Norland, S. (1978). Sex roles and criminality: Science or conventional wisdom. *Sex Roles* 4: 111–125.

Simon, R.J. (1975). *Women and crime*. Lexington, MA: D.C. Heath/Lexington Books.

Simpson, S S. (1989). Feminist theory, crime, and justice. *Criminology* 27: 605–631.

——— (1991). Caste, class, and violent crime: Explaining differences in female offending. *Criminology* 29(1): 115–135.

Singer, S.I., & Levine, M. (1988). Power-control theory, gender, and delinquency: A partial replication with additional evidence on the effects of peers. *Criminology* 26: 627–647.

Smart, C. (1989). *Feminism and the power of law*. New York: Routledge.

Steffensmeier, D.J., & Allan, E.A. (1988). Sex disparities in arrests by residence, race, and age: An assessment of the gender convergence/crime hypothesis. *Justice Quarterly* 5: 53–80.

Steffensmeier, D.J., & Streifel, C. (1991). Age, gender, and crime across three historical periods: 1935, 1960, and 1985. *Social Forces* 69: 869–894.

Steffensmeier, D.J., Allan, E., & Streifel, C. (1989). Development and female crime: A cross-national test of alternative explanations. *Social Forces* 68: 262–283.

Thompson, K.M. (1989). Gender and adolescent drinking problems: The effects of occupational structure. *Social Problems* 36: 30–47.

Tillman, R. (1987). The size of the "criminal population": The prevalence and incidence of adult arrest. *Criminology* 25: 561–579.

Toby, J. (1957). The differential impact of family disorganization. *American Sociological Review* 22: 505–512.

Wattenberg, W.W., & Saunders, F. (1954). Sex differences among juvenile offenders. *Sociology and Social Research* 39: 24–31.

Wells, L.E., & Rankin, J.H. (1988). Direct parental controls and delinquency. *Criminology* 26: 263–285.

Wiatrowski, M.D., Griswold, D.B., & Roberts, M.K. (1981). Social control theory and delinquency. *American Sociological Review* 46: 525–542.

Wilkinson, K. (1974). The broken family and juvenile delinquency: Scientific explanation or ideology. *Social Problems* 21: 726–739.

Appendix A
Delinquency Index Reliabilities and Factor Loadings

Delinquent Acts (each item is coded 0 for noncommission or 1 for commission of a nontrivial incident within the last year). Alpha = .62	
1. Purposely damaged or messed up something not belonging to you.	.52
2. Hurt or injured someone on purpose	.68
3. Took something not belonging to you (worth less than $5).	.45
4. Went on someone's property when you knew you were not supposed to.	.54
5. Took part in a fight where a bunch of your friends were against another bunch.	.65
6. Carried a gun or knife besides an ordinary pocket knife.	.49
7. Threatened to hurt or injure someone.	.50
Inter-item correlations range from 0.11 to 0.30, with a mean of 0.20, and all are significant.	
Status-Substance Abuse Acts (each item is coded 0 for noncommission or 1 for commission of a nontrivial incident within the last year). Alpha = .71	
1. Skipped a day of school without a real excuse.	.71
2. Tried to get something by lying about who you were or how old you are.	.68
3. Smoked marijuana.	.75
4. Drank beer, wine, or liquor without your parents' permission.	.75
Inter-item correlations range from 0.33 to 0.48, with a mean of 0.38, and all are significant.	

Appendix B
Parental Controls Index Reliabilities and Factor Loadings

Indirect Parental Controls

Affectional Attachment to the Father (response format is a 5-point scale from "never true" to "almost always true"). Alpha = .85

1.	My father accepts and understands me as a person.	.64
2.	My father gives me the right amount of affection.	.77
3.	I want to be like my father.	.51
4.	I feel close to my father.	.82
5.	My father makes it easy for me to confide in him.	.77
6.	My father and I do things together that we both enjoy doing.	.71

Inter-item correlations range from 0.35 to 0.61, with a mean of 0.48, and are all significant. Scores on this factor range from 6 to 30.

Affectional Attachment to the Mother (response format is a 5-point scale from "never true" to "almost always true"). Alpha = .83

1.	My mother gives me the right amount of affection.	.68
2.	I want to be like my mother.	.55
3.	I feel close to my mother.	.76
4.	My mother makes it easy for me to confide in her.	.81
5.	As I was growing up, my mother tried to help me when I was scared or upset.	.66
6.	My mother and I do things together that we both enjoy doing.	.66

Inter-item correlations range from 0.34 to 0.61, with a mean of 0.46, and are all significant. Scores on this factor range from 6 to 30.

Identification with Parents' Lifestyle (response format for the first item is a 3-point scale ranging from "different" to "in between, or 50-50" to "same." Response format for the second item is a 7-point scale ranging from "everything different" to "everything same"). Alpha = .83

1. These days some young people have ideas about the way they expect to live when they get older that are different from their parents' ideas. . . . That is, some young people want to follow a different lifestyle when they are adults than the lifestyle of their parents. Do you think your lifestyle as an adult will be like that of your parents or different? .97
2. The second item is a summary item indicating the degree of difference in seven role-related lifestyle areas: spouse, parent, family-provider, worker, religious believer, citizen, and sex role. .96

Inter-item correlation is 0.89. Scores range from 2 to 10.

Agreement with Parents' Ideas and Opinions (response format is a 5-point scale ranging from "never true" to "almost always true"). Alpha = .59

1. I agree with my father's ideas and opinions about things. .67
2. I agree with my mother's ideas and opinions about things. .68

Inter-item correlation is 0.42. Scores range from 2 to 10.

Consideration for Parents (response format is a 5-point scale ranging from "strongly disagree" to "strongly agree"). Alpha = .42

1. When young people make important decisions they should think first about their parents' wishes. .77
2. I would be unhappy living away from my parents when I get older. .64

Inter-item correlation is 0.26. Scores range from 2 to 10.

Direct Parental Control

Need to Obey Parents' Rules (response format is a 5-point scale ranging from "never true" to "almost always true"). Alpha = .77

1. My father makes rules that I have to obey. .82
2. My mother makes rules that I have to obey. .86

Inter-item correlation is 0.63. Scores range from 2 to 10.

Stealing and Dealing: The Drug War and Gendered Criminal Opportunity

Nanci Koser Wilson
Indiana University of Pennsylvania

In the last decade, the United States Government has waged an increasingly vigorous war on drugs. A more intensive law enforcement effort has had the effect of enlarging the "crime tariff" (Packer 1968), and foreign policy has stimulated the growth of cocaine importation (Beirne & Messerschmidt 1991); Weisheit 1990). As cocaine flowed more freely into the United States and as legitimate opportunities for employment among the underclass decreased during the 1980s, an enormous demand for crack cocaine was created. Ghetto entrepreneurs were able to make large amounts of money selling this highly addictive drug.

To what extent has this new criminal opportunity altered the ways in which American men and women make a living at crime? Has the emergent opportunity affected men and women differently? In this essay, the different methods in which men and women make money at crime will be examined. Then their experiences in the 1970s and the 1980s will be compared. These two decades present a good opportunity to analyze this phenomenon because during the latter decade the introduction of crack cocaine opened a new criminal option in drug dealing that had not existed in the previous decade.

The Gendered Shape of Income-Productive Crime

Crime and, in particular, income-productive crime can best be understood within the context of an economic analysis. Since the economy of the underworld mirrors that of the upperworld, or the legitimate economy, it is important to understand the gendered nature of the American economy (especially when sex differences in crime are noted).

The United States economy is tripartite. Its first leg is the domestic economy, which is composed of unpaid labor performed in the home, mostly by women, and within which few cash exchanges take place. Instead, economic exchange is by barter, gift, loan, and borrowing, all of which are mediated by friendship, kinship, and neighborliness, and made possible by the stable home base which women create through their child-care responsibilities. It is estimated that women produce more than 40% of the gross domestic product through this labor (Morgan 1984), which is not accounted for in United States accounting systems like the GNP (Gross National Product) or in the UNSNA (see Waring 1988). Instead, this economy is invisible because its labor is unpaid, because its transactions are not mediated by cash, and because the labor of women in the home is a taken-for-granted commodity, "a natural resource, freely available like air and water" (Mies 1986). The most distinctive feature of the domestic economy is its cooperative relations of production and distribution.

The second part of the economy is that of the commercial labor market (CLM), in which all transactions are cash. In the CLM, women's work *is* accounted for, but this part of the economy is hierarchically and patriarchally structured. Its most distinctive feature is competitive relationships. Women run the domestic economy, but the CLM is run by men. Women who work in the CLM have significantly lower wages than men, partly as a result of the intensive sex segmentation of this labor market. In the CLM, male jobs assume a person with no home-care responsibilities, are highly paid, and involve responsibility over other workers, particularly female workers. Female jobs, less well paid, supervised by men, and with little chance for upward career mobility, assume a worker with home-care responsibilities (see Sokoloff 1980). Thus, the nature of the CLM is shaped by the domestic economy.

These two parts of the economy—the domestic economy and that of the CLM—meet in the sexual alliances men and women form in marriage, in common-law marriage, and in other arrangements for the sharing of households. Thus, the family constitutes the third part of the economy. After a split in the alliance, children produced from such alliances typically stay with the woman who continues to maintain the family household. Single men rarely maintain such households for their offspring, who often become in effect "ex-children." Accordingly, many families are composed of an older single women, some of her grown children, and *their* children.

The work of the domestic economy is centered around the child; the work of the market economy is structured to provide gendered opportunity. As noted before, male jobs in the CLM assume a person with no or minimal responsibilities in the home, and female jobs allow for a worker who maintains such responsibility. Therefore, male jobs can require mobility, long and/or unpredictable hours, and integration into an established "good old boys" network of contacts, including customers, sponsors, and potential partners.

The domestic economy meshes neatly with the CLM economy. The women who provide domestic labor have sometimes in the past and, typically today, also brought in cash income through CLM work. But, importantly, this work never takes up so much of their time and energy as to prevent their performance of domestic work. The cash income needed to make the family, as an economic unit, work effectively is provided *in toto* or in part by a male "family wage earner."

American divorce law and welfare policy recognize the nature of this tripartite economy and reproduce it in providing alimony, child support, aid to families with dependent children, rent subsidies, and food stamps for single mothers who maintain households for their offspring. Criminal justice system policy mirrors this policy in its lesser willingness to imprison "familied" women (see Daly 1987; Wilson 1985).

Thus, the United States economy is based upon a deep sexual division of labor, a mesh between women in the home and men in "male" jobs that meets in the family. Men can do male work because of women's homework, and most women are restricted to "women's work" in the CLM because of their homework.

The criminal, or underworld, economy mirrors that of the straight- or upperworld. Because of the tripartite economy and the deep sexual division of labor it implies, men's and women's work depend upon one another and are deeply intertwined. Women's criminal work cannot be understood apart from men's criminal work nor apart from their legitimate work.

The differing patterns of male and female criminal work are revealed strikingly in *Uniform Crime Reports* (*UCR*) arrest data, which provide nationwide arrest information for 10 income-productive crimes. These include offenses that the FBI, and indeed most criminologists, would categorize as property crime—larceny-theft, auto theft, burglary, fraud and embezzlement, forgery, and receiving/possessing stolen merchandise. Also included are armed robbery, which is largely motivated by the desire for income (see Conklin 1972), drug offenses, and prostitution. The latter two are classified by most as victimless, public order, or (in the case of prostitution) sexual offenses, but their motivation is clearly economic (see James 1976). These offenses may be seen as alternate routes to producing income.

For the purposes of this analysis, the 10 income-productive crimes are further recombined into four categories: prostitution, drug offenses, professional or subcultural theft, and amateur theft. The latter two categories are comprised as follows: (a) subcultural theft, which includes burglary, armed robbery, auto theft, and fencing (receiving/possession of stolen merchandise) and (b) amateur theft, which includes forgery, fraud, embezzlement, and larceny-theft. The categories are not watertight. Certainly there are professional shoplifters, for example, whose arrests would fall in the larceny-theft category. And certainly, there are amateur armed robbers and burglars. However, the crimes in the amateur category are those which are most frequently and easily engaged in by amateurs and/or as part-time work, whereas, the other offenses require immersion in a subculture for eventual success.

The requirements of burglary, armed robbery, auto theft, and fencing include physical and geographical mobility, discretionary time, an appropriate mesh with legitimate work, and access to a wide network of contacts. Amateur theft can be engaged in without the acquisition of any special skills; it does not require a network of associations; and it can be done part-time. Prostitution, like subcultural theft, requires immersion in a subculture, but it does not connect with other subcultural theft networks and is limited both by demand and by its unappealing nature (Wilson 1983).

The two worlds—straight- and underworld—interact with and shape one another. The patterns of male and female choice in criminal work are comprehensible only when seen in this larger context.

First, subcultural crime is particularly unattractive to women because they lack discretionary time and mobility. It is estimated that American men have some 50% to 75% more discretionary time than women (Bernard 1979). The work women do in the straight world leaves little time for anything other than part-time work at crime. Their limited mobility further restricts their participation in crime.

Second, women who can enter a criminal subculture are usually pulled into prostitution, partly because of the similarity of prostitution to straight-world female work and partly through coercion.

Third, subcultural theft is often connected with straight-world employment as the owner of a small business, as a trucker, or as a mechanic. These are occupations which few women enter. To the extent that straight-world occupations provide an entree to the criminal subculture of theft, this avenue is closed to women. And, importantly, the subculture of prostitution does not link itself to the subculture of theft. An older retired prostitute may buy a small business such as a hair-dressing salon or, in another era, own or operate a house, but she does not acquire the connections and skills necessary to professional theft through her career as a prostitute.

Finally, there is evidence that underworld networks, which are controlled by men, exhibit a bias against women and effectively keep them out (Pettiway 1987; Steffensmeier 1986).

As the data in Tables 1 and 2 indicate, throughout the two decades covered by this study, women have been less involved than men in subcultural theft, which comprises less than 10% of women's total income-productive (I-P) crime as opposed to up to 38% for men. Women's arrest rates (see Tables 3 and 4) for these crimes are never

Table 1
Male Income-Productive Crime 1970–1989
(Types of I-P Crime as a Percentage of All I-P Crime*)

	Amateur Theft	Subcultural Theft	Prostitution	Drugs
1989	39.60	26.71	1.00	32.67
1988	41.91	27.19	1.03	29.87
1987	43.22	27.81	1.41	27.55
1986	44.35	28.94	1.43	25.27
1985	44.25	28.52	1.32	25.91
1984	44.43	29.54	1.36	24.67
1983	44.84	30.64	1.54	22.99
1982	44.99	32.23	1.41	21.37
1981	44.19	33.67	1.13	21.01
1980	43.87	34.90	1.13	20.10
1979	42.34	35.29	1.21	20.15
1978	41.04	35.58	1.24	22.14
1977	40.92	35.23	1.05	22.80
1976	41.15	35.28	.90	22.67
1975	40.13	37.34	.65	21.89
1974	37.59	37.14	.82	24.45
1973	34.99	37.20	.73	27.09
1972	37.89	37.66	.75	23.70
1971	38.80	38.41	77	22.09
1970	39.30	38.68	.74	21.29

* Totals will not add up to 100% because of rounding.

Table 2
Female Income-Productive Crime 1970–1989
(Types of I-P Crime as a Percentage of All I-P Crime*)

	Amateur Theft	Subcultural Theft	Prostitution	Drugs
1989	63.51	9.04	7.10	20.34
1988	66.44	8.95	7.14	17.47
1987	68.15	8.49	8.19	15.17
1986	69.33	8.69	8.52	13.46
1985	69.32	8.24	9.44	13.00
1984	68.15	8.64	10.25	12.96
1983	67.49	8.51	11.83	12.18
1982	68.45	8.95	11.43	11.17
1981	69.12	9.24	10.71	10.95
1980	70.27	9.14	9.14	10.95
1979	70.53	9.87	8.70	10.89
1978	68.91	9.75	9.08	12.27
1977	68.51	9.61	7.92	12.94
1976	70.24	8.89	8.94	12.96
1975	69.74	9.96	7.05	13.25
1974	64.68	9.85	9.77	15.70
1973	63.01	9.88	8.90	18.22
1972	63.94	9.80	8.72	17.54
1971	61.85	9.88	11.05	17.23
1970	62.32	9.39	11.87	16.42

* Totals will not add up to 100% because of rounding.

Table 3
Female Arrest Rates 1970–1989

	Amateur Theft	Subcultural Theft	Prostitution	Drugs
1989	546.77	77.87	61.08	175.81
1988	530.51	71.45	57.04	139.53
1987	538.21	67.03	64.67	119.83
1986	519.29	65.10	63.81	100.84
1985	508.53	60.43	69.24	95.41
1984	456.48	57.89	68.62	86.84
1983	476.32	60.05	83.49	85.96
1982	504.06	65.87	84.17	82.23
1981	456.21	60.98	70.63	72.24
1980	440.51	60.50	57.33	68.68
1979	444.51	62.21	54.83	68.65
1978	443.42	62.71	58.40	78.92
1977	421.47	59.13	54.98	79.59
1976	419.51	53.08	47.26	77.36
1975	411.71	58.79	41.63	78.20
1974	397.70	60.57	60.08	96.53
1973	312.73	49.04	44.16	90.40
1972	303.05	46.44	41.33	83.12
1971	298.03	47.59	53.22	83.04
1970	271.04	40.82	51.64	71.43

Table 4
Male Arrest Rates 1970–1989

	Amateur theft	Subcultural theft	Prostitution	Drugs
1989	1091.89	737.46	35.12	905.61
1988	1066.67	692.02	26.30	760.32
1987	1069.82	688.22	35.11	681.89
1986	1046.47	682.96	33.81	596.31
1985	1019.37	657.09	30.41	596.97
1984	969.60	644.63	29.60	538.34
1983	1031.49	704.91	35.36	528.85
1982	1096.90	785.72	34.51	521.12
1981	999.55	761.50	25.59	475.08
1980	967.92	769.89	25.10	443.35
1979	944.13	768.71	26.38	438.99
1978	922.59	799.70	27.92	497.66
1977	887.16	763.74	22.75	494.29
1976	895.06	767.29	19.57	493.05
1975	896.71	834.18	14.43	489.01
1974	894.73	884.14	19.43	582.08
1973	690.19	733.93	14.30	534.44
1972	729.02	723.06	14.45	454.99
1971	767.68	759.83	15.29	435.68
1970	711.75	700.53	13.46	385.56

Table 5
Percentage of Females among Income-Productive Crime 1970–1989

	Amateur Theft	Subcultural Theft	Prostitution	Drugs	Total I-P
1989	33.37	9.55	68.97	16.3	23.78
1988	33.22	9.36	68.44	15.5	23.88
1987	33.47	8.88	64.81	14.9	24.19
1986	33.17	8.70	65.37	14.5	24.10
1985	33.28	8.42	69.48	1.8	24.15
1984	32.01	8.24	69.86	13.9	23.49
1983	31.59	7.85	70.25	14.0	23.48
1982	31.49	7.74	71.02	13.6	23.20
1981	31.34	7.41	73.41	13.2	22.59
1980	31.28	7.29	69.56	13.4	22.13
1979	32.01	7.49	67.51	13.5	22.44
1978	32.46	7.27	67.66	13.7	22.26
1977	32.21	7.19	70.73	13.9	22.10
1976	31.91	6.47	70.72	13.6	21.54
1975	31.47	6.59	74.26	13.8	20.90
1974	30.77	6.41	75.57	14.2	20.53
1973	31.18	6.27	75.54	14.5	20.10
1972	29.41	6.04	74.10	15.4	19.80
1971	27.97	5.89	77.69	16.0	19.59
1970	27.58	5.51	79.33	15.6	19.36

higher than 77 per 100,000 as compared to male peaks of almost 900 per 100,000. And the percentage of females involved in the category is less than 10% in even the most recent years (see Table 5).

Women have been much more involved in amateur theft, and this is where most of the increase in female Income-Productive crime has occurred not only from 1970 to 1989 (where 64% of the arrest increases are produced by amateur theft) but also from 1960 onward (see Wilson 1983). There is, of course, a high percentage of female involvement in prostitution (always close to 70% female), but prostitution arrest rates are fairly stable, fluctuating around a median of 57.87 with a range from 41.83 to 84.17. This reflects, most probably, the fact that prostitution is responsive to demand and not to female need for income, for as the number of women in poverty increases, they are more likely to engage in theft than in prostitution.

In general, gender differences in criminal work may be summarized as follows:

1. Women are less involved than men in subcultural theft, because these crimes require
   a. a network of partners;
   b. physical and geographical mobility;
   c. long, unpredictable hours away from home;
   d. freedom from other daily responsibilities, like child care; and
   e. occasional lengthy absences (for work, for prison terms).
2. Women are more involved than men in amateur theft, which
   a. can be done solo (without hooking into male crime networks);
   b. can easily be combined with child- and home-care responsibilities;
   c. does not require physical and geographical mobility; and
   d. can be performed in hours that mesh with home-care responsibilities.
3. Women's participation in prostitution does not increase incrementally over time, as does their participation in theft, and this may well reflect a stable male demand for prostitution combined with a pronounced female unwillingness to engage in

prostitution. (Often, in fact, the pimp-prostitute relationship is held together by force [see Barry 1984]).

Women's Economic Situation in the 1970s and 1980s as Reflected in Income-Productive Crime Arrests

As Table 6 shows, from 1970 to 1989, women's arrest rates for income-productive crimes climbed steadily, as did men's. The women's rates doubled, however, while the male rates increased only by 1.5 times, an indication that women's economic situation worsened more than men's. And, in fact, during this time period women's share of income-productive crime arrests steadily increased (see Table 5). In 1970 such arrests were 19.36% female; by 1989 they were 23.78% female.

In a comparison of the two decades, rates of increase in arrests for income-productive crime were very similar, and this is so for both men and women (Tables 6 and 7). The male rates of increase was 1.2 for the 1970s and 1.26 for the 1980s. The female rate of increase was 1.45 for the 1970s and 1.38 for the 1980s.

But startling differences between rates of increase for drug crime and other Income-Productive crimes emerged in the 1980s for both men and women. During the 1980s, arrests for drug crime doubled for men and increased 2.56 times for women. Rates of increase for career theft, amateur theft, and prostitution were lower in the 1980s than in the 1970s. Apparently, drug dealing has replaced theft as an income producer among the underclass.

The Impact of Cocaine on Women's Income-Productive Crime Involvement

During the 1970s, drug arrests made up approximately 20% of male Income-Productive crime arrests and from 10% to 18% of

Table 6

Arrest Rates per 100,000 for Income-Productive Crime 1970–1989

	Male	Female
1989	2771.78	864.98
1988	2545.32	798.98
1987	2475.03	789.73
1986	2359.56	749.28
1985	2303.83	733.62
1984	2182.18	669.85
1983	2300.61	705.82
1982	2438.11	736.35
1981	2262.13	660.05
1980	2206.27	627.03
1979	2178.20	630.19
1978	2247.87	643.46
1977	2167.95	615.19
1976	2174.98	597.21
1975	2234.33	590.34
1974	2380.39	614.90
1973	1972.86	496.35
1972	1919.83	473.95
1971	1978.49	481.90
1970	1811.29	434.93

Table 7
Changes in Arrest Rates for Two Decades

Men						
	1970	1979	Increase	1980	1989	Increase
All I-P	1811.29	2178.20	x1.20	2206.27	2771.98	x1.26
Drugs	385.56	438.99	x1.14	443.35	905.61	x2.04
S-C theft	700.53	768.71	x1.10	769.89	737.46	x 0.96
A. theft	711.75	944.13	x1.33	967.92	1091.90	x1.13
Prost.	13.55	26.38	x1.95	25.11	27.48	x1.09
Women						
	1970	1979	Increase	1980	1989	Increase
All I-P	434.93	630.19	x1.45	627.03	864.98	x1.38
Drugs	71.43	68.65	x 0.96	68.68	175.81	x2.56
S-C theft	40.82	62.21	x1.52	60.50	77.87	x1.29
A. theft	271.04	444.51	x1.64	440.51	546.77	x1.24
Prost.	51.64	54.83	x1.06	57.33	61.08	x1.07

women's Income-Productive crime arrests (see Table 1 and 2). During this time period, both male and female drug arrest rates (see Tables 3 and 4) fluctuated a good deal, but female arrests never exceeded 100, nor male arrests 600, per 100,000 during the decade. Yet, as noted, arrests for income-productive crime during this decade increased fairly steadily for both men and women (Table 6).

What would have happened during the 1980s if cocaine had not come on the scene in such large amounts? If, overall, income-productive crime had kept increasing in the 1980s as a function of increasing poverty and decreasing legitimate opportunities and dealing cocaine had not presented itself as a criminal opportunity (i.e., if the crime tariff were nonexistent), then the rates of both subcultural and amateur theft would be much higher than they now are (see Table 8). Instead, because the rate of increase for theft during the 1980s was less

Table 8
I-P Arrest Rate Predictions for 1989,
Based on Increases during 1970s

Offense	Predicted Rate	Actual Rate
	Men	
All I-P	2647.00	2771.98
Drugs	505.39	905.61
S-C theft	846.88	737.46
A. Theft	1287.33	1091.89
Prost.	49.20	35.12
	Women	
All I-P	909.19	864.98
Drugs	65.93	175.81
S-C theft	90.75	77.87
A. Theft	704.82	546.77
Prost.	60.77	61.08

than during the 1970s, these crime rates are much lower in 1989 than one would have predicted at the start of the decade. In contrast, drug arrests are almost twice as high as predicted for men and more than two and one-half times higher for women. From the beginning of the decade to its end, the percentage of all male income-productive crime accounted for by drugs alone increased from 21.02% to 32.67%, and for women the percentage nearly doubled, moving from 10.95% to 20.34% (see Tables 1 and 2). For both men and women, increases in the percentage contribution of drug arrests to income-productive crime and drug arrest rates (Table 3 and 4) increased steadily, compared to the fluctuating pattern of the previous decade.

The new criminal opportunity appears to have had more impact on women's crime than on men's. In spite of being almost locked out of subcultural theft, women have moved readily into drug dealing, also a subcultural crime. Why? The answer to this question lies in the nature of the criminal networks needed to sustain drug dealing and in their difference from subcultural theft networks.

Generally, it would appear that the movement into drug dealing is facilitated by existing street networks. Evidence for this assertion comes from the decreasing rates of subcultural theft evident for men, who have always been much more involved in these networks than women. There appears to be a replacement effect. The pattern is particularly pronounced for burglary, where the male arrest rates declined during the 1980s (from 432.30 in 1980 to 325.64 in 1989). That this is not merely a function of differential law enforcement attention is evidenced by the fact that burglaries known to the police have declined during the decade (FBI, *UCR*) as have burglaries known to the National Crime Survey (NCS) (Johnson & DeBerry 1990).

Further evidence for this interchangeability, or flexibility of street networks to accommodate various kinds of crime, comes from data which indicate that most of those arrested for theft have had experience at least as users (National Institute of Justice 1990) and that most drug users among the arrest population have committed crimes of theft (Anglin & Hser 1987). Further, burglars and robbers are the most likely arrestees to be drug users (Conklin 1986). Research also indicates that (a) virtually all sellers are users of drug(s) sold, (b) the more frequent the use of a specific drug, the higher the probability of selling it and selling it at high rates, and (c) regular sellers frequently consume some of the drugs sold (Johnson, Kaplan, & Schmeidler 1990).

An economic analysis of drug dealing as a business enterprise indicates that it requires the following: (a) production and distribution networks; (b) marketing; and (c) services, which include credit, enforcement of contract, places to conduct business, communication facilities, and advertising (Schelling 1967).

The illegal drug industry "operates like importing, wholesaling and retailing business [and is] structurally [similar to] the garment industry" (Beirne & Messerschmidt 1991: 22). Thus, there are many sources of raw materials and many importers. Cocaine is "probably the most economically valuable agricultural product in the world . . . . It produces up to $1 billion of hard currency annually in countries such as

Bolivia, Peru and Columbia. ... Given the high U.S. demand ... the international cocaine trade may be the most significant transfer of wealth between affluent and less economically developed countries in the world today (McBride & Swartz 1990: 158).

Both heroin and cocaine are marketed through long vertical distribution systems (Simon & Witte 1982) with many syndicates that service a small number of customers below them. Hellman (1980) suggests that there are as many as six distribution stages between the producer, or manufacturer, and the consumer. He suggests that the distribution chain may be unusually long because the substance is illegal. This minimizes the information each link has about the people at the top of the chain and minimizes sellers' risks by decreasing the number of transactions each dealer makes. Thus, as one moves down the distribution chain, the number of dealers or firms increases, market power diminishes, and price markups get smaller, while the risk of arrest increases because the number and frequency of transactions increase. At the street dealer level, the bottom of the distribution chain, there are many small firms because "there are fewer barriers to entry at this level ... [and] capital requirements are smaller. ... Many dealers at this level are also addicts, so their opportunity costs in the legal sector are relatively low ... and the stigma [is likewise] lower at lower levels, where dealers are also users. ... [Thus] a large supply of retailers is created (Hellman 1980:148–149).

The business of drug dealing is a good deal different from the stealing and selling of goods. For both enterprises partners are needed, customers are needed, and the work requires long and unpredictable hours, with significant career time subtracted for occasional prison sentences.

However, production and distribution networks are central to drug dealing and not to burglary, armed robbery, and other forms of theft. For theft, the only distribution system necessary is the fence, and no production is necessary—here there is only transfer. For drugs, the criminals must link up to a production system, because that in itself is illegal. Drug dealers are thus both buying and selling, unlike thieves who steal goods, so that no dickering is involved and sources of merchandise are known, not hidden. A thief may obtain tips, but he/she does not need a business partnership with the supplier, quite the contrary. The thief's only need for connections is a need for working partners and a fence or receiver. A wider network of connections is thus necessary to dealing than to stealing, just in the production aspect.

Distribution presents further problems of making connections, for customers must be obtained. Unlike the thief who can peddle all his/her goods to one or, at most, two fences, the drug dealer needs to sell to the user of the goods directly—at least at some point in the distribution network. As drugs are a black market commodity in which both the seller and the buyer are aware of the illegality of the transaction, somewhat different problems may arise (Schelling 1960). A fence can peddle his/her merchandise along with straight merchandise and thus can display it directly, operating out of a legitimate store (Klockars 1974; Steffensmeier & Tonry 1986; Walsh 1977). Advertising and marketing are, accordingly, more difficult for the business of drugs, as compared to the market in stolen property. Drug dealing also requires some services not necessary to theft: a place to conduct business, credit, communication facilities, and the ability to enforce contracts.

Because of these unique characteristics of drug dealing, it is much easier for drug networks than for theft networks to employ women as well as men, for some aspects of the work lend themselves to the services a woman might provide to the dealing enterprise *just because* she often maintains a stable base in the home, from which, because of child-care responsibilities, she does not range far.

Women can provide (a) a place to conduct business, (b) credit (e.g., cash loans), and (c) communication facilities (a telephone can provide a way to receive and relay messages). All of these things require or are enhanced by a stable base and/or a stable income. They are not things which a stable base or daily responsibilities would impede.

Men are more able to (a) enforce contracts, (b) engage in direct sales, and (c) import and do midlevel wholesaling. These are aspects of drug dealing that require mobility, long/unpredictable hours, connections with a network, and possibly violence. None of these aspects of the drug trade requires a stable base.

The two aspects, however, merge together very well in the sexual alliance of a man and a woman. Not only can the woman do the sorts of work that a stable base enables rather than impedes, but men are very unlikely to form crime partnerships with women unless they are sexually involved with them. The discrimination evident in street networks does not apply to such arrangements.

The crime networks that men have established for subcultural theft involve mostly other men, as Miller (1986), Pettiway (1987), and Steffensmeier (1986) have demonstrated. They are composed of men one has met in prison, in bars, on the street, and as working partners in theft itself. But they are ultimately reliant on female support, just as the executive or professional male is reliant on his wife taking care of the family. Men rely on women's work in the home in several ways related to its provision of a stable base: it provides a place to crib, a place for storage, a place to hide, a place to eat, a place to come home to after prison, and a place where children are reared. But women are largely excluded from direct work in the male-dominated networks of subcultural theft, because nothing else they can provide is needed. In drug networks, however, women do enter as direct workers. Their role is different from men's, but the two form one system.

What women provide is stability, be they welfare women or other housewives. Regardless of what other work they do, their homework is their first priority. Other work must mesh with it, and thus in the nature of the case, they maintain a stable base for themselves and their children—which can then be used by men as a base of operations, an integral part of "taking care of business." The American welfare system reproduces the American family structure; it lends stability to the ghetto. It was intended to do so and has done so remarkably well. What Block (1980) had to say about women in the Mafia corresponds to this—crime is always a "family business."

Men may use different women's homes for this—their mothers', sisters', aunts', girlfriends'—drifting from one to another as one or another place gets "hot." It is this base that enables them to steal or, alternately, to deal drugs.

As in the upperworld, the men of the ghetto are freed by women's work in the domestic economy to participate in work requiring mobility, networking, long/unpredictable hours, and occasional lengthy absences (for criminal men some of these absences are for imprisonment). For this reason, men have predominated in the world of subcultural theft. Through their work in burglary, auto theft, armed robbery, and fencing, they have built up networks of contacts for working partners, of receivers for their stolen goods, of tipsters, and of relatively trustworthy co-workers and clients. Through their prison sentences they have built up further contacts and reputations as "real men" or "real thieves" (Klockars 1974; Walsh 1977).

These networks are readily converted to drug distribution networks into which women can be more easily integrated than theft networks. The mesh between women's provision of a home base and their lack of mobility and men's lack of a home base but high mobility may be a combination that works well for a sexually integrated drug network. Women's astonishing increase in drug arrests may reflect an equal opportunity crime.

Dealing Drugs and Stealing Goods—Some Implications for the Economic Health of the Underclass

One thing the arrest rates for income-productive crime demonstrate is that the size of the criminal class is steadily increasing. The male arrest rates are now one-half again as large as they were 20 years ago, and the female arrest population is twice as large, proportionate to the population. In absolute terms, of course, the increase is even greater. There are twice as many men and 2.6 times as many women arrested for income-productive crimes now as there were two decades ago.

The introduction of crack cocaine into the economy of the ghetto has had a pronounced effect on the further criminalization of this class. During the 1980s, arrest rates for drug offenses increased at a steeper rate than for other offenses. The drug arrest population for males doubled and for females increased by 2.5 times. In absolute terms, there are now three times as many men and 3.2 times as many women in this population. At the same time, the rate of increase for career theft, amateur theft, and prostitution decreased for both men and women, while the rate of increase for drug arrests climbed dramatically.

In a very real sense, however, cocaine certainly has not been an income-producer for the underclass, for this same class is a major consumer of the drug—the net gain in cash income probably has been about zero. Arrest data conflate use and sales, because United States drug policy has been to criminalize both user and seller by prohibiting possession. Interactionally, this makes a good deal of sense because the line between use and sales is fuzzy at best. At the higher reaches of the drug trade, substantial income can be produced even if the seller is himself/herself a user. But at the level of street dealing and midlevel wholesale distribution, where most arrests are made, the user is a dealer, the dealer a user. Many, if not most, dealers will smoke up all their profit (Anglin & Hser 1987; Johnson, Kaplan, & Schmeidler 1990).

The drug-crime connection has been debated for many years (see the summary in Beirne & Messerschmidt 1991). So far as the experience of the last decade with cocaine is concerned, however, the drug economy is a closed loop. While some of the increase in amateur theft for both men and women may be accounted for by increased need of income to purchase drugs, for the most part the user can support his/her habit simply by sales, and the new dealers who have taken advantage of a new criminal opportunity have quickly become users whose fantasied profit was spent on drug use. In short, users deal to obtain drugs, and sellers quickly learn to use. Dealing causes use as much as use causes dealing—a closed loop.

This loop is closed not only for the individual user/dealer but also for the economy of the ghetto as a whole. Income produced by drug sales, after a profit goes to large importers, stays in the ghetto, but as it is used to buy more drugs, it does not increase the overall economic productivity of this class. Nor does it, like burglary or robbery, whose targets are often middle or upper class, redistribute income.

The economic health of the underclass remains at the same low level as it was in 1970, while the size of this class has steadily increased. The criminalization of drug use creates a previously nonexistent income producer, to be sure, through the crime tariff (Packer 1968). But it stabilizes the economy and the life chances of the underclass. Effectively, it does not produce income for this class.

Meanwhile, it has a disastrous effect on their morbidity. Reports from almost every large city with heavy drug traffic suggest that the increase in male-on-male assault and homicide is the direct result of disputes over drug deals (McBride & Swartz 1990). Some have speculated that an apparently mystical property in the chemical substance itself accounts for this. More likely it is simply that an increased number of users for a drug high, which lasts a very short time, produces an increased amount of transactions. With each transaction, the potential for dispute is very high. It is likely that the rate of lethal dispute per transaction has not increased while the number of transactions has increased. Cocaine's impact on the health of mothers and their children is also pronounced.

It appears obvious that this new commodity has affected the criminal activity of men and women, by altering dramatically the types of offenses for which the criminal class is being arrested, most likely increasing the size of this class. What these changing patterns of crime commission reveal is the shape of criminal networks within the underclass and the manner in which public policy interacts with them to reproduce and reinforce class, caste, and gender inequalities.

The gendered patterns of crime mirror the patterns of straight-world economic activity. Criminal men take care of business, and their women take care of children and the home. The introduction of the cocaine opportunity does not alter this but follows established patterns of normal crime networks, which feature men on the streets in sales and women working, even at drug sales, much closer to home base and in conjunction with the men to whom they are tied. So long as women maintain a stable home base for themselves and their children, they continue to provide the possibility for criminal men to work at career theft or alternately drug sales. The households they make available as places to crash, to eat, to live intermittently; the child care they perform for the fathers of their children; and the welfare aid they receive because they head families with dependent children allow their men to engage in crime without living continuously on the street and to do time intermittently without losing their home base. Thus, welfare policy and criminal justice system policy reproduce and even reinforce the gender inequities seen among the criminal class which in themselves mirror gender inequities in the straight-world classes.

These policies also reinforce and reproduce class and racial disparities in the American economy and social structure. The spiraling criminalization of drug use is particularly effective in this regard. As numbers of criminologists have noted, drug policy has always been driven by ethnic prejudice (see, e.g., the discussion and citations in Beirne and Messerschmidt [1991]). A "yellow peril" criminalized opium, a fear and hatred of Mexicans criminalized marijuana, and an intense fear of the burgeoning underclass in American ghettoes combined with a backlash against affirmative action policies in the face of a worsening economy increased the crime tariff for cocaine. The alternative—to treat cocaine addiction as a health problem—would require facing squarely the lack of legitimate economic opportunity for the underclass (see Hellman 1980). The lack of desire to do so, and the specter of roving, out-of-control black and Spanish-speaking drug gangs effectively displaces fears onto the very victims of the economy.

Yet the productive classes are enabled to continued improving their economic situation through the sales of acceptable consumer drugs for humans such as tranquilizers, sleeping pills, stimulants, and mood elevators and acceptable agricultural chemicals (e.g., pesticide use *increased* after DDT was banned ([Hynes 1990]). Through such regulations as FIFRA, through the continued production of CFCs (chlorofluorocarbons) and the approval of so-called safe substitutes in the form of HCFCs (hydrochlorofluorocarbons), chemicals so dangerous that they have poked two holes in the sky and thinned the ozone layer generally continue to be produced and used. The production, sale, and use of such chemicals are not prohibited as is cocaine but regulated and accommodated (Schelling 1967). Seen as a whole, United States drug policies reproduce inequities and further concentrate wealth in the hands of the wealthiest class. Regulatory justice system policy simply reinforces these inequities (see Yeager 1987).

Class and ethnic inequities are intimately intertwined, but drug policies also reflect the intertwining of gender and class inequities. The drug wars have become an occasion to further constrain women's lives through their reproductive capacities. This has been used as an excuse to be terrified of crack babies and thus to send a further warning to women that their bodies are not their own. The specter of irresponsible ghetto women producing defective children haunts middle- and upper-class women's striving for equity, and the specter of lazy, sensuous black and brown ghetto teen-agers with uncontrollable drug appetites haunts the aspirations of black and Spanish-speaking citizens.

In this regard, Weisheit's (1990) comments are: "The war is not against drugs, but against people who . . . take particular actions regarding drugs. The significance of this point cannot be overstated, for it means that any war on drugs is really a civil war in which the forces of society are marshaled against some of its own citizens" (p. 2).

If we think of legitimate drugs for both human and nonhuman consumption as part of the total chemical picture, it can be seen that the war on drugs includes an attack of one class against another, of one sex against another, one ethnic group upon another, and finally, one species (human beings) against all other species on the planet. This civil war will not end nor "will peace be made with the planet" (Commoner 1990) until United States drug policies are altered radically. This includes, but is not limited to, cocaine policy. It must involve all the toxic chemicals—dioxin as well as heroin, chlorofluorocarbons as well as cocaine. It is not too far-fetched to suggest that the same desire—that for total control—underlies all chemical policy and that it is this which must be altered.

References

Anglin, M.D., & Hser, Y. (1987). Addicted women and crime. *Criminology* 25:359–397.

Barry, K. (1984). *Female sexual slavery.* New York: New York University Press.

Bernard, J. (1979). Policy and women's time. In J. Lipman-Blumen & J. Bernard (eds.), *Sex roles and social policy* (pp. 303–333). Beverly Hills, CA: Sage.

Beirne, P., & Messerschmidt, J. (1991). *Criminology*. New York/San Diego: Harcourt, Brace, Jovanovich.

Block, A. (1980). Searching for women in organized crime. In S.K. Datesman & F. Scarpitti (Eds.), *Women, crime and justice* (pp. 192–213). New York: Oxford University Press.

Commoner, B. (1990). *Making peace with the planet*. New York: Pantheon Books.

Conklin, E. (1972). *Robbery and the criminal justice system*. Philadelphia: Lippincott.

——— (1986). *Criminology*. New York: Macmillan.

Daly, K. (1987). Discrimination in the criminal courts: Family, gender, and the problem of equal treatment. *Social Forces* 66(1): 152–175.

Federal Bureau of Investigation (1970–1979). *Uniform Crime Reports*. Washington, DC: U.S. Government Printing Office.

Hellman, D.A. (1980). *The economics of crime*. New York: St. Martin's Press.

Hynes, P.H. (1990). *The recurring silent spring*. New York: Pergamon.

James, J. (1976). Motivations for entrance into prostitution. In L. Crites (ed.), *The female offender* (pp. 177–205). Lexington: D.C. Heath.

Johnson, B.D., Kaplan, M.A., & Schmeidler, J. (1990). Days with drug distribution: Which drugs? How many transactions? With what returns? In R. Weisheit (Ed.), *Drugs, crime and the criminal justice system* (pp. 1–8). Cincinnati, OH: Anderson Publishing.

Johnson, M., & DeBerry, M. (1990). Criminal victimization (1989 NCS Report). Washington, DC: U.S. Department of Justice.

Klockars, C. (1974). *The professional fence*. New York: Free Press.

McBride, D.C., & Swartz, J.A. (1990). Drugs and violence in the age of crack cocaine. In R. Weisheit (ed.), *Drugs, crime and the criminal justice system* (p. 158). Cincinnati, OH: Anderson Publishing.

Mies, M. (1986). *Patriarchy and accumulation on a world scale*. London: Zed Books.

Miller, E.M. (1986). *Street woman*. Philadelphia: Temple University Press.

Morgan, R. (Ed.) (1984). *Sisterhood is global*. Garden City, NY: Anchor Books.

National Institute of Justice (1990). *Drug use forecasting*. Washington, DC: U.S. Government Printing Office.

Packer, H. (1968). *The limits of the criminal sanction.* Stanford, CT: Stanford University Press.

Pettiway, L.E. (1987). Participation in crime partnerships by female drug users: The effects of domestic arrangements, drug use, and criminal involvement. *Criminology* 25(3): 741–766.

Schelling, T.C. (1967). Economic analysis and organized crime, In President's Commission on Law Enorcement and the Adminstration of Justice, (Appendix D). Washington, DC: U.S. Goverment Printing Office.

Simon, C.P., & Witte, A.D. (1982). *Beating the system: The underground economy.* Boston: Auburn House Publishing.

Sokoloff, N.J. (1980). *Between money and love: The dialectics of women's home and market work.* New York: Praeger.

Steffensmeier, D. (1986). *The fence: In the shadow of two worlds.* Totowa, NJ: Rowman and Littlefield.

Steffensmeier, D., & Tonry, R.M. (1986). Institutional sexism in the underworld. *Sociological Inquiry*; 309–323.

Walsh, M. (1977). *The fence.* Westport, CT: Greenwood Press.

Waring, M. (1988). *If women counted.* San Francisco: Harper & Row.

Weisheit, R.A. (1990). Declaring a "civil" war on drugs, In R. Weisheit (ed.), *Drugs, crime and the criminal justice system* (pp. 1–10). Cincinnati, OH: Anderson Publishing.

Wilson, N.K. (1983). Making a living at crime: Differences in male and female criminal work. Paper presented at the American Society of Criminology annual meetings, Denver, CO.

——— (1985). Witches, hookers and others: Societal response to women criminals and victims. Paper presented at the American Society of Criminology annual meetings, San Diego.

Yeager, P.C. (1987). Structural bias in regulatory law enforcement: The base of the U.S. Environmental Protection Agency. *Social Problems* 34(4): 330–344.

Sister Against Sister: Female Intrasexual Homicide

Coramae Richey Mann
Indiana University, Bloomington

At a recent national criminology conference, considerable discussion was generated during a debate on whether women were as violent as men. The basic theme of that discourse was domestic violence, but other types of female violence, were broached, such as women who commit assault and homicide. For a number of years, arrest trends have revealed annual increases in the number of females arrested for aggravated assault. For example, 1978–1987 female arrest trends for aggravated assault reveal an increase of 35.5% with the male increase only slightly larger at 37.6%. Female arrests over the time period for "other assaults" (no weapon or serious victim injury is involved) were up 80.8%, much larger than the 67.8% increase for males for this violent crime (Federal Bureau of Investigation, 1988). Similar to most female deviance, aggravated assault committed by females was rarely studied until recently; yet many of these assaults are against other women.

It has also been noted that "female-on-female homicide is a rare form of patterned behavior . . . that has been totally ignored by the scholarly community" (Goetting, 1988:181). Although there has been little variation in female arrests for homicide over the years, there are indications that same-gender–directed violent behavior may be increasing. Unfortunately, homicide statistics do not usually disaggregate females who kill by the gender of their victims, and even more importantly, such statistics are not disaggregated by victims' gender and age to afford separate analyses of women who slay their children from those who kill men. Since women historically have been recorded as the predominant killers of their children, infanticide and filicide cannot be considered the true measures of female violence. However, one possible test (used in the study reported here), is a comparison of female homicide offenders by the gender of their adult victims. As Silverman and Kennedy (1987) keenly observe, "An interest in the female perpetrator of homicide requires a knowledge of the victim-offender relationship and a more thorough knowledge of victim-offender interaction than can be provided by national aggregate data" (p. 18).

It is clearly established that women are frequent victims of violence at the hands of their men (e.g., Browne 1987; Saunders 1989; Straus, Gelles, & Steinmetz 1980; Straus & Gelles 1986), and conversely, men are the usual victims of women (e.g., Goetting 1988; Mann 1988; Weisheit 1984; Wolfgang 1975); therefore, the implications of increasing numbers of females as potential victims at the hands of their "sisters" warrants closer examination. If it is shown that women are as likely to kill other women as they are to kill men, violence can then be viewed as the human issue it is (McNeely & Mann 1990) and not solely as the gender issue it has become. The limitations of the exploratory research on which the contents of this essay are based render any theoretical assumptions woefully short of the criteria requisite to the construction of a theory of gender and crime (Daly & Chesney-Lind 1988), but it is hoped that the results will provide building material toward that end for future researchers. Even more important perhaps is that these findings on women who kill other women will increase concern for the debilitating effects of violence in society.

The fact that young black men and women are those most likely to die from homicide in the United States is a social problem that has been identified as having "epidemic proportions" (Mann 1987:158). In his use of vital statistics to study women victims of homicide, Farley (1980) notes that "homicide is currently the leading cause of death of black men and women aged 25 to 34 (p. 181). These appalling statistics demand that a more intense examination be made for solutions to reduce such intraracial violence.

Definitional problems introduce an additional limitation to this essay. *Homicide*, or the killing of one human being by another, includes *murder*, or criminal homicide. Since the homicide files that were studied use the terms murder, homicide, and criminal homicide interchangeably, they are reported accordingly throughout the essay. The victim-offender relationship in homicides is also diverse and contains "little conceptual guidance and almost no methodological research on the measurement issues" (Loftin et al. 1987:259). Such relationships include, for example, killings that are intrafamilial; homicides of loved ones who are not family members; and slayings that involve strangers, friends, or acquaintances. Closely related to the definitional quandary is the previously observed finding that since homicide statistics and other reports on female homicide offenders do not disaggregate by the victim-offender relationship, comparisons across studies are difficult.

Previous Research

Very little has been reported on females who kill other females. A number of homicide studies report their findings by gender but give few details on the characteristics of the female offender, her female victim, or the circumstances of intragender homicide. The extant research on the topic indicates that earlier studies merely gave female offender–female victim homicide statistics and the proportions they represented compared to the majority group of male-male homicides. Fortunately, studies reported predominantly in the 1980s provide more particulars about the persons and circumstances involved in the homicides.

The most frequently cited study of homicide is that of Wolfgang (1975) in Philadelphia from 1948 to 1952. Although this pivotal study of homicide laid the empirical groundwork for later explorations of this violent crime, the specifics related to female homicide offenders, their female victims, and the offense are not fully addressed. The omission plagued most of the homicide research that followed, which, like that of Wolfgang, documented and emphasized the *intersexual* nature of homicide. Nonetheless, the *incidence* of female intragender homicide is available from a few of the limited number of homicide studies that describe what Goetting (1988) refers to as "the exceptional case."

Among the 105 female homicide offenders Wolfgang (1975) identified in 1958, 16.2% killed other females, which is a higher proportion than the 11% reported 16 years later by Suval and Brisson (1974). In her six-city study of black homicide in the United States, McClain (1982–1983) found that, in 1975, 14.5% were female victims in the 119 cases where women were the killers. By 1980, Willbanks (1982) reports that nationally, female homicide victims of other females comprised of 19.7% of such incidents, the highest recorded proportion up to the time of this writing. Among homicides known to the Chicago police from 1965 to 1981, Block (1985) reports 15% are female victims of female assault homicide offenders and slightly less in homicides resulting from an armed robbery (12%) committed by females. Although these studies provide only a sketchy picture of female intragender homicide, they do roughly circumscribe the proportions of female victims who were killed by other females in their reports, which indicate a range of 11% (Subal & Brisson 1974) to 19.7% (Wilbanks 1982). Interestingly, a Canadian study of 948 females who committed homicide between 1961 and 1983 revealed an even higher proportion of female victims (23%) than any United States study (Silverman & Kennedy 1987). However, it is still not known whether the females killed were minors or adults. More recent investigations provide a clearer picture.

Blackbourne (1984) offers more details of female-female homicide phenomenon in his description of homicide in Washington D.C., from 1972 to 1980. Of the 200 cases examined in detail, 21 were female-female killings (10.5%) among which Blackbourne describes four as the result of alcohol altercations, five concerned love triangles, and three involved homosexual disputes. Applying a routine activities approach—"the convergence of likely offenders, suitable targets, and the absence of capable guardians," Block (1986) notes that "gender remains a successful predictor of certain features of homicides" (p.4). She found that over a 10-year period (1974–1984) in Baltimore, similar to their male counterparts, most women killed only males; nonetheless,

17.1% of the female killers had female victims. Further, when women killed women, 13.6% of the offenses involved concurrent felonies—a practice Block found more common among white than black women.

The remaining available studies that include female intragender homicide vary in their contributions to the paucity of research on this phenomenon. In a three-state study (Alabama, Illinois, and Texas), Hazlett and Tomlinson (1988) used state supplementary homicide data to compare patterns of female homicide across states from 1980 to 1984. Among cases involving offenders and victims who were both female (6%) there was little variation among the states—Illinois had the largest percentage (6.3%), followed by Alabama (5.9%) and Texas (5.8%). Hazlett and Tomlinson report the mean age of the female homicide offenders as 33 years and that they were predominantly black (71.8%) but offer little additional information about the victims.

The differences between men and women convicted of nonvehicular homicide in Maricopa County (Phoenix), Arizona, between 1979 and 1984 was the focus of a study by Winn, Haugen, and Jurik (1988), who compared men and women homicide offenders on demographic data, their victims, their roles in the offense, the circumstances of the offense, and the final disposition. Winn, Haugen, and Jurik comment that women made up a "very small percentage" (actual percentage not given) of all the homicides committed over the 6-year period ($n = 50$) and that they were more likely to kill men than other women, but unfortunately, the researchers did not separately report any findings on women who killed women.

Finally, although the number is small ($n = 15$), Goetting (1988) provides the most detailed characterization of females who kill other females, the circumstances of their offenses, and the outcomes of their crimes:

> The construction of a statistical profile describing the population of 15 females arrested for killing other females in the predominantly black city of Detroit, Michigan, during 1982 and 1983 yields the image of a locally born black, 30-year-old Detroit mother who is Protestant, married, and living with her family. She is an undereducated, unemployed, welfare recipient with an arrest record, in the passion of anger in a private residence on a weekend between 8:00 P.M. and 1:59 A.M. (186)

Methods

The Sample

This subgroup of 57 female homicide offenders whose victims were also females is part of a larger aggregated sample of 296 cleared homicide cases where females were the perpetrators in six U.S. cities in 1979 and 1983.[1] The cities—Atlanta, Baltimore, Chicago, Houston, Los Angeles, and New York—were selected because they had homicide rates equal to or higher than the national rates, and additionally, they provided modest regional representations of homicides for the years selected. While there was a decrease in the proportion of females arrested for female homicide from 1979 (56.1%) to 1983 (43.9%) overall, for the 2 years combined, these 57 female killers represent 19.3% of the total study sample.

Procedure

The data were collected over a two-year period through field visits to each of the cities where minute examinations of police department homicide files and criminal court records were recorded on a previously designed research schedule (see Mann 1984b). To insure the offenders' anonymity, case numbers were assigned. The modified schedule included selected demographic and social characteristics of the offenders and victims, information concerning the homicide, criminal justice data on the offenders and victims, and the final legal dispositions of the cases. For comparability, every attempt was made to include all of the variables indicated in previous studies of intragender homicide. A number of additional variables omitted in earlier studies was also included in order to explore the following research questions.

1. Is the *profile* of a female homicide offender differentiated by her victim's gender?
2. Is the *role* of a woman who kills circumscribed by her victim's gender?
3. Do women's *motives* for killing differ by the gender of the victim?

4. In the comission of homicide are women *more violent* toward men than they are toward women?
5. Does *"southernness"* distinguish women who kill men from those who kill women?
6. Are women who kill men less *"officially" criminal* than women who kill other women?
7. Does the criminal justice system accord *differential treatment* to female killers of other females compared to women who kill males? More specifically, does the criminal justice system more severely sanction female homicide offenders whose victims are male rather than female?

The two primary goals of the investigation reported here were (a) to provide a profile of the female who kills another female and (b) to compare women who kill other women with those women who kill men. In order to accomplish the last task, victim's age was recorded to include only adult victims (18 years of age or older). Since the intent of the study was exploratory and the majority of the variables were nominal, data analyses were best suited to the application of nonparametric statistical procedures, namely, descriptive statistics (frequencies) and measures of association through cross-tabulations using the chi-square statistic.

Study Limitations

One of the first observations made during data collection was that police arrest files and homicide records frequently omit a great deal of information. Consequently, on some variables, particularly those related to social characteristics, there are more missing data than recorded data. Also, even though the total sample of 296 female homicide offenders represents 42.9% of all women arrested for homicide in the six cities in 1979 and, similarly, 42.3% for 1983, the small number of cases of female-female homicide (n = 57) limits generalization to the larger offending population. Finally, because of research time restrictions that limited field visits to a maximum of 7 to 10 days per city, males arrested for homicide were not a part of this study. As a result of this limitation, comparisons between male and female homicide offenders cannot be made.

Findings

Female-Offender–Female Victim Homicide

As indicated in an earlier section, up to now the profile of female homicide offenders described in the estimable Detroit study reported by Goetting (1988) offered the most comprehensive picture of this offender population and is, therefore, used here as a model for comparison. This association is obviously speculative because the two data bases differ: Goetting's study aggregated cases in one city from 1982 and 1983, whereas this study aggregates cases from 1979 and 1983 in six cities. But since Goetting provides the only study that includes substantially the same variables, in order to understand the phenomenon under examination there is a logical justification for employing the following compare/contrast method.

Both studies reveal that females arrested for killing other females are predominantly nonwhite, undereducated, unemployed, have arrest records and their homicides were committed in residences. There are also some interesting differences between the findings of the two studies which are seen in Table 1.

Interestingly, with the exception of marital status, the demographic *profiles* of the female homicide offender in both studies are highly similar. Goetting found that more than half the offenders in her study were married (53.3%), whereas in this study, 53.8% were single. This is a particularly intriguing difference, since common-law marriage relationships (5.8%) were included in the category "ever married" which also consisted of offenders who were married (19.2%), separated (11.5%), and divorced (9.6%). With this anomaly noted, the primary findings in the two studies seem to diverge on the circumstances and consequences of the homicide.

Table 1
Comparison of Two Recent Female-Female Homicide Studies*
(in percentages)

Characteristic	Goetting (n = 15)	Mann (n = 57)
Offender		
Age	(range = 19 to 45 yrs.) (mean = 29.9 yrs.)	(range = 12 to 63 yrs.) (mean = 28.3 yrs.)
Black	73.3	73.7
Married	53.3	19.2
High school	61.0	50.0 (only 20 cases)
Unemployed	66.7	78.0
Prior arrests	50.0	50.9
Victim		
Age	(range = less than 1 yr. to 66) (mean = 21.4 yrs.)	(range = less than 1 yr. to 64) (mean = 22.2 yrs).
Black	75.0	68.4
The homicide		
Victim precipitated	20.0	48.1
Victim is a child	43.8	30.4
Committed alone	66.7	76.8
In a residence	93.3	73.7
Time		
2 :00 A.M.–7:59 P.M.	NA	17.9
8:00 A.M.–1:59 P.M.	NA	28.6
2:00 P.M.–7:59 P.M.	26.0	32.1
8:00 P.M.–1:59 A.M.	50.0	21.4
Criminal justice outcome		
Most serious final charge:	("felony murder") 81.9	(murder/vol. manslaughter) 67.5
Prison sentence	88.9	41.1
Mean years to serve	11.6	6.4

* Neither study includes missing data.

First, in contrast to Goetting's results, a female victim more likely precipitated her death, a possibility supported largely by the victim-offender relationship. Unlike Goetting's female killers whose predominant victims were their children (43.8%), the females in the six-city study were slightly more likely to kill an acquaintance (39.3%), friend (10.7%), or homosexual lover (8.9%) with these three categories accounting for 58.9% of the victims. A possible explanation for the difference may be found in the high incidence of single offenders in this study (53.8%), only 14% of whom were single mothers who killed their offspring. Further, the female offenders in this study were more likely to commit the homicides alone (76.8% vs. Goetting's 66.7%) and to premeditate the crime (55.7%).[2]

A second major difference between the two studies concerns the day and time of the homicide. Goetting's finding that "homicide is concentrated on weekends, peaking on Saturdays" (p. 185) and usually late at night coincides with previous studies (e.g., Wolfgang 1975). In contrast, in the six-city study, the women who killed were equally likely to commit the offense on a Wednesday as a Saturday (17.5%, respectively), or a Tuesday as a Sunday (15.8%, respectively). Further, Goetting reports that half of the victims died between 8:00 P.M. and 1:59 A.M., or that the murders were night crimes, where as only 21.4% of the homicide deaths occurred during this time frame in the study reported here. The peak time was between 2;00 P.M. and 7:59 P.M. (32.1%) with the 12-hour period between 8:00 A.M. and 7:59 P.M. accounting for 60.7% of the female-female homicides. In other words, female intragender homicide appeared to be predominantly a daytime-to-early evening event, and not a night crime. Moreover, the finding that 26.3% of these homicides took place outside of a residence with the majority of those outside the residence occurring in a street, alley, or yard (21.1%) implies a different picture of this offending group than Goetting's or earlier studies characterize. A case example illustrates this point:

> In this homicide (#2218) the offender was a petite (4'11"), 20-year-old black woman who was employed as a shoe salesperson, but received food stamps. On the day of the homicide, she and the victim were in line at the food stamp office and got into an argument.

According to one witness there was a long-standing feud between the two women over a man they both loved who was currently in prison. Eight other witnesses stated that the 21-year-old victim, who was also black, taunted the offender by calling her names and threatening to "get" her when they got outside. The victim swung her purse at the offender who responded by jumping over a desk between them and stabbing her one time in the chest with a 4-inch lock-blade knife. She then fled as relatives of the victim pursued her. The offender claimed self-defense, had no previous arrests, and her case was subsequently dismissed.

Finally, as seen in Table 1, processing by the criminal justice system was much harsher for the females who killed other females in the Goetting Detroit study than in this one. Her defendants were more likely to receive very serious final charges, were more than twice as likely to be sentenced to prison (88.9% vs. 41.1%), and once sentenced were given more years to serve in prison (11.6 vs. 6.4 years). These differences in homicide outcomes between the two studies might be explained by the fact that Goetting reports more child victims and found far less victim precipitation. Further, in the six-city study 80.6% of the female homicide offenders denied responsibility for the crime by, for example, claiming self-defense (23.6%), that the homicide was an accident (21.8%), or that they were innocent (16.4%). Presumably the court believed them.

Comparison by Gender of Victim

Although no age controls were imposed on the female offender group, in order to compare women who killed women with those who killed men, victim age was controlled to include only the analyses of females whose victims were 18 years of age or older, thereby eliminating the child victims typically found to be the primary targets of female killers.

A recent essay by Daly and Chesney-Lind (1988) on feminism and criminology offers a superb and long overdue treatise on gender and crime in which the authors conclude the following:

> Most theories of crime suggest the "normalcy" of crime in the light of social processes and structures, but have barely examined the significance of patriarchal structures for relations among men and for the forms and expressions of masculinity. Gender differences in crime suggest that crime may not be so normal after all. Such differences challenge us to see that in the lives of women, men have a great deal more to learn. (527)

As previously noted, since male homicide offenders were not included in the sample, these data do not lend themselves to analyses of gender differences in homicide, nor is there an attempt to "build" a general theory of gender and crime (Daly & Chesney-Lind 1988). The gender ratio is not an issue of concern here, although the fact that women are less involved in both crime and criminal justice system processing should be an important and necessary part of any theory-generating agents. However, there is a deep heuristic concern about the nature of crime and a belief that the motives for crime are not gender related. Women commit property crimes, and some vice crimes (e.g., prostitution or selling drugs), for the same reasons that men do; they are economically motivated. Also, like men, women feel emotions such as rage, jealousy, and revenge that often result in violent personal crimes. It is reasoned that if women who take another's life are different than men who do, one beginning approach is to examine whether women who kill women differ from women who kill men. The research questions and conceptualizations listed earlier will now be addressed.

Is the profile of a female homicide offender differentiated by her victim's gender?

This first question addresses social and demographic characteristics of the two groups. As seen in Table 2, members of both groups—those with adult female victims (the *study group*) and those with adult male victims (the *comparison group*)—tend to be mothers, are largely unemployed, and have attained about the same number of years of education (11 years). The comparison group is slightly more likely to be younger, ever married, and composed of more whites, whereas the study group of females who kill women are more

Table 2

Offender and Victim Characteristics by Gender of Victim[1]

Characteristic	Female victim ($n = 35$)	Male victim ($n = 219$)
Offender		
Age	(range = 30.4 yrs.)	(range = 31.9 yrs.)
Under 30	48.6	52.1
30 and over	51.4	47.9
Race		
Nonwhite	94.3	88.1
White	5.7	11.9
Marital status		
Single	53.3	37.6
Ever married[2]	46.7	62.4
Mother		
Yes	65.0	66.7
No	35.0	33.3
Education	(mean = 10.6 yrs.)	(mean = 10.8 yrs.)
Grammar school	5.7	2.7
Jr. high & above	94.3	97.3
Employed		
Yes	31.0	33.3
No	69.0	66.7
Arrest record		
Yes	57.6	57.3
No	42.4	42.7
Violent history		
Yes	50.0	34.3
No	50.0	65.7
Victim		
Age	(mean = 33.4 yrs.)	(mean = 38.5 yrs.)
Under 30	42.9	32.0
30 and over	57.1	68.0
Race		
Nonwhite	85.7	86.3
White	14.3	13.7
Arrest record		
Yes	40.0	71.2
No	60.0	28.8
Violent history		
Yes	36.4	48.5
No	63.6	51.5

* $p = .005$, $X^2 = 7.67$ @ 1df.

1 Does not include missing cases.

2 "Ever Married" includes marrried, common-law married, divorced, separated, & previously widowed.

Table 3
Homicide Characteristics by Gender of Victim (in percentages)[1]

Characteristic	Female Victim ($n = 35$)	Male Victim ($n = 219$)
Day		
Weekend	31.4	47.9
Weekday	68.6	52.1
Location		
Region		
Non-South	48.6	46.1
South	51.4	53.9
Locale		
Residence	71.4	75.2
Other	28.6	24.8
Location in residence		
Inside	74.1	84.6
Outside	25.9	15.4
Victim-offender relationship		
"Family"[2]	32.4	69.6*
Non-family	67.6	30.4
Offender's role		
Alone	80.0	85.6
With others	20.0	14.4
Victim precipitation		
Yes	71.9	75.2
No	28.1	24.8
Premeditated		
Yes	68.8	58.4
No	31.3	41.6
Motive claimed		
Responsible	19.4	19.9
Not responsible	80.6	80.1
Victim's condition		
Helpless[3]	31.0	26.9
Not helpless	69.0	73.1

Characteristic	Female Victim	Male Victim
Alcohol use involved		
Offender		
Yes	36.4	41.3
No	63.6	58.7
Victim		
Yes	40.0	56.4
No	60.0	43.6
Drug use involved		
Offender		
Yes	18.2	12.4
No	81.8	87.6
Victim		
Yes	20.0	12.4
No	80.0	87.6
Method		
Gun	45.7	52.1
Knife	48.6	42.5
Other	5.7	5.5
Number of wounds		
Single	60.0	54.2
Multiple	40.0	45.8
Homicide outcome		
Final charge		
Murder	85.2	80.6
Manslaughter	14.8	19.4
Disposition		
Prison	44.1	42.6
No prison	55.9	57.4
Years to serve	(mean = 6.7 yrs.)	(mean = 7.2 yrs.)
5 years or less	22.9	18.7
Over 5 years	77.1	81.3

* $p = .00002$, $x^2 = 17.81$ @ 1 df.

1 Does not include missing cases.

2 "Family" includes relatives, in-laws, lovers, ever married. Non-family victims are friends, acquaintances, strangers, and employer.

3 "Helpless" includes ill or infirm, asleep, drunk, and bound or tied.

frequently nonwhite, single, and more likely to have violent arrest histories, although the groups tend equally to have prior arrest records. None of these differences is statistically significant; therefore, it tentatively can be concluded that the profile of female homicide offenders is not differentiated by the gender of their victims. Put another way, the profile of women killers does not vary based on the gender of their adult victims; women criminal homicide offenders appear to be the same regardless of who they kill.

With the lone exception that male victims had more violent arrest histories than female victims and were significantly more likely to have arrest records, gender also did not distinguish the victims. Both male and female victims tended to be nonwhite and older than their assailants. Not surprisingly, since female victims tended to be nonfamily members, predominantly friends and acquaintances, the women killed were closer to the age of their female killers (mean = 33.4 years) than the men who were victims (mean = 38.5 years).

Is the role of a women who kills circumscribed by her victim's gender?

To answer the second research question the part played by the homicide offender was measured by (a) whether she committed the crime alone or in some way was assisted by another person, (b) if the crime was premeditated, and (c) if the victim precipitated his/her own death. It generally has been found that females tend to commit homicide unassisted. The women in this sample were no exception, although, as seen in Table 3, they were slightly more likely to kill a man alone (85.6%) than to kill another woman unassisted (80.0%). It was also somewhat surprising to find that the slayings of women were preplanned or premeditated more frequently than those of men (68.8% vs. 58.4%, respectively). Finally, men were more likely to instigate their deaths (75.2%) than women (71.9%), but again this difference is not statistically significant.

Other characteristics of the homicide, such as whether the victim was helpless[3] or if either the victim and/or offender were under the influence of alcohol or narcotics prior to the homicide, yielded no significant differences related to the victim's gender. Alcohol use by both the offender and her victim was more frequently involved when the victim was a man. However, drug use predominated in cases involving female offenders and female victims.

While both male and female victims were more likely to be killed in a residence, women appeared more often to be slain outside, for example, on a porch or in a yard (25.9% vs. 15.4%). There was also a slight tendency for women to be killed outside of a residence in places such as taverns or on the street more so than men (28.6% vs. 24.8%). Weekdays were more common than weekends for both victim groups, but weekday homicides were found more frequently in the study group cases ($s = .06$). Previous research indicates that most murderers take place on weekends, especially on Saturday nights, so the finding that the women in this study were more likely to commit homicide during the weekdays suggests that being unemployed may have contributed to this time-frame finding.

Do women's motives for killing differ by the gender of the victim?

Motive is generally believed to be closely related to the offender-victim relationship in cases involving female homicide offenders. The relationships between offenders and victims were significantly different according to gender of the victim, with women more frequently killing male family members or females who were nonfamily.[4] Since women usually kill someone with whom they are intimately involved, most often a man, the rationale for the homicide is commonly innocence, self-defense, or an accident. Such was the case with both groups regardless of the victim's gender. For example:

> A 28-year-old Latina (#2106) apparently planned the killing of her 23-year-old sister because of jealousy and rage, since her sister was the lover of the offender's husband and had his baby. Around noon, the offender went to the victim's residence to kill them both. The two women fought, with the victim apparently winning, until the offender pulled out a .22 and fired three shots, killing her sister with one shot to the chest. The offender then took the victim's baby, went to her husband's job, shouted to him of the killing, and threatened to kill

> him also, but he was able to disarm her of the gun, and a knife. The husband's attorney stated that the offender had tried to kill her husband several times at his job and that he was divorcing her. With no prior record, she received 10 years probation.

In a similar case, involving a male victim of jealousy:

> (#5118) At 1:35 A.M, the offender, age 41, shot her lover of four years, a 56-year-old, disabled, black male who died three days later from the shot in the throat. The offender, who was also black, claimed she pointed the gun at him and it went off accidently [sic]. However, a witness stated that the previous evening the offender had threatened the victim with a gun in his place of business. The offender, who had one previous arrest for felony assault, pled guilty to attempted manslaughter and was sentenced to 18 to 54 months in prison. She was paroled in less than three years.

Cross tabulations of the motive variable by degree of responsibility[5] appear to provide a negative answer to the third question, since no significant differences were found between the reasons given by women who killed men and those who killed women. A noteworthy majority of the female homicide offenders claimed they killed in self-defense, among other disclaimers of responsibility for the crime.

In the commission of homicide, are women more violent toward men than they are toward women?

The primary variables examined in an effort to answer this question were the method used in the killing and the number of wounds inflicted. It is suggested that the use of a knife indicates a more violent means of killing because of the necessity to get close to the victim in order to stab, slash, or cut him/her. Clubbing, strangling, drowning, or stomping someone to death also requires close proximity to the victim, but these methods were involved in only 11 out of 219 cases where males were victims and 2 out of 35 female victim cases, or about 5% for each victim group. A gun, however, implies the possibility of distancing from the victim. The number of wounds administered is believed to reflect the degree of brutality in the homicide and measures whether a single knife puncture or one gunshot or multiple wounds by knife or bullets were inflicted. Accordingly, multiple wounds indicate the more vicious crime.

> In case #2120, both the offender and her victim were black and were rumored to have been involved in a homosexual relationship for over 15 years. Although the offender denied that she was homosexual, she admitted that the victim was homosexual. A school teacher with whom the offender had been living as a lodger for a little over a week stated that the victim, age 35, had broken into the house earlier and was waving a gun around. The police were called, and came, but had left. On the victim's next attempt to enter the house at 9:00 A.M., the offender fired six shots at her with a .22 caliber gun inflicting three wounds to the chest and two in the back. The 34-year-old offender, who was 5'3" and 122 pounds, claimed self-defense because she feared a beating from the victim who was 5'8" and weighed 207 pounds. There was a documented history of the victim's mental illness. No bill was filed in the case.

Guns were more frequently the weapons of choice in the slaying of men (52.1%), whereas the killing of women more often involved knives (48.6%). In terms of distancing, this is a logical finding; it would appear that a man was seen as more of a threat. This assumption is partially supported by the slight tendency for males to be the victims of multiple wounds more so than female victims.

Does "southernness" distinguish women who kill men from those who kill women?

A modest effort was made to explore the "southern subculture of violence" long debated by, among others, Hackney (1969), Gastil (1971, 1978), Loftin and Hill (1974, 1978), Doerner (1975, 1978), and more recently, Messner (1983), Dixon and Lizotte (1987, 1989), Ellison and McCall (1989), and Corzine and Huff-Corzine (1989). This perspective assumes that southern, particularly Civil War, states have a tradition of lethal violence that is an integral part of southern culture. This alleged cultural pattern includes the habit of carrying guns (Hackney 1969), an exaggerated sense of honor with resultant duels, interfamily feuds, and disregard for life. The devaluation of black lives is believed to be rooted in slavery and demonstrated by the lynchings and other violent acts of the Ku Klux Klan and other violent whites (Gastil 1971).

Compared to the nonsouthern cities, slightly higher proportions of both males (53.9%) and females (51.4%) were the victims of women in the southern cities studied—Atlanta, Baltimore, and Houston—but the question of whether southern women are more violent than their nonsouthern counterparts cannot be answered from these data on the basis of this single variable. Other explorations comparing southern with nonsouthern cities (Chicago, New York, and Los Angeles) were inconclusive because of the small numbers involved in the cross tabulations; nonetheless, the results offer interesting research pathways for future studies on southern female homicide offenders. Characteristics such as the victim-offender relationship, the extent of involvement of alcohol and narcotics in the murder, circumstances of the homicide (e.g., when and where it occurred), and the homicide method selected suggest that regional differences might exist.

A rough picture of the southern female homicide offender and her victim reveals that she is more likely to be employed than her nonsouthern counterpart whether her victim is a man or a woman. Whereas here male victim is someone close to her, her female victim tends to be nonfamily. Nonsoutherners, however, were more likely to kill female family members. Another indicator of "traditional" violence is seen in the finding that, compared to nonsouthern women, southern female killers of men did so on weekends usually under the influence of alcohol or drugs. Additional tentative support for the southern violence perspective is suggested by the more frequent use of guns in the homicide. However, multiple wounds were slightly more often inflicted by nonsouthern female homicide offenders, particularly against female victims. Both male (59.4%) and female (52.2%) victims in the southern cities tended to precipitate their deaths compared to nonsouthern instances of victim precipitation, 40.6% and 47.8%, respectively. Southern women who killed other women more frequently had prior arrest records (63.2% vs. 36.8%) and violent arrest histories (53.3% vs. 46.7%) than nonsouthern women with female victims.

A final look at whether southern women are more "traditional" (i.e., more socially stable, nonviolent) than nonsouthern women or whether they reflect the southern culture of violence compared the female homicide offenders by region controlling for prior arrest records, violent arrest histories, and marital status. More than half (53.1%) of the 49 women who were single and had previous arrest histories were southern women. Whereas these offenders were equally likely to kill a man as nonsouthern women, they were twice as likely to kill another woman (66.7% vs. 33.3%). The case for ever married southern women was more dramatic. Among the 61 ever married women with arrest histories, 35 or 57.4%, were found in the southern cities. These women were more likely to kill both males and females than nonsouthern female killers, especially other women (75% vs. 25%). Violent arrest histories again differentiated the ever married women from southern cities, 71.4% of the female victims and 53.1% of the male victims were killed by ever married southern women who had previous arrests for violent crimes. These differences were not statistically significant but do suggest that violence may be related to "southernness" among female criminal homicide offenders.

Are women who kill men less "officially" criminal than those who kill other women?

Evidence of a prior arrest record is generally recognized as a standard measure of "official" criminality. A second indication of previous involvement in the criminal justice system used to address the question of "official" deviance was whether an offender had a former arrest for a violent crime. Convictions are obviously better measures than arrests, but such information was rarely available for either offenders or victims. Prior arrest history had little influence when the gender of the victim was examined, since both types of victim gender groups were equally "officially" criminal as measured by arrest histories. Although 50% of the female-female homicide offenders had been previously arrested for a violent crime and only 34.3% of the male-male killers had such records, this was not a statistically significant difference.

Another idea pursued was that if female killers of male victims are married, or at least have some form of stable, intimate relationship in their personal lives, they would be less likely to have been involved in the criminal justice system. It has already been seen that 62.4% of the women who killed men were more likely to be ever married (Table 2) and that relationships with their male victims were significantly more of a "family" type than when women were their victims (Table 3). Also, 53.3% of the study group was single women who killed women who were not family members.

Comparisons by victim's gender controllng for prior record and marital status offer little support for the idea that an ever married status is less associated with prior arrest experience since single offenders were only slightly more likely (58.3%) to have previous arrests than ever married offenders (55.0%). The same was true for prior violent arrest histories: 36.7% of single women arrested for homicide had prior arrests for violent crimes as did 35.1% of ever married women killers. Interestingly, among those ever married women with either prior arrests or violent arrest histories, the victims were more likely to be other women. Put another way, among the women killed by ever married women, 61.5% of their assailants had prior arrests; for male victims, the proportion was 54.1 percent. Similarly, when previous violent arrests were indicated, 53.8% of the female victims compared to only 32.7% of the male victims were killed by an ever married offender.

Does the criminal justice system more severely sanction female homicide offenders whose victims are male rather than female?

The final question is related to the Marxist feminist perspective discussed by Daly and Chesney-Lind (1988) when they depict the causes of gender inequality as "deprived from hierarchial relations of control with the rise of private property and its inheritance by men. Class relations are primary; gender relations, secondary" (p. 537). Daly and Chesney-Lind also note "a master-slave relationship applied to husband and wife" (p. 537). Or as Bannister (1989) notes, "The status of women in relation to men in the United States is characterized by domination, intimidation, and violence" (p. 3). Thus, similar to historically disadvantaged minorities and the poor, as members of an oppressed, lower-status group, application of this perspective suggests that women would receive harsher penalties for killing men than for killing other women. Hawkins (1986) suggests that the official sanctioning of homicide offenders reflects a higher valuation of the lives of white victims than black victims. A modification of the Hawkins perspective leads us to the question: Are the men's lives more highly valued than women's lives?

In discussing women who kill their male abusers, Bannister (1989) finds that the state incarcerates women "(1) to deter other women from believing that they can similarly resist; (2) to reinforce in women the belief that they have no right to their own bodies' integrity and no right to defend against or resist male attacks; and (3) to protect and assert men's power over women" (p. 4).

It has already been established that the motive, the extent of violence in the homicide, prior arrests, and previous violent histories did not differentiate the female-female killers from the male-male killers. Therefore, any differences in official processing based on victim's gender should suggest that men's lives are valued more highly and/or that the criminal justice system more likely discriminates against female killers of men for the reasons outlined by Bannister (1989) due to women's inequality (Daly & Chesney-Lind 1988).

Table 3 reveals that none of these characteristics—final charge, a prison sentence, years to serve in prison—significantly distinguishes the two victim groups. Final charge was examined to see if defendants were tried on lesser charges because of the gender of their victims. A majority of women with female victims (85.2%) as well as those with male victims (80.6%) received the more serious final charge of murder or manslaughter the same as the original charge. Women who killed women were slightly more likely to be accorded a prison sentence (44.1%) than those who killed men (42.6%). The range in years of prison sentence was from 1 year to 25 years in female victim cases and from less than a year to life imprisonment in male victim cases. No women were sentenced to life in prison for killing other women, but in the five cases in which life sentences were assigned, men were the victims. Finally, although the difference is also not statistically significant, women whose victims were men received slightly harsher prison sentences (mean = 7.2 years) than when their victims were women (mean = 6.7 years).

It appears that gender of the victim is not a major factor in criminal justice outcomes when murder is committed by a female perpetrator. The sentencing findings—i.e., life sentences and number of years to serve in prison—do suggest a tendency to treat women who kill men more harshly, but on the basis of these data no definitive answers can be reached to the questions posed concerning devaluation of women or gender inequality.

Discussion

One of the primary aims of this exploratory investigation of urban female homicide offenders who kill other females was to generate a profile of such offenders in an attempt to partially fill a gap in the research literature on this largely ignored group of homicide offenders. Also, it is felt that if one can assume that there is no substantial difference between male and female homicide offenders, a clearer picture of the causes of violence may be obtained through a more in-depth examination of female killers. The second objective was to determine if the gender of their victims differentiated the women killers by attempting to answer a number of research questions and applying modest tests of notable hypotheses in the literature concerning devaluation of female victims' lives and gender inequality in official processing.

In contrast to earlier reports of women who kill, which suggest women are more likely to kill their spouses and their children, these women who committed intragender homicide were single and more likely to kill acquaintances, friends, or female lovers. The killing of one's children, especially infants, is an age-old practice that has been studied more intensively than the phenomenon of women slaying other women. An earlier comparison of the women in this data set who killed their preschool children with the remaining female homicide offenders in the sample did not distinguish the two groups (Mann, forthcoming);

therefore, the findings reported here exclude child victims and focus only on females whose victims were 18 years of age or over.

It was found that women who kill other women basically resemble the portrait depicted over the past two decades by previous researchers: they are young, black, undereducated, and unemployed. Thus, they reflect the current American portrait of an expanding group of women of color who are marginal to the larger society. Anger, arguments, and fights which could take place at any time or any place were most often the precipitating factors that led to the killing of another woman, who, in many instances, instigated her own death. Possibly because of the victim's contributory role in her homicide, prison sentences were assigned in only 41.1% of the cases, and time to be served in prison averaged only 6.4 years.

As to the second purpose of this analysis, the research questions posed in the comparison of women by the gender of their victims concerned a homicide offender profile, role, motive, extent of violence, the influence of "southernness," prior criminality of the offender, and the criminal justice outcome for the murder. None of these characteristics significantly distinguished women who killed women from women who killed men, which suggests that perhaps the process of violence may be identical for men and women.

For a number of years, I have found the notion of a *unisex* approach to crime appealing, or that "criminologically there is no difference between males and females" (Mann 1984a:268). After an extensive review of the extant theories of female deviance, it was concluded that "the previous emphases on differences assumed to be peculiar to women, are precisely why none of the theoretical perspectives outlined in this book have been fruitful in explaining the origins of crime" (p. 268).

Although the results of this study appear to yield some support for a unisex theory of female homicide commission, the race and class statuses of the offenders suggest that the critical (devaluation of life) perspective cannot be dismissed. Since the majority of the female homicide offenders were women of color, predominantly black, and their victims were also primarily black, it is suggested that a black or

Hispanic life, whether male or female, is not as highly valued as a white life in the administration of United States justice.

Reliance upon a critical feminist perspective, or that women's class domination by men results in a devaluation of their status and a concomitant higher valuation of men's lives, assumes that female homicide offenders with female victims would be differentiated from those with male victims by less severe sanctions by the criminal justice system. Although the killers of men received slightly longer prison sentences than those who murdered other women, and further, only women with male victims were assigned life sentences, these differences were not statistically significant. Obviously more research is required to address sufficiently the questions and hypotheses posed here.

Future research directions should include larger and more representative samples with more attention devoted to comparisons across time and across urban as well as suburban areas. Rural jurisdictions should be included, particularly to test the southern culture of violence thesis. In order to verify if the process of violence is the same for men and women, male homicide offenders must be incorporated in future research efforts. Further explorations of the gender inequality perspective should contain explanations of possible connections between changes in women's lifestyles and lifestyles and life circumstances. Finally, the problem of missing data which is legendary in police files is somewhat reduced when homicide files are used as was the case in this study, but more descriptive data demand the utilization of alternate sources of information such as newspaper accounts and court records on the homicide cases studies.

Notes

1. Because of the large numbers of cases and the research time restrictions involved, random samples were obtained from Chicago, Houston, New York City, and Los Angeles. The number of cases in Atlanta and Baltimore were small enough to include all of the cases in these cities.
2. Goetting did not report this variable.
3. "Helpless" is defined as ill or infirm, asleep, drunk, bound, or tied up.

4. "Family" includes relatives, current and former in-laws, lovers, and spouses. Nonfamily victims were friends, acquaintances, strangers, and employers.

5. "Not responsible," included in Table 3, refers to innocent, self-defense, defense of others, accident, under the influence, another's fault, and justifiable.

References

Bannister, S. (1989). Another view of political prisoners. *The Criminal Criminologist*. 1(4): 3–4, 14.

Blackbourne, B.D. (1984). Women victims of homicidal violence. Unpublished paper received from author.

Black, C.R. (1985). *Lethal violence in Chicago over seventeen years: Homicides known to the police, 1965–1981*. Chicago: Illinois Criminal Justice Information Authority.

Block, K.J. (1986). Life stages, routine activities and homicides: Women in Baltimore, 1974–1984. Paper presented at the American Society of Criminology annual meeting, Atlanta.

Browne, A. (1987). *When battered women kill.* New York: Free Press.

Corzine, J., & Huff-Corzine, L. (1989). On cultural explanations of southern homicide: Comment on Dixon and Lizotte. *American Journal of Sociology* 95(1): 178–182.

Daly, K.B., & Chesney-Lind, M. (1988). Feminism and criminology. *Justice Quarterly* 5(4): 497–538.

Dixon, J., & Lizotta, A.J. (1987). Gun ownership and the "southern subculture of violence." *American Journal of Sociology* 93(2): 383–405.

——— (1989). The burden of proof: Southern subculture-of-violence explanations of gun ownership and homicide. *American Journal of Sociology* 95(1): 182–187.

Doerner, W.G. (1975). A regional analysis of homicide rates in the United States. *Criminology* 13: 90–101.

——— (1978). The index of southernness revisited. *Criminology* 16: 47–56.

Ellison, C.G., & McCall, P.L. (1989). Region and violent attitudes reconsidered: Comment on Dixon and Lizotte. *American Journal of Sociology* 95(1): 174–178.

Farley, R. (1980). Homicide trends in the United States. *Demography* 17: 177–188.

Federal Bureau of Investigation (1988). *Crime in the United States.* Washington, DC: U.S. Department of Justice.

Gastill, R.D. (1971). Homicide and a regional culture of violence. *American Sociological Review* 36: 412–427.

——— (1978). Comments. *Criminology* 16: 60–66.

Goetting, A. (1988). When females kill one another. *Criminal Justice and Behavior* 15: 179–189.

Hackney, S. (1969). Southern violence. *American Historical Review* 74: 906–925.

Hawkins, D.F. (1986). *Homicide among black Americans.* New York: New York University Press.

Hazlett, M.H. & Tomlinson, T.C. (1988). Females involved in homicides: Victims and offenders in three U.S. States. Paper presented at the American Society of Criminology annual meeting, Chicago.

Loftin, C., & Hill, R.H. (1974). Regional subculture and homicide: An examination of the Gastil-Hackney thesis. *American Sociological Review* 39: 714–724.

——— (1978). Comments. *Criminology* 16: 56–50.

Loftin, C., Kindley, K., Norris, S.L., & Wiersema, B. (1987). An attribute approach to relationships between offenders and victims in homicide. *Journal of Criminal Law and Criminology* 78(2): 259–271.

McClain, P. (1982–1983). Black females and lethal violence: Has time changed the circumstances under which they kill? *Omega* 13(1): 13–25.

McNeely, R.L., & Mann, C.R. (1990). Domestic violence is a human issue. *Journal of Interpersonal Violence* 5(1): 129–132.

Mann, C.R. (1984a). *Female crime and delinquency.* Tuscaloosa: University of Alabama Press.

——— (1984b). Race and sentencing of women felons: A field study. *International Journal of Women's Studies* 7(2): 160–172.

——— (1987). Black women who kill. In R.L. Hampton (Ed.), *Violence and the black family* (pp. 157–186). Lexington, MA: D.C. Heath.

——— (1988). Getting even? Women who kill in domestic encounters. *Justice Quarterly* 5(1): 33–51.

——— (1992). Maternal filicide of preschoolers. In A.V. Wilson (Ed.), *The dynamics of the victim-offender interaction* (pp. 227–246). Cincinnati, OH: Anderson.

Messner, S.F. (1983). Regional differences in the economic correlates of the urban homicide rate. *Criminology* 21(4): 477–488.

Saunders, D.G. (1989). Who hits first and who hurts most? Evidence for the greater victimization of women in intimate relationships. Paper presented at the American Society of Criminology annual meeting (41st), Reno, NV.

Silverman, R.A., & Kennedy, L.W. (1987). *The female perpetrator of homicide in Canada*. Edmonton, Alberta, Canada: Centre for Criminological Research.

Straus, M.A., & Gelles, R.J. (1986). Societal change and change in family violence from 1975 to 1985 as revealed by two national surveys. *Journal of Marriage and the Family* 48: 465–479.

Straus, M.A., Gelles, R.J., & Steinmetz, S. (1980). *Behind closed doors: Violence in the American family*. Newbury park, CA: Sage.

Suval, E.M., & Brisson, R.C. (1974). Neither beauty nor beast: Female homicide offenders. *International Journal of Crime and Penology* 2(1): 23–24.

Weisheit, R. (1984). Female homicide offenders: Trends over time in an institutionalized population. *Justice Quarterly* 1(4): 471–489.

Wilbanks, W. (1982). Murdered women and women who murder: A critique of the literature. In N.H. Rafter & E.A. Stanko, (Eds.), *Judge, lawyer, victim, thief: Women, gender roles, and criminal justice* (pp. 151–180). Boston: Northeastern University Press.

——— (1983). The female homicide offender in Dade County, Florida. *Criminal Justice Review* 8(2): 9–14.

Winn, R.G., Haugen, L.M., & Jurik, N. (1988). A comparison of the situational determinants of males and females convicted of murder. Paper presented at the Academy of Criminal Justice Sciences annual meeting, San Francisco.

Wolfgang, M.E. (1975). *Patterns in criminal homicide*. Montclair, NJ: Patterson Smith.

Prostitution in the Netherlands: It's Just Another Job![*]

Ineke Haen Marshall
Chris E. Marshall
University of Nebraska at Omaha

The topic of this essay is prostitution policy in the Netherlands. A dormant issue since the early part of the century, it was not until the late 1950s that prostitution once again became an issue of public policy debate in the Netherlands. The reason for this arousal of interest was mostly because of a concern with the psychosocial problems of the people involved in prostitution: the focus was upon rehabilitation and help for prostitutes (Boutellier 1991). In the mid-1970s, public order problems associated with the burgeoning sex industry began to strain the precarious relationship between the world of prostitution and the status quo, thereby causing policymakers, researchers, and government officials to take a closer look at the how, the why, and the what of Dutch prostitution control strategies. This reexamination resulted in a proposal to look at prostitution as "just work" and to abolish the legal prohibition of the active promotion of prostitution.

* An earlier version of this essay was presented at the 1990 meeting of the Academy of Criminal Justice Sciences. The authors of this essay are grateful to Jan H. Visser of the Mr. De Graaf Stichting (Amsterdam, the Netherlands) for his assistance in identification of publications and for sharing some of his insights. We also thank Professor Frank Bovenkerk of the Willem Pompe Instituut of the University of Utrecht, the Netherlands, for his helpful comments.

In this essay, we will examine the movement toward a new Dutch prostitution policy for the 1990s. Any public policy in a modern democracy has many and varied sources and influences including historical, political, legal, social, economic, cultural, and so on. Therefore, the choice of where to create the boundaries for the discussion of such a policy is largely an arbitrary one; moreover, this particular policy is a work in progress: the related legislation is yet to be passed.** We will, therefore, provide some of what we conceive to be the more important highlights of current policy—its aims, its origins, its contexts—knowing that the policy itself is in flux.

Toward a New Prostitution Policy for the 1990s

Legal-Historical Context

Prior to 1911, prostitution was not against the law in the Netherlands. The Dutch penal code of 1886 contained no criminal prohibition of prostitution, except in cases where minors were involved. During those times, keeping a brothel was, in a legal sense, viewed as a proper occupation. Prostitutes and brothels were registered with the police, and prostitutes had to be under medical supervision (Gieske 1990).

Throughout most of the twentieth century, Dutch prostitution policy has been shaped by antiprostitution legislation enacted in 1911, (Article 250bis of the public morality act of the Dutch penal code).[1] In the early part of the century, a strange coalition developed between ultraconservative Roman Catholics and the liberal, progressive women's movement. The enactment of Article 250bis was largely a result of this strong anti-prostitution movement,[2] heavily influenced by its conservative religious members. This movement viewed the customary earlier practice of registration of prostitutes as a form of tacit legitimization (Boutellier 1987). The antiprostitution movement viewed prostitutes as victims in need of protection from unscrupulous, immoral, profit-seeking entrepreneurs. Although the main behavior

---

** The law was passed since the writing of this essay.

defined criminal by this act was brothel keeping, the major objective of the legislation was clearly to get rid of prostitution. There was no prohibition against using the services of a prostitute. Rather, a general prohibition of the "business of prostitution" was part of this 1911 legislation. The law was aimed against third parties, including pimps, gaining financially from prostitution.[3]

In 1985 the government introduced a change of Article 250bis in the Dutch Parliament. Under the revised Article 250bis, only prostitution using force, coercion, or deception would remain illegal.[4] In the revised statute, the formal legal obstacle prohibiting the active promotion or "profiting from" prostitution, proscribed in the 1911 act, would be removed. The main difference between the old and the new version of Article 250bis is that, in the old version any form of exploitation of prostitution by a third party was prohibited; in the new version, exploitation of *voluntary* prostitution is no longer illegal. This revision has important consequences: "It opens the way to look at prostitution as 'just work'" (Boutellier 1991:201).

At the time of this writing, the revision of Article 250bis is still under discussion in the States General, the Dutch legislative body.[5] There is little doubt, however, that the formal abolition of the old "anti-brothel law" will be realized in the very near future. Powerful forces are at work to bring this about: for example, both the Minister of Justice and the Under-Secretary of Emancipation have formally and publicly endorsed the abolition of the old version of Article 250bis. Furthermore, numerous local and national work groups have written position papers and prepared draft regulations in anticipation of the formal enactment of the revised law. Most larger cities and some of the smaller towns are already in the process of adjusting their policies to the criteria of the proposed revision (De Boer & Wissenburg, 1990:15).

Public Policy Context

The Dutch Principle of Restrictive Tolerance

Dutch public policy in the 1980s was guided by the principle of "restrictive tolerance." This principle on the design and implementation of public policy takes a central place in Dutch policy, especially in potentially divisive and controversial areas such as drugs, pornography, gambling, euthanasia, and prostitution policy. Restrictive tolerance involves two key notions: (a) reluctance to use criminal law and the criminal justice apparatus and (b) the emphasis upon pragmatic concerns in the design and implementation of public policy rather than moral concerns.

Reluctance to Use Criminal Law

For the Dutch, the role, scope, and task of the criminal law should be limited: "The Dutch prefer a policy of encirclement, adaptation, integration and normalization, rather than a policy of social exclusion through criminalization, punishment and stigmatization" (Ruter, 1986:152). It is believed that like drugs, pornography, abortion, and gambling, prostitution is simply not controllable through criminal justice measures. Consequently, with respect to prostitution, enforcement of the old version of Article 250bis has been viewed as a last resort;[6] preference is given to administrative and civil measures mandated by local ordinances.

A crucial element in shaping Dutch prostitution policy has been the "expediency principle" laid down in Articles 167 and 242 of the Code of Criminal Procedure, which empowers the Public Prosecutor's department to refrain from bringing criminal charges if there are weighty interests to be considered (e.g., "grounds deriving from the public good") (Pieterman 1985). This legal principle in Dutch law allows "the public interest" to dictate law enforcement policy. The principle of expediency is used to develop local and national guidelines for the investigation, prosecution, and sentencing of entire categories of offenses (e.g., traffic offenses, drug violations). At the local level, investigation and prosecution priorities are typically determined through the process of "triangular consultation" between the mayor, the chief of police, and the Prosecutor's office. This legal principle has allowed Dutch city officials to develop local policies of non-enforcement of criminal statutes regarding prostitution.

Pragmatism, Not Moralism

The Netherlands prides itself on being a pragmatic society. That it simply is not practical to base government policies entirely on moral or ideological grounds is an important premise of the Dutch political system. Dutch society has sharp religious and ideological differences, but through a political system based on tolerance and compromise, conflicting views and opinions typically are reconciled in workable policies (Marshall, Anjewierden, & Van Atteveld 1990). This pragmatic approach, guided by cost-benefit principles, is reflected in Dutch policies with regard to drugs, pornography, abortion, euthanasia, and prostitution. This pragmatism includes the belief that prostitution will always be part of society. The government's role is simply to make sure that people are not exploited and that no public order problems result from prostitution; this is where government's responsibility ends.

Local Government's Role in Prostitution

Article 168 of the Dutch municipal code allows municipalities to develop their own ordinances in the interest of public order, morality, and health. Amid complaints in the 1970s about nuisance and public order problems related to prostitution, many municipalities moved to restrictive tolerance methods to control prostitution (Gieske 1990). Versions of this approach included control of times and places where prostitution would (or would not) be allowed. Amsterdam's municipal prostitution policy is a good example of the application of restrictive tolerance: in 1979, this city created internal guidelines stating that the police would take action against prostitution only in cases of public order disturbances, criminality, hard drugs, involvement of minors, and so on (Gieske 1990).

Local government's ability to set local policy was seriously hampered by a provision in Article 250bis that made the *promotion* of prostitution illegal. Although local government could decide *not* to enforce the antibrothel article, it was not permissible for the city council, in any way, to take active control of the sex business. In other words, "the state should not be a pimp." This constraint on the local or city governments included efforts to design a permit system or use city funds to purchase properties for the purpose of prostitution. Typically, then, local policies were characterized by *ad hoc* decisions in response to public order problems (Scholtes 1987).

Local Variations in Prostitution Policy

Role of the city. There is no such thing as "the" Dutch prostitution policy. Local policy varies widely, ranging from complete denial, or extremely restrictive, to very permissive. Municipalities differ with respect to the role the city government plays in shaping local prostitution policy. Some cities have taken action only when undesirable developments occurred by banning bothersome prostitution activities from certain streets; the prohibition to solicit at certain times and in certain areas (*tippelverbod*) is used in several cities (De Winter 1990; Serrarens & Spronken 1991).[7]

Alternatively, the city of The Hague has taken a more active stance and uses local ordinances to concentrate prostitution in one area. The Hague's local ordinance, based on "the exemption rule," states that window prostitution is prohibited everywhere except in certain streets.

Perhaps the most aggressively pro-active prostitution policy attempted is that of Rotterdam in the 1980s. The city of Rotterdam has tried to act as an active (in)direct entrepreneur involved in prostitution by making two proposals: (a) a permit system and (b) concentration of prostitution on "sex-boats" in the Rotterdam harbor. These proposals never came to fruition, however, because adjacent neighborhoods protested and because judicial arguments based upon the old version of Article 250bis were raised (Boutellier 1991: 206).

Concentration policy. A common thread of local prostitution policy in most larger cities has been to restrict prostitution activities to certain areas. Larger cities such as Amsterdam, Utrecht, and The Hague have designated "areas of tolerance" (*gedoogzones*), where prostitution is permitted. While many cities have some form of zoning policy with regard to prostitution, this is not true for all cities (Overman 1982).

Concentration policies have been used primarily for the control of "open," or public, prostitution (i.e., street prostitution and window prostitution). Other, more "closed," or private, forms of prostitution (e.g., brothels, sex clubs, call girls, or escort services) typically are not limited to a particular area of town (Scholtes 1987).

Although the 1911 article on brothel keeping prohibits the exploitation of prostitution by cities, several city councils have participated in the relocation of illegal prostitution businesses in order to keep the "sex business" contained in a particular area of town (Scholtes 1987). Under public pressure, street prostitution has been relocated in Rotterdam, The Hague,[8] Amsterdam, Utrecht, and Groningen.[9]

Regular contacts with the vice squad. Most larger cities have a special police branch, the vice squad, to deal with prostitution (Overman 1982). The main task of this branch is to conduct regular checks of establishments involved in prostitution. Although there is no legal ground legitimating these regular checks, most businesses allow them, primarily because it gives them some semblance of legality (Scholtes 1987). The police limit checks to such easily observable phenomena such as age of employees, use of alcohol, conduct of patrons, and so on. Members of the vice squad attempt to know all the prostitutes. If they see a new face, they will check to see if the person is a juvenile or if there is reason to believe that the prostitute is being forced to engage in the trade.

The primary objective of the police is not to arrest prostitutes and/or their customers. Rather, provided that prostitution remains in accepted areas and times, the police stay informed about the prostitution world in order to clear up criminal cases that may arise; they are interested in knowing the prostitutes and the entrepreneurs and what the working conditions and so on are. Moreover, the police try to prevent abuse of juvenile and foreign prostitutes, many of whom are non-Dutch speaking; they deal with problems of public order and nuisance.

Registration of prostitutes. The old antibrothel law does not demand registration of prostitutes. In most cities, however, the police check the clubs and neighborhoods, often using a camera. Each new prostitute identified by the police is registered. The stated reason for this is that it increases the safety of the prostitute and the controllability of prostitution (Stichting De Rode Draad 1987). Most prostitutes do not realize that they are *not required* to cooperate with the request for registration; however, they do it for their own safety. The police do not report the women's names to other agencies such as the internal revenue service or welfare.

Interest Group Context

Prevailing Problems Stir Movement to Decriminalize Prostitution among an Unlikely Coalition of Forces[10]

In the mid-1980s, according to the law, making a profit by providing opportunities for prostitution was still illegal. Local policies, however, more and more reflected the de facto decriminalization of the prostitution business. There was an increasingly urgent demand for a revision of the "brothel law" by a diversity of groups, organizations, and interests.

Neighborhood Groups Protest Public Order Problems Associated with Prostitution

Because of the introduction of hard drugs in 1971, open street prostitution became more prevalent. Prior to the introduction of hard drugs, streetwalkers were usually able to establish a peaceful co-existence in a neighborhood (Scholtes 1987). Drugs changed this precarious balance. By the mid-1980s, a substantial segment of the street prostitutes were addicts. The public order problems created by this unstable group of prostitutes, combined with the noise and pollution caused by the increase of traffic, resulted in frequent complaints by the affected neighbors. Moreover, as a byproduct of the sexual revolution, the 1970s and 1980s witnessed a greatly expanded sex industry (i.e., peep shows, movie theaters, sex paraphernalia shops, and so on). Areas traditionally accepted for these kinds of activity widened and became much more visible. A strange new phenomenon emerged: sex farms in the countryside.

Because of increased local problems and pressure by neighborhood groups, officials in several large cities decided a more active stance with regard to prostitution was needed. As mentioned before, the city's ability to set local policy was seriously hampered by the old version of Article 250bis, which made the promotion of prostitution illegal. This obstacle became important in cultivating support for decriminalization of organized prostitution among local government officials: they simply needed more latitude to develop a pro-active prostitution policy and thereby meet the demands of their constituents.

Prostitution Stands in the Way of Urban Planners' Renewal Activities

Often window prostitution was located in the older parts of the city and interfered with plans to renovate and restore these areas.[11] Some urban renewal plans demanded a concentration or outright relocation of prostitution (J. Visser n.d.; Horde 1987), such as in Rotterdam and in The Hague. The brothel law stood in the way of urban planners' desire to redesign their cities.

Public Health Officials See Health Concerns Associated with Prostitution

Prevention of the spread of sexually transmitted diseases has always been a major public health concern in the Netherlands, particularly as it relates to prostitution. As long as prostitution remains a deviant occupation, prostitutes will have more difficulty accessing medical services. With increasing intravenous drug use and AIDS, public health officials have expressed a renewed concern about the health hazards associated with prostitution.

One of the mainstays of Dutch drug policy has been to keep the drug addict population visible and accessible to service providers through the availability of low-threshold, easily accessible treatment services (Marshall, Anjewierden, & Van Atteveld 1990). This easy accessibility of medical services is also considered a crucial requisite for keeping prostitutes healthy. The old brothel law was viewed as an obstacle to ensuring adequate preventive health care for prostitutes. Complete decriminalization of organized prostitution would enable public health officials to impose minimum health standards on those involved in the prostitution business. Good health and safe sex would no longer be the responsibility of the individual prostitute only;

employers could be held responsible for maintaining minimum health standards among their employees, the prostitutes.

Feminists Conceive of Prostitution as a Flashpoint for Broader Women's Rights Agenda

The feminist movement has had an impact on the proposed complete decriminalization of prostitution in two main ways: (a) the growth of political and public support of equal rights for women, led by feminists, forced the government to create an official emancipation policy and (b) the prostitutes themselves have become politicized.

Under the old Article 250bis, the prostitute had no rights. According to feminists, the very existence of social sexual inequality is thought best reflected in the act of sexual prostitution (J. Visser n.d.). Proponents of equal rights saw an urgent need to improve the social and legal position of the prostitute (Scholtes 1987). Complete decriminal–ization of all voluntary prostitution was viewed as necessary to protect the interests of the prostitute better.

Many feminists feel better protection of prostitutes' physical and economic security is only one argument in favor of complete decriminalization. The more forceful argument is that not only have prostitutes the right to expect equal protection, they also have the right to self-determination. This right of self-determination includes the right to choose prostitution as a profession. Corollary to this position is that prostitution be viewed as an ordinary job arising in an ordinary economic marketplace because a legitimate demand for service exists, a supplier for those services materializes, and the invisible hand of the marketplace sets the price.

The Dutch organization of prostitutes, The Red Thread (*De Rode Draad*), promotes the view of prostitution as a voluntarily chosen legitimate form of work. They do not see a need for government regulation. Like United States (COYOTE, Call Off Your Old Tired Ethics) and English (Collective of Prostitutes) counterparts, members of The Red Thread have participated in recent international prostitutes' conventions, the general theme of which was the abolition of discrimination and end of stigmatization of prostitutes and ex-prostitutes. The Red Thread rejects the view that prostitution is a "necessary evil," to be tolerated as a marginal phenomenon. Instead, prostitution should be viewed as work. Those who choose to work as prostitutes should have the same rights, privileges and duties (e.g., paying taxes) of any other worker (Belderbos &Visser 1987).

At this point, we want to stress that the proposed decriminalization of prostitution is consistent with official Dutch emancipation policy. The government memorandum accompanying the proposed legal change presented as a formal rationale the desire to (a) protect better the prostitute by making cities responsible for enforcing conditions related to the health and safety of the prostitutes and (b) improve the vulnerable position of the prostitute by allowing contractual agreements between prostitutes and third parties (employer or landlord) (MvA [Memorie von Antwoord] 18202, Nr. 5, in Gieske 1988).

So What is This New Proposed Dutch Prostitution Policy?

The core of the proposed legal change is that a legal business of prostitution will become a possibility. Exploitation of prostitution will no longer be illegal. The prostitution business will become subject to all laws, rules, and regulations that exist for any other business (Scholtes 1987).

The national government will not provide a general framework for the regulation of the prostitution business.[12] Instead, it will be left explicitly to the local authorities to develop their own regulatory system. The new law holds cities responsible for the development of a prostitution policy. A passive policy based on restrictive tolerance is no longer acceptable (Horde 1987). The cities would have a direct regulating role. Prostitution businesses must meet certain minimum requirements. Cities will have the additional authority to demand special conditions associated with operating a business of prostitution. The decriminalization of prostitution allows local "brothel ordinances" with "brothel licenses." Already existing "gentlemen's agreements" between city council and sex bosses will have legal basis and, consequently, be open to judicial review (Mensing van Charente 1988).

As we noted before, there is virtually unanimous support for the abolition of the old brothel law among local and national policy makers, government and police officials, and feminists.[13] Recent discussions about the actual implementation of the proposed new policies reflect more and more dissension among the affected parties. Points of disagreements, not surprisingly, reflect the differing interests of the involved parties. Most controversial are the specific features of the proposed licensing systems.

Licensing of People and Places Involved in Prostitution

In theory, municipalities can choose from three possibilities: (a) a system of permits, (b) a system of exemptions, and (c) a local ordinance with an absolute prohibition of brothel keeping (C. Visser 1988). Most of the larger cities have chosen for the first option, while smaller towns tend to prefer the second. It appears that the system of permits is most beneficial for the improvement of the position of the prostitute, for local government has to take a pro-active role including creating establishment standards, making inventories, and so on. However, a system based on exemptions is reactive, where a city official waits for exempation requests (C. Visser 1988).

First attempts. The four largest Dutch cities (Amsterdam, Rotterdam, Utrecht, and The Hague) in conjunction with the Association of Dutch Municipalities have attempted to develop a model licensing system for prostitution. Although philosophical differences and differences in local conditions related to prostitution interfered with the development of a uniform licensing system, the collaborative effort did result in a prototype licensing system that can be adjusted to accommodate local conditions.

The Hague is perhaps most advanced in its attempt to develop a licensing system. After formal abolition of the article on brothel keeping, all sex businesses in this city (including approximately 50 to 60 private houses and sex clubs, and about 400 "windows") will have to obtain a license in order to continue doing business. Applicants will be checked for public order problems and working conditions of the prostitutes (Gemeente Den Haag 1988; C. Visser 1988).

In 1988, Rotterdam rejected a licensing system mainly because of the anticipated enforcement problems. Unlike the The Hague, Rotterdam has not been successful in its concentration policy. After the city got rid of window prostitution in a particular neighborhood (Katendrecht), it failed to provide a workable alternative, and consequently, prostitution became dispersed over the entire city. Prostitution in Rotterdam is neither concentrated nor clearly visible; therefore, the city will initially follow an "adjusted closing policy" which involves closing those establishments that cause public order problems. Only after a certain time period will Rotterdam move in the direction of a licensing system (Van de Poel, cited in C. Visser 1988).

What type of prostitution shall we license? A main issue of the licensing approach concerns exactly which forms of prostitution are to be included in the licensing system. The model ordinance developed by the Association of Dutch Municipalities limits its regulatory focus to those forms of prostitution that are "publicly recognizable." The Hague, comparatively, proposes a more inclusive definition of prostitution (i.e., any exchange of sexual services for money). The Hague argues that a more limited definition (i.e., only "public" prostitution) would result in an "undesirable escape into other forms of prostitution" of those who do not want to be regulated (Gemeente Den Haag 1988:14).

According to Gieske (1988), revised Article 250bis is limited to prostitution in a building (i.e., brothels, window prostitution, and sex clubs). Thus, those businesses operating out of a building and publicly trying to attract customers should be subject to rules because of the potential for public nuisance (Gieske 1988). The ordinance developed by The Hague goes further by adding those involved in prostitution as intermediaries (i.e., escort services, or women who receive customers at home through the intervention of a third party).

Many people feel that streetwalkers should be exempted from any new licensing system (Gemeente Den Haag 1988; Scholtes 1987). One objection to the proposed city regulations is the apparent neglect of streetwalker working conditions. The prostitutes' union challenges the government's assumption that prostitutes want to work in a club; rather, many prostitutes want to work independently, which may even become a trend in order for them to escape these proposed systems of regulation. For independent prostitutes, particularly streetwalkers, the areas of tolerance (*gedoogzones*) as they currently exist in Amsterdam, Utrecht, and The Hague provide relatively safe and easy working conditions:

> You don't feel so pressured. Before you get into the car with a customer, you first can negotiate. For example, about the use of a condom. Without these *gedoogzones*, you have to work more hurriedly, get into the car faster, and start your negotiations only after you are in the car. That does not promote safety. (Margot, quoted in *Het Niewsblad van het Zuiden* :6)

That these *gedoogzones* remain safe, well-lit, and patrolled is an important concern for prostitutes and their advocates.

It is feared (particularly by prostitutes and their advocates) that the proposed decriminalization will result in more stringent rules for the prostitutes (Stichting De Rode Draad, 1987). The local authorities' preoccupation with the development of licensing systems may actually result in a weakening of the prostitutes' position (Van der Zijden 1988). One major concern is the proposed mandatory registration of prostitutes.

Registration of Individual Prostitutes

Despite serious disagreement in law enforcement circles about mandatory registration of prostitutes, the police have generally supported this issue in order that they may deal more effectively with the problems of juvenile and forced prostitution. This type of crime control, however, has not appealed to the city of The Hague, whose proposed licensing system states explicitly that mandatory registration is *not* desirable (Gemeente Den Haag 1988).

Prostitutes and their advocates, through The Red Thread, are vehemently opposed to mandatory registration of prostitutes. They argue that, as long as there is a social stigma attached to prostitution, prostitutes should be able to remain anonymous. Moreover, if there is a need for registration, the police should not be involved. Mandatory registration opponents also point out that some prostitutes will never want to be registered (e.g., juveniles, illegal immigrants, and "part timers") (Stichting De Rode Draad 1987). This clearly shows that the whole legal enterprise of decriminalization is based on an abstract concept of what a professional prostitute is (Bovenkerk 1992, personal communication).

Medical Controls

Some have suggested that mandatory medical checkups become part of the registration system, but cheap, easily accessible medical services for the prostitutes is a more generally accepted alternative. It is viewed as the responsibility of the licensee (or operator) of a prostitution business to take the necessary measures. For example, licensees in The Hague must provide condoms to the prostitutes and ensure regular access to a medical doctor for tests and preventive information.

In addition to the issue of whether regular medical checkups should be required, the question of who should pay the associated costs has also been raised, arguing that public health concerns are mainly focused on the prostitute's *customers*, not the prostitutes themselves (Bruins Slot, 1988).

Role of the Police

The new law allows the development of a licensing system comparable to that used in the regulation of other "normal" businesses. The prostitution business, having historically operated outside the boundary of the law, would be subject to the scrutiny of a large number of social control agencies (i.e., government bodies involved in the collection of income tax, enforcing labor conditions, and so on). The police would no longer be the sole agent of social control responsible for prostitution. A major unresolved issue related to the decriminalization of prostitution deals with the proper role of the police and their relationship to other agencies (Kraft 1988; Mensing van Charente 1988).

One main objective of the decriminalization of prostitution is to better protect the large number of foreign prostitutes (estimated to be approximately 60% of the total) against coercion, force, and abuse. When the police find a foreign prostitute working under conditions that are "considerably worse than those of a Dutch colleague," the police will be authorized to take action against the employer. Unfortunately, increasing police pressure on the sex "managers" may have the "trickle down" effect of putting more pressure on the women involved (Blad 1990:390).

Application of Labor Law to Prostitution

Under the revised legislation, prostitution is a legitimate occupation. Prostitutes in the Netherlands historically have had to pay income taxes, but they were not eligible for the benefits normally associated with having a job (i.e., unemployment, disability, or health insurance). Now that prostitution is defined as "just another job," prostitutes are eligible to join labor unions.[14]

Two pieces of national legislation regulating labor relations may be applicable to prostitution under the new policy. First, the 1919 Labor Act (*Arbeidswet*) is limited to those instances where there is an authority relationship between the worker and the employer. Second, the Labor Conditions Act (*Arbeidsomstandighedenwet*), which regulates the safety, health, and well-being of workers, is also limited to employer-employee relationships. Whether labor law is applicable depends on the type of prostitution involved, which raises key questions: Is the prostitute a freelancer responsible only to herself? Does she rent a room from a third party? Have two parties entered into a contract, resulting in an employer-employee relationship? (C. Visser 1988).

Still, there appears to be considerable confusion concerning the degree of control local authorities should have in determining labor conditions (Gemeente Den Haag 1988; Wassenberg & Van Kemenade 1990). For example, The Hague imposes minimum standards for the exploitation of a prostitution business (i.e., the size of the work rooms, the size of the windows, the presence of bathroom facilities, ventilation of the rooms, the presence of a kitchen and "day room," hygienic conditions, and so on). However, this city does not feel it has the authority to regulate employer-employee relationships (i.e., wages and so on); in its view, those relationships are within the sole jurisdiction of the Labor Conditions Act.

The Red Thread recommends that the local licensing system set demands regarding the safety (alarm bells, fire extinguishers, emergency exits) and hygiene (place to wash, clean linens, condoms) of the workplace. The main concern, though, should be the protection of the women's physical integrity and safety. They should be able to decide whether to take a customer and what kind of sexual activities will be permitted.

Decriminalization: A Wolf in Sheep's Clothing?

Legalization of prostitution will result in stricter regulation (Coenen 1988); business owners and individual prostitutes also will be subject to increased rules, regulations, and surveillance. Brunott (1986) fears that the revised law allows local government intervention too much control, particularly with regard to the individual prostitute.

Reflecting this concern, the Red Thread[15] recently formulated several demands for future prostitution policy in the Netherlands. First, a spokesperson for The Red Thread has argued that under the old brothel-keeping article with no system of permits, a prostitute was able to work in a club under her "artist name" (*Het Nieuwsblad van het Zuiden*:6). However, as soon as a permit system is initiated, prostitutes will have to provide identification to their employers.

The Red Thread also has argued that the proposed system of permits actually implies protection of those already involved in the business. The Red Thread spokesperson states:

> The managers of window prostitution, for example, request permits based on the number of windows they are currently exploiting. In the past years, cities have anticipated the to-be-implemented permit system. For example . . . the number of windows has been expanded by making the rooms for the prostitutes smaller in size. They are now covered with an expensive marble floor to satisfy [future] fire codes. All this has made these rooms very expensive, not affordable for women who want to work for themselves and because of this the

manager has a monopoly. Everything is already divided. (*Het Nieuwsblad van het Zuiden*:6)

The Mr. De Graaf Stichting, an organization devoted solely to studying and promoting the well-being of Dutch prostitutes, argues that most of the cities have approached the implications of the revised law from a public order perspective, rather than focusing on it as an improvement of the position of the prostitute (Scholtes cited in C. Visser 1988).[16] Amsterdam, however, is a notable exception. A broadly based working group in Amsterdam that includes representatives of The Red Thread and the Mr. De Graaf Stichting has chosen a system of permits with a detailed set of norms and demands related not only to issues of public order but also to the working conditions of the prostitutes (C. Visser 1988).

For many of the smaller Dutch municipalities, prostitution still remains a taboo topic, proposed changes in national legislation notwithstanding. These smaller communities' prostitution policies tend to emphasize a public order approach with minimal inclination to improve the position of the prostitute (C. Visser 1988). These communities tend to prefer the reactive approach with a system based on exemptions, rather than the pro-active approach of a system based on permits favored by the larger cities.

We do not want to suggest that the Dutch, at this point in time, are completely satisfied with the draft permit systems and related policy suggestions. In all fairness, even the most diehard Dutch government bureaucrats recognize that the implementation of regulation should proceed very gradually; most believe it naive to expect that anybody can produce overnight (or even in a period of a few years) a full-fledged, detailed licensing plan that meets the varied and conflicting needs of prostitutes, prostitutes' customers, prostitutes' landlords and employers, urban planners, health officials, feminists, law enforcement officials, political parties, and community organizations.

Notes

1. Article 250bis WvS reads as follows: "Whoever makes it his habit or profession to intentionally promote or arrange sexual contacts of others with third parties may be punished with incarceration of no longer than one year or a fine of the third category." Related is Article 250ter WvS: "Trade in women and trade in male minors may be punished with incarceration of no longer than five years or a fine of the fourth category."

2. For a description of the social forces involved in the antiprostitution movement in the Netherlands, see Boutellier (1987, 1991).

3. Related Article 432 WvS reads as follows: "Whoever publicly begs for alms, is vagrant without means of support, or profits from a woman's fornication as her pimp, may be sent to jail for no longer than 12 days or may get a fine of the first category."

4. The proposed revision of Article 250bis is: "Anybody who through force or coercion, or through threat with force or coercion, or through misuse of power or deception makes a profit from the sexual activities of another person, may be punished with a prison sentence of maximum 18 months or a fine of the fourth category." One of the main topics of discussion currently is that the use of force or coercion is already unlawful under other statutes. So why keep a special law relating commercial sex and the use of force if you want to abolish the first (Bovenkerk 1992, personal communication)

5. The delay is, in part, due to the increasingly complicated system of proposed regulations accompanying the discussion of the bill (Gieske 1990), its relation to another article concerning the trafficking in women (Boutellier 1991), and proposed increased penalties for unauthorized brothel exploitation (C. Visser 1988).

6. As a rule, Article 250bis is only used to prosecute someone who is involved in other criminal behavior that cannot be proven (Visser n.d.:5). Horde (1987) points out that the infrequent use of Article 250bis is partly explained by the rather stringent standards of evidence required for successful criminal prosecution of this statute.

7. There are great differences in the manner in which municipalities make use of the so-called *tippelverbod*. For example, in the town of Heerlen, the "prohibition to solicit" is used in an extremely repressive manner. The pertinent local ordinance (July 7, 1987) states that it is prohibited to solicit (i.e., stand still or walk back and forth) "in the entire inner city and surrounding areas, between 14.00 and 06.00 hours" (Serrarens & Spronken 1991:5). This local ordinance has been challenged in court on constitutional grounds (Serrarens & Spronken 1991). What is different about the Heerlen case is that johns are being

prosecuted as well. Other cities have a much more tolerant policy, with a *tippelverbod* for a narrowly defined area for a particular time period.

8. Relocation of the areas where prostitution is allowed has sometimes included the establishment of "support services" in or near the designated area. For example, city officials in The Hague published a report outlining the conditions that would have to be met to make the place acceptable to the prostitutes: a "livingroom project" (a place to go and have coffee during the night), better lighting, and garbage cans (Scholtes 1987). Regular evaluations of the area would be required to make sure the conditions are met. The city of The Hague has indeed implemented these recommendations; the same is true for Amsterdam, Rotterdam, and Utrecht.

Window prostitution is primarily a big-city phenomenon. Several local governments have taken active measures to limit the nuisance problems for the neighborhoods. In The Hague, citizens living in window prostitution areas received monetary compensation to help them move into another neighborhood. This resulted in a monopoly position of window prostitution in certain areas. The next step was then to concentrate all window prostitution in one designated neighborhood. Window prostitution businesses outside the designated area were bought and offered a place in the newly designated area. Cars were no longer allowed in the area—the area was designated for pedestrians only. According to Scholtes (1987), The Hague has the most successful window prostitution business of the Netherlands.

9. Local authorities in Groningen, a mid-size city in the northern part of the Netherlands, also played an active role in the relocation of window prostitution. The city bought buildings to resell to people interested in the prostitution business. The buildings are sublet using contracts specifying that the building will be used for prostitution. The city has also purchased existing prostitution businesses, paying a certain amount for "good will" (Scholtes 1987:57).

10. This section draws heavily on J. Visser (n.d.), Belderbos and Visser (1987), Scholtes (1987), Horde (1987), and Boutellier (1987, 1991).

11. It is not unusual to encounter arguments in favor of including prostitution as an explicit consideration in urban planning: "Prostitution . . . is/may be a part of the services needed in a big city" (Horde 1987:296).

12. A common theme of reformers in the 1980s in many Western nations has been the call for decentralization of government function. This theme was notably present in the United States; it was a centerpiece of President Ronald Reagan's candidacy and his subsequent terms of office. This theme was also present in the Netherlands, representing itself as an increased role for local and municipal governments—rather than the national—in the regulation of prostitution.

13. It should be noted that there is not much support for the revised legislation within the sex world itself. The Red Thread has actually very little influence in this subculture (Bovenkerk 1992, personal communication).

14. Starting January 1, 1990, prostitutes have been eligible to join the national union FNV (De Boer & Wissenburg, 1990:15).

15. In a recent newspaper article (*Nieuwsblad van het Zuiden*:4), representatives of The Red Thread complained that they were never asked for their opinions about the proposed system of regulations. However, it should be noted that the Mr. De Graaf Stichting, an organization devoted solely to studying and promoting the well-being of Dutch prostitutes, has been involved in various activities and work groups on the implementation of the revised prostitution law. The Mr. De Graaf Stichting has a close working relationship with The Red Thread. Furthermore, the Minister of Justice, during the parliamentary discussion about the proposed abolition of the article on brothel keeping, emphasized that it was important for local government to include prostitutes or organizations of prostitutes in discussions about planned policies (C. Visser 1988).

16. It should be noted that the Dutch police are not uniformly in favor of the public order approach with minimal attention for the improvement of the position of the prostitute. For example, the chief of police of Heerlen, a town with a very repressive prostitution policy, stated in a 1985 published report that a municipal policy aimed primarily toward preventing harmful effects of prostitution on the public order is much too narrow (Serrarens & Spronken 1991:8). He argues in favor of a policy based on the premise that prostitution is a socially accepted fact and that the "interests of the prostitutes are considered together with the interests of the other parties" whenever measures are taken in the area of public order and urban renovation (Berends, cited in Serrarens & Spronken 1991:8-9). The notion that the needs and rights of prostitutes are at least as important as the need for public order is certainly not uncommon among Dutch law enforcement officials.

References

Beeren, M. (1988). Gemeenten krijgen mogelijkheid prostitutie te reguleren. *De Nederlandse Gemeente* 42: 76–77.

Belderbos, F., and Visser, J. (eds.) (1987). *Beroep: prostituee*. Utrecht, The Netherlands: Stichting Welzijns Publikaties.

Blad, J. (1990). Civilisering van prostitutie als instrument tegen vrouwenhandel. *Nederlands Juristen Blad* 65: 390–395.

Boutellier, J.C.J. (1987). Prostitutie en moraal. *Justitiele Verkenningen* 13: 7–35.

——— (1991). Prostitution, criminal law and morality in the Netherlands. *Crime, Law and Social Change* 15:201–211.

Bruins Slot, V.H. (1988). Ambities en illusies. *Bestuursforum* 12: 196–198.

Brunott, L. (1986). Prostitutie: beheerste ontucht. *Nemesis* 2: 173–175.

Coenen, H. (1988). Prostitutie als daad van ontkleding. In *Prostitute in banen.* Report on a meeting on local prostitution policy in Rotterdam on December 16, 1987, City of Rotterdam.

De Boer, M., & Wissenburg, K. (1990). Slechte arbeidsomstandigheden leiden tot steunfraude. *Sociaal Bestek* 52: 15–16.

De Winter, R. (1990). Het Heerlens tippelverbod: de Hoge Raad als feitenrechter. *Nederlands Juristenblad* 65 : 1681.

Foucault, M. (1979). *Discipline and punish: The birth of the prison* trans. A. Sheridan, 1977. New York: Vintage House. (Original work published 1975).

Gemeente Den Haag (1988). *Discussienota. Naar een vergunningenstelsel voor de Haagse prostitutie.* The Hague, the Netherlands: Author.

Gieske, H. (1988). Vergunningenbeleid en lokale regelgeving. In *Prostitutie in Banen.* Report on a meeting on local prostitution policy in Rotterdam on December 16, 1987, City of Rotterdam.

——— (1990). Prostitutieverordening. *De Gemeentestem* 140: 193–201.

Horde, M. (1987). Prostitutie: een stedelijke voorziening. *Rooilijn* 20: 294–299.

Kraft, D. (1988). Mogelijkheden voor een gemeentelijk prostitutiebelied blijven in de praktijk beperkt. *Binnenlands Bestuur* 9: 14–15.

Marshall, I.H., Anjewierden, O., & Van Atteveld, H. (1990). Toward an "Americanization" of Dutch drug policy? *Justice Quarterly* 7(2): 391–420.

Mensing van Charente, D.B. (1988). Vergunningenbeleid en politiebeleid. In *Prostitutie in Banen.* Report on a meeting on local prostitution policy in Rotterdam on December 16, 1987, City of Rotterdam.

Mr. A. De Graaf Stichting & Stichting De Rode Draad (n.d.). *Prostitutie Geregeld.* Amsterdam, the Netherlands: Author.

Overman, L. (1982). *Prostitutie in woonwijken.* Amsterdam, the Netherlands: Mr. A. De Graaf Stichting.

Pieterman, R. (1985). Opportuniteit: Een kenmerk van de strafvervolging in Nederland. *Sociologisch Tijdschrift* 12: 339–367.

Prostituees bang voor opheffen bordeelverbod (1991, May 15). *Het Nieuwsblad van het Zuiden,* 6.

Ruter, F. (1986). Drugs and the criminal law in the Netherlands. In J. van Dijk, C. Haffmans, F. Ruter, and S. Stolwijk (Eds.), *Criminal law in action.* Arnhem, the Netherlands: Gouda Quint.

Scholtes, J.T.I. (1987). Recente ontwikkelingen rond prostitutie. *Justitiele Verkenningen* 13(1): 45–71.

Serrarens, J., & Spronken, T. (1991). Tippelen in Heerlen. *Nemesis* 7: 4–9.

Spronken, T. (1987). Prostitutie. *Nemesis* 3(4): 220–223.

Stichting De Rode Draad (1987). Prioriteiten bij een nieuw prostitutiebeleid gezien vanuit de belangenorganisatie van prostituees. (unpublished report). Amsterdam, the Netherlands: Author.

Van Der Zijden. (1988). Vergunningenstelsel en positie van de prostituee. In *Prostitutie in banen.* Report on a meeting on local prostitution policy in Rotterdam on December 16, 1987, City of Rotterdam.

Visser, C. (1988). Berucht `bordeelverbod verdwijnt, prostitutie mag voortaan: maar gemeentelijk beleid buiten de grote steden komt moeizaam op gang. *Binnenlands Bestuur 9*: 24–31.

Visser, J. (n.d.). *Getemde ontucht: prostitutiebeleid tussen gedogen en reguleren.* Unpublished paper available from The Mr. A. De Graaf Stichting, Amsterdam, the Netherlands.

Wassenberg, J., & Van Kemenade, E. (1990). Prostitutie: Het beroep.*Nemesis* 6: 10–17.

Female Serial Killers

Jack Levin
James Alan Fox
Northeastern University

Because of well-publicized cases such as the recent slayings of five students in Gainesville, Florida, and the macabre crimes of Milwaukee's Jeffrey Dahmer, the term "serial killer" has fast become part of everyday vocabulary. Serial killers like David Berkowitz, ("Son of Sam"), Kenneth Bianchi, ("The Hillside Strangler"), and Theodore Bundy are now featured in prime-time television docudramas and mass market paperbacks.

Not all multiple homicides are serial, even though the serial form of multiple murder surely receives an inordinate amount of publicity. In a *massacre*, such as the mass shooting at a Luby's Cafeteria in Killeen, Texas, an offender slays a number of victims simultaneously; in a *serial murder*, the perpetrator takes the lives of a number of victims on separate occasions over a period of time—weeks, months, years, or even decades. In this essay, we will focus primarily on serial homicide, with occasional passing references to mass murder for the sake of comparison.

In this essay we also discuss the role of women in serial murder. Before examining female serial killers and why there are so few of them, we need to review some basic characteristics and a typology associated with this type of crime.

Profile of Serial Killers

Typically, serial killers are white males in their late 20s or 30s, who span a broad range of human attributes including appearance and intelligence. Most are fairly average at least to the casual observer. That is, they do not appear to be different from most other people; clearly, they are not the "glassy-eyed lunatics" seen in slasher films like *Friday the Thirteenth* or *Texas Chainsaw Massacre*. But there is one trait that tends to separate serial killers from the norm: they are exceptionally skillful in their presentation of self, so that they appear beyond suspicion. This is part of the reason why they are so difficult to apprehend.

In the modern mythology of serial murder, the killer is characterized as a nomad whose compulsion to kill carries him hundreds of thousands of miles a year as he drifts from state to state and region to region leaving scores of victims in his wake. This may be true of some well-known and well-traveled killers like Ted Bundy and Henry Lee Lucas, but not for the majority (Levin & Fox 1985). According to Hickey (1990b), less than one-quarter of the serial killers operating since 1975 crossed state lines in their murder sprees. John Wayne Gacy, for example, killed all of his 33 young male victims at his Des Plaines, Illinois, home, burying most of them there as well. Gacy, like Wayne Williams, David Berkowitz, and Angelo Buono, had a job, friends, and family but secretly killed on a part-time basis.

In terms of motivation, most serial murderers kill not for love, money, or revenge but for the pleasure of it. That is, they enjoy the thrill, the sexual satisfaction, or the dominance that they achieve over the lives of their victims. Not only do they savor the act of murder itself, but they rejoice as their victims scream and beg for mercy. As another expression of their need for power, serial killers often crave the publicity given to their crimes. It is not just the celebrity status that they seek; more importantly, they are able to control the lives of thousands of area residents who are held in their grip of terror.

Unlike most other types of murderers, the serial killer hardly ever uses a firearm. A gun would only rob him of his greatest pleasure—exalting in his victim's suffering. The serial killer satisfies his hunger for power and control by squeezing from his victim's body its last breath of life or by literally beating the life out of him/her.

Contrary to popular view, most serial killers are not insane in either a legal or medical sense (see Levin & Fox 1985; Leyton 1986). They know right from wrong, they know exactly what they are doing, and they can control their desire to kill, but they choose not to do so. They are more cruel than crazy.

Psychologically, the serial killer is a sociopath (or antisocial personality), which is a disorder of character rather than of the mind. The serial killer lacks a conscience, feels no remorse, and cares exclusively for his/her own pleasures in life. Other people are seen merely as tools to fulfill his own needs and desires, no matter how perverse or reprehensible (see Harrington 1972).

Modifying a scheme proposed by Holmes and De Burger (1988), we suggest that serial murders can be classified into three major categories, each with two subtypes:

1. Thrill
   a. Sexual sadism
   b. Dominance
2. Mission
   a. Reformist
   b. Visionary
3. Expedience
   a. Profit
   b. Protection

Most serial killings can be classified as thrill killings. The so-called "lust killer" (Hazelwood & Douglas 1980), a sexual sadist, is perhaps the most common form of all. In addition, a growing number of murders committed by hospital caretakers have in recent years been exposed; while not sexual in motivation, these acts of murder are perpetrated for the sake of dominance nevertheless.

A less common form of serial killing consists of mission-oriented killers who murder in order to further a cause. Through killing, the reformist type attempts to rid the world of filth and evil, such as slaying prostitutes or skid-row derelicts. Most self-proclaimed reformists are actually motivated by thrill-seeking but simply try to rationalize their murderous behavior. For example, Donald Harvey, who worked as an orderly in Cincinnati-area hospitals, confessed to killing over 80 patients over a period of years. Although he was termed a mercy killer, Harvey actually enjoyed the dominance he achieved by "playing God" with the lives of other people.

In contrast to the pseudo-reformist, the visionary killer is rare but genuinely believes in his/her mission. He/She hears the voice of the devil or God instructing him/her to kill. Driven by these delusions, the visionary killer tends to be psychotic, confused, and disorganized. Because the killings are impulsive and even frenzied, the visionary rarely remains on the street long enough to become a prolific serial killer.

The third category of serial murderer, those who kill for the sake of expediency, is the least common of all. It is important to note that we exclude career criminals who on rare occasion may kill (e.g., a drug dealer who once in a while must eliminate a competitor or a subordinate). By contrast, the expedience type of serial killer systematically murders as a critical element of his/her overall plan (e.g., the Lewington brothers systematically robbed and murdered 10 people throughout central Ohio).

Why Are There So Few Female Serial Killers?

Murder is essentially a masculine crime. Approximately 85% are committed by men. Yet, the disproportionate participation of men in violent crime is magnified even more in the case of homicides involving four or more victims. In fact, less than 5% of all such mass murders are committed by females, perhaps even fewer in the case of serial killings (Levin & Fox 1985).

Both motivation and personality may help explain the relative absence of female serial killers. Regarding motive, most serial killers possess an inordinate need for power and dominance, which they satisfy by torturing, raping, and killing their victims. When sex is involved, it is usually one expression of the much larger need to control and dominate other people. The male sex role continues to include an expectation of control and violence not sanctioned for females (Edwards-Short 1991).

The women's movement may have actually increased the salience of the need for masculine power by threatening it (Levin & McDevitt 1993). There is reason to believe that a number of men feel that their masculine advantage has been eroded by competition from women in jobs and education. The anger of men against women can be seen in many ways, including the growing number of R-rated slasher films in which women are depicted as victims of brutal attacks, popular music—especially rap and heavy metal—whose lyrics suggest that "women are only asking for it anyway" when they are the victims of sexual violence, and the rise of "attack comedians," who belittle women in their stand-up routines. Perhaps as another indicator of a more widespread masculine resentment, women are particularly likely to be victimized by serial killers. In addition, at least two of the largest massacres in American history—Marc Lepine's 1989 mass killing at the University of Montreal and George Henard's 1991 mass killing in Killeen, Texas, seem to have been motivated, at least in part, by profound hatred toward women (Levin & McDevitt 1993).

In terms of character or personality, serial killers tend to be sociopaths. It has been estimated that 3% of all males in our society could be considered sociopathic (for a discussion of the prevalence of antisocial personality disorder, see American Psychiatric Association 1987). Of course, most sociopaths are not violent: they may lie, cheat, or steal, but rape and murder are not necessarily appealing to them.

Characteristics of Female Serial Killers

Criminologists with a psychiatric bent have argued that women choose their weapons of homicide based on a passive-aggressive personality posture, that is, they prefer not to confront their victims in a violent way. Even if this is so, female mass killers may also have more "practical" reasons. Because of their relatively small physical stature, women are less likely to be able to do to men what male serial killers often do to their female victims. It would generally be harder for the average female to strangle or suffocate her male victim. This may partially explain why women frequently use less physical means—for example, poisoning—when they commit homicide. Indeed, though only 15% of all homicides are committed by females, more than 40% of all homicides by poisoning are committed by them. According to Hickey (1990a), female serial killers are more likely to target males than females, when their victims are adults. He also suggests that 52% of all female serial killers in the United States have used poison in order to slay their victims. Just as males have unequal access to and training in the use of firearms because of the male role, so females tend to have unequal access to and training in the use of poisons (and poisoned medications) by virtue of their traditional role as homemakers.

Aside from the impact of their physical stature, female serial killers may choose their weapons based on motivation. Physical contact is very important to many male serial killers, especially those motivated by dominance and control. In order to achieve a feeling of superiority, they torture. Few male serial killers would, therefore, consider using either a firearm or poison; such weapons only distance them from their victims and reduce physical contact.

Women Killing for Profit and Protection

By contrast, female serial killers are more often motivated by profit or protection. To collect her victims' social security checks, Sacramento landlady Doreathea Puentes allegedly poisoned as many as nine elderly roomers. The first victim was initially thought to have committed suicide by an overdose of codeine; her body was found in Puentes' home. The body of the second victim, an old boyfriend of Puentes, was discovered floating in a wooden box downriver. In the fall of 1989, seven bodies, in varying stages of decomposition, were found buried in the yard in front of Doreathea Puentes' rooming house.

Thirty-five-year-old ex-prostitute Aileen Wuornos recently confessed to having killed seven men. Prosecutors charged that, in 1989–1990, Wuornos conducted a 13-month serial-killing spree along Florida's highways. Her motive: greed. Typically, she would be picked up by a stranger, have sex with him, ask for payment, shoot him several times, take his money, and then dump his body. After being found guilty of first-degree murder in the 1989 killing of a Florida businessman, Wuornos whispered in the direction of the jurors as they filed out of the courtroom, "I am innocent. . . . I was raped." She then shouted to departing jurors, "You are the scumbags of America."

Some profit-motivated female serial killers have targeted their family members, usually spouses, as victims. Betty Lou Beets murdered her fifth husband, a Dallas firefighter, to collect his $100,000 insurance benefits. She was also suspected in the mysterious deaths of her former spouses. For example, she was charged with murder when the body of her fourth husband was discovered buried behind a tool shed in the backyard. In 1985, she was sentenced to death.

The profit motive occasionally takes a more metaphysical form, where serial killers believe that their ritualistic murder will protect them from the law. Sara Maria Aldrete was believed to have been the "witch" for a devil-worshipping gang of Mexican drug smugglers who, in 1989, engaged in ritualistic human sacrifice to bring them immunity from bullets as well as criminal prosecution. The 24-year-old honor student at Texas Southmost College apparently aided in the murder and human sacrifice of 15 people. Yet, according to one of her professors, "Sara was a model, respectful student. Little did we know that she was apparently leading a double life."

Women Killing for Dominance

Dependent patients, particularly those in hospitals and nursing homes, represent a class of victims that is at the mercy of a different kind of serial killer, called "angels of death." Recent revelations about female serial killers working as nurses and nurses' aides have horrified even the most jaded observers of crime. In 1987–1988, two Grand

Rapids, Michigan, nurses' aides—Gwendolyn Graham and Catherine Wood—suffocated to death at least five elderly patients just for the thrill of it. The two women later confessed that their murders had formed the basis for a lovers' pact—a shared secret that was meant to bind their love forever. In November 1989, Graham was sentenced to life imprisonment without eligibility for parole. Her accomplice, who admitted serving as a lookout while the murders were being committed by her partner, was sentenced to 20 to 40 years in prison.

Another "angel of death" was Genene Jones, a licensed vocational nurse in San Antonio, Texas, who may have been responsible for the deaths of numerous children who died mysteriously while on her shift. Although some of her colleagues suspected that she was responsible for the deaths, they could never collect the conclusive evidence needed to make a formal accusation. Moreover, other staff members at the hospital regarded Jones as a meticulous nurse whose medical procedures were beyond question.

It wasn't until she left her job in the San Antonio hospital in 1982 to take a position in a pediatric clinic in nearby Kerrville's downtown business district that Genene Jones' murderous behavior was finally discovered. One of her first patients in the clinic, 15-month-old Chelsea McClelland, mysteriously died after a routine physical examination. Eight months later, medical examiners found in the infant's body traces of a powerful muscle relaxant, Anectine, which caused her respiratory system to stop. In fact, during the 6-week period in which Jones had worked for the town's new pediatrician, six children had stopped breathing and were rushed to the hospital for resuscitation. Nurse Jones was reportedly euphoric when she was able to administer CPR to help save their lives. She was "playing God." In January 1984, Genene Jones was tried for first-degree murder. It took the jury only 3 hours to find her guilty and sentence her to 99 years in prison.

Not all female serial killers motivated by dominance victimize patients. According to Hickey (1990a), husbands are usually selected as victims by female serial killers, who target members of their own family for "the thrill of it." In 1954, Nannie Bragg admitted to police that she had killed four of her five husbands simply because she enjoyed killing. For the same reason, she also murdered her two sisters, her mother, two of her children, a grandson, and a nephew. All of her victims died agonizing deaths after sampling Bragg's home cooking—food laced with rat poison.

Women Teaming Up with Male Serial Killers

We have already noted the presence of female serial killers in crimes of dominance without sex and in crimes of expedience, for profit or protection. Although the number of such killers is relatively small, female serial murderers do occasionally team up with males in crimes committed for the thrill of it. In some cases, these women participate in the crimes in order to please their murdering mates; in others, they develop their own sense of satisfaction from killing. Regardless, it is often assumed, in analyzing such offenses, that the male was the major culprit, while his female companion was merely an accomplice who deferred to her lover in order to preserve their relationship.

According to the state of California, in 1980, Douglas Clark—the man known as the "Sunset Strip Killer"—and a female accomplice murdered and mutilated at least seven people. Some of the victims were adults, others were juveniles. Some were prostitutes, and one was a male. All were slain in an unusually brutal manner, including decapitation.

To this day, Clark argues that he was victimized by a shoddy legal defense and by a secret plea bargain with the woman whom the prosecution claimed was his accomplice. That woman, Carol Bundy (no relation to Ted), was able to convince the court by her testimony that Douglas Clark was the main culprit in their killing spree and that, mesmerized by his charm, she merely went along to please her lover. Despite assurances to the jury that the district attorney would go for the death penalty, Carol Bundy received a parolable sentence; Doug Clark is scheduled to die in the gas chamber.

Whether he is actually innocent or guilty, Douglas Clark's argument on his own behalf directs attention to the use of a controversial procedure in the prosecution of certain killers, especially serial killers. In order to secure a conviction, one of the defendants is convinced by the prosecuting attorney to turn state's evidence in return for a lesser sentence. From the prosecution's standpoint, it makes sense to convict at least one defendant on the word of another, rather than to convict no one at all.

But this advantage is not always properly weighed against its potential for abuse. How much credibility should the court give to the testimony of an accomplice who is eager to escape the gas chamber or a lifetime behind bars? To what extent does a plea bargain with accomplices actually promote lying and perjury? The importance of such questions is highlighted by the fact that some 30% of all serial murders are committed by teams of assailants—usually brothers, cousins, friends, lovers, or co-workers. If they are caught and tried, one defendant often ends up informing on the other. This was true, for example, in the nursing home killings committed by Graham and Wood (Levin & Fox 1985).

In the Sunset Strip Killer case, one defendant, Douglas Clark, was a man; the other, Carol Bundy, was a woman. The prosecutor chose to plea bargain with the female rather than the male defendant, to use Carol Bundy's version of the crimes against Douglas Clark.

This is nothing new. In fact, there seems to be a consistent willingness for juries, prosecuting attorneys, and citizens generally to side with female defendants who stand accused of committing heinous crimes. At least in some of these cases, longstanding prejudice against women—the stereotype according to which they are capable of nothing more than submissively following orders—may become the basis for discriminating against men.

In 1958, for example, Charles Starkweather and Caril Fugate went on an 8-day killing spree across Nebraska and Wyoming that resulted in the slaughter of 10 victims. Jurors heard testimony that implicated both defendants. Yet only Starkweather went to the electric chair. His female partner was released from prison in 1976, following an outpouring of public sentiment on her behalf.

The Future for Female Serial Murderers

During her trial in Deland, Florida, television and newspaper accounts suggested that the presence of Aileen Wuornos, "America's first female serial killer," marked the incipient stage of a trend toward growing numbers of women who commit serial murder. Clearly, Wuornos is not alone among women who have killed on a continuing basis. Just as clearly, she will not be the last.

But data from the Supplementary Homicide Reports are not consistent with the expectation of a growing presence of females among killers. Since 1976, the proportion of homicide offenders who are females has actually declined somewhat—from 16.5% in 1976 to 12.1% in 1989. Thus, almost 88% of all homicides are committed by men.

Serial killers typically target total strangers as their victims. Thus, gender differences in homicides committed by strangers are particularly revealing. If women are becoming more involved as the perpetrators of serial murder, then they should probably also become more involved in killing strangers generally. Yet the percentage of female offenders in such homicides decreased from 4% in 1976 to only 2.2% in 1989. Thus, more than 98% of all homicides against strangers are committed by men, and their presence in such crimes seems to be growing.

One might project that as sex-role distinctions blur and women increasingly refer to their careers for self-definition, more of them will also be motivated by the masculine goal of being powerful and dominant in their relationships. To some extent, this social change might reasonably be expected to produce larger numbers of female serial killers motivated by the need for dominance and control. At this juncture, however, the evidence indicates instead that, at least for the foreseeable future, men will continue to monopolize serial murder.

Despite the low prevalence of female serial killers, or perhaps because of it, the American public seems to be inordinately fascinated with the notion of a female killing machine. At this time, curiously, a number of Hollywood films about female serial killers are in various stages of production.

Unquestionably, the significant media attention devoted to the Wuornos case is a result of her gender. Indeed, in the mind of the typical observer, women are supposed to be nurturers, not murderers. But there may be one other reason why the female serial killer has become so intriguing to Americans: We can be fascinated without being afraid. Nearly everyone, at some level or another, fears being victimized by a serial killer. But when we analyze our fears, there is little question that the nightmarish figure hiding in the shadows is not named Sue.

References

American Psychiatric Association (1987). *Diagnostic and statistical manual of mental disorders* (3rd edition revised). Washington, DC: American Psychiatric Association.

Darrach, B., & Norris, J. (1984). An american tragedy. *Life Magazine* 7: 58–74.

Edwards-Short, V. (1991). Serial killers: A by-product of our patriarchal society. Paper presented at the American Society of Criminology annual meeting, San Francisco.

Egger, S.A. (1984). A working definition of serial murder and the reduction of linkage blindness. *Journal of Police Science and Administration* 12: 348–357.

——— (1986). Utility of the case study approach to serial murder research. Paper presented at the of the American Society of Criminology annual meeting, Atlanta.

——— (1990). *Serial murder: An elusive phenomenon.* New York: Praeger.

Fox, J.A. (1989, January 29) The mind of a murderer. *Palm Beach Post,* B1.

———, and Levin, J. (1985, December 1). Serial killers: How statistics mislead us. *Boston Herald,* 45.

Harrington, A. (1972). *Psychopaths.* New York: Simon & Schuster.

Hazelwood, R.R., & Douglas, J.E. (1980). The lust murder. *FBI Law Enforcement Bulletin* (April): 1–5.

Hickey, E.W. (1990a). *Serial murderers and their Victims.* Pacific Grove, CA: Brooks/Cole.

——— (1990b). The etiology of victimization in serial murder: A historical and demographic analysis. In S.A. Egger (Ed.), *Serial murder: An elusive phenomenon* (pp. 53–72). New York: Praeger.

Holmes, R.M., & De Burger, J. (1988). *Serial murder.* Newbury Park, CA: Sage.

Howlett, J.B., Haufland, K.A., & Ressler, R.K. (1986). The violent criminal apprehension program—VICAP: A progress report. *FBI Law Enforcement Bulletin* 55: 14–22.

Jenkins, P. (1988). Myth and murder: The serial killer panic of 1983–5. *Criminal Justice Research Bulletin* 3: 1–7.

Kiger, K. (1990). The darker figure of crime: The serial murder enigma. In S.A. Egger (Ed.), *Serial murder: An elusive phenomenon* (pp. 35–52). New York: Praeger.

Levin, J., & Fox, J.A. (1985). *Mass murder: America's growing menace.* New York: Plenum Press.

Levin, J., & McDevitt, J. (1993). *Hate crimes: The rising tide of bigotry and bloodshed.* New York: Plenum Press.

Leyton, E. (1986). *Compulsive killers: The story of modern multiple murderers.* New York: New York University Press.

Magid, K., & McKelvey, C.A. (1988). *High risk: Children without a conscience.* New York: Bantam Books.

Norris, J. (1988). *Serial killers: The growing menace.* New York: Doubleday.

Ressler, R.K., & Burgess, A.W. (1985), Violent crime. *FBI Law Enforcement Bulletin* Special Issue: 54.

Ressler, R.K., Burgess, A.W., & and Douglas, J.E. (1988). *Sexual homicide: Patterns and motives.* Lexington, MA: Lexington Books.

Schwartz, T. (1981). *The hillside strangler: A murderer's mind.* New York: Doubleday.

Starr, M., et al. (1984, November 26). The random killers. *Newsweek,* 100–106.

Trial starts for accused serial killer (1992, January 16). *Palm Beach Post,* 10A.

Vetter, H. (1990). Dissociation, psychopathy, and the serial murderer. In S.A. Egger (Ed.), *Serial murder: An elusive phenomenon* (pp. 73–92). New York: Praeger.

Women and Crime in the United States: A Marxian Explanation

Polly F. Radosh
Western Illinois University

Abstract

The essay briefly reviews the leading theories of female crime causation that surfaced in the twentieth century and proposes an alternative, theoretical orientation using a Marxian approach. This explanation uses existing theoretical and empirical studies to account for (a) the means by which women are defined as criminal, (b) the class relationship between female criminals and general population of women, and (c) the system by which control over both the population of female criminals and the general population of women is legitimized. The essay also examines the relationship between the victimization of women and the opportunity structure as class based.

Theories of female crime causation have surfaced periodically for most of the twentieth century and have called attention to some of our basic assumptions about women's lives. Most of the theories about women's involvement in criminal activities have proposed that female criminality is the result of atomized, feminine traits (Klein 1973) rather than of social, structural problems such as poverty or access to opportunity. Individual female characteristics, such as physiological, psychological, or universally "feminine" characteristics, have been perceived to be the antecedents to female criminality.

Lombroso's (1903) theory of atavistic causation pointed to physiological factors that surfaced in women and girls but also elaborated the social stereotypes of his time period—that feminine characteristics were de facto inferior characteristics: "Women have many traits in common with children; that their moral sense is deficient; that they are revengeful, jealous. . . . In ordinary cases these defects are neutralized by piety, maternity, . . . sexual coldness, weakness, and an underdeveloped intelligence" (p. 151).

Thomas (1907, 1923) believed female criminality was endemic to women who were lower in the biological hierarchy than men but who had learned to control their basic urges for the sake of domestic harmony. He perceived the instigation of female crime to be residual in women's sexuality, with the criminal behavioral patterns emergent only when traditional, social restraints broke down (Smart 1976). Factors that might initiate a rise in female criminality were seen as present in social change that permitted women to seek employment outside of the home or to otherwise increase their social autonomy (Smart 1976).

Many of the earliest theories of female crime causation addressed the "ubiquitous nature of women" as a foundational premise. In addition to the biological determinism theorized by Thomas (1907, 1923) and Lombroso (1903), others such as Freud (1933), Davis (1971), and Pollak (1961) proposed that factors hidden in the unique "nature of women" cause some women to commit crimes. These hidden factors were stimulated by environmental, psychological, or situational variables but were potential in all women.

Pollak (1961), in particular, developed the idea of residual factors that triggered female crime periodically. He believed that women are inherently manipulative, secretive, and passionless. He suggested that women are innately deceitful, providing a biological propensity to commit crime, which requires deceit: "Our sex mores force women to conceal every four weeks the period of menstruation. . . . They thus make concealment and misrepresentation in the eyes of women socially required and must condition them to a different attitude toward veracity than men" (p. 11).

Others (Cowie, Cowie, & Slater 1968; Konopka 1966; Morris 1965; Rosenblum 1965) have proposed that there is either something inherent in the "nature of women" or in the nature of the socialization of women that gives rise to female crime.[1] The undercurrent of these theories is a monolithic explanation of female crime that places the origins of individual crime within the context of basic or natural feminine etiology. The theoretical directions that these theories delineate as the foci of crimes committed by women have been ultimately deterministic. These theories express and ideological unity, which proposes that women commit crimes because there are factors in their physiological or psychological makeup that make the crimes irresistible.

After the etiology of women theories (circa 1900–1970), two authors in the mid-1970s modernized the monolithic discourse on female crime patterns. Adler's *Sisters in Crime* (1975) proposed that the unique social changes triggered by increased autonomy, access to opportunities, and free lifestyles for women in the 1970s and into the future would cause a masculinizing of female crime.[2] She predicted that as women's lives become more emancipated the differences between male and female crime patterns would dissipate.

> The forces behind equal employment opportunity [and] women's liberation movements . . . have been causing and reflecting a steady erosion of the social and psychological differences which have traditionally separated men and women. It would be natural to expect parallel developments in female criminality. . . . But what is clear is that as the position of women approximates the position of men, so does the frequency and type of their criminal activities. (251)

Adler's (1975) empirical evidence to support her theory has been discounted as inaccurate or misinterpreted (Smart 1979). Most notably, Steffensmeier (1978) used national data from the Federal Bureau of Investigation (FBI) to illustrate the statistical fallacy of Adler's assertions. Nevertheless, this work continues as a frequently cited, authoritative exploration of female crime causation.

Similarly, Simon (1976) proposed that women's work outside of the home would provide greater opportunities to commit fraud and embezzlement, that increased independence would foster new images of women's potentialities, and that property offenses would rise as a consequence. She predicted that women's occupational opportunities would increase women's involvement in white-collar offenses, in particular. Yet, as Smart (1979) pointed out, it is not the "liberated" woman who comprise the roles of female criminals. Rather, poor and working-class women, who have always worked outside of the home, are those most likely to be involved in crime. Increased employment opportunities for middle-class women would likely have a negligible impact on the illegitimate opportunity structure for these women.

Many recent authors have been critical of these theories (see Bowker 1985; Price & Sokoloff 1982; Rafter & Stanko 1982; Schur 1984; Smart 1976). The implicit message in all of the theories from Lombroso (1903) to Pollak (1961), and up to Adler (1975) and Simon (1976) is that female crime is residual in the character of women's lives. The theoretical orientations throughout the twentieth century have been succinct in their delineation of monocausal explanations for female crime that have attached primary importance to factors present in the lives of women, in the biology or psychology of women, or in the rejection of traditional status differentials.

The subliminal message has been that because men commit most crimes, then there must be something atypical about women who commit crimes. Crime is defined as male; therefore, women who commit crime must possess characteristics that make them distinct from other women. Simon (1976) and Adler (1975) further delimited the monocausal philosophy by suggesting that women who commit crimes are an expression of the equalizing of the roles for men and women. This is, of course, a further attempt to draw attention to a single detail in all women's lives that might initiate criminal activity in some women.

Traditional explanations of male crime, such as anomie theory, control theories, or the labeling perspective also have had inadequate applicability to female crime. The emphasis in these theories is on the nature of social rules and labels or on the social reaction to individuals who break rules. According to these theories, the deviant is endowed with a variety of choices. For example, in anomie theory the actor chooses whether to pursue culturally prescribed goals by legitimate means or through criminal means. In the social control theories the pull between inner controls and other-directed social pressure leaves the individual with the choice between restraints or groups acceptance. In this case, social control is determined by the strengths of such moral inducements as family responsibility or socialization into middle-class normative patterns. With labeling theory, the decision to engage in deviance is triggered by societal reaction to initial rule-breaking behavior. In all of these theories, as well as other central, sociological theories, the wider origins (social structural factors) that act as determinants of social behavior and societal reaction are not adequately elucidated (Taylor, Walton, & Young 1973). With regard to crimes committed by women, this is an especially crucial omission. The social structural placement of women is more embracing as a causal explanation than any current sociological theories propose.

Although the traditional explanations of female crime have failed to account adequately for social structural factors that influence some women to commit crime, Marxist theories also have failed to illustrate social structural factors that distinguish male crime from female crime. Currently, there is no convincing account of female crime. Because the general theories of crime are male based and the traditional theories of female crime are too individualistic, Marxist theory offers the most promising explanation. The following section briefly summarizes the Marxian theory of crime causation.

Marxist View of Criminal Behavior

Marxist criminology developed from Marx's general theory of society because Marx did not develop a theory of crime. The interpretation of the writings of Marx, in this regard, have focused on the fact that the capitalist mode of production demoralizes workers. Capitalism is built on the labor of workers employed to pursue the productive effort. The competition between the owners or controllers of the productive effort (capitalists) and the workers polarizes the two groups and encourages exploitation of the workers by the capitalist class. As the exploitation exacerbates, the alienation and demoralization among the workers increases (Marx 1967:763).

Marx believed human potential was fulfilled only when people engaged in productive lifework (Marx & Engels 1965:365–367), but that as industrialization under capitalism increased, the numbers of people unemployed or underemployed would also increase. Because these unemployed people are not engaged in productive work, they become demoralized and are subject to crime. Marx called this group the "lumpenproletariat" (Marx & Engels 1965:367).

Others in the Marxist tradition, most notably Bonger (1916), argued that the capitalist system encourages people to be greedy, selfish, and to pursue their own interests at the expense of others. Crime is centralized among the lower classes because the system of justice criminalizes greed among the poor and allows the wealthy legal opportunities to pursue selfish desires. Quinney (1980:59–62) described lower-class economic crimes as an "accommodation" to the inequities of capitalism. People engage in crime as a response to the unequal distribution of wealth endemic to the conditions of capitalism. Gordon (1971) also argued that crime committed by the poor is a rational response to the chronic problems of unemployment or underemployment in low-paying and demeaning jobs among the lower classes.

Marxian theories of crime have excluded crimes committed by women from the explanations. As with most of Marxian theory, gender issues are either ignored or summarized as problems connected to the general issue of class (Messerschmide 1986:8). The Marxist notion that women's problems arise from their status as instruments of reproduction has been the focus of much of the literature relating Marxist principles to the status of women (Eisenstein 1979: 11). Women have been perceived as victims of the division of labor under capitalism. The separation imposed by the sexual division of labor implied no special distinction for Marx or Marxian theorists (Eisenstein 1979; Matthaei 1982). Likewise, women's crime has been subsumed under the general explanation of the economic determinism endemic to class relations. This essay proposes a separation of male and female crime categories and explains female crime from a Marxian perspective.

Being Female in Capitalist Society: A Marxian Account

As suggested earlier, the main problem with most of the theories concerned with female crime patterns is that they have failed to consider social structural requisites and they have infrequently included a historical analysis of women's crimes. Many of the descriptive or historical studies of women's relationship to crime have used social structural explanations to illustrate the enduring relationship, for women, between social status and crime; but these works have been essentially atheoretical (see Feinman 1986; Freedman 1984; Rafter 1985).

The early theories of women's crime placed the criminal activity within the social order, but failed to see that the crimes might result from the social order. The omission furthered the view that female crime was episodic and thus controllable, if the causal factor could be isolated. Whether the causal factor was atavism (Lombroso 1903) or feminism (Adler 1975), the implication was that it was transitory rather than an outgrowth of long-term social structural and historical developments.

The final factor, which has been absent from many of the theories or descriptions of female crime patterns, is a dialectical analysis of the impact of a social structural construction of the sexual division of labor on the generation of crime patterns. For example, theorists may ask whether the capitalist sexual division of labor has any historical relationship to reduced or increased crime. Perhaps crime is an outgrowth of specific control procedures (Spitzer 1975) that are endemic to changes in the sexual division of labor. A dialectical examination of the capitalist division of labor and its relationship to women may provide the most insight into female crime patterns.

The capitalist sexual division of labor is so fully incorporated into social understandings that it is not recognizable as a contrived arrangement. In all known societies, the socialization process dictates the division of social activities along sex lines (Tavris & Wade 1984). The biological makeup of men and women ideally suits both sexes to certain types of activities, but factors prohibiting a merger of the roles are often socially controlled. For example, females who are tied to domestic roles are initiated into such roles by their biological capacity to bear and nurse children. Males, who possess greater muscle mass and upper body strength, may initially have been best suited to warrior or hunting roles. The causation of a sexual division of labor may be initially biological, but people comply with the established roles because they hold the behaviors to be proper to each sex, not because biology forces compliance. Males may, biologically, engage in domestic or nurturing roles and females may pursue aggressive, breadwinning roles without biological loss of sexual identity, even though social roles may be marginalized.

The sexual division of labor turns males and females, who are biologically differentiated, into masculine men and feminine women, who are social beings differentiated on the basis of social activities. "Womanhood" and "manhood" become conceptualizations within which males and females strive to realize their actions. As a result, each sex develops a psychic structure that makes undertaking activities of the opposite sex difficult or impossible (Matthaei 1982). Social differentiation of the roles appropriate to each sex is so complete that it creates separate male and female worlds. These separate spheres were previously attributed to human nature or God, as the creator of the natural order of things.

The merger between biological sex and socially dictated roles had been so complete, historically, as to provide the rationale for exclusion of women from full social participation. Women were prohibited from entering professions, getting an education, or securing the right to vote, because the biological roles for women were merged with the social expectations for women (Tavris & Wade 1984). In addition, criminal definitions, which are grounded in biological definitions of behavior as feminine, are established because they create a disjuncture between social behavior and biological expectations.

Social constructs that dictate sex-specific social behavior contribute to a subjective understanding of reality that is at odds with the objective facts. People tend to equate the merger of social and biological sex as appropriate and in the best interest of society. Society understands the sexual division of labor to be a product of nature. The strength of this belief is illustrated by the taboo against participation in the work of the opposite sex. Society requires "proof" that the activities are social and not biological (Matthaei 1982). Failure to achieve the appropriate role within the sexual division of labor leads to a questioning of one's biological sex, rather than the sexual division of labor (for example, male ballet dancers are stereotyped as homosexual, and female executives are stereotyped as using sex to get to the top).

The sexual division of labor underlies marriage roles. An interdependence is created in the traditional marriage under capitalism, which dictates that a man needs a woman to do the "women's work" or domestic work in the marriage, and a woman needs a man for economic support. An interdependent relationship is established, with the economic needs of the wife indicating greater dependence on her part. Women's work is intrafamilial and domestic; men's work is interfamilial and public, which places the ranked importance of the man's work hierarchically above that of the woman (Matthaei 1982). Universal subordination of women's work derives from the content of feminine activities as private, intrafamilial, and child centered. Women as a cross-national class of people with similar labor requirements are integrated into a unified caste or group, which cross-cuts traditional economic definitions of class membership.

Under capitalism, this caste membership is exaggerated by economic mandates, which encourage female affiliation with the fringe of the occupational status hierarchy. The importance of maintaining an occupational hierarchy that permits only token female participation at the highest ranks is central to containment of current economic distributions. Under United States capitalism, 80% of the women are employed in approximately ten occupational categories (Tavris & Wade 1984) that are low status, receive low remuneration, and have little opportunity for advancement. Women in the United States have been generally unskilled or have comprised the requisite reserve labor force. Although they have been agitating for increased freedom and accessibility to scarcities for most of the history of modern capitalism, their struggle has been dismissed as the "women problem" rather than a prototype of capitalist domination.

Under capitalism, where the dominant ideological constructs focus attention on accumulation of capital as the natural motivation for human behavior, full equality is not possible and the sexual division of labor becomes the epitome of economic inequality. The sexual division of labor becomes a model for domination of the economically wealthy over those who have no access to wealth. The ideology that the relationship between the owners of the means of production and the workers represents a natural evolution of competency in that pursuit of profit is patterned after the natural division of labor between the sexes, which differentiates competitors from domestics. The ultimate dichotomy is a differentiation between the producers of material products and the reproducers of future generations of producers. In effect, the sexual division of labor creates a system of control that preserves the current system.

The fact that women experience special vulnerability to certain types of crime, such as incest, rape, domestic abuse, or sexual harassment (Armstrong 1977; Brownmiller 1975; Price & Sokoloff 1982; Robin 1977), that the legal system has frequently failed to take seriously crimes committed against women,[3] and that the social system has failed to take seriously aspirations or accomplishments of women (see Tavris & Wade 1984) have all conspired to exacerbate the lack of control that has characterized women's lives in the modern capitalist sexual division of labor. This, combined with capitalist economic control engendered in the competition between the classes, has sealed the suppression of women as a specific caste.

Many of the contradictions in the collective advancement of women's opportunities have obscured the issue of control, but it is still an undercurrent of women's lives. Critics of the control thesis will point to the fact that women are advancing in business, government, and the professions in unprecedented numbers. Herein lies the contradiction. Although women have moved into business, they have not moved into executive or manegerial positions in appreciative numbers, and they are consistently compensated at a lower salary rate than men in the same or similar positions (Fishman 1987; Hewlett 1987). This is also true of women who have made it into professional occupations (Hewlett 1987; Tavris & Wade 1984). Women have been elected into government, but hold only 2% of Senate seats and only 5% of House seats.[4] The widespread belief in American society that women have finally achieved equality in the occupational marketplace is indicative of, and contributes to, the false consciousness associated with the ideological hegemony of capitalism. The fact is that the ranks of the poor have been increasingly swelled by women since World War II (U.S. Bureau of the Census 1987), and only a small percentage of women have achieved occupational equality with men.

Production of Female Crime in Capitalism[5]

For a Marxian theory of female crime causation to hold explanatory potential it should account for (a) the means by which women are defined as criminal, (b) the class relationship between female criminals and the general population of women, and (c) the system by which control over both the population of female criminals and the general population of women is legitimized. All aspects of the process of criminal behavior must be understood, as well as definitional properties of individual criminal acts.

Criminal Definitions

As Engels (1972:136) pointed out, "The legal inequality of the two partners [men and women] . . . is not the cause but the effect of the economic oppression of women." The fact that women have historically occupied a suppressed class is the result of an economic order that thrives on exploitation. The cause of female oppression does not rest in sexism alone, but in capitalism, which is fed by sexism.

It is the capitalist system that is supported by and grows because of the historical subservience of women in monogamous, nuclear families. Women have been the girding, institutional support for the pursuit of profit by men. The sexual division of labor has assured that women have remained unpaid laborers in the family, whose primary responsibilities have been to nurture future generations of capitalists and workers. The commerce-based power structure has exploited the labor of women at the same time that the ideological hegemony has convinced society that this system is the most appropriate humanitarian mechanism for perpetuating the human race. For working-class women this has often meant that they could and should perform unpaid labor for the benefit of the family at the same time that they worked for subservient wages for the benefit of the capitalists.

Historically, women who have not cooperated with the sexual division of labor in the capitalist family system have been defined as criminal or deviant. Women who did not adopt sexual mores appropriate to monogamous, domestic service were social outcasts. And, of course, the most ubiquitous crime among women, prostitution, has always been a flagrant affront to the nuclear family (see Rosen 1982). Women who have lived outside of the social definitions of morality (whether they were raped, made a choice to do so for economic reasons, or they simply preferred an alternative lifestyle) have been labeled by society as "sick" and in need of rehabilitation. The prevailing ideological hegemony has been that sexual alternatives are understandable for men but intolerable for women. The presumption has always been that if women's sexuality were loosened, the nuclear family would fall, and society (capitalism) would decay. As a result, the moral bolster of capitalism has rested on the sexual loyalty of women. Any woman who transgressed the social definitions of morality was eligible for a criminal label.

The evidence in the literature to support the relationship between female sexuality and criminal labels is overwhelming (see Price & Sokoloff 1982; Rafter & Stanko 1982; Schur 1984:51–131). Most of the early theories of female criminality proposed that some residual sexual, physiological, or psychosexual characteristic motivated female crime. Not only have parochial rationales for female crime relied on sexuality as explanatory, but the academic and intellectual theories also have relied on this as at least as a residual cause, if not a motivation for female criminality. Even crimes that were obviously motivated by economic factors (or perhaps thrill), such as shoplifting, were believed to have underlying sexual motivation (Pollak 1961). The violations were not only criminal, but an affront to the sexual division of labor and ultimately to female biological requisites.

Crimes other than those that included some moral significance have been most often rooted in social structural factors for women. Most women who are arrested, tried, and punished in the United States are convicted of crimes that reflect the general status of women in society. Most women who commit crimes are lower class and often on welfare, and they become involved in crimes as a result of frustration, anger, and economic necessity (Price & Sokoloff 1982). The legal framework, which is created by male judges and legislators, interpreted by male judges, and administered by predominantly male correctional officials, is the epitome of the class-based structure of capitalism.[6] Not only is the law created and implemented by the protectors of capitalism, but it is symbolic of justice, fairness, and constitutional protections (Rifkin 1980), which furthers the ideological hegemony of capitalism.

The law, then, is implemented against those of the lower classes as a protection of the property rights of the capitalists. Crimes committed by the upper classes are punished less severely, if they are punished at all (Gordon 1971; Quinney 1980). This is the common differentiation between street crime and white-collar crime that places greater importance on crimes committed by the poor than on crimes committed by the rich. The fact that the ranks of poor Americans have been continually increased by poor women for at least the last 25 years (Scott 1984) has meant that the law has also been implemented against women with increased frequency (see U.S. Dept. of Justice 1986).

Thus, capitalism has defined women as criminal in two ways. First, to protect the nuclear family and the sexual division of labor, which is the cornerstone of capitalism, women's sexuality has been closely controlled. Deviation from the moral proscriptions of society has been labeled as criminal. Although males have been allowed to survey freely alternative sexuality (for example, buying the services of a prostitute), females have been strictly regulated. Deviance has attracted criminal sanctions (for example, being a prostitute).[7]

Second, the class structure has protected the rights and property of the capitalists, while the lower classes have been closely scrutinized and sanctioned. Women, who are increasing the ranks of the poor in record numbers (Scott 1984; Hewlett 1987), are among the closely monitored poor. The types of crimes committed by women are especially representative of their position in the social structure.

For example, women are most likely to commit crimes that directly reflect their level of economic opportunity (welfare fraud, passing bad checks, prostitution, and drug offenses) and that require little skill or education (Feinman 1986:19). The lack of opportunity for economic security is cited as the most frequent motivation for female crimes (Feinman 1986; Price & Sokoloff 1982).

Economic opportunities for poor women have declined significantly in the last decade, and predictions are that by the year 2000 the poverty population will be composed solely of women and their children (Rodgers 1987:7). Currently, 78% of welfare recipients, who continually depend on welfare for more than half of their income, are women (Duncan 1984:79–82). Since 1970, the number of single women heading households has increased by 97%; 20% of all American children live with one parent—usually the mother (U.S. Bureau of the Census 1984).

The burden of supporting a family is especially difficult for single mothers. One reflection of the problem is demonstrated by the fact that full-time, yearly statistics for female workers averaged $16,843 in 1986, as compared with $25,894 for male workers (U.S. Bureau of the Census 1987:432). This, combined with the fact that only 48% of single mothers receive the full child support they are entitled to ("Average Child Support Payment Drops by 12%" 1987), has increased the financial burden of poor women and decreased legitimate opportunities for economic security. Women who commit crimes most frequently come from the ranks of the poor, who are frustrated by declining economic opportunity.

Class Status of Women

Class societies are based on an indispensable conflict between groups, with harmony achieved through domination of one specific class (Spitzer 1975). Those singled out as criminal are those who create problems for the ruling class (see Gordon 1971). Those who make up the criminal class may vent their aggression on those outside of the dominant class, but the basis for their criminal label resides in their challenge to the class rule (Spitzer 1975).

Although most women (and most men) occupy a position in the social structure that restricts access to opportunity and capital, by virtue of the sexual division of labor in the capitalist system, women as a group represent a clear subgroup of the permanent underclass. One of the most important social supports of capitalism is sexism, because it requires the nonpaid labor of women to insure high capital gain in a commerce-based society. The nuclear family perpetuates the system whereby women have two jobs: one paid at a wage determined by the capitalist class, and one unpaid service to the family (Engels 1972). Capitalism promotes sexism in the simple wage distribution and in all of its institutional supports from religion to education to politics to law. The ideological hegemony that protects the sexual division of labor either perpetuates the false understanding that times have changed and women are now treated equally, or it reinforces the traditional approach as the most appropriate mechanism for rearing children, governing the country, or creating laws. With either approach, attention is directed away from the most salient issue, the permanent status of women in society, and focuses either on how much equality has already been achieved or how little needs to be done to ensure equality with men. This creates a definitional smoke screen; the real focus of change should not be equality with men—because men are oppressed by capitalism—but a redefinition of class lines to eliminate the domination of one group by another.

Women singled out as criminal in a capitalist society are those who represent the poorest of the underclass. They seek solace in drugs, write bad checks, engage in prostitution, and commit petty property offenses (Rafter & Natalizia 1982). Female members of the upper classes are not singled out, except for the most flagrant law violations, because they have moved into occupational positions of responsibility, and they perpetuate the myth of increased equality. Poor women, like poor men, commit crimes of frustration and necessity. All women are inextricably linked to the capitalist caste of women, but only poor women are singled out for criminal sanctions. This perpetuates the ideological hegemony that poverty, and not the capitalist system, breeds crime. The capitalist economic system is actually perceived as offering unique opportunities for escape from poverty.

Thus, women labeled as criminal are those who commit offenses that threaten the distribution of property (Gordon 1971) or the sexual division of labor (Matthaei 1982). The fact that ownership of property, no matter how unequally distributed, is defensible at all costs under the capitalist system perpetuates the hegemony that those who attempt to take the property of others must be sanctioned. The fact that this "universal" rule only applies to the lower classes, that sanctions are disproportionately distributed according to class, and that women who commit petty property offenses often receive penalties more severe than those assigned to men (Rafter & Natalizia 1982; Schur 1984; Smart 1986) attests to the strength of the threat these crimes hold for the ruling class. Women, in particular, are sanctioned severely because their crimes threaten property rights, and their involvement in crime is a symbolic threat to the reification of the nuclear family and the sexual division of labor as sacred to capitalism.

Women who commit crimes not only violate the legal protections of property distributions, but they also overlap the moral requirements of loyalty to the family. They are perceived as oblivious to the effects of their potential incarceration on their children,[8] and they have thus committed a moral offense that may be even less pardonable than the criminal offense (Price & Sokoloff 1982). Hence, women frequently receive more severe sentences than those assigned to men for similar offenses (Bowker 1985; Moyer 1985; Rafter & Stanko 1982; Price & Sokoloff 1982).

The System of Control

The capitalist control of women as a caste has been embodied the basic precept of domination, in that women have been historically viewed as "support personnel," those whose domestic service made possible the full participation of men in the productive enterprise. As women have moved into the commerce base of capitalism, their support function has not diminished. Women are viewed as the most recent contributors to the economic system, but as members of the reserve labor force they are called on only as production necessitates. The explicit, social ideal of full or equal participation with men in the work force perpetuates a satisfaction with the "progress" that has been made toward securing female equality with males. With limited exceptions, however, women's work has been "ghettoized" into specific categories. For example, 99% of all secretaries, 97% of all receptionists, 97% of child care workers, and 96% of registered nurses are women (U.S. Bureau of Census 1984).[9] Women are now employed in the labor force in greater numbers than at any other time, but they are employed in jobs aligned with the traditional, sexual division of labor and are associated with low status, low remuneration, and little professional authority.

The relative permanency of the position of women in the economic system is legitimized by the adage that "progress is slow," and even though many women have "made it," society must be patient for complete equality to materialize. This serves as a pacifier to those who advocate full, sex-based equality. As more middle-class white women and a few minority women move into positions of responsibility, the level of satisfaction with the present economic and social system increases. The contradiction rests in the fact that opportunities for women are available only in the privileged classes and the advancement of women into business and government has not meant full equality with men, even at this level (Anderson 1983; Hewlett 1987; Tavris & Wade 1984).

Women's opportunities are controlled by the availability of opportunity under capitalism. The capitalist, ideological hegemony that all people have equal opportunity under the law has been legitimized, subjectively, by litigation that has proven and eradicated discrimination. The objective fact is that opportunity for women has been regulated by the level of profit available. If the productive effort requires the work of the reserve labor supply, women will have increased access to the labor force (see Tavris & Wade 1984:252–296). In effect, the quality of women's lives is controlled by economic factors. Although this is true for men also, women's social positions are especially vulnerable to economic fluctuations, and women are likely to suffer more intensely in the face of unemployment (Hewlett 1987; Scott 1984; Tavris & Wade 1984). The control of women's experience under capitalism is legitimized by the productive effort. In periods of unemployment, women are often perceived as expendable labor sources (Scott 1984). As members of the reserve labor force, women, who are not needed in the productive effort, increase the ranks of those living in poverty (Hewlett 1987; Piven & Cloward 1982; Scott 1984). As previously stated, 78% of those who depend on welfare for at least half of their income are female heads of households.

Women who have lived on the fringe of economic stability have increased vulnerability and have an increased propensity to commit crime. As women have increased the ranks of the poor, they have also increased the ranks of the incarcerated (Scott 1984; U.S. Dept. of Justice 1986, 1988). Although poverty may be the direct antecedent of increased crime among women, the dialectic of the capitalist sexual division of labor holds a more ultimate explanation. Poverty among women is not a recent phenomenon, and token representation in positions of responsibility may project hope for some women, but creates anger, frustration, and alienation for others, as the gap between the classes widens (Lekachman 1982).

The system of laws under capitalism focuses on the subjective pathologies of individual criminals (as opposed to exploitative systems, corporate immorality, or human rights issues) at the same time that objective equality under the law is advocated. As the judiciary settles each case as an individual violation of the law, patterns of violation that illuminate the systemic nature of the criminal behavior are not obvious. The fact that women are committing the same crimes that they have committed since the birth of capitalism and that only the volume of crime, and not the variety, has increased attests to the controlling influence of capitalism in the lives of women. Women commit crimes that are offensive to the moral character of capitalism and petty property offenses, with only a minority of women involved in serious, violent, or white-collar crime (Price & Sokoloff 1982).

Systems of control over female criminals, or those who have been viewed as vulnerable to crime, have historically proposed that female criminality could be reduced by training women to be better housewives and mothers (Freedman 1984; Price & Sokoloff 1982) or to otherwise epitomize the sexual division of labor as central to capitalism. Consequently, most corrections for women during the twentieth century have worked to legitimize the prevailing belief that women's proper place in the social structure is as a wife and mother. The ideal is, of course, an intimate support of the capitalist economy and an unrealistic expectation for poor women. The ideological hegemony that controls women's access to opportunity under capitalism has also been the modus operandi for treatment of women who could not gain access to opportunity under the capitalist system.

Although the overt sexism in this style of management of female criminals has faded into the backdrop of corrections, women are still provided with inadequate training for educational programs in prisons (Baunach 1985; Feinman 1986; Glick & Neto 1982), which restricts their opportunity for postrelease success. Not only are women denied training and education in prison, but the training that is provided is not comparable to that provided for men in similar institutions. Alpert (1982) details the legal rationale for failing to provide women with comparable treatment programs available to incarcerated men. The argument is ultimately reduced to the fact that states must have reasonable, as opposed to arbitrary, reasons for failure to provide equal programming under the Equal Protection Clause of the Constitution (Alpert 1982:177). This leaves the provision of equal treatment as a phenomenon to be interpreted in the best interests of the state. Because the states have had only minimal interest in the minority of female prisoners, women have had little training or education available.

Women's lives, which are ultimately controlled by economic factors, are further controlled by state interests after they have been convicted of crime. The interests of capitalism, which strengthen the caste relationship among women, are the same interests that prohibit most women from attaining meaningful status in society and that further restrict the opportunities of convicted women. Women's domination under the control network of corrections is the prototype of women's domination under capitalism: those women who are members of society's privileged class will received more ameliorative treatment from the judiciary (Rafter & Natalizia 1982) than those who live on the fringe of the economy.

Conclusion

Marx viewed capitalism as a system that undergoes continual change (Spitzer 1975). The system is in constant need of productive increase for survival, and it must continually adapt new modes of production and plan for expansion. The productive increase is accomplished by increasing the ratio of technology to workers, so that as technology advances, human laborers become increasingly redundant (Marx 1967:641). As technology advances under modern capitalism, more laborers are removed from productive activity for longer periods of time (Spitzer 1975). Institutionalized mechanisms (such as mandatory retirement) insure the removal of certain workers, but others are denied access to employment because there are not enough jobs available. Those most severely affected by the increased use of technology in production are unskilled laborers, or those who have been traditionally viewed as a surplus labor supply.

Women living what has been called the "feminization of poverty" (Scott 1984) are among the surplus laborers increasingly frustrated by the failure of the economic system to absorb their labor potential. According to Duncan (1984), 78% of recipients continually dependent upon welfare sources for more than half of their income are women, and the vast majority of those living in poverty are female (Duncan 1984). As technology advances, the percentage of people who make up the surplus labor supply steadily increases. During the years of the most rapid advancement of capitalism, the ranks of women living in poverty have paralleled the increase. In 1959, female heads of households living in poverty accounted for 26% of the nation's poor; by 1986 the figure had risen to 52% (Pearce & McAdoo 1982; U.S. Bureau of the Census 1987:434). As productive technology has become more specialized and advanced, the demand for unskilled labor has declined, and those exempted from the labor pool have become a permanent group.

At the same time that large percentages of unskilled or low skilled workers have been forced out of the labor pool, openings in the technocratic character of capitalism have permitted some women to merge in the class of economically secure workers. This infiltration of women into the ranks of high status, high prestige occupational categories has masked the downward mobility of large numbers of women (Moore 1986). Those few women who have achieved high occupational status reinforce the capitalist ideal that success requires only hard work and perseverance. The fact that women in the permanent underclass occupy a fixed position in the social structure further delineates the demarcation between "productive" citizens (Spitzer 1975) and those who are parasitic to the system. Problems of drug addition and a departure from middle-class moral standards or lifestyles among the poor further stigmatize the poor as a population that needs to be controlled.

The rate of incarcerated women per 100,000 population has risen most significantly since 1980 (U.S. Dept. of Justice 1988), and opportunities under capitalism have decreased significantly for women (Moore 1986). The fact that most women have limited opportunity for capital accumulation has meant that the ideology of equality, which legitimizes the economic system, has been threatened. In order to control the threat, it is necessary for the economic system to define women who live outside the opportunity structure as a social burden and to reinforce the opportunity potential for all others. Women who pose a threat to the ideological hegemony of equality of opportunity or who directly threaten property distributions become eligible for imprisonment. Meanwhile, victimizations (both individual and societal) of these women is permitted and even tacitly encouraged,[10] because it legitimizes the control function of the state and rationalizes slow progress toward equality. At the same time, the ideology-generating mechanisms downplay the threat of victimization by blaming the victim rather than the perpetrator or the social system that gives rise to behavior.

Crimes committed by women further the legitimization of control, because these are generally moral offenses or property crimes. Unlike men, who commit crimes in both the capitalist classes and the underclasses, and who commit wide ranges of both socially immoral and illegal behaviors, women's crimes are associated with their social structural restrictions. The fact that women who engage in crimes are predominantly from the same social class and engage in similar types of offenses (Price & Sokoloff 1982) makes the inclination to rely on a monolithic explanation tempting. However, it is the complexity of the obvious that underlies a full understanding of female crime. Women's crimes are tied to the complexities and contradictions endemic to the sexual division of labor in a capitalist society.

Female crime patterns are not related to the etiology of women (Lombroso 1903; Pollak 1961) or to the emancipation of women (Adler 1975). Women commit crimes because the economic system controls their access to scarcities such as prestige, status, independence, middle-class standards of opulence, or even economic security. Women's behavior is often labeled as criminal according to the moral implications of capitalism, but real criminal perpetration among women reflects the class differential of the economic system. Certain women occupy intergenerational positions outside of the legitimate system of rewards, which assures that a perpetual underclass, within the caste of women, suffers from alienation and frustration. This factor, more than any other social, psycholgoical, or physical characteristic, produces female crime.

Women's rates of involvement in crime have increased for those crimes that provide relief from the pressures of escalating capitalism—petty property and drug offenses (Steffensmeier 1978; U.S. Dept. of Justice 1988). With capitalism's unprecedented expansion during the Reagan years, opportunities for women have declined and the incarceration of women has increased. Constant capitalism produced a rate of women's incarceration that fluctuated between 6 and 8 incarcerated women for every 100,000 population between 1925 and 1979; since 1980, the rate has increased to 20 per 100,000 population (U.S. Dept. of Justice 1988). As capitalism expands, the likelihood that women's rates of incarceration will increase is enhanced.

Notes

1. Even crimes *against* women have been seen in this light.

2. This, of course, ignores the fact that most women's work is either low paid or unpaid labor.

3. For example, the "blaming the victim" orientation has been, historically, the most common approach taken with regard to crimes specifically perpetrated against women. This has been true of both the popular and legal response to these crimes (see Brownmiller 1975).

4. Figures derived from *Time.* "Why Not a Woman?" (1984, June 4), 28.

5. Female crime does exist in noncapitalist societies. Prostitution is, of course, a worldwide phenomenon. However, rates for other types of crimes committed by women are unavailable. Current, cross-cultural analysis of crime (e.g., Archer & Gartner 1984) do not even mention female crime. Obvious sources, such as the *Demographic Yearbooks* or *Statistical Yearbooks*, do not catalog crime rates for any nation. Neither the Soviet Union nor China publishes crime statistics for either sex. A comparison of rates of female crime in capitalist and noncapitalist countries is, therefore, not possible with current data sources.

6. According to Freeman (1986) 8% of federal judges and 4% of state judges are female, and approximately 10% of federal correctional officers are female.

7. This is also true for the men who have been criminally sanctioned for being homosexual and thus not properly procreating to build and supply future workers for the economic system.

8. It is true that 70% of incarcerated women have dependent children (Glick & Neto 1982), but people do not commit crimes with the intention of getting caught.

9. Other job classifications in the "women's ghetto" are 88% of billing clerks, 88% of waiters, 87% of librarians, 84% of health technicians, 83% of elementary school teachers, 81% of bank tellers, and 70% of retail salesclerks (U.S. Bureau of the Census 1984).

10. Such as by a failure of the legal system to respond to crimes against women (see Price & Sokoloff 1982) and by the presence of sexism in society.

References

Adler, F. (1975). *Sisters in crime: The rise of the new female criminal.* New York: McGraw-Hill.

Alpert, G. (1982). Women prisoners and the law: Which way will the pendulum swing? In B. Price & N. Sokoloff (eds.), *The criminal justice system and women* (pp. 171–182). New York: Clark Boardman.

Anderson, M.L. (1983). *Thinking about women: Sociological and feminist perspectives.* New York: Macmillan.

Archer, D., & Gartner, R. (1984). *Violence and crime in cross-national perspectives.* New Haven: Yale University Press.

Armstrong, G. (1977). Females under the law: Protected but unequal. *Crime and Delinquency* 23: 109–120.

Average child support payment drops by 12% (1987, August 26). *New York Times,* 23.

Baunach, P.J. (1985). Critical problems of women in prison. In I.L. Moyer (Ed.) *The changing roles of women in the criminal justice system* (pp. 95–110). Prospect Heights, IL: Waveland.

Bonger, W. (1916). *Criminality and economic conditions.* Boston: Little, Brown.

Bowker, L.H. (1985). *Women and crime in America.* New York: Macmillan.

Brownmiller, S. (1975). *Against our will: Men, women and rape.* New York: Bantam.

Cowie, J., Cowie, V., & Slater, E. (1968). *Delinquency in girls.* London: Heinemann.

Davis, K. (1971). *Prostitution.* In R. Merton and R. Nisbet (Eds.), *Contemporary social problems* (3rd ed.) (pp. 341–351). New York: Harcourt Brace Jovanovich.

Duncan, G.J. (1984). *Years of poverty, years of plenty.* Ann Arbor: Institute for Social Research, University of Michigan.

Eisenstein, Z.R. (1979). *Capitalist patriarchy and the case for socialist feminism.* New York: Monthly Review Press.

Engels, F. (1972). *The origin of the family, private property, and the state.* New York: International.

Feinman, C. (1979). Sex role stereotypes and justice for women. *Crime and Delinquency* 25: 87–94.

——— (1986). *Women in the criminal justice system.* New York: Praeger.

Fishman, W.K. (1987). The struggle for women's equality in an era of economic crisis: From the morality of reform to the science of revolution. *Humanity and Society* 11: 519–522.

Freedman, E.B. (1984). *Their sister's keepers: Womens' prison reform in America, 1830–1930.* Ann Arbor: University of Michigan Press.

Freud, S. (1933). *Femininity.* In *The standard edition of the complete psychological works of Sigmund Freud* (pp. 122–135). London: Hogarth.

Glick, R.M., & Neto, V. (1982). National study of women's correctional programs. In B. Price & N. Sokoloff (Eds.), *The criminal justice system and women* (pp. 141–154). New York: Clark Boardman.

Gordon, D.M. (1971). Class and the economics of crime. *Review of Radical Political Economics* 3: 51–72.

Hewlett, S.A. (1987). *A lesser life: The myth of women's liberation in America.* New York: Warner.

Klein, D. (1973). The etiology of female crime: A review of the literature. *Crime and Social Justice: Issues in Criminology* 3: 3–30.

Konopka, G. (1966). *The adolescent girl in conflict.* Englewood Cliffs, NJ: Prentice-Hall.

Lekachman, R. (1982). *Greed is not enough: Reaganomics.* New York: Pantheon.

Lombroso, C. [1903] (1920). *The female offender.* New York: Appleton.

Marx, K. [1872] (1967). *Capital* (Vol. 1). New York: International.

Marx, K., & Engels, F. (1965). *The German ideology.* London: Lawrence and Wishart.

Matthaei, J.A. (1982). *An economic history of women in America: Women's work, the sexual division of labor, and the development of capitalism.* New York: Schocken.

Messerschmide, J.W. (1986). *Capitalism, patriarchy, and crime: Toward a socialist feminist criminology.* Totowa, NJ: Rowman and Littlefield.

Moore, L.L. (1986). *Not as far as you think: The realities of working women.* Lexington, MA: D.C. Heath.

Morris, R. (1965). Attitudes toward delinquency by delinquents, non-delinquents and their friends. *British Journal of Criminology* 5: 249–265.

Moyer, I.L. (1985). *The changing roles of women in the criminal justice system.* Prospect Heights, IL: Waveland.

Pearce, D.M., & McAdoo, H. (1981). *Women and children: Alone and in poverty.* Washington, DC: U.S. Government Printing Office.

Piven, F.F., & Cloward, R.A. (1982). *The new class war: Reagan's attack on the welfare state and its consequences.* New York: Pantheon.

Pollak, O. (1961). *The criminality of women.* New York: A.S. Barnes.

Price, B.R., & Sokoloff, N.J. (1982). *The criminal justice system and women.* New York: Clark Boardman.

Quinney, R. (1980). *Class, state and crime* (2nd ed.). New York: Longman.

Rafter, N.H. (1985). *Partial justice: Women in state prisons.* Boston: Northeastern University Press.

Rafter, N.H., & Natalizia, E.M. (1982). Marxist feminism: Implications for criminal justice. In B. Price & N. Sokoloff (Eds.), *The criminal justice system and women* (pp. 465–484). New York: Clark Boardman.

Rafter, N.H., & Stanko, E.A. (1982). *Judge, lawyer, victim, thief: Women, gender roles and criminal justice.* Boston: Northeastern University Press.

Rifkin, J. (1980). Toward a theory of law and patriarchy. In P. Beine & R. Quinney (Eds.), *Marxism and law* (pp. 295–302). New York: Wiley.

Robin, G.D. (1977). Forcible rape: Institutionalized sexism in the criminal justice system. *Crime and Delinquency* 23: 136–153.

Rodgers, H.R., Jr. (1987). *Poor women, poor families.* Armonk, NY: Sharpe.

Rosen, R. (1982). *The lost sisterhood: Prostitution in America, 1900–1918.* Baltimore: Johns Hopkins University Press.

Rosenblum, K.E. (1975). Female deviance and the female sex role: A preliminary investigation. *British Journal of Sociology* 26: 169–185.

Schur, E.M. (1984). *Labeling women, gender, stigma, and social control.* New York: Random House.

Scott, H. (1984). *Working your way to the bottom: The feminization of poverty.* London: Pandora.

Simon, R.J. (1976). American women and crime. *Annals of the Academy of Political and Social Science* 423: 31–46.

Smart, C. (1976). *Women, crime and criminology: A feminist critique.* London: Routledge and Kegan Paul.

——— (1979). The new female offender: Reality or myth? *British Journal of Criminology* 19: 50–59.

Spitzer, S. (1975). Towards a Marxian theory of deviance. *Social Problems* 22: 638–651.

Steffensmeier, D.J. (1978). Crime and the contemporary woman: An analysis of changing levels of female property crime, 1960–75. *Social Forces* 57(2): 566–584.

Tavris, C., & Wade, C. (1984). *The longest war: Sex differences in perspective.* New York: Harcourt Brace Jovanovich.

Taylor, I., Walton, P., & Young, J. (1973). *The new criminology.* New York: Harper Torchbooks.

Thomas, W.I. (1907). *Sex and society.* Boston: Little, Brown.

——— (1923). *The unadjusted girl.* New York: Harper & Row.

U.S. Bureau of the Census (1984). Money, income, and poverty status of families and persons in the U.S. *Current Population Reports* (Sen. P-60, No. 145). Washington, DC: U.S. Government Printing Office.

——— (1987). *Statistical abstract of the United States, 1988.* Washington, DC: U.S. Government Printing Office.

U.S. Department of Justice (1986). *State and federal prisoners, 1925–1985.* Washington, DC: U.S. Government Printing Office.

——— (1988). *Sourcebook of criminal justice statistics—1987.* Washington, DC: U.S. Government Printing Office.

Why not a woman? (1984). *Time* (June 4): 28–30.

Female Criminality: An Economic Perspective

Martin Milkman
Murray State University
Sarah Tinkler
Weber State University

Introduction

Most researchers in the field of female criminality have not utilized the insights and findings that economists have contributed to the field of criminal justice. There are several possible reasons for this. First, until the late 1960s, economists did not focus on criminality research. Because of the time lags involved in the dissemination of research findings and approaches, many criminologists and other researchers who focus on the criminal justice system are today only vaguely aware that extensive research literature exists that examines criminal justice systems from an economic perspective. Second, economists have not addressed directly the issue of female criminality. This perhaps is due to the methodology that economists have adopted when examining the criminal justice system. However, an economic approach to crime and punishment does yield several significant insights that contribute to our understanding of female criminality. This essay reviews the economics of crime literature so that researchers in the area of female criminality will begin to develop an understanding of the methodology employed by economists and the major research contributions of economists in the criminal justice area. The essay then narrows its focus to the specific area of empirical analysis of female criminality. An attempt is made to extend the findings of the broader economics of crime literature to issues raised in female criminality research. We view the insights offered in this essay as preliminary. Economic research in the area of female criminality is in its infancy and there are many interesting research questions that we hope will be pursued in the future. Therefore, we conclude this essay with several suggestions for future research.

The Economic Approach to Human Behavior

Because economists, when examining criminal behavior, do not make any distinction between the behavior of criminals and other individuals, a brief review of the basic assumptions that economists make when examining any sort of human behavior is helpful in understanding the economics of crime literature. Economic models of human behavior are based upon two basic assumptions. First, resources are scarce, due to limited resources and unlimited wants. Individuals who do not have the resources to meet all of their wants are forced to make choices but are constrained by resource availability. Second, individuals are assumed to make these choices rationally in an attempt to maximize expected utility or satisfaction. These two assumptions about human behavior underlie predictions about how individuals respond to various incentives.

The Economic Model of Female Criminality

The standard economic approach to criminal behavior is to view a criminal as a rational individual who, when deciding whether or not to commit a crime, weighs the costs and benefits of all alternative legal and illegal options open to her. Becker (1974) says, "Some persons become criminals . . . not because their basic motivation differs from that of other persons, but because their benefits and costs differ." Therefore, economic theory predicts that if the expected costs and benefits of crime and legitimate work differ for women and men, then the level of participation in criminal activity will differ for women and men. Furthermore, if women's and men's benefits and costs of crime change over time, then their relative participation in crime will change too.

The economic model of crime evaluates female criminals as rational individuals who respond predictably to the incentives they face. The economic model does not use assertions about female psychology to account for the rise in women's criminality. Therefore, economists would reject in theory a hypothesis that "blames" women's increased labor market participation for the rapid increase in women's crime. Since increased female participation in the labor force results in higher wages, the economic model of crime would predict that increased labor force participation should result in reduced female participation in illegal activities if all other factors remained unchanged (Bartel 1979).

An economic analysis of women's participation in crime must begin with an evaluation of the benefits and costs of that participation. After evaluating the benefits and costs, the empirical evidence collected by economists on the determinants of women's criminality will be described.

Crime (except perhaps white-collar crime) does not require substantial investment in human capital. ("Human capital" is a term used by economists to describe any sort of investment in workers that increases their productivity. Two examples would be formal education and on-the-job training.) However, investment in human capital is rewarded with higher wages in legitimate activities. Therefore, individuals with lower levels of investment in human capital will be at a "comparative advantage" in criminal activities compared to legitimate activities. While white women have similar years of formal education as white men, they traditionally have spent substantially less time in the labor force than white males and, therefore, accumulated less experience (Corcoran & Duncan 1979). Women also receive less on-the-job training than men (Kaufman 1991). Furthermore, women and men do not obtain the same types of qualifications: men still dominate high-paying fields. In 1989, 8% of engineers and 84% of elementary school teachers were women (Kaufman 1991:354). These statistics, which probably result from a combination of individual choice and discrimination, are the primary reasons that in 1988 white women still earned only 65% of the earnings of white men, while black women earned 81% of the earnings of black men (Kaufman 1991).

The economic model predicts that women are attracted to crime because of poorer legitimate market opportunities. In addition, women have less to lose from unsuccessful criminal activity than men, in terms of legitimate wages and opportunities that lead to imprisonment and/or loss of employment opportunities in the future.

However, not all women are dependent solely on their own economic activities for income. A husband's income raises household income, which reduces participation in *all* labor market activities, both legal and illegal, by married women. This leads to an increase in the demand for all normal goods, such as leisure. Therefore, the increase in income will result in an increase in the amount of leisure consumed and a reduction in the amount of time devoted to labor. As a result married women will be less likely to participate in crime than single women. However, married women invest less in their human capital than single women. For this reason, married women will be more predisposed to commit crimes than single women (Bartel 1979). At a theoretical level, therefore, the relative tendencies to commit crime for married and single women are ambiguous, and empirical investigation is required.

Increasing divorce rates and childbearing by unmarried women are predicted to increase women's participation in crime because there will be a reduction in income sharing with higher paid men. In 1988 one-third of all female-headed households and half of black female-headed households were classified as below the poverty line by federal standards (Kaufman 1991). The increase in poverty among female-headed households is a potent precursor to increased crime by women.

Unemployment is another predictor of criminal activity. If women differ in their experiences of unemployment than men, then their tendency to be involved in crime will differ. Typically, men's and women's experiences of unemployment have been similar in times of economic prosperity, while men have tended to experience higher unemployment than women during recessions. This difference reflects the fact that in the past men have been employed in more cyclically sensitive occupations than women. In "good" years, men and women face the same push to crime resulting from unemployment, but in recessionary years men appear to face greater incentives to commit crimes than women. One caution should be noted here: Government unemployment figures probably understate the level of women's unemployment since women with a spouse present (and hence an alternative source of support) are more likely to be classified as "discouraged workers" than either men or single women. (Discouraged workers are those individuals without jobs who would like to work, but since they are not "actively seeking work," they fail to be recorded in government unemployment statistics.)

In terms of the economic experience of women, we might conclude that their poorer legitimate market opportunities make crime an attractive alternative. However, women choose between three alternative activities—legal work, crime, and household duties—whereas most men choose between legal work and crime only. Most women are constrained by what Phillips and Votey (1984) refer to as "committed leisure," or household obligations. To the extent that household obligations are pressing (particularly likely if young children are present in the home), women have a high marginal value of time spent in the home and will substitute away from both legal work and crime. However, Bartel (1979) disputes that crime competes with other activities for a woman's time. It is possible that some crime is "jointly produced" with some legal activities (specifically, shoplifting may be "jointly produced" with shopping for the family). This modifies the standard economic model in which crime must compete with other uses of a woman's time and, if true, will increase married women's participation in shoplifting, since time spent shoplifting does not compete with household obligations.

Analysis of women's time allocation decisions between legal work, crime, and (possibly) household activities suggests that the incentives to commit crime may differ between men and women. However, the crime rate in a particular community is determined by the *interaction* of individual incentives to commit crime (described above) and the deterrence effects of law enforcement activities. If the costs to women and men criminals differ due to differences in the treatment of men and women by law enforcement agencies, then the economic model of crime would predict differential responses of men and women in similar circumstances. As other essays in this collection have noted, there seem to be substantial differences in the probability of arrest, in the probability of conviction if arrested, and the sentencing practices across gender. These gender differences in enforcement seem to be a function of the type of crime committed, and these differences may help to explain the fact that gender differences in criminal activity differ depending on crime type.

It was noted above that women will be less deterred by incarceration of a particular duration, since the cost in terms of foregone income is lower than for men. In the case of fines, assuming diminishing marginal utility of money (meaning that better off people place a lower value on an additional dollar than do the poor), women will be more deterred by a fine of given size than men. Even if courts set fines for men and women equally, we would expect a greater deterrence effect on women for crimes that are punished by a fine (Chiplin 1976).

However, the evidence is strong (see Culliver 1989:11–16) that men and women *do not* face identical probabilities of apprehension, conviction, and punishment for identical crimes. One of the major distinctions between legal and illegal activity is the degree of uncertainty associated with both the costs and benefits of criminal activity. This difference is crucial. Women, from the available evidence, would seem to be treated more leniently than men for similar offenses, particularly if young children are present in the home.

This may result from two factors. First, Culliver (1989) describes the "chivalry hypothesis" (attributable to Pollak), that is, the tendency for criminal justice officials to display reluctance to apprehend, convict, or punish women compared to their greater zeal in pursuing male criminals. Second, a lower emphasis on the processing of female criminals may be a rational response by law enforcement agencies to a scarcity of law enforcement resources. If women's criminality is relatively trivial (or unusual) compared to men's criminality, then women are not likely suspects in any given (anonymous) crime and are less likely to come under suspicion and be apprehended even if they have committed the crime (Chiplin 1976). However, the dramatic rise in women's involvement in felonies, particularly burglary and larceny, raises the probability that a woman will be investigated, which increases the potential payoff to law enforcement agencies. Overall, lower probabilities of arrest, conviction, and punishment for women lower the *expected cost* (cost multiplied by probability of incurring that cost) of criminal activity and, hence, increase the attractiveness of criminal activities to women.

Another possible cost of involvement in criminal activity is social embarrassment if apprehended. If society dictates that the shame of criminal behavior is felt more strongly by women than men, then women will be more discouraged from crime than men. If, however, society perceives women criminals to be victims (stealing to feed children) or pawns of male criminals, then their social disgrace may be lessened. Therefore, different psychic costs (if any) may be felt by apprehended male and female criminals. Since a wider range of roles for women have become acceptable in society over the past several decades, any differences in psychic costs to crime between men and women can be expected to narrow.

Women appear to face fewer costs (apart from possibly psychic costs) to crime than men—probabilities of arrest, conviction, and punishment are lower (but increasing) and the loss of market earnings associated with incarceration are lower. They may, however, be constrained by their household obligations.

Since few crimes involve physical strength, men have no obvious advantage over women in criminal activities. In addition, since most crimes require little investment in human capital, there is no a priori reason to expect that the benefits to a particular criminal activity will differ greatly between men and women. However, the costs of criminal activity do differ between men and women. Therefore, the rational man will select a different level of criminal activity than the rational woman. Crime, which is greatly motivated by poor economic circumstances and low probability of apprehension, conviction, and punishment, might, if anything, prove to be more of a temptation to women than men.

The Empirical Evidence

What does the empirical evidence suggest about the motivations for women's criminal activity? Bartel (1979) reports that, in 1960, 11% of persons arrested were women, whereas by 1974 that figure had jumped to 20%. The rise in women's criminal behavior is even more dramatic if what economists call "income-producing" crimes are considered separately from "consumption" crimes.

Stigler (1974) distinguishes between "consumption" crimes (such as assault), which provide direct satisfaction, and "income-producing" crimes, which substitute for other forms of economic activity. Assault committed by a rational individual with no expectation of financial gain must provide some level of satisfaction (at least initially), whereas assault to obtain a wallet is an income-producing crime; however, assault may have consumption components if the criminal enjoys the activity.

Arrests of women for income-producing crimes have been growing at rates three times those of men for comparable offenses, whereas arrests of women for consumption (personal) crimes have been growing at rates comparable to those of men (Phillips & Votey 1984). It is the increase in the participation of women in income-producing crime that needs to be explained. (One proviso: most women offenders commit larceny, principally shoplifting, which is considered an income-producing crime. However, some shoplifters take items they do not need or which are very cheap relative to their family income suggesting that shoplifting may be a consumption crime [one that provides thrills] for some offenders.)

A look at which costs and benefits associated with women's crime have changed since the early 1960s accounts for the increase in women's criminal activity. Bartel (1979) attempts to explain differences in female arrest rates among states for the year 1970. Although states differ in some of the key determinants of women's crime, it still is possible to decide which determinants are most important. Changes over time (rather than across states) in these determinants also lead to changes in women's crime.

Bartel (1979) finds that the presence of young children in the home increases the amount of time spent in the home and decreases all income-generating activities, including crime. According to Bartel, "The decrease in the average number of preschool children per husband-wife family that took place between 1960 and 1970 . . . accounted for more than half of the increase in female property crime that occurred during that decade" (p. 29). The probabilities of arrest and conviction as well as the severity of the average penalty serve to deter women; however, the deterrence effect is weaker for larceny than for other property crimes and weaker yet for personal crimes. Married women are more likely to commit property crimes (e.g., shoplifting) than single women, because such crimes are jointly produced with household tasks. The degree of income inequality in a state (measured by the percentage of families with incomes below one-half the median income in the state) explains much crime but is not a factor in explaining shoplifting. This supports a perception that shoplifting is popular among middle- and upper-class women, suggesting that shoplifting also may be a consumption crime. In addition, rising labor force participation by women does not appear to be an important determinant of women's crime.

Phillips and Votey (1984) analyze participation in crime by black women who face problems common to all women in terms of unemployment, restricted labor market opportunities, and absence of spouse; however, these problems are magnified for black women. Women who head households have particular incentives to commit crime. Low wages and financial obligations of female heads of households often necessitate more than 40 hours of work per week. When suitable second jobs are not available, income is often supplemented through criminal activity. By the same token, women with small children who wish to work less than 40 hours a week may resort to crime because of its flexible hours.

Phillips and Votey (1984) also attribute some crime by women who head households to the incentives created by the welfare system. Since work in the marketplace results in loss of welfare benefits, crime for many women is a tempting alternative since "unreported (illegal) income cannot reduce eligibility for welfare support" (p. 294).

The standard economic model of criminal behavior can be applied to women offenders. Women, like men, evaluate the costs and benefits associated with participating in a range of activities, both legal and illegal. The dramatic rise in women's participation in some types of illegal activities can be attributed to changes in the circumstances facing women. Divorce and single parenting, reduced fertility rates, low wages, and the incentives inherent in the welfare system all make criminal activity increasingly attractive to women.

At the same time, increasing recognition of female criminals, coupled with increased resources to arrest, convict, and punish women, results in a reduction in female criminality because women (and men) respond to the incentives inherent in the criminal justice system. Unfortunately, there is a lack of empirical work in the economics literature on women offenders, so data on individual female offenders are difficult to find. This leads researchers to focus their attention on differences in crime rates between geographical regions. The number of women offenders in a given data set is often small, making it difficult to analyze women's crime separate from men's. Empirical studies, however, support the idea that women criminals, as rational individuals, adjust their level of activity in all sectors in response to changes in their incentives.

Suggestions for Future Research

The economic model of crime should be attractive to researchers investigating issues related to female criminality. The model is complementary to the general approach that modern researchers have adopted. It is consistent with other research that relates to gender issues in that it takes into consideration the explicit and implicit constraints facing women in a sexist society. Two key determinants in this model are the lesser labor market opportunities and the increased burden of household production, indicating that economic models applied to female criminality are not the same models that are applied to male criminality.

There are two areas that need extensive research. First, as mentioned above, there exists only limited empirical research that attempts to validate the predictions of economic models relating to female criminality. One explanatiton for this lack of empirical work is the lack of data on a national level. One priority of future research funds should be the gathering of data relating to female criminality so that more detailed empirical studies of female criminality can be undertaken.

A second area of research that needs to be explored is the development of theoretical models that help us to understand the gender differences in enforcement behavior. A formal economic model of gender differences in enforcement practices has not been developed.

Finally, the economic research on female criminality has taken place in an isolated environment. Economists have not taken advantage of other studies investigating issues relating to female criminality, and criminologists have not allowed economists' research of female criminality to influence their research. The interdisciplinary nature of female criminality makes such collaboration essential if a better understanding of female criminality is to be achieved.

References

Bartel, A.P. (1979). Women and crime: An economic analysis. *Economic Inquiry* XVII: 29–51.

Becker, G.S. (1974). Crime and punishment: An economic approach. In G.S. Becker & W.M. Landes (Eds.). *Essays in the economics of crime and punishment*. New York: National Bureau of Economic Research.

Chiplin, B. (1976). Sexual discrimination: Are there any lessons from criminal behavior? *Applied Economics* 8: 121–133.

Corcoran, M., & Duncan, G.J. (1979). Work history, labor force attachment, and earnings differences between the races and sexes. *Journal of Human Resources* 14: 3–20.

Culliver, C. (1989). Female criminality: The state of the art. Paper presented at the Mid-South Sociological Conference, Baton Rogue, LA.

Kaufman, B.E. (1991). *The economics of labor markets* (3rd ed.). Chicago: Dryden.

Phillips, L., & Votey, H.L. (1984). Black women, economic disadvantage and incentives to crime. *American Economic Association Papers and Proceedings* 74: 293–297.

Stigler, G.J. (1974). The optimum enforcement of laws. In G.S. Becker & William M. Landes (Eds.), *Essays in the economics of crime and punishment*. New York: National Bureau of Economic Research.

PART III

The Criminal Justice Systems' Response to Female Offenders

An Examination of Gender Issues That Were Observed in the Proportion of Arrests over Time*

Benjamin S. Wright
University of Baltimore

There is an expanding body of research that seeks to explore issues related to observed gender differences in the criminal justice process. Unfortunately, very little of this research has addressed instances of differential processing at the arrest phase. Upon examining research that was conducted in criminal justice, investigations of the sentencing phase appeared to dominate the literature. Several such inquiries examined the effects of racial differences between males relative to the type of sentence received (Gibson 1978; Hagan 1974; Hawkins 1986; Kleck 1981; Spohn, Gruhl, & Welch 1981–1982; Welch, Spohn, & Gruhl 1985; Zatz 1984). Other researchers have addressed issues related to disparate offending levels based on racial and ethnicity differences between males (Messner & South 1988; Petersilia 1984; Peterson & Hagan 1984; Tinker, Quiring, & Pimentel 1985). Many other researchers have considered the combined effects of gender, race, and ethnicity on the decision-making process in criminal justice (Chilton & Datesman 1987; Daly 1989; LaFree 1980; Spohn, Gruhl, & Welch 1987; Spohn, Welch, & Gruhl 1985; Steffensmeier & Allan 1988; Young 1980).

* This is a revised version of a paper presented at the 1990 annual meeting of the American Society of Criminology.

Shifting the research focus to one specific stage in the criminal justice process, the arrest stage, very few investigations have addressed variations in the arrest rate on the basis of gender and race influences. A close scrutiny of the literature revealed that several researchers had examined the question of race as a prominent factor in the police decision to make an arrest (Chilton & Datesman 1987; Jefferson 1988; Smith & Visher 1981; Visher 1983). In another instance, the researcher examined the combined effects of gender and race but focused on incidence rates of offending, as opposed to arrest rates generated by police (Hindelang 1981). Based on Hindelang's observations, it was suggested that offending rates for some categories of personal crimes could be estimated more effectively through the use of the National Crime Survey since it provided more extensive data on between-group differences.

A review of the literature also revealed minimal empirical evidence to assist in explaining gender differences based on the proportion of offense-specific arrests for each gender subgroup rate. Gender disparity research closely paralleled several investigations conducted on the question of racial disparity in the criminal justice process in that several of these inquiries were conducted at the sentencing stage (Crump 1987; Erez 1988; Farrington & Morris 1983; Kruttschnitt 1980–1981; Spohn, Welch & Gruhl 1985; Wilbanks 1986; Young 1986) rather than at either the pretrial judicial stage (Bishop & Frazier 1984; Daly 1987, 1989; Kruttschnitt 1984) or the arrest stage (Chilton & Datesman 1987; Hindelang 1979; Steffensmeier 1978, 1980). Even among the few studies that have investigated gender differences at the arrest stage, the findings often contradict previous research, which creates a lingering doubt relative to understanding and interpreting fully the level of gender variation that appears in the arrest data.

In an attempt to expand the current level of understanding on gender differences as observed in arrest statistics, the present essay proceeds on three premises. First, in order to understand fully how gender differences affect arrest statistics, the more serious felony offenses should be observed at more than one point in time. Time-related effects could cause significant fluctuations in the gender-specific proportion of arrests that would be difficult to detect in a cross-sectional analysis. Second, it is important that gender influences be examined as one more step toward fully appreciating the impact of fixed variables on outcomes in the arrest stage. Researchers are continuously grappling with questions of bias and inequality in the criminal justice process. In some investigations, gender differences were examined in order to determine if the criminal justice process reacts in a discriminatory manner relative to the suspect's gender. Third, in an attempt to mitigate some shortcomings in prior research, the present study examined gender effects on six of the *Uniform Crime Report* (*UCR*) Part I offenses. The *UCR* Part I offenses were utilized because of the manner in which researchers rely on these data to observe trends in the proportion of arrests on specific demographic subgroups at the national and local levels of government.

Data and Methods

Data for the present study were collected from the *Uniform Crime Reports*. Adult arrest data were collected based on the gender of the suspects for eight time points that included 1950, 1955, 1960, 1965, 1970, 1975, 1980, and 1985. Several time points were incorporated into the investigation's design in an attempt to reduce the static nature of cross-sectional analyses. Arrest data for the indicated study period were collected for murder, rape, robbery, aggravated assault, burglary, and motor vehicle theft (U.S. Department of Justice 1985). Larceny-theft was eliminated from further study consideration because the arrest statistics displayed very little gender variation during the study period. Arson, a recent addition to the *UCR* Part I offenses, was not included in the present study because it was not designated as a Part I offense for the entire study period; this particular offense category was reclassified as a Part I offense in the late 1970s.

The *Uniform Crime Report* was identified as a rich source of data containing the gender of those suspects who were arrested in order to resolve outstanding criminal complaints. By relying on the *Uniform Crime Report*, data were collected for all six offenses. The proportion of arrests was calculated for each gender subgroup over the study period by dividing the total number of each of the six Index Offenses cleared by an arrest on a yearly basis by the total number of arrests for each gender subgroup, such that a male and female proportion of arrests was derived for murder, rape, robbery, aggravated assault, burglary, and motor vehicle theft.

The difference of means test was used to analyze gender variation for each of the eight time positions under investigation. This method was judged superior for detecting whether or not there were significant differences among the arrest rate figures for the gender subgroups that were the subject of this inquiry. The difference of means test is a procedure that incorporates *t*-test pairwise comparisons within and between the specified gender subgroups, which allows the reporting of a difference of means between the pairs and a significance level (Blalock 1979; Jendrek 1985).

There are those who would question the continued use of the *UCR* arrest data for analytical purposes. In response to such criticism of the *UCR*, several reasons are offered to illustrate the important role that these official crime statistics play in the criminal justice research process. First, *UCR* statistics are the most accurate measure of reported crime that is collected at the national level (Gove, Hughes, & Geerken 1985; Sampson & Cohen 1988). Second, arrest rates are a valid indicator of police ability to reduce the level of reported crime during any one period of time (Galvin & Polk 1982; Kitsuse & Cicourel 1963; Skogan 1974). Third, the *UCR* closely parallels the level of crime reported in victimization surveys (Eck & Riccio 1979; Hindelang 1981; Messner & South 1988; Young 1986). The continued use of *UCR* crime statistics for analytical purposes is justified since it is widely accepted as a source of crime data known by police. Police administrators continue to utilize *UCR* data to make budgetary and personnel allocation decisions. An informed public has the perception that the *UCR* is a valid indicator of reported crime in their individual communities. Based on these factors, *UCR* gender-specific arrest proportions were incorporated into the present study for analytical purposes.

Results

The annual proportion of arrests based on the gender of those individuals arrested is presented in Table 1. Annual proportionate arrests for the eight reporting periods, 1950–1985, are displayed for murder, rape, robbery, aggravated assault, burglary, and auto theft for males and females. It was observed that males consistently had a greater involvement in all six Part I offenses than did females. The greater involvement of males in the Part I offenses is based entirely upon the assumption that males are much more physically aggressive than females as evidenced by, for example, the much greater involvement of males in aggravated assaults such that their proportion of arrests for this offense varied from 84% to 89% over the study period. So, at any one point in time, female involvement in this particular offense category did not exceed 20% for the study period. In several instances, males were arrested 100% of the time in order to clear incidences of reported rape. However, for this specific offense category, the overrepresentation of males was due much more to legal and statutory limitations for which the gender subgroup could conceivably complete the statutory requirements for rape. Reflecting the current mood of the country in the mid-1970s, the *UCR* definition for rape was changed to include female involvement in this Part I offense. But, even with the inclusion of female involvement in reported rape in the latter study period, males were still arrested about 99% of the time for 1975, 1980, and 1985 in order to clear rape offenses. Overall, these findings were not wholly unexpected based on the current state of the literature. With the exception of several specific offense-related arrest rates, these results very closely mirror findings from prior research.

Table 2 shows the yearly fluctuations in the proportion of arrests for females during the entire study period. The rationale that prompted the inclusion of Table 2 was to report the intragender variations in the annual proportion of arrests. When female involvement in murder is examined, for example, it is found that there is as much as a 5% increase (1950 to 1955) and a low level of involvement of about 4%

Table 1
Proportion of Gender Arrests for Six Offense Categories, 1950–1985*

Variable Name	Variable Description	Annual Proportion of Arrests			
		1950	1955	1960	1965
PMURML	Murder clr.—Male	.87	.82	.82	.82
PRAPML	Rape clr.—Male	1.00	1.00	1.00	1.00
PRBML	Robbery clr.—Male	.96	.96	.95	.95
PASML	Agg. assault clr.—Male	.89	.84	.85	.86
PBGML	Burglary clr.—Male	.97	.98	.97	.96
PATML	Auto theft clr.—Male	.97	.97	.96	.96
PMURFM	Murder clr.—Fem.	.13	.18	.21	.18
PRAPFM	Rape clr.—Fem.	.00	.00	.00	.00
PRBFM	Robbery clr.—Fem.	.04	.04	.05	.05
PASFM	Agg. assault clr.—Fem.	.11	.16	.17	.14
PBGFM	Burglary clr.—Fem.	.03	.02	.04	.04
PATFM	Auto theft clr.—Fem.	.03	.03	.04	.04
		1970	1975	1980	1985
PMURML	Murder clr.—Male	.85	.84	.87	.88
PRAPML	Rape clr.—Male	1.00	.99	.99	.99
PRBML	Robbery clr.—Male	.94	.93	.93	.92
PASML	Agg. assault clr.—Male	.87	.87	.88	.87
PBGML	Burglary clr.—Male	.95	.95	.94	.93
PATML	Auto theft clr.—Male	.95	.93	.91	.91
PMURFM	Murder clr.—Fem.	.15	.16	.13	.12
PRAPFM	Rape clr.—Fem.	.00	.01	.01	.01
PRBFM	Robbery clr.—Fem.	.06	.07	.07	.08
PASFM	Agg. assault—Fem.	.13	.13	.12	.13
PBGFM	Burglary clr.—Fem.	.05	.05	.06	.07
PATFM	Auto theft clr.—Fem.	.05	.07	.09	.09

clr. = cleared by arrests

Table 2

Observed Yearly Fluctuations in the Proportion of Females Arrested, 1950–1985

Offense Type	Annual Fluctuations			
	1950	1955	1960	1965
PMURFM	———	.0461	.0321	–.0370
	(.1348)*	(.1809)	(.2130)	(.1760)
PRAPFM	———	.0000	.0000	.0000
	(.0000)	(.0000)	(.0000)	(.0000)
PRBFM	———	.0007	.0088	.0013
	(.0429)	(.0422)	(.0510)	(.0523)
PASFM	———	.0541	.0049	–.0299
	(.1064)	(.1604)	(.1645)	(.1355)
PBGFM	———	.0027	.0132	.0013
	(.0254)	(.0227)	(.0359)	(.0372)
PATFM	———	.0008	.0163	–.0007
	(.0268)	(.0260)	(.0423)	(.0416)
	1970	1975	1980	1985
PMURFM	–.0218	.0019	–.0285	–.0031
	(.1542)	(.1561)	(.1276)	(.1245)
PRAPFM	.0000	.0098	–.0006	.0018
	(.0000)	(.0098)	(.0092)	(.0109)
PRBFM	.0087	.0094	.0017	.0038
	(.0610)	(.0704)	(.0722)	(.0760)
PASFM	–.0091	.0042	–.0066	.0107
	(.1263)	(.1305)	(.1239)	(.1346)
PBGFM	.0096	.0075	.0074	.0127
	(.0468)	(.0544)	(.0618)	(.0744)
PATFM	.0094	.0186	.0167	.0069
	(.0509)	(.0695)	(.0863)	(.0932)

* Figures in parentheses indicate annual proportion of males arrested.

from 1960 to 1965. Also of interest is that female involvement decreased for the time periods 1965–1970, 1975–1980, and 1980–1985. There were small decreases in female involvement in murder that varied from less than 1% to about 3% for this offense category. However, the yearly differences appear to be more offense-specific, rather than a general trend of increased female involvement in Part I offenses. For example, the yearly differences for female involvement in burglary shows a slight decrease for the period 1950–1955 (–.002%) and small, insubstantial increases of about 1% for the other time periods.

Table 3 presents the yearly differences in the proportion of arrests for males. Observed differences in male involvement in the six *UCR* Part I offenses appear to parallel female involvement in the same offense categories. For all offenses, the yearly fluctuations during the study period do not reveal any substantial increases or decreases in the proportion of males committing these particular offenses. When male involvement in murder is examined, for example, the amount of decrease varied from about 5% (1950 is compared to 1955) to less than 1% for the periods 1955–1960 and 1970–1975. A similar pattern was observed for the other offenses cleared by arrest. No wide fluctuations were observed during the study period that would lead to a finding suggesting a substantial increase or decrease in male involvement in the six *UCR* Part I offenses.

Table 4 shows the proportionate differences that existed between those males and females who were arrested for each of the study periods addressed in this analysis. For all eight periods, the male proportion of crime was significantly higher than for females. From 1950 to 1970, 100% of the rapes cleared by arrest were committed by males. However, this finding is more a result of the way that rape offenses were reported prior to 1970. As mentioned earlier, pre-1970 statutory definitions for this offense made rape a crime that almost exclusively involved males. As a result of a major impetus by state legislatures to update criminal sexual statutes, post-1970 rape was primarily defined as an offense capable of being committed by either

Table 3

Observed Yearly Fluctuations in the Proportion of Males Arrested, 1950–1985*

Offense Type	Annual Fluctuations			
	1950	1955	1960	1965
PMURML	———	.0461	–.0010	.0060
	(.8652)*	(.8191)	(.8181)	(.8240)
PRAPML	———	.0000	.0000	.0000
	(1.000)	(1.000)	(1.000)	(1.000)
PRBML	———	.0007	–.0035	–.0066
	(.9571)	(.9578)	(.9543)	(.9477)
PASML	———	.0541	.0075	.0174
	(.8936)	(.8396)	(.8471)	(.8645)
PBGML	———	.0027	–.0054	–.0092
	(.9746)	(.9773)	(.9720)	(.9628)
PATML	———	.0008	–.0099	–.0056
	(.9732)	(.9740)	(.9641)	(.9584)
	1970	1975	1980	1985
PMURML	.0218	–.0019	.0285	.0031
	(.8458)	(.8439)	(.8724)	(.8755)
PRAPML	.0000	.0098	.0006	–.0018
	(1.000)	(.9902)	(.9908)	(.9891)
PRBML	–.0087	–.0094	–.0017	–.0038
	(.9390)	(.9296)	(.9278)	(.9240)
PASML	.0091	–.0042	.0066	–.0107
	(.8737)	(.8695)	(.8761)	(.8654)
PBGML	–.0096	–.0075	–.0074	–.0127
	(.9532)	(.9456)	(.9382)	(.9256)
PATML	–.0094	–.0186	–.0167	.0069
	(.9491)	(.9305)	(.9137)	(.9068)

* Figures in parentheses indicate annual proportion of males arrested.

Table 4
Annual Proportionate Differences in Arrest by Gender, 1950–1985*

	1950	1955	1960	1965
PMURML with PMURFM	.730	.638	.605	.648
PRAPML with PRAPFM	1.000	1.000	1.000	1.000
PRBML with PRBFM	.914	.915	.903	.895
PASML with PASFM	.787	.679	.681	.729
PBGML with PBGFM	.949	.954	.936	.925
PATML with PATFM	.946	.948	.921	.916

	1970	1975	1980	1985
PMURML with PMURFM	.691	.687	.744	.751
PRAPML with PRAPFM	1.000	.980	.981	.978
PRBML with PRBFM	.878	.859	.855	.848
PASML with PASFM	.747	.739	.752	.730
PBGML with PBGFM	.906	.891	.876	.851
PATML with PATFM	.898	.861	.827	.813

* Denotes significance at the .05 level, two-tail probability.

males or females. So, in the 1975 arrest statistics, it is noted that there is some female involvement in the rape offense category. However, the results still indicate a significant involvement in rape by males. Most of the fluctuation in the proportion of females arrested was for murder, aggravated assault, and robbery, which are those types of offenses most often associated with crimes against the person. For example, the percentage of females arrested for aggravated assault varied from a low of 11% up to a 17% high for the eight time periods under investigation. This small amount of variation was found to be insignificant. Regardless of offense type, gender differences in the arrest statistics consistently favored a much higher male involvement in the *UCR* Part I offenses than female involvement.

Discussion and Conclusions

The purpose of the present study was to determine if there were time-related gender differences that were apparent in the proportion of male and female arrests for *UCR* Part I offenses. One premise of this inquiry was that there is a significant amount of instability in the proportion of male and female arrests from one time period to the next time period. Based on the gender of the arrested person, there was a significant difference in the proportion of arrests. The overall pattern that emerged was that males were consistently arrested much more often than female suspects. The five-year interval between each study time period did not reveal any statistically significant fluctuations in proportionate arrests for male or female suspects. However, a closer inspection of the modest percentage increases and decreases from one time period to the next provides some support for analyzing more than just the first and last time periods, where there is a wide time band, in order to identify patterns in official arrest statistics. The findings in the present investigation illustrate that there are time-related effects that create fluctuations in the gender-based proportion of arrests, such that if arrest data are collected for only one time period it may create the false impression that one gender subgroup is either more or less involved in committing some *UCR* Part I offenses when compared with the other gender subgroups.

Another issue addressed in this inquiry is the question of whether or not there are real gender differences identified in the proportion of arrests. These findings closely paralleled several prior studies where the investigators concluded that there is more of a male dominance in the commission of some *UCR* Part I offenses (Boritch & Hagan 1990; Hindelang 1979; Simpson 1991; Steffensmeier 1980; Steffensmeier & Allan 1988; Young 1986). They also questioned the findings of several researchers who have concluded that there was a substantial increase in the proportion of females arrested for the more serious crimes, usually operationalized as *UCR* Index Offenses (Adler 1975; Crump 1987; Simon 1975). According to Steffensmeier (1980), females have made some arrest gains on males, but those gains were really statistical artifacts, which were especially well documented when consideration is given to the small proportion of females, relative to males, who are arrested; the change in criminal reporting procedures, and law enforcement practices. Once these factors were included in the analysis there was very little change in the gender-specific crime rate.

The present analysis spans several earlier and later time periods than did the Steffensmeier investigation, and yet, the basic findings on the effects of gender on the proportion of arrests are very similar. In every instance, the proportion of males arrested was significantly higher than for females. Participation in some *UCR* Part I offense categories is still predominately a male-type activity. These findings provide continuing support for the position that males and females are socialized differently. Many of the gender-role differences that exist between males and females are very prominently exhibited in the gender-specific proportion of arrests. Evidence is accumulating which suggests that gender-role socialization makes some very real distinctions in the type of behavior with which males and females should align themselves. Traditional gender-role differences persist and these differences were evident in the significant differences observed in the higher proportion of males arrested for each of the offense categories across the eight study periods.

In conclusion, the present investigation was conducted in order to provide an understanding of gender-specific arrests when those arrests are examined at several different time points. The proportion of arrests for six *UCR* Part I offenses was most often higher for males than for females. These findings provided some support for analyzing arrest statistics at several different time periods with relatively narrow intervals between those time periods. Examining arrest statistics at only one time period leads to the false conclusion that one gender subgroup is committing serious offenses at either a higher or a lower rate than another gender subgroup. These findings also revealed that the commission of *UCR* Part I offenses is restricted to traditional gender roles. Fluctuations were observed in the proportion of arrests for males and females over the study period. With either modest increases or modest decreases in the gender-related proportion of arrests the most consistent pattern identified in the present study was that participation in some *UCR* Part I offense categories was dominated by male suspects.

References

Adler, F. (1975). *Sisters in crime: The rise of the new female criminal.* New York, NY: McGraw-Hill.

Bishop, D., & Frazier, C. (1984). The effects of gender on charge reduction. *Sociological Quarterly* 25(3): 385–396.

Blalock, H. (1979). *Social statistics*. New York: McGraw-Hill.

Boritch, H., & Hagan, J. (1990). A century of crime in Toronto: Gender, class, and patterns of social control, 1859 to 1955. *Criminology* 28(4): 567–599.

Chilton, R., & Datesman, S. (1987). Gender, race, and crime: An analysis of urban arrest trends. *Gender and Society* 1(2): 152–171.

Crump, A. (1987). Women and crime—A contemporary controversy. *International Journal of Offender Therapy and Comparative Criminology* 31(1): 31–40.

Daly, K. (1987). Discrimination in the criminal courts: Family, gender, and the problem of equal treatment. *Social Forces* 66(1): 152–175.

——— (1989). Neither conflict, nor labeling, nor paternalism will suffice: Interactions of race, ethnicity, gender, and family in criminal court decisions. *Crime and Delinquency* 35(1): 136–168.

Eck, J., & Riccio, L. (1979). Relationship between reported crime rates and victimization survey results: An empirical and analytical study. *Journal of Criminal Justice* 7(4): 293–308.

Erez, E. (1988). The myth of the new female offender: Some evidence from attitudes toward law and justice. *Journal of Criminal Justice* 16(6): 499–509.

Farrington, D., & Morris, A. (1983). Sex, sentencing and reconviction. *British Journal of Criminology* 23(3): 229–248.

Galvin, J., & Polk, K. (1982). Any truth you want: The use and abuse of crime and criminal justice statistics. *Journal of Research in Crime and Delinquency* 19(1): 135–165.

Gibson, J. (1978). Race as a determinant of criminal sentences: A methodological critique and case study. *Law and Society Review* 12(3): 455–478.

Gove, W., Hughes, M., & Geerken, M. (1985). Are uniform crime reports a valid indicator of the index crimes? An affirmative answer with minor qualifications. *Criminology* 23(3): 451–501.

Hagan, J. (1974). Extra-legal attributes and criminal sentencing: An assessment of a sociological viewpoint. *Law and Society Review* 8(3): 357–384.

Hawkins, D. (1986). Race, crime type and imprisonment. *Justice Quarterly* 3(3): 251–269.

Hindelang, M.J. (1979). Sex differences in criminal activity. *Social Problems* 27(2): 143–156.

——— (1981). Variations in sex-race-age specific incidence rates of offending. *American Sociological Review* 46(4): 461–474.

Jefferson, T. (1988). Race, crime, and policing: Empirical theoretical and methodological issues. *International Journal of the Sociology of Law* 16(4): 521–539.

Jendrek, M. (1985). *Through the maze: Statistics with computer applications.* Belmont, CA: Wadsworth Publishing.

Kitsuse, J., & Cicourel, A. (1963). A note on the uses of official statistics. *Social Problems* 11(2): 131–139.

Kleck, G. (1981). Racial discrimination in criminal sentencing. *American Sociological Review* 46(6): 783–805.

Kruttschnitt, C. (1980–1981). Social status and sentences of female offenders. *Law and Society Review* 15(2): 247–265.

——— (1984). Sex and criminal court dispositions: The unresolved controversy. *Journal of Research in Crime and Delinquency* 21(3): 213–232.

LaFree, G. (1980). The effect of sexual stratification by race on official reactions to rape. *American Sociological Review* 45(5): 842–854.

Messner, S., & South, S. (1988). Estimating race-specific offending rates: An intercity comparison of arrest data and victim reports. *Crime and Justice* 11(2): 25–45.

Petersilia, J. (1984). Racial disparities in the criminal justice system: Executive summary of Rand Institute study, 1983. In D. Georges-Abeyie (Ed.), *The criminal justice system and blacks* (pp. 225–253). New York: Clark Boardman.

Peterson, R., & Hagan, J. (1984). Changing conceptions of race and sentencing outcomes. *American Sociological Review* 49(1): 56–70.

Sampson, R., & Cohen, J. (1988). Deterrent effects of the police on crime: A replication and theoretical extension. *Law and Society Review 22*(1): 163–189.

Simon, R. (1975). *The contemporary woman and crime*. Washington, DC: U.S. Government Printing Office.

Simpson, S.S. (1991). Caste, class, and violent crime: Explaining differences in female offending. *Criminology* 29(1): 115–135.

Skogan, W. (1974). The validity of official crime statistics: An empirical investigation. *Social Science Quarterly* 55(1): 25–38.

Smith, D., & Visher, C. (1981). Street level justice: Situational determinants of police arrest decisions. *Social Problems* 29(2): 167–177.

Spohn, C., Gruhl, J., & Welch, S. (1981–1982). The effect of race on sentencing: A re-examination of an unsettled question. *Law and Society Review* 16(1): 72–88.

——— (1987). The impact of the ethnicity and gender of defendants on the decision to reject or dismiss felony charges. *Criminology* 25(1): 175–191.

Spohn, C., Welch, S., & Gruhl, J. (1985). Women defendants in court: The interaction between sex and race in convicting and sentencing. *Social Science Quarterly* 66(1):178–185.

Steffensmeier, D. (1978). Crime and the contemporary woman: An analysis of changing levels of female property crime, 1960–75. *Social Forces* 57(2): 566–584.

——— (1980). Sex differences in patterns of adult crimes 1965–77: A review and assessment. *Social Forces* 58(4): 1080–1108.

Steffensmeier, D., & Allan, E. (1988). Sex disparities in arrests by residence, race, and age: An assessment of the gender convergence crime, 1960–75. *Social Forces* 57(2): 566–584.

Tinker, J., Quiring, J., & Pimentael, Y. (1985). Ethnic bias in California Courts: A case study of Chicano and Anglo felony defendants. *Sociological Inquiry* 55(1): 83–96.

U.S. Department of Justice. (1965). *Uniform crime report.* Washington, DC: U.S. Government Printing Office.

——— (1970). *Uniform crime report.* Washington, DC: U.S. Government Printing Office.

——— (1975). *Uniform crime report.* Washington, DC: U.S. Government Printing Office.

——— (1980). *Uniform crime report.* Washington, DC: U.S. Government Printing Office.

——— (1985). *Uniform crime report.* Washington, DC: U.S. Government Printing Office.

Visher, C.A. (1983). Gender, police arrest decisions, and notions of chivalry. *Criminology* 21(1): 5–28.

Welch, S., Spohn, C., & Gruhl, J. (1985). Convicting and sentencing differences among black, Hispanic, and white males in six localities. *Justice Quarterly* 2(1): 67–80.

Wilbanks, W. (1986). Are female felons treated more leniently by the criminal justice system? *Justice Quarterly* 3(4): 517–529.

Young, V. (1980). Women, race, and crime. *Criminology* 18(1): 26–34.

——— (1986). Gender expectations and their impact on black female offenders and victims. *Justice Quarterly* 3(3): 305–327.

Zatz, M. (1984). Race, ethnicity and determinate sentencing: A new dimension to an old controversy. *Criminology* 22(2): 147–172.

The Role of Gender in Pretrial Decision Making*

Noreen L. Channels
Sharon D. Herzberger
Trinity College

Gender has been of only peripheral interest in most research designed to discover the way that bond decisions are made within the criminal justice system. Most of the research has used samples of men only or has simply included gender as one among many independent variables in the model. In research of this type, gender has not been the primary focus, and researchers often either have failed to investigate how findings might differ for women had they been included in the sample or have failed to accompany their reports of gender effects with any further analysis designed to determine what these differences might indicate about the criminal justice system.

In this essay, we present analyses of the decisions made about men and women at the bond-setting stage. We look first at the sample as a whole to determine the significance of gender and then conduct separate analyses to identify the factors that are considered when bond is set for men and for women. Finally, we look at the pretrial release status of individuals with financial bond, a decision that is reflective of the amount of bond as well as other factors that fall outside the scope of the criminal justice system. Here, too, we analyze the sample as a

* Inquiries may be addressed to Dr. Channels at the Department of Sociology, Trinity College, Hartford, CT 06106. We would like to thank Dr. Adam Grossberg of Trinity College and Dr. Randy Brown of Econometrica for their helpful comments on the analytical approach to this study.

the amount of bond as well as other factors that fall outside the scope of the criminal justice system. Here, too, we analyze the sample as a whole and then men and women separately. Our data show that previous claims about the workings of these early steps in the criminal justice system are largely based on information about how the system works for men. Decision making regarding women is a considerably different process.

The question of whether or not women are treated with leniency and, if so, whether this pattern applies to all women has dominated the literature on gender and the criminal justice system. The most persistent findings about the treatment of men and women are that women are given more lenient treatment than are men in decisions about sentencing, especially in response to serious offenses (Chesney-Lind 1987). Nagel and Hagan (1983) described a pattern of leniency toward women when the options clearly differed in severity (e.g., in pretrial release and sentencing), with the less serious options selected for women. In summarizing the literature, Spohn, Gruhl, and Welch (1987) found that the observed pattern of leniency occurs most consistently in the formal, "visible" decisions—conviction and sentencing.

Men and women are treated differently in some aspects of bond decision making as well. Nagel (1983) and Nagel and Hagan (1983) found that women are more likely than men to be released on their own recognizance. No gender differences were found, however, in the bond amount, once a financial bond is required. Similarly, Steury and Frank (1990) found differences between men and women in bond type but not in the bond amount or the consequences of court decisions—pretrial release, length of time in pretrial detention, appearance at trial. Thus, the most persistent finding of bail-stage leniency for women seems to occur at the decision regarding bond type.

Much of the research directed at the question of leniency has simply documented some areas of advantage to women, with little attention to understanding the *process* that leads to any differences in treatment. A number of researchers (e.g., Daly 1987; Kruttschnitt & Green 1984; Steffensmeier 1980; Steury & Frank 1990; Visher 1983) found that the issue of how women are treated throughout the system is more complicated than one of simple leniency. These researchers suggested that gender per se does not affect the decision but that gender interacts with other aspects of the situation. When leniency is granted, it is not granted to all women but is offered to those women who conform to expectations of appropriate behavior for women. From this sex-role stereotype perspective then, women's crime and personal characteristics are viewed and evaluated in the context of cultural norms and expectations. A common test of this perspective has been to determine whether women are accorded different treatment on the basis of their crime type, especially whether they have committed "female" or "male" types of crime (e.g., Kruttschnitt & Green 1984; Steffensmeier 1980; Steury & Frank 1990).

Other studies have expanded this perspective by moving beyond crime-related behavior to other aspects of expected behavior for women that may influence judicial decision making. For example, Visher (1983), in her research on arrest decisions, found that women who violate "typical middle-class standards of traditional female characteristics and behaviors (i.e., white, older, and submissive) are not afforded any chivalrous treatment during arrest decisions" (pp. 22–23). Kruttschnitt (1980–1981) found that disposition for women is more severe for those in lower economic ranks, those on welfare, and those with a prior criminal record. In this, the courts appear to be acting so as to support female dependency, an informal mechanism of social control of women. Kruttschnitt suggested further attention to the interactive role of gender with social status variables such as employment, economic dependency, and marital status (see also Kruttschnitt 1982; Kruttschnitt & Green 1984). In interviews with court personnel, Daly (1987) learned that judicial decisions are not based on traits of the women per se, but on a woman's family situation. Daly suggested that the social and economic costs of punishing women with families are considered to be too high; concern for the punishment of dependent children by removing the mother from the situation and the cost of supporting children while the mother is imprisoned mitigate against a decision to imprison. "Family paternalism," more than "female paternalism," Daly found, is the motivational root of leniency for particular women as they pass through the criminal justice system. While for the present study, we were unable to analyze the effect of having children, we tested this argument by examining the role of marital status, which in itself confers family responsibility.

The theme throughout these findings is that gender is interacting with other variables that measure women's conformity to stereotypes of appropriate behavior. These findings make clear the importance of continuing to identify the specific factors that differentially influence the treatment of men and women within various stages of the criminal justice system. In our research, by conducting separate analyses for men and women, we focus on the differing effects that crime-related factors and other, personal traits have in decision making about men and women.

Method

The Data Set

The original sample for the current study included a random selection of 2,336 people who were charged with a felony and who were interviewed by the State Bail Commission in 1983–1984. To this core sample, criminal history was added from state police files, information on the current case and its disposition was gathered from the Judicial Department files, census block group (for an income proxy) was taken from the 1980 United States Census, and prison time served was obtained from the Department of Corrections.[1] Disposition and sentencing are not included in the analysis reported here, and the sample size is considerably reduced because of missing information, especially on details of the crime and on the income estimate.

The strengths of our data for this analysis are several. We have information about the separate steps in the bond-setting decisions, allowing us to separate bond type from bond amount. We have information about pretrial release, which can be examined with amount of bond controlled. Our sample is not limited to those who progress beyond the bond-setting stage to disposition and sentencing; we also have data from those whose cases are, for example, dismissed or dropped. Thus, we are able to eliminate the potential bias incurred by examining the early bond decisions only for those who continue on in the criminal justice system.

The Dependent Variables and Approach to Analysis

As noted previously, we focus here on the three steps in the process that determine whether an accused individual will obtain pretrial release: First, we examine *bond type*, the decision to require either a financial bond or to release the individual without financial constraint; second, we analyze the decision about the *amount of bond* imposed upon individuals who have been required to post a financial bond; and, third, we focus on whether or not the individual obtains a *pretrial release*.

In our state criminal justice system, it is often the police or the bail commissioner at the police station who release accused individuals on their own recognizance. If the person is denied a nonfinancial bond, the bond amount is initially set at the police station, reviewed and perhaps changed by the bail commissioner, and then examined again by the judge, who in some but not all instances makes the final determination. Individuals who meet the conditions set may gain release before final judicial involvement. In our sample, 28% did so (usually after the bail commissioner's recommendation). There is a strong correlation ($r = .83$, $p < .0001$) between the bond amount recommended by the bail commissioner and that set by the judge. Thus, the bond-setting phase of the criminal justice system is actually a number of distinct but related steps, usually involving several different decision makers, each making a determination with information about prior decisions available. In the analysis here, we have used the final bond amount.

For analysis of the first two dependent variables, bond type and bond amount, we used a Tobit regression analysis that simultaneously estimates the determinants of bond type and bond amount. As described by McDonald and Moffitt (1980), the Tobit coefficients for each independent variable can be disaggregated into two segments: (a) the extent to which each independent variable changes the probability of having a financial bond and (b) the change in the amount of the financial bond if a financial bond is required. In the results reported here, we have presented this decomposition for the analyses of men and women separately. For the analysis of the sample as a whole, we have presented only the Tobit coefficients and their significance. An advantage of Tobit analysis is that we can avoid the sample selection problems that would occur if we dropped from analysis of bond amount those individuals granted a nonfinancial bond.

We based our analyses of the third decision, pretrial release, on the distinctions of Steury and Frank (1990), who identified two separate categories of variables: *court decisions* (financial or nonfinancial bond and amount of bond) and *consequences* of court decisions (pretrial release, length of pretrial confinement, and appearance at one's trial). These variables are expected to be related, so that it is important to understand the impact of bond amount on whether or not the individual subsequently gains release. We use a type of probit analysis that eliminates the sample selection bias that would occur if disparities between men and women in bond type were ignored in this analysis. In this analysis of pretrial release, we include only those who have been required to pay a financial bond, and the bond amount is included as an independent variable in this estimate of pretrial release.

The findings reported here are based upon two types of analyses. First, *the entire sample* was used to identify the factors that influence the decisions in the criminal justice system. From this analysis we can determine the extent to which gender plays a role in determining bond type, bond amount, and pretrial release. Second, *the sample was divided by gender*, and separate regression analyses were performed on each group. It is quite likely that decision makers are influenced by the gender of an individual in a way that is less direct than a simple harsh or lenient response to the question of bond type or bond amount. Instead, the decision maker may be more or less sensitive to *other* crime-related or personal characteristics of the individual when confronted with the case of a man or a woman. By conducting separate analyses for the men and women in the sample, we are able to discover the differences in the effects of various predictors in determining outcomes for men and for women. In essence, this separate analysis lets us explore the possibility of gender interacting with all other independent variables in the model.

Independent Variables

Table 1 shows the independent variables used in the study, along with their coding. As noted, we included information about the characteristics of the current crime, the individuals' criminal history, and demographic information. Also, as discussed above, we included bond amount in analysis of pretrial release.

Results

Type and Amount of Bond

In this analysis, *type of bond* is a dichotomous variable, including financial bond (full surety and a 10% surety deposit) and nonfinancial bond (promise to appear and other forms of conditional release). Sixty percent of the women in the sample (55 of 92) were required to post a financial bond, as were 74% (609 of 821) of the men. When no other factors are controlled, the average *amount of bond* required is higher for men ($8,313) than for women ($6,448). However, the difference between men and women in bond type and amount must be further analyzed with the control variables introduced. As discussed above, these results are obtained from the decomposition of the Tobit coefficients, where the influence of each independent variable on the probability of receiving a financial bond and on the amount of bond is calculated.

Direct effects of gender. In a Tobit analysis of bond type and amount (Table 2), for the sample as a whole, we found that the coefficient for gender is not significant, indicating that once the controls are introduced, *women are not more likely than men to receive a nonfinancial bond* and *men and women with financial bonds do not differ in the amount of money they are required to post in order to gain*

Table 1
Variables Used for Regression Analysis and Their Direction

Variable	Notes on Codes
Decisions	
Type of bond	nonfinancial = 0, financial = 1
Amount of bond	in $1,000s
Pretrial release	no = 0, yes = 1
Independent variables	
Weapon use	no = 0, yes = 1
Personal injury	no = 0, yes = 1
Relationship to victim	no = 0, yes = 1
Property damage	no = 0, yes = 1
Most serious current charge	7 levels coded from 1 to 7: C, B, or A misdemeanor; D, C, B, or A felony
Number of counts	at time of arraignment
Source of bond decision	Bail Commissioner = 1, Judge = 2
Severity of prior convictions	within the last five years none = 0, misdemeanor = 1, felony = 2
Known prior convictions	total number
Current status	none = 0; on parole, probation, or having outstanding warrant = 1
Race/ethnicity	divided into three groups: white, black, Hispanic
Marital status	single = 1, other = 2
Age	in years
Income	median household income of census block group
Gender	male = 1, female = 2

Table 2
Predicting Decisions about Bond Type and Bond Amount: Tobit Analysis

Independent variable	*Coefficient*
Intercept	–27.1382***
Weapon use	3.83210*
Personal injury	5.21223**
Relationship	–7.12782**
Property damage	1.65452
Most serious charge	4.31050***
Number of counts	1.13294**
Source of decision	5.91328***
Severity of priors	1.16015
Number of priors	0.22870*
Current status	2.26543[a]
Black	1.71491
Hispanic	2.93649[a]
Marital status	3.45614[a]
Age	–0.02704
Income	–0.013241
Gender	–2.74094

[a] $p < .10$, *$p < .05$, **$p < .01$, ***$p < .0001$. Sample size = 909.

pretrial release. Thus, the apparent difference between men and women in these decisions is explained by their differences on other factors in the model.[2]

Indirect effects of gender. In spite of the insignificance of the gender coefficient in analyses of bond type and amount, there are disparities in the treatment of men and women. By conducting separate analyses, we are able to ascertain whether the expected predictors work in the same direction and with the same importance for men and women. Our analyses show that the criteria used in making these decisions for men and women differ dramatically. The Tobit coefficients and the results of the decomposition of the coefficients are presented in Table 3.

For men, *bond type and bond amount* are significantly affected by characteristics of the current crime: the severity and number of counts in the current crime, whether or not the judge set the final bond, and other characteristics of the crime (weapon involvement, personal injury, and being related to the victim). Also, for men, there is a trend toward significance of criminal history, both in the number of priors ($p < .09$) and the severity of priors ($p < .08$), and a trend toward significance for Hispanics ($p < .07$).

For women, however, *none* of the characteristics of the current crime and *none* of the criminal history variables included in the model are significant criteria in making these decisions (although there is a trend toward significance of number of priors, $p < .06$). For women, but not for men, *marital status* plays a significant role, in that women who are married are *more likely* to be given a financial bond and to pay a higher amount, once so required. None of the other demographic factors was significant for women.

As the decomposition of the Tobit coefficient shows, the jeopardy to married women in terms of bond type is far from trivial: *being married increases by 43% the probability that a woman will receive a financial bond*. And we can see the predicted increase in the bond amount for married women: to secure release from pretrial detention, *married women were required to pay $6,746 more than comparable women who were not married*. (In contrast, as noted above, being married did not contribute significantly to this decision for men;

married men paid $740 more than single men, about one-tenth of the difference that exists for women.)

Pretrial Release

In these analyses, we examine whether there is a difference in rates of pretrial release between men and women who have been given a financial bond. In the sample as a whole, with no other factors taken into account, 89% of the women obtain a pretrial release, 59% by meeting their financial bond. Overall, women appear to be advantaged compared to men, where 71% are free pending resolution of their cases, 66% on a financial bond.

The sample as a whole. With the control variables introduced, however, the data show that *comparable men and women do not differ significantly in the likelihood that they will meet their financial bond and obtain a pretrial release* (Table 4). In this, we see no support for advantage to women in the ability to meet their financial bond requirements.

Separate analyses of men and women. In the models used in these analyses, several independent variables are dropped for both men and women in order to avoid a substantially diminished sample size for women. We retained information about the severity of prior criminal history but deleted the number of prior offenses; we retained information about the severity and extensiveness of the current crime but deleted some particular characteristics of the crime (use of a weapon, personal injury, and property damage). Also, age and income have been omitted from the models.

In these analyses, we find the same pattern of results as for bond type and amount (Table 4). For men, there is a greater likelihood of a pretrial release for those with more severe current crimes, with less severe past crimes, and with no relation to their victims. Hispanic men are significantly more likely to be released pretrial. As expected, but important because of the absence of significance of this variable for women, a higher financial bond amount decreased the likelihood of pretrial release for men.

Table 3

Tobit Models and Decomposition, Predicting Decisions about Bond Type and Bond Amount for Men and Women

	Men			Women		
Independent Variable	Tobit Coefficient	Change in Probability of Financial Bond	Increase in Bond Amount	Tobit Coefficient	Change in Probability of Financial Bond	Increase in Bond Amount
Intercept	–30.57280***	–0.76517	–11.6760	–27.93140[a]	–0.81259	–12.8206
Weapon use	4.50434**	0.11273	1.7202	3.17981	0.09251	1.4595
Personal injury	6.53516***	0.16356	2.4958	–2.53148	–0.07365	–1.1620
Relationship	–7.26940*	–0.18194	–2.7762	–4.11371	–0.11968	–1.8882
Property damage	1.18364	0.02962	0.4520	4.47069	0.13006	2.0521
Most serious charge	4.42235***	0.11068	1.6889	3.12345	0.09087	1.4337
Number of counts	1.17275**	0.02935	0.4479	.64305	0.01871	0.2952
Source of decision	6.42750***	0.16087	2.4547	1.42048	0.04133	0.6520

	Men			Women		
Independent Variable	Tobit Coefficient	Change in Probability of Financial Bond	Increase in Bond Amonut	Tobit Coefficient	Change in Probability of Financial Bond	Increase in Bond Amount
Severity of priors	1.50665[a]	0.03771	0.5754	–.76099	–0.02214	–0.3493
Number of priors	.19605[a]	0.00491	0.0749	.48214[a]	0.01403	0.2213
Current status	1.77424	0.04441	0.6776	5.49912	0.15998	2.5241
Black	1.99375	0.04990	0.7614	.33532	0.00976	0.1539
Hispanic	3.08765[a]	0.07728	1.1792	.06433	0.00187	0.0295
Marital status	1.94760	0.04874	0.7438	14.69770*	0.42759	6.7463
Age	–.04882	–0.00122	–0.0186	.24555	0.00714	0.1127
Income	–.01599	–0.00040	–0.0061	–.05932	–0.00173	–0.0272
Sample size		818			91	

a $p < .10$, $*p < .05$, $**p < .01$, $***p < .0001$.

Table 4

Probit Models Predicting Release from Pretrial Detention

	Entire Sample		Men		Women	
Independent Variable	Coefficient	Transformed	Coefficient	Transformed	Coefficient	Transformed
Intercept	–0.46259	–0.18379	0.07841	0.03128	–0.48622	–0.07483
Weapon use	0.07362	0.02916	—	—	—	—
Personal injury	0.14697	0.05796	—	—	—	—
Relationship	–0.62862*	–0.24251	–0.36831[a]	–0.14383	–0.36703	–0.06770
Property damage	0.04321	0.01713	—	—	—	—
Most serious charge	0.12597*	0.05005	0.11412**	0.04552	0.47219	0.07267
Number of counts	–0.00580	–0.00230	0.03394	0.01354	–0.04002	–0.00616
Source of decision	–0.12837	–0.05075	–0.17752	–0.07067	–0.60753	–0.07798
Severity of priors	–0.25978**	–0.10321	–0.31662**	–0.12630	–0.16336	–0.02514

	Entire Sample		Men		Women	
Independent Variable	Coefficient	Transformed	Coefficient	Transformed	Coefficient	Transformed
Number of priors	–0.01379	–0.00548	—	—	—	—
Current status	0.00065	0.00026	–0.04644	–0.01852	–0.25005	–0.03989
Black	0.21415[a]	0.08477	0.05418	0.02161	1.08043	0.16860
Hispanic	0.36874*	0.14357	0.30286**	0.12000	0.18180	0.02552
Marital status	0.54420*	0.20438	0.27304	0.10801	0.19611	0.02746
Gender	0.24411	0.09703	—	—	—	—
Age	–0.00236	–0.00094	—	—	—	—
Income	0.01679*	0.00667	—	—	—	—
Bond amount	–0.02323***	–0.00923	–0.02391***	–0.00954	–0.03357	–0.00517
Sample size		615		831		68

a $p < .10$, $*p < .05$, $**p < .01$, $***p < .0001$. Also, "—" indicates the exclusion of this independent variable from the regression model.

For women, none of these variables—nor any of the others in the model—was a significant predictor of pretrial release. The factors generally assumed in the literature to be predictors of this outcome are not relevant for women.

Summary

Our analysis of bond type and amount leads to several conclusions. The initial appearance of leniency for women, both in bond type and bond amount, is not supported by the analyses that take into account the current crime, criminal history, and other personal characteristics of the individuals in the sample. From these analyses, it would appear that the decision-making process identified with our data analyses reflects the legally supportable pattern, with attention to current and prior crime and inattention to personal characteristics, including gender.

However, these whole-sample analyses can be misleading, in that men and women are treated differently in the *criteria considered* by decision makers. Separate analyses for men show that criminal behavior, current and past, is given significant weight in determining bond type and amount. For women these characteristics have no significant influence; the immediate and past criminal behavior is irrelevant to those who are making these decisions for women. Also, among the personal factors, marital status is given significant weight in making these crucial judgments about women, with harsher treatment given to married women.

In the analysis of pretrial release, which is one of the most important consequences of the decisions about bond type and amount, similar findings prevail. When the controls are introduced, comparable men and women do not differ in the likelihood of obtaining a pretrial release. However, the separate analyses show that the consequences for men are, at least in part, due to the constraints imposed by the criminal justice system. For women, no such pattern exists. In fact, we were not able to identify any significant regularity in the pretrial release of women.

Discussion

In our study of the direct effects of gender, with the controls introduced, we found no leniency toward women either in bond type or bond amount. However, the separate analyses of men and women show that the foundations of these decisions differ substantially. For men, the decision to require a financial bond and the amount of that bond are influenced by the factors we have come to expect from earlier research and from the policies that guide bond decisions: characteristics of the current crime and criminal history. For women, however, neither current nor past crime-related behavior is found to be of importance to decision makers.

The analyses of the sample as a whole result in essentially the same findings as the analysis of men alone, due, of course, to the large proportion of men in the criminal justice system. However, this consequence of the gender distribution in the sample can lead to a mistaken understanding of the workings of the criminal justice system, where the significant predictors for men are seen as predictors for women as well. Our findings highlight the importance of continuing to examine the differences in treatment of men and women, not simply by examining the decisions but also by analyzing the criteria used in making these decisions.

In regard to this lack of significant predictors in the analyses of women, it is not necessarily the case that decision makers are using no systematic criteria, since factors not available to us might be regularly considered. However, it is of serious concern that, at the least, a separate set of criteria is used in making decisions about men and women and that the expected crime-related factors are not among the criteria in decisions made about women.

Further, in the analysis of women, we found that marital status is of significant influence, with a disadvantage to married women. In neither bond type nor bond amount is marital status a significant predictor for men in the sample. This pattern is consistent with earlier research that finds more attention to the personal traits of women than men (Daly 1987; Kruttschnitt 1980–1981; Nagel, Cardascia, & Ross 1982). In this finding, we see support for the sex-role stereotype perspective that sees women as doubly disadvantaged in the criminal justice system when their crime or personal characteristics violate the cultural expectations of social position as well as the law.

However, our findings of a disadvantage to married women in these early phases of the criminal justice system are the reverse of other findings of advantage to married women in sentencing, especially in imprisonment. In sentencing decisions, the advantage to married women has been explained as a desire on the part of decision makers to maintain the household or to reward women for fulfilling their traditional role (Daly 1987; Nagel, Cardascia, & Ross 1982). In regard to our findings, we speculate that bond decisions result only indirectly in imprisonment, as a result of an individual's inability to meet financial bond. Thus, these consequences of the decision are not as obvious and may not be considered by the judicial decision maker. Also, this disadvantage to married women is consistent with the sex-role stereotype perspective in that married women have been accused both of illegal activities and of behavior inappropriate to their "station" as married women. These women are, our data show, disadvantaged by two types of deviance. These findings also raise the question of whether the courts do in fact act so as to reward women who fulfill traditional role expectations of women as wives or, as our data show, are more harsh with women who then do not act in a manner deemed appropriate for this role.

In the analysis of the sample as a whole, men and women were found to obtain pretrial release with equal frequency. But, as before, we found that the process leading to release is not the same for men and women. None of the crime-related factors was predictive for women, and neither was the bond amount. But these variables are significant for men. While release is expected in part to be a function of bond amount and other factors within the criminal justice system, release also may depend upon the individual's resources and his or her own decision making. It is important to note that these other possible determinants, such as personal resources, ability to raise money, family ties, and support of family and friends, are usually not included in research on pretrial release, a serious omission if men and women are different in these ways (Steury & Frank 1990).

Several areas for further research are suggested by our analyses. Importantly, further research should focus on ascertaining the extent to which there are systematic criteria used in determining bond type and amount and pretrial release for women and, if found, what role these criteria play. It is also important to obtain further information on the factors outside the criminal justice system that influence pretrial release and, as mentioned above, to ascertain whether these factors are differentially available for men and women. The assumed value of "equality of treatment" requires further debate. It is not obvious that a goal in criminal justice processing is or should be identical treatment of men and women (Daly & Chesney-Lind 1987), especially if gender differences in absconding or jumping bail, which, after all, underlie bond decisions, are not taken into consideration (Steury & Frank 1990). It would be beneficial to repeat this study with a larger sample, especially with more women. This would allow a replication of our research within specific crime categories and would allow further investigation of variables that interact with gender, such as marital status and other aspects of the female sex-role stereotype. Finally, attention must be paid to recasting our assumptions about the workings of the criminal justice system, since these are shown to be primarily assumptions that describe experiences for men and not for women.

Notes

1. There is some bias introduced by the absence in our sample of accused felons who were released by the police prior to a Bail Commission interview, a figure that is not known by the state. All offenses are bailable, so the sample is not further limited by denial of bail to some.

2. The reader should note that we also estimated probit regressions for bond type, with the whole sample and for men and women separately. The results of the analyses are substantially the same, with no important differences in significant variables or in sign changes.

References

Chesney-Lind, M. (1987). Female offenders: Paternalism reexamined. In L.L. Crites & W.L. Hepperle (Eds.), *Women, the courts, and equality* (pp. 114–139). Newbury Park, CA: Sage.

Daly, K. (1987). Structure and practice of familial-based justice in a criminal court. *Law and Society Review* 21: 267–290.

Daly, K., and Chesney-Lind, M. (1988). Feminism and criminology. *Justice Quarterly* 5(9): 497–535.

Frazier, C.E., Bock, E.W., & Henretta, J.C. (1980). Pretrial release and bail decisions. *Criminology* 18: 162–181.

Goldkamp, J.S., & Gottfredson, M.R. (1979). Bail decision making and pretrial detention: Surfacing judicial policy. *Law and Human Behavior* 3: 227–249.

Kruttschnitt, C. (1980–1981). Social status and sentences of female offenders. *Law and Society Review* 15(2): 247–265.

——— (1982). Women, crime, and dependency: An application of the theory of law. *Criminology* 19: 495–513.

———, & Green, D.E. (1985). The sex-sanctioning issue: Is it history? *American Sociological Review* 49: 541–551.

McDonald, J.F., & Moffitt, R.A. (1980). The uses of Tobit analysis. *Review of Economics and Statistics* 62: 318–321.

Myers, M.A. (1982). Common law in action: The prosecution of felonies and misdemeanors. *Sociological Inquiry* 52: 1–15.

Nagel, I.H. (1983). The legal/extra-legal controversy: Judicial decisions in pretrial release. *Law and Society Review* 17: 481–515.

Nagel, I.H., Cardascia, J., & Ross, C.E. (1982). Sex differences in the processing of criminal defendants. In D.K. Weisberg (Ed.), *Women and the law: A social historical perspective: Vol. 1, Women and the Criminal Law* (pp. 259–282). Cambridge, MA: Schenkman Publishing.

Nagel, I.H., & Hagan, J. (1983). Gender and crime: Offense patterns and criminal court sanctions. In M. Tonry & N. Morris (Eds.), *Crime and justice: An annual review of research* (Vol. 4) (pp. 91–144). Chicago: University of Chicago Press.

Spohn, C., Gruhl, J., & Welch, S. (1987). The impact of the ethnicity and gender of defendants on the decision to reject or dismiss felony charges. *Criminology* 25(1): 175–191.

Steffensmeier, D.J. (1980). Assessing the impact of the women's movement on sex-based differences in the handling of adult criminal defendants. *Crime and Delinquency* 26: 344–357.

Steury, E.H., & Frank, N. (1990). Gender bias and pretrial release: More pieces of the puzzle. *Journal of Criminal Justice* 18: 417–432.

Visher, C.A. (1983). Gender, police arrest decisions, and notions of chivalry. *Criminology* 21(1): 5–28.

Gender and Crime: Different Sex, Different Treatment?

Frank H. Julian
Murray State University

If she hasn't committed murder and she has children at home, she walks.—Criminal Defense Counsel

It's difficult to send a mature woman to prison. I keep thinking. . . . Hey! She is somebody's mother!—Criminal Court Judge

I knew I wouldn't do no hard time. No way. Not for a little stealin'.—Female Felon

It is a puzzle that has challenged dozens of researchers for decades. If a man steals cash from the register of a convenience store on any given evening in a major U.S. city, while a woman steals cash from another convenience store elsewhere in town on that same night, why is it that the woman is likely to be treated with greater leniency by the criminal justice system? Research extending over three decades has studied this phenomenon, and the results are distinctly varied. Much of the research conducted in the 1960s and 1970s, and even some from the 1980s, supports the view that women are treated with greater leniency than men accused of the same crime. However, some research conducted more recently, and especially research conducted from a feminist perspective, has found a number of holes in the theory. The differences seem to be evaporating.

Still, very few researchers have concluded that the pro-female bias does not exist at all. Interviews conducted in connection with this essay seem to suggest that the issue just will not die and will not go away no matter how much research is undertaken on the subject. Interviews with police officers, judges, attorneys, even offenders themselves lead to the conclusion that a certain amount of leniency is, in fact, granted female offenders.

Note the quotations used to open this essay. These are statements made in the 1990s by people closely involved with the criminal justice system in three states. The findings of numerous researchers suggest that these statements reflect a diehard reality. Chivalry lives.

There is that word—chivalry. Is it an antiquated relic of a bygone era or a modern reality? In medieval Europe, chivalry represented a system of values, ideals, and acceptable forms of conduct. Interestingly, history credits women with the development of chivalrous values.

Specifically, European noblewomen of the twelfth century are believed to have developed standards of conduct whereby they expected much from knights. This was viewed by women as great progress, because women in much of Europe at this time were little more than "chattel personal," the property of men. These noblewomen found men willing to fight bravely on the battlefield and in tournaments to win their hearts. As medieval times progressed, noblewomen came to expect more refined standards of behavior from men, deference for women, social skills, even talent in music. The Renaissance added education and cultural polish to the list of expectations. By the eighteenth century, it was these very traits by which one judged a male as a "gentleman."

However, as twentieth-century women can attest, what passed for progress in the twelfth century became a frustrating gilded cage for women who hoped to achieve equality. Gentlemen, it seems, had thoroughly internalized their roles in society over the course of the centuries, and they did not instantly accept role changes. In fact, many men resisted women's desires for a "different but equal" status in society. Sociologists have suggested that men's resistance was due to parallel concerns: loss of special male privileges and role confusion. Whatever the reason, the twentieth century has been a "sorting out" century, a century in which sex roles have changed in fits and starts but clearly irrevocably.

So what does chivalry have to do with America's criminal justice system very late in the twentieth century? Perhaps a great deal. Without reference to the history of chivalrous relations between the sexes, it is difficult, if not impossible, to explain the different treatment which at least some women receive in the criminal justice process.

Of course, gender differences do not explain all of the differences in treatment researchers have observed. Some differences seem clearly based on race, some on age, criminal history, even community status. Still, none of these other factors seems as potent as gender.

In preparation for this essay, several interviews were conducted. The views of a policewoman, two judges, several criminals, a past and current prosecutor, and a defense counsel were sought. Several were women. All agreed that gender can be a powerful judicial tool as noted in the following statements:

"If my client listens to me and does as I suggest," a defense counsel said, "her chances of avoiding jail time are excellent."

"Look and act like a responsible person. Dress conservatively. Avoid violence and swearing. Be contrite and deferential in court. Stay at home at night," advises a defense attorney.

One might suggest that this is probably good advice for any defendant, regardless of gender. "It sure is," the defense attorney responds, "but it works like a magic charm for women. It seems to affect some judges and jurors, even some prosecutors. I hate to say this, I really do, but a young, attractive, feminine, demure woman is a cinch to defend."

Does the physical appearance and demeanor of a female defendant affect the prosecutor's judgment? "It probably does, much as I hate to admit that I could be taken in by appearances," says a prosecuting attorney. "It's hard to make yourself want to throw the book at someone who looks as if she's a good person who just lost her way for awhile. Looking back, I think this is particularly true in cases of nonviolent crime. It's definitely true for victimless crimes."

And what about men who look and sound beatific? "I'm not so easily taken in by men," claims the prosecutor. "Of course, some men deserve and receive assistance rather than punishment," said a criminal court judge.

Historical gender roles overlaid with an instinct for protection of motherhood create a powerful anti-incarceration elixir. "I have never slept well after a day in which I have ordered a mother of young children to be incarcerated," said a criminal court judge.

What if the woman has no children? "In my court I think they receive the same treatment as a man," says the judge. "But I don't see that many women in my court, at least not for truly serious crimes . . . and it seems most of the ones I do see have kids."

How often does the small-town policewoman arrest a woman for a serious infraction of the law? "Not very often. Maybe an occasional drug dealer, that sort of thing. Mostly it involves less serious violations, you know, DUI's, writing cold checks, shoplifting."

Obviously, anecdotal evidence is clearly insufficient to support the view that chivalry is still alive and kicking in the criminal justice system; however, numerous researchers have found at least some evidence to support the viewpoint that women are receiving more lenient treatment than men during some phases of the criminal justice process.

Anderson (1976) and Feinman (1980) found support in their research for the "chivalry theory," which is sometimes referred to as "judicial paternalism." Gibbons and Prince (1962); Baab and Furgeson (1967); Nagel and Weitzman (1971); Moulds (1978); Curran (1983); and Frazier, Bock, and Henretta (1983) all found that women were less likely to be incarcerated than were men. Various studies have reported that only one-half to one-fourth as many women are in prison as one would predict based upon arrest records.

Allegedly women commit far more crimes than are reported, but individuals are much less likely to report crimes when they know the perpetrator is a woman. If this allegation is true, it would seem to lend additional support to the chivalry theory. Perhaps the influence of chivalry begins long before a woman faces the criminal justice system.

Others claim that women tend to commit minor crimes, the type that are less likely to result in incarceration or even in prosecution, such as shoplifting, writing bad checks, or public intoxication. National crime reports (Federal Bureau of Investigation 1991) support the view that while women's share of crime is growing, it is still a relatively small part of the total and largely confined to lesser crimes.

Another closely related explanation for low female incarceration rates reasons that women tend to commit minor crimes and police are too busy solving major crimes to pursue minor crimes; hence, little attention is devoted to solving women's crimes. Police officers vociferously disabuse this theory.

"Pure bunk," says the small-town policewoman. "In a small town we actively pursue solutions to *all* crimes. Usually, small crimes are all we have."

And what percentage of those arrested are women in this town? "Maybe 10, 15%. Tops." What about the incidence of women and violent crime? "Other than occasional domestic violence, arrest of a woman for a violent crime would be a rarity here," answers the policewoman. "But," she adds, "we don't have much non-domestic violence, period."

Kruttschnitt (1984) suggested an alternative explanation, as noted earlier by Crites in her 1978 study of women criminals. Women are frequently accomplices to crimes being committed by men so the courts may not view them as the instigators of the crime. They are led more by an emotional tie to their man than motivated by anger, rebellion, or economic gain. Hence, the actions of the women are viewed by the criminal justice system as more forgivable, more remediable, and more deserving of less severe retribution by society. That women are far more likely to commit victimless crimes, such as prostitution and drug use, is another explanation for low arrest rates of females.

The FBI's (1991) national crime statistics for 1990 offer blunt support. Men represented 95% of all people arrested for murder or manslaughter, 89% of those arrested for arson, and 92% of burglary arrests. But, women comprised one-third of those arrested for forgery and fraud and nearly half of all alleged embezzlers. Except for prostitution, the only crime for which more females were arrested than males was running away from home.

Despite whatever flaws may exist in the national crime data, it can be concluded that criminality is an area where women have not kept pace with men. However, it is also true that female criminality has been increasing as a portion of total crime for the past 25 years. Twelve percent of all violent crimes are now committed by females, up slightly over 1% in the past 10 years. The only increases in female violent criminal activity have been in the areas of motor vehicle theft (up 70.1%), aggravated assault (up 56%), and theft (up 9.5%), offsetting decreases in all other categories of violent crimes. Increases in female nonviolent criminal activities were most pronounced in the areas of embezzlement (up 88.6%), other assaults (up 86.7%), and weapons possession (up 53.5%).

Despite the "New Woman" image which has emerged over the past 25 years, women in American society are still imbued with a sense of nonviolence; women tend to be less aggressive, especially physically. While many men express their social or emotional deviance in the form of violence toward others, women tend to exhibit deviant behavior in inward ways (depression and suicide, for instance), ways society accepts as a problem to be solved medically, not through punishment (e.g., Steffensmeier 1980a; Kruttschnitt 1982b). Whether this inclination away from externally directed violence and toward cooperativeness is cultural, genetic, or hormonal, it shows up in the crime statistics. It is also one likely explanation of leniency toward female criminals.

This may help explain the study by Krohn, Curry, and Nelson-Kilges (1983) in which it was discovered that police are simply less likely to refer women for prosecution. Across nearly all offense categories, women were less likely than men to be referred by the police for prosecution. The difference was great when misdemeanors were involved, but only slight when felonies were involved.

Nagel and Weitzman (1971) and Simon (1975) concluded that female offenders receive "preferential treatment" from both the federal and state criminal justice systems. Nagel and Weitzman also noted that women who committed more "manly" offenses, such as assault, were more likely to serve time than were women who committed larceny.

A number of analysts have argued that these two studies from the 1970s, as well as some earlier studies, are flawed. They have pointed out that neither study controlled for prior arrest records or seriousness of offenses, two variables believed to contribute substantially to sentence length, (e.g., Steffensmeier 1980b; Fenster & Mahoney 1981; Frazier, Bock, and Henretta 1983).

However, Mould's (1978) study of California's sentencing practices in felony cases controlled for race, offense, and prior record, and this study still found that fewer women were incarcerated than were their male counterparts. Baab and Furgeson reported similar results from their work in Texas in 1967, as did Frazier, Bock, and Henretta from their 1983 study in Florida.

Frazier, Bock, and Henretta controlled for a dozen social and legal variables and still found that men in their study were 23% more likely to be incarcerated than women who committed the same crime. An interesting aspect of the study was the impact on sentencing of the recommendation of probation officers. The researchers found that irrespective of the gender of the probation officer, women offenders were more often viewed as suffering from psychological or emotional problems, or as victims of family problems, bad marriages, or dependent relationships. Only one man in their study had been described in such terms by the probation officers. Men were more likely to have their cases judged in view of the seriousness of the offense committed, employment history, and prior record.

In other words, the reason for the commission of the crime in the first place was considered inherently different. In yet another twist on traditional views of chivalry, women offenders were much more likely to be viewed as victims of personal relationships or of society, suffering from emotional difficulties which more or less forced them down the road to crime. However, the officers' reports on male offenders were quite likely to describe them as being aggressive, acquisitive, and irresponsible, traits that led them somewhat more naturally to commit criminal acts.

Naturally, these probation officers were far more likely to recommend non-incarceration for offenders who were suffering from emotional and family problems (read: women). Offenders who were considered more dangerous, less responsible, less stable (read: men) were far more likely to face recommendations of imprisonment.

Importantly, when the researchers matched pairs of male and female offenders who shared the same offense, race, marital status, children, age, and prior record, the apparent decisive factor in the sentencing decision of the judge seemed to be the probation officer's reports. Since these reports were more likely to favor nonincarceration for women offenders, fewer women were actually sentenced to serve time in jail. In fact, Frazier, Bock, and Henretta concluded that independent of a long list of other potential influences on the sentencing decision, being female reduced the likelihood of an incarceration recommendation from the probation officer by 22%. Hagan had noted in his 1975 study that probation officers were more likely to consider extralegal variables when they were given a formal advisory role in the court.

Fenster and Mahoney (1981) used a similar matched pair procedure, noting only insignificant differences in sentencing when a woman's prior record and offense were truly similar to a man's. However, they noted that when differences were detected, the more lenient treatment was received by female offenders. Also, the tendency of courts to treat men and women differently grew markedly as the women received distinctly more lenient treatment when their records and offenses were less severe than the men in the study.

Curran (1983) conducted an in-depth study in the courts of Dade County, Florida. She investigated the treatment of women at four stages in the criminal justice process: negotiation, prosecution, conviction, and sentencing. Curran used multiple regression analyses to control for race, age, gender, and occupational status of those who were arrested, as well as their prior arrest records, the seriousness of their offenses, and the total number of counts brought against them. Curran reported that while it did not appear to be advantageous to be female at the negotiating, prosecuting, or convicting stages, it was an advantage to be a woman when it came time for judgment to be pronounced.

Nagel and Hagan (1983) reported similar results, although they determined that women were more likely to be released pending trial than were men. However, gender did not seem to affect the size of the bail that the courts required for release. Like previous researchers, Nagel and Hagan reported finding no difference between men and women at the negotiating, prosecuting, and convicting stages of the criminal justice process. Of course, like many other researchers, they did find some preferential treatment for females at the sentencing stage, although they further reported that the severity of the crime and the defendant's prior record seemed to have a greater effect on the court's sentencing decision than the defendant's gender.

Kruttschnitt's (1984) study of theft, forgery, and drug offenses in Minneapolis attempted to control for a large number of variables, such as offense severity, number of defendants, prior arrests, education, gender, race, age, education, family composition, and employment. They found that the following factors seemed to lead to leniency:

- gender (female)
- race (Caucasian)
- employment (employed)
- prior arrests/pending cases (few or none)
- parental status (children at home)
- offense severity (light maximum statutory penalty)
- age (young)

Kruttschnitt then attempted to pinpoint the factors leading to apparent leniency given to female defendants with regard to pretrial release and sentence severity. She found that when both men and women who have minimal arrest histories are employed, and if they pleaded guilty, they are likely to gain their freedom prior to adjudication. Women who have children at home and who commit less serious crimes are more likely than men to go free at this stage of the criminal process. In the Minneapolis study, 25% of the women were single parents; none of the men was. Herein may lie a significant part of the difference in pretrial treatment of men and women.

Kruttschnitt's findings seem to be borne out in comments made by a small group of female offenders in Nashville, Tennessee. When asked if they expected to be freed prior to trial, each responded affirmatively. (None had committed a crime more violent than assault.) "Hey, the jails is really crowded," said a small-time crack user and seller. "Ain't no room for the likes o' me in there."

One woman was upset that she had been held in jail for several hours following her arrest for receiving stolen property and that her arrest had been publicized. "I told 'em I hadn't personally done nothin' wrong. Joe (not his real name) was just keepin' stuff at my place, that's all. I didn't know where it came from. So why they want to make me lose my job, huh?" Then an older woman summed up the feelings of all simply and directly: "Only 'real' criminals and stupid women sit in jail."

Kruttschnitt then studied factors leading to leniency for women in sentence severity. She concluded that judges weigh offense severity and arrest history as the two most important factors in determining appropriate sentence length. Therefore, it is only logical that women be treated with greater leniency because they tend to commit less serious crimes and have shorter "rap sheets."

One of the Nashville women who had been arrested relayed a story whose outcome Kruttschnitt probably would have predicted. "It was my first offense. I felt embarrassed and dumb. I was scared something terrible. A woman who claimed to have been arrested more times than she could count asked me what I was in for. When she found out no one was hurt and I'd never been arrested before, she told me not to 'break a sweat'—that's what she said, not to 'break a sweat'—'cause they'd end up letting me go. And though they scared me a lot, she was right. They let me go."

Kruttschnitt also suggested that a woman's social status and respectability in the community may affect how she is treated throughout the criminal justice procedure. When a small-town judge was asked about a local significant shoplifting case which resulted only in a small fine and neither publicity nor criminal record for the prominent woman involved, the response merely was, "She had learned her lesson."

When it was suggested that the outcome of the case may have been attributable to the offender's gender and community position, the judge replied, "I'd have done the same thing if it had involved her husband." While the response turned aside the gender preference claim, it merely reinforced the community standing issue.

Some researchers would agree with the judge that gender plays little, if any, role in the criminal justice system and have concluded that chivalry virtually does not exist in the police and court structures. For instance, Ghali and Chesney-Lind's (1986) study of criminal records accumulated during 1979–1980 in Honolulu concluded that police were actually tougher on women than on men. They concluded that police were more likely to press for prosecution of arrested women, that prosecutors were likely to continue this bias against women, that women were more likely to plead guilty, that dismissal of cases was no more likely for women, and that sentencing results were indistinguishable between men and women. However, even this study concluded that women do, in fact, receive preferential treatment when it comes to imprisonment for felonious activities. Prison sentences were, in a word, shorter for women than for men.

One must note that Ghali and Chesney-Lind's study took place in Hawaii. It is impossible to know whether the Hawaiian culture had a role to play in the results of this study. American subculture had no perceptible effect on a study done by Daly (1989b). She interviewed 20 male judges and three female judges in New York and Massachusetts. Daly found that women were generally less likely to receive long prison sentences than men. She found "paternalistic attitudes" to be fairly pervasive, but the paternalism was directed less at women than at their families. The judges seemed to deem mothers who care for children as "good" and women who did not take care of their children as "irresponsible." "Good" women were likely to be treated with judicial leniency, while "irresponsible" women were not.

Likewise, Daly discovered this family protection motivation alive and well when it came time to sentence men. Since these judges rated the direct care of children as their highest consideration and financial support of a family as their second most important concern, male defendants who had jobs and supported their families were also treated with greater leniency than those without jobs and families. These same judges rated men and women who had families as better probation risks than single people without families. Daly reasoned that the judges considered the substantial social costs of sending men and women to jail when those men and women were responsible for the support of families.

In a separate study, Daly (1989a) compared the sentencing differences between black, Hispanic, and white (Anglo) men and women in the courts of Seattle and New York. She reportedly found a consistent leniency in sentencing toward men and women, irrespective of race or culture, if the defendants were supporting families. However, the courts in these two locales tended to be even more lenient in sentencing women who were supporting families than men who were supporting families. In Seattle, Daly found that women who were separated or divorced also received sentencing leniency if they had children or some other type of family ties.

This fairly consistent finding—that women receive preferential treatment in sentencing—may have little to do with traditional chivalry theory or paternalistic judicial systems. Steffensmeier (1980a) and Parisi (1982) concluded that difference in sentencing may represent nothing more than pragmatism. Since so many convicted females are single parents, it only makes sense that the courts would not want to break up families and do more harm than good by injuring innocent children through lengthy sentences for mothers. "If she (the offender) appears to be a decent mother," says a judge, "sentencing her to jail time would probably just exacerbate the harm that her criminal activity has already caused."

Steffensmeier's study is particularly interesting, because he studied sentencing patterns in Arizona after the state passed a determinate sentencing statute that should have eliminated much of the gender-based differences in sentencing. Nonetheless, Steffensmeier, who controlled for prior record, weapon use, injury to victim, and severity of offense, reported finding favorable treatment toward women when it came time to negotiate the charge(s) with the prosecutor, when sentence length was announced, and when probation was granted rather than prison confinement. Only women convicted of the most serious and violent felonies received no preferential treatment.

In fact, Bernstein, Cardascia, and Ross reported in 1979 that sentencing for women in their study was actually more severe if they were convicted of violent crimes; the type of crimes not normally committed by women. Women who commit "counter-type" or atypical crimes—crimes normally committed by men—are not likely to receive kid-glove treatment in the criminal justice system.

In 1987 Johnston, Kennedy, and Shuman studied the sentencing of 2,500 felony offenders in Arizona (Phoenix) under the state's determinate sentencing law. Despite the intent of the sentencing law to assure uniform treatment of criminals, determinate sentencing laws do not work as intended because prosecutors negotiate with criminal offenders for reduced charges. A felon will not be sentenced to a life sentence for a Class 1 (sometimes called a Class A) felony, when the prosecutor agrees to forego a trial in return for a guilty plea to a Class 2 (Class B) felony. Hence, plea bargaining has a major impact on sentencing and jail time, especially in a state with a determinate sentencing law.

The 2,500 offenders in the Phoenix study were divided almost equally between men and women. Approximately 90% of the cases in Phoenix during the study years (1979–1983) were determined by guilty pleas to the original or reduced charges. Women were significantly more likely than men to plead guilty to a reduced charge rather than the more serious original charge. Consequently, with the direct link between charge and sentencing, it is not surprising that women also were far less likely to do any jail time. In fact, in the study, men were almost twice as likely as women to be incarcerated. The percentage of men who were incarcerated exceeded the percentage of women incarcerated across all conviction offense categories. Furthermore, men were more likely to receive longer sentences than women, although the differences diminished greatly when women committed truly serious crimes.

Charge reduction and the effect of gender on the plea negotiation process was studied by Bishop and Frazier (1984). They studied plea negotiation in one Florida judicial district and concluded that women fared no better than men in this criminal justice stage. They conceded, however, that it is possible that women in the study had originally been undercharged, that is, charged with a lesser offense than a man would be charged with under similar circumstances. Therefore, it would not be likely that a further reduction in the charges would be forthcoming.

Nonetheless, studies of crime data from Washington, D.C., by Simon and Sharma (1979) and Figueiria-McDonough (1982) suggest that it is no advantage to be female when charged with a crime in the nation's capital. In fact, since men are more likely to commit serious crimes, and since these crimes tend to be plea bargained, women appeared to be at some disadvantage since their charges were seldom plea bargained. In addition, men who pleaded guilty received lighter sentences than men who pleaded guilty to lesser charges or who pleaded innocent. The same was not true for women offenders.

Obviously, since these studies took place in Washington, D.C., it seems appropriate to ask if a degree of racism may be entering the picture, clouding the results. Spohn, Welch, and Gruhl (1985) reviewed many of the major studies of the treatment of women offenders by the courts and also wondered if race played a factor in the outcome. Therefore, they studied 50,000 of the 12 most common crimes committed over an 11-year period in a major city in the Northeast, which they called "Metro City." They compared the cases based on the answers to the following questions.

1. What is the defendant's race?
2. What is the defendant's sex?
3. What is the defendant's prior criminal record?
4. Was the accused defended by a public defender or a private attorney?
5. Did the accused plead guilty or not guilty?
6. Was the accused released on bail or detained?
7. If the accused was released on bail, what was the size of the bail?
8. Was the charge reduced from the original charge?
9. What was the sex of the sentencing judge?

The researchers did not attempt to control for three variables that they concede could have made a difference in the outcome: marital status of accused, number of children the accused supported, and the recommendation of the parole officer.

This extensive study found that women were about half as likely as men to be incarcerated, even though the study did not control for marital status and children. However, race seemed to play a role in the incarceration rates of black men, 25% of whom were sentenced to time in jail. This finding comes as no surprise when one considers that a black man is roughly three times as likely as a white man to find himself imprisoned at some point in his life. Incarceration rates for black women (18%) and white men (17%) were roughly the same. Both groups were, statistically speaking, significantly less likely to be sentenced to incarceration than were black males. Perhaps the difference in the incarceration rates of black men and women does not so much represent chivalrous treatment of women as it does discrimination against black males, since black women and white men were sentenced similarly.

Meanwhile, the number of white female offenders was too small to use in conducting statistical comparisons, but that fact itself speaks volumes about the apparent low criminality rates (or, at least, low prosecution rates) for white females. The few white women whose cases were part of the study received the most lenient treatment, with only 15% being incarcerated.

> A woman offender who was interviewed for this essay had helped her boyfriend rob a store. She sat staring out the window, smoking a cigarette, talking. "I know he's in for a long time, and I'm out here waitin' for him. Don't get me wrong. I'd rather be out here, but somethin' just don't seem right. We went into that store together."

Conclusion

Two hundred years ago Edmund Burke announced to the world that "[t]he age of chivalry has gone." Maybe so, maybe not. In America's criminal justice system the remnants of chivalry may yet be waving its banner, however diminished. While a number of researchers have effectively argued against its continued existence, it seems they cannot quite extinguish the final flickering flames.

A large body of research exists which at least suggests that women receive more lenient treatment than men at various stages of the criminal justice process. Are women less likely than men to be arrested, less likely to be charged; more likely to be charged with a lesser crime, more likely to be freed pending trial, less likely to be convicted, and more likely to be sentenced to probation or a short period of incarceration? While no one would contend that all women receive more lenient treatment than men, or more lenient treatment at every phase of the criminal justice process, it does appear that some women do receive "special treatment." Is this the result of chivalry or paternalism? Who can say? We can say only that preferential treatment sometimes exists for some women.

Clearly, white women receive greater deference than women of color or men. Women of maturity, status, respectability, and mothers of minor children all appear to receive some leniency. In addition, women who commit less serious crimes, nonviolent crimes, and victimless crimes all appear to benefit from a degree of favoritism exhibited by the police, prosecutors, and the courts. Call it chivalry or call it pragmatism: it results in the exact same outcome. Men, especially black men, are more likely to be incarcerated than are women. Only women who commit counter-type, "manly" offenses are as likely as men to serve lengthy sentences.

References

Adler, F. (1975). *Sisters in crime: The rise of the new female criminal.* New York: McGraw-Hill.

Anderson, E. (1976). The "chivalrous" treatment of the female offender in the arms of the criminal justice system: A review of the literature. *Social Problems* 23: 350–357.

Armstrong, G. (1977). Females under the law—protected but unequal. *Crime and Delinquency* 23: 109–120.

Baab, G., & Furgeson, W. (1967). Texas sentencing practices: A statistical study. *Texas Law Review* 45: 471–503.

Bernstein, I., Cardascia, J., & Ross, C. (1979). Defendant's sex and criminal court decision. In R. Alvarez & K. Letterman and Associates (eds.), *Discrimination in organizations*. San Francisco: Jossey-Bass.

Bernstein, I., Kick, E., Leung, J., & Schultz, B. (1977). Charge reduction: An intermediary stage in the process of labeling criminal defendants. *Social Forces,* 56: 362–384.

Bishop, D., & Frazier, C. (1984). The effects of gender on charge reduction. *Sociological Quarterly* 25(3), 385–396.

Burney, E. (1985). All things to all men. *Criminal Law Journal* 9: 284–293.

Cernkovich, S.A., & Giordano, P. C. (1979). A comparative analysis of male and female delinquency. *Sociological Quarterly* 20: 131–145.

Chesney-Lind, M. (1973). Judicial enforcement of the female sex role: The family court and the female delinquent. *Issues in Criminology* 8: 51–59.

——— (1977). Judicial paternalism and the female offender: Training women to know their place. *Crime and Delinquency* 23: 121–130.

——— (1986). Women and crime: The female offender. *Sigma: Journal of Women in Culture and Society* 12: 78–96.

——— (1987). Female offenders: Paternalism re-examined. In L.L. Crites & W. Hepperle (Eds.), *Women, the courts, and equality* (pp. 114–139). Newberry Park, CA: Sage.

Crites, L. (1978). Women in the criminal court. In W.L. Hepperle and L. Crites (eds.). *Women in courts.* Williamsburg, VA: National Center for State Courts.

Curran, D. (1983). Judicial discretion and defendant's sex. *Criminology* 21: 41–58.

Daly, K. (1989a). Neither conflict nor labeling nor paternalism will suffice: Interactions of race, ethnicity, gender, and family in criminal court decisions. *Crime and Delinquency* 35(1): 136–168.

——— (1989b). Rethinking judicial paternalism: Gender, work-family relations, and sentencing. *Gender and Society* 3(1): 9–36.

Federal Bureau of Investigation (1991). *Crime in the United States: Uniform crime reports—1990*. Washington, DC: U.S. Department of Justice, Bureau of Justice Statistics.

Feinman, C. (1980). *Women in the criminal justice system*. New York: Praeger.

Fenster, C., & Mahoney, A. (1981). The effect of prior record upon the sentencing of male-female co-defendants. *Justice System Journal* 6: 262–271.

Figueiria-McDonough, J. (1982). Gender differences in informal processing: A look at charge bargaining and sentence reduction in Washington, D.C. Paper presented at the American Society of Criminology, Toronto, Canada.

Foley, L., & Rasche, C. (1976). A longitudinal study of sentencing patterns for female offenders. Presented at the annual meeting of the American Society of Criminology, Chicago, IL.

Frazier, C., Bock, E., & Henretta, J. (1983). The role of probation officers in determining gender differences in sentencing severity. *Sociological Quarterly* 24: 305–318.

Ghali, M., & Chesney-Lind, M. (1986). Gender bias and the criminal justice system: An emperical investigation. *Sociology and Society Research* 70: 164–171.

Gibbons, T.C.N., & Prince, J. (1962). *Shoplifting*. London: ISTD.

Hagan, J. (1975). The social and legal construction of criminal justice: A study of the presentence process. *Social Problems* 11(June): 620–637.

Johnston, J.B., Kennedy, T.D., & Shuman, I. (1987). Gender differences in the sentencing of felony offenders. *Federal Probation* 51: 49–55.

Julian, F. (1990–1991). Interviews with anonymous misdemeanants and felons, a judge, prosecuting attorney, defense counsel, and police officer in Tennessee, West Virginia, and Kentucky.

Krohn, M.D., Curry, J.P., & Nelson-Kilger, S. (1983). Is chivalry dead? An analysis of changes in police dispositions of males and females. *Criminology* 21: 417–438.

Kruttschnitt, C. (1982a). Respectable women and the law. *Sociological Quarterly* 23 221–234.

———(1982b). Women, crime, and dependency. *Criminology* 19: 495–513.

———(1984). Sex and criminal court dispositions: The unresolved controversy. *Journal of Research in Crime and Delinquency* 21(3): 213–232.

Lombroso, C. (1899). *The female offender.* New York: Appleton Publishers.

Miller, J., Rossi, P., & Simpson, J. (1986). Perceptions of justice: Race and gender differences in judgments of appropriate prison sentences. *Law & Society Review* 20(3): 313–334.

Mould, E. (1978). Chivalry and paternalism-disparities of treatment in the criminal justice system. *Western Political Quarterly* 31: 416–430.

Nagel, I., Cardascia, J., & Ross, C.E. (1982). Sex differences in the processing of criminal defendants. In D.K. Weisberg (Ed.), *Women and the law, A social historical perspective: Vol. 1, Women and criminal Law* (pp. 121–148). Cambridge, MA: Schenkman.

Nagel, I., & Hagan, J. (1982). Gender and crime: Offense patterns and criminal court sanctions. In M. Tonry & N. Morris (Eds.), *Crime and justice: An annual review of research* (Vol. 4) (pp.91–144). Chicago: University of Chicago Press.

Nagel, S., & Weitzman, L. (1971). Women as litigants. *Hastings Law Journal* 23: 171–198.

——— (1972). Double standard of American justice. *Society* 9: 18–25.

Parisi, N. (1982). Are females treated differently? In N. Rafter & E. Stanko (Eds.), *Judge, lawyer, victim, thief.* Boston: Northeastern University Press.

Simon, R. (1975). *Women and crime.* Lexington, MA: D.C. Heath.

Simon, R.J., & Sharma, N. (1979). *The female defendant in Washington, D.C.: 1974 and 1975.* Washington, DC: Institute for Law and Social Research.

Simpson, S. (1989). Feminist theory, crime, and justice. *Criminology* 27(4): 605–621.

Smart, C. (1976). *Women, crime, and criminology: A feminist critique.* London: Routledge and Kegan Paul.

Spohn, C., Welch, S., & Gruhl, J. (1985). Women defendants in court: The interaction between sex and race in convicting and sentencing. *Social Science Quarterly* 66(1): 178–184.

Spohn, C., Gruhl, J., & Welch, S. (1987). The impact of the ethnicity and gender of defendants on the decision to reject or dismiss felony charges. *Criminology* 25(1): 175–191.

Steffensmeier, D. (1980a). Assessing the impact of the women's movement on sex-based differences in the handling of adult criminal defendants. *Crime and Delinquency* 26: 344–357.

——— (1980b). Sex differences in patterns of adult crimes, 1965–77: A review and assessment. *Social Forces* 58(4): 1080–1108.

Thomas, D. (1988). Sentencing: Some current questions. *Current Legal Problems* 41: 115–133.

Tjaden, P., & Tjaden, C. (1981). Differential treatment of the female felon: Myth or reality? In M. Warren (Ed.), *Comparing female and male offenders.* Beverly Hills: Sage.

Visher, C.A. (1983). Gender, police arrest decisions, and notions of chivalry. *Criminology* 21(1): 5–28.

Zimmerman, S., Van Alstyne, D., & Christopher, S.D. (1988). The national punishment survey and public policy consequences. *Journal of Research in Crime and Delinquency* 25: 120–149.

A Comparative Analysis of Female Felons: Some Recent Trends in Sentencing Severity Compared with a Matched Sample of Male Offenders

Dean J. Champion
California State University, Long Beach

Abstract

An analysis of female felons in six states (Florida, Georgia, Alabama, Virginia, Tennessee, and Kentucky) for the period 1983–1988 discloses several trends, including increased sentencing severity proportionately for females compared with a matched sample of male offenders, a general shift in the nature of female offending from property crimes to more violent offenses, and proportionately longer lengths of incarceration.

A profile of offenses is provided on a year-by-year basis, as well as an analysis of recent trends through interviews with prosecutors and judges in the jurisdictions examined. No evidence is presently available about whether crime among females is increasing, although female offenders in these jurisdictions appear to receive comparatively harsher sentences in later years compared with past years. Thus, although females continue to receive less-harsh sentences from judges compared with matched samples of males with similar prior records, social histories, and personal characteristics, the harshness of sentences imposed by judges upon convicted female offenders is gradually increasing. Some convergence of sentencing severity for both males and females is apparent.

According to the 1989 *Uniform Crime Reports*, women accounted for 18% of all index offense arrests (U.S. Department of Justice 1990). For those more serious index offense categories, women accounted for 11% of all violent crime arrests and approximately 24% of all property crime arrests. In 1986, women accounted for only 4% of inmates of jails and prisons (Stephan 1987), although this figure increased to approximately 9% by 1989 (Bessette 1990a, 1990b). Furthermore, 12% of all probationers in 1989 were women, while females accounted for nearly 15% of all parolees.

While it is difficult to draw absolute conclusions from these figures, two implications are that (a) proportionately larger numbers of women are diverted from the criminal justice system annually and (b) disproportionately larger numbers of convicted females who remain within the criminal justice system consistently receive less-severe punishments at most stages compared with their male counterparts. Viewed another way, crime for crime, there are proportionately fewer incarcerations of females compared with males, and proportionately greater numbers of females are involved in nonincarcerative conditional punishment programs, including probation and parole.

There are inconsistent reports, depending upon the source, about how women are treated in the courts. For instance, a 1986 report by the New York State Task Force on Women in the Courts concluded the following:

> Women are often denied equal justice, equal treatment, and equal opportunity. Women, uniquely, disproportionately, and with unacceptable frequency, must endure a climate of condescension, indifference, and hostility. Female litigants have limited access to the courts, are denied credibility, and face a judiciary underinformed about matters integral to many women's welfare. (pp. 1–3)

Figueira-McDonough's (1985) study noted:

> Most previous studies of gender disparities have focused on sentencing and have found no discrimination, . . . that women were less able to plea bargain and more willing to plead guilty than men, . . . that concerning the other aspect of plea bargaining, sentence reduction, women were also less comparative losers in the process, in

that judges did not reward women as frequently as men for their guilty pleas by imposing more lenient sentences. (pp. 102–103)

However, the preponderance of evidence in the research literature suggests that gender differences do exist, that they exist in sentencing as well as in plea bargaining, and that they overwhelmingly show substantial judicial leniency toward women compared with men who are charged with and/or convicted of similar crimes. For example, a study of 2,500 male and female first-offenders in Arizona conducted by Johnston, Kennedy, and Shuman (1987) showed that women received greater leniency in charge bargaining, prison confinement, and sentence length.

Also, Kruttschnitt and McCarthy (1985) studied over 2,900 male and female offenders during the period 1965–1980 in Minneapolis and found evidence of gender-based leniency in pretrial release and incarceration decisions favoring women. A study of sentencing of men and women in Pennsylvania by Kempinen (1983) also showed that women consistently received more-lenient sentences than men, when similar crimes had been committed. Kempinen did note, however, that gender-based sentencing disparities appeared to be diminishing in later years compared with comparative sentencing differences in previous years. Finally, Zingraff and Thomson (1984) studied 9,500 male and female felons in North Carolina for the period 1969–1977. They found that women consistently received shorter sentences compared with men when convicted of the same crimes.

The Present Study

In view of previous research, the present investigation sought to determine (a) whether women in selected jurisdictions receive greater leniency in sentencing compared with males convicted of similar offenses, (b) whether any observed sentencing leniency patterns have continued over the years, (c) whether any observed sentencing leniency is associated with particular kinds of offenses, and (d) whether there are any trends that would suggest diminishing gender-based sentencing disparities over time.

Sentencing data were available from trial court records in Florida, Georgia, Alabama, Kentucky, Virginia, and Tennessee for the years 1983–1988. Compared with other states, these jurisdictions have fairly high rates of female incarcerations, although several states other than those investigated here have substantially higher female incarceration rates. California presently has the highest rate of female incarcerations and the highest rate of female inmate prison and jail populations, while Florida ranks second in the rate of female incarcerations. By comparison, Kentucky has the smallest number of female incarcerations among the present sample of investigated jurisdictions.

Random samples of convicted female felons were obtained for each of the jurisdictions for the years 1983–1988. Available sentencing data for each year disclosed information about sentencing severity and whether or not these convicted offenders were incarcerated. The measure of sentencing severity used in the present research was determined by identifying the *actual sentence imposed (AS)* (numbers of months) against the statutory *maximum possible sentence (MS)* (again, calculated in numbers of months) the judge could impose for each conviction offense. This yielded an "actual sentence" (AS) and "maximum sentence" (MS) ratio, or an *AS/MS ratio.* Probation or any other nonincarcerative alternative (shock probation, intermediate punishments) was counted as a "0" for purposes of determining the amount of sentencing severity.

A second computation was made only for those female felons who received a sentence of incarceration. This was again calculated in terms of numbers of months and was *the ratio of the actual number of months sentenced to incarceration against the statutory maximum number of months of incarceration that the judge could impose.* To distinguish this ratio from the former AS/MS severity measure, the designation *ASI (actual sentence of incarceration)/MSI (maximum sentence of incarceration)* was used, or simply, the *ASI/MSI ratio.*

In order to determine general trends, aggregate figures were examined, regardless of the individual state selected. Table 1 shows overall AS/MS ratios for the samples of 3,943 female felons for the years 1983–1988. Furthermore, AS/MS ratios are shown according to whether violent or property crimes were the particular conviction offenses.

Table 1
AS/MS Ratios (Sentencing Severity) for 3,943 Convicted Female Felons in Six Southern States, by Violent or Property Offense, 1983–1988

	All Offenses	Conviction Offenses	
Year	Overall AS/MS Ratio	Property Crime %	Violent Crime %
1983	.14	.14	.19
1984.	.14	.16	.20
1985	.17	.15	.22
1986	.17	.18	.23
1987	.18	.19	.23
1988	.23	.18	.25
Totals: (*n*) =	3,943 (100%)	3,723 (83%)	670 (17%)

Table 1 shows a systematic increase in the overall AS/MS ratio in these jurisdictions for these female felons, rising from 0.14 in 1983 to 0.23 in 1988. On the basis of property versus violent offenses, although both AS/MS ratios increased during this same time period, the greater gain was for violent offenses, from 0.19 to 0.25 in 1988. The AS/MS ratio for property crimes fluctuated between 0 14 and 0.19. Approximately 83% of these women were convictec of property offenses, while about 17% were convicted of violent crimes.

Table 2 shows ASI/MSI ratios for those women incarcerated as the result of sentences imposed. Again, figures are shown for all offense categories and for property/violent categories.

Table 2 shows systematic increases in incarceration rates for the period 1983–1988, although the overall incarceration rate for all 3,943 convicted female felons is low or about 11%. Compared with national figures, the 11% incarceration rate is somewhat high, although several of these states have large numbers of incarcerated women in their prison and jail populations. For different offense categories, violent female offenders were incarcerated at a greater rate and for longer periods compared with property offenders. Increases in incarceration rates were observed for both offense categories over the years, and the rate differences remained fairly consistent.

Table 2
ASI/MSI Ratios for Female Felons According to Property and Violent Offenses, 1983–1988

			Conviction offense			
			Property		Violent	
Year	Overall ASI/MSI Ratios	*n*	ASI/MSI Ratio	*n*	ASi/MSI Ratio	*n*
1983	.05	45	.03	17	.08	30
1984	.07	55	.03	15	.08	39
1985	.07	62	.04	22	.10	49
1986	.08	67	.06	29	.13	47
1987	.10	75	.08	42	.14	48
1988	.13	132	.10	40	.16	58
Totals(*n*) =	436 (100%)		165 (38%)		271 (62%)	

In order to see whether male offenders convicted of similar crimes and with similar prior records and social backgrounds received similar sentences in the same jurisdictions, the female offenders for each year were matched on selected salient variables with samples of male offenders, controlling for race, conviction offense, prior record, age, and several other demographic and socioeconomic variables. Male matches for sentenced female felons were drawn exclusively from those courts where the same judges sentenced both offenders. Thus, no contamination was introduced by comparing males sentenced by one judge with females sentenced by another judge within the same jurisdiction. No attempt was made to randomize the selection of male offenders. Once a match for a particular female felon was found, the next match was sought. ASI/MSI ratios were computed for all incarcerated male offenders, compared with the original female sample for the six-year period. These ratios are shown overall and for both property and violent offense categories, by year and gender, in Table 3.

Table 3
Matched Samples of Male Offenders Compared with 436 Incarcerated Female Offenders for the Years 1983–1988, by Year and Gender

	Overall		Conviction offense			
	ASI/MSI Ratios		Property		Violent	
Year	Males	Females	Males	Females	Males	Females
1983	.18	.05	.18	.06	.36	.08
1984	.18	.06	.20	.06	.38	.10
1985	.17	.05	.20	.07	.34	.09
1986	.16	.08	.22	.09	.32	.12
1987	.15	.10	.24	.10	.31	.13
1988	.15	.11	.29	.10	.31	.16
Averages	.24	.09	.22	.07	.33	.12

Table 3 discloses substantial incarceration rate differences for male and female offenders convicted of similar offenses and having similar prior records and other salient characteristics. Overall ASI/MSI ratios for the matched samples of male and female offenders were 0.24 and 0.09, respectively. Interestingly, in both the property and violent offense categories, males compared with females had substantially higher ASI/MSI ratios, more than twice as large for property offenses and almost three times as great for violent offenses.

higher ASI/MSI ratios, more than twice as large for property offenses and almost three times as great for violent offenses.

However, between 1983 and 1988, the overall magnitude of differences for each offense category tended to decrease. Despite this decrease, marked disparities in sentences imposed for all offense categories according to gender continued to exist. In 1988, the overall male ASI/MSI ratio was 0.15 compared with 0.11 for females. For property offenses, the ASI/MSI ratio for males was 0.22 compared with 0.07 for females, and for violent offenses, these differences were 0.33 and 0.12, respectively. Thus, it appears that for the samples of male and female felons examined here, judges seem more likely to impose more-severe sentences for males than for females, at least in terms of sentence lengths. This severity and disparity also extends to the rate of incarceration as well.

Discussion and Commentary

It is still too early to tell whether these figures are representative of most U.S. jurisdictions. First, there is some question about whether these jurisdictions are generally typical of other U.S. jurisdictions, since there are proportionately larger numbers of incarcerated female offenders in these state and local prison and jail facilities compared with many other states. Second, the matching process in research is always risky, since there are always variables that may be overlooked and that are more important than those used for matching purposes here. However, it was believed that matching these convicted felons according to their age, race, socioeconomic characteristics, prior records, and other pertinent demographic data, together with controlling for the judges who sentenced both types of offenders, did much to equate the two samples compared.

Furthermore, other measures of sentencing severity exist which may be more reliable than those used here. However, the construction and application of these measures seemed reasonable and disclosed sentencing disparities consistent with those found in other research.

The primary conclusions drawn here are that (a) female offenders continue to receive greater leniency in sentencing compared with matched samples of male felons convicted of the same crimes; (b) these disparities in sentencing appear to be decreasing over the years examined, although not at a rate that would allow us to say that judges are totally uninfluenced by gender in their sentencing practices; and (c) the rate of female incarcerations in these jurisdictions appears to be increasing. This latter finding is consistent across all offense categories.

Drastic changes have occurred in the type of sentencing system used in each of these jurisdictions which are designed to minimize sentencing disparities, so that offenders, regardless of whether they are male or female, will be subject to the same criminal penalties, including incarceration, and for similar durations. Some indication is provided here that sentencing reforms in these jurisdictions are bringing disparate sentences of males and females closer together, although there are still considerable discrepancies observed in view of these sentencing reforms.

Disparities in sentencing, where similar crimes are committed by offenders with similar backgrounds, are not wholly assignable to judicial biases. Prosecutors and others earlier in the criminal justice system, such as the police, share some of the blame for perpetuating gender-based discrepancies between how male and female offenders are treated. Police officers, for instance, continue to display an inordinate amount of conventionalism relating to arrests of female suspects. Many prosecutors continue to view female felon prosecutions as generally unpopular among the public, and such prosecutions seem to be unpopular. Executions of female felons for capital crimes are rare, although many females have been convicted of first-degree murders in various states with death penalty provisions. Jury sympathy is extended more often toward females than toward males, since often, female offenders have children and are portrayed by their defense counsels in motherly roles. If juries are persuaded toward leniency for females convicted of serious crimes, why should judges be excluded from possessing similar sentiments? In view of existing research, there is a strong empirical basis for linking judicial discretion, gender-based justice, and maternal influence (Zingraff & Thomson 1984).

Plea bargaining is undoubtedly susceptible to gender influence, and this influence continues to be exhibited in many jurisdictions. More research is needed across a greater variety of jurisdictions in order to make more definitive conclusions about the impact of gender and other related variables upon sentencing generally. There is no question that gender-based sentencing disparities presently exist. Also, there is no question that many of the recently undertaken sentencing reforms from indeterminate to determinate sentencing and to guidelines-based sentencing are intended to rectify these gender-based disparities as well as disparities attributable to race and socioeconomic status. The question is whether there is any indication that these disparities will be eliminated in the near future, or if gender-based differential treatment in the criminal justice system will continue.

References

Bessette, J.M. (1990a). *Jail inmates 1989*. Washington, DC: U.S. Department of Justice.

——— (1990b). *Prisoners in 1989*. Washington, DC: U.S. Department of Justice.

Brantingham, P. (1985). Sentencing disparity: An analysis of judicial consistency. *Journal of Quantitative Criminology* 1: 281–305.

Figueira-McDonough, J. (1985). Gender differences in informal processing: A look at charge bargaining and sentence reduction in Washington, DC. *Journal of Research on Crime and Delinquency* 13: 101–133.

Gertz, M.G., & Price, A.C. (1985). Variables influencing sentencing severity: Intercourt differences in Connecticut. *Journal of Criminal Justice* 13: 131–139.

Ghali, M., & Chesney-Lind, M. (1986). Gender bias and the criminal justice system: An empirical investigation. *Sociology and Social Research* 70: 164–171.

Greenfeld, L.A. (1989). *Prisoners in 1989*. Washington, DC: U.S. Department of Justice.

Johnston, J.B., Kennedy, T.D., & Shuman, G.I. (1987). Gender differences in the sentencing of felony offenders. *Federal Probation* 51: 49–55.

Kempinen, C. (1983). Changes in the sentencing patterns of male and female defendants. *Prison Journal* 63: 3–11.

Kruttschnitt, C., & Green, D.E. (1985). The sex-sanctioning issue: Is it history? *American Sociological Review* 49(1): 541–551.

Kruttschnitt, C., & McCarthy, D. (1985). Familial social control and pretrial sanctions: Does sex really matter? *Journal of Criminal Law and Criminology* 76: 151–175.

New York State Task Force on Women in the Courts (1986) *Report*. New York: New York State Unified Court System.

Peterson, R.D., & Hagan, J. (1984). Changing conceptions of race: Towards an account of anomalous findings of sentencing research. *American Sociological Review* 49(1): 56–70.

Pollack, H., & Smith, A.B. (1983). White collar v. street crime sentencing disparity: How judges see the problem. *Judicature* 67: 174–182.

Pruitt, C.R., & Wilson, J.Q. (1983). A longitudinal study of the effect of race on sentencing. *Law and Society Review* 17: 613–635.

Stephan, J.J. (1987). *1984 Census of state correlational facilities.* Washington, DC: U.S. Department of Justice.

U.S. Department of Justice (1987). *Uniform crime reports.* Washington, DC: U.S. Government Printing Office.

——— (1990). *Uniform crime reports.* Washington, DC: U.S. Government Printing Office.

Welch, S., Gruhl, J., & Spohn, C. (1984). Sentencing: The influence of alternative measures of prior record. *Criminology* 22: 215–227.

Zatz, M.S. (1987). The changing forms of racial/ethnic biases in sentencing. *Journal of Research on Crime and Delinquency* 24: 69–92.

Zingraff, M., & Thomson, R. (1984). Differential sentencing of women and men in the U.S.A. *International Journal of the Sociology of Law* 12: 401–413.

Women in Prison

Rita J. Simon
The American University

In 1987, about 22 out of 100 persons arrested for serious crimes were women. In the same year, about 10 out of 100 persons convicted of serious crimes were women, but only about 5 out of every 100 persons sentenced to a federal or state prison were women. As of December 1987, of the approximately 580,000 inmates in state and federal prisons, 29,000 were women. At the present time, there are 5 federal institutions for women, 24 for men, and 7 that are coed. There are 51 state institutions for women, 536 for men, and 19 that are coed.

Table 1 shows the percentage of women compared to men who were sentenced to all of the federal and state institutions for the years 1971–1987. Note that for the past one and a half decades, the percentage of women in federal prisons has ranged from 3.7 to 6.3; and in state prisons, in which the bulk of inmates are housed, the percentage of women has remained virtually unchanged at 4.8. These data indicate that the rate of commitment to prison has not kept up with the rate of female arrests because the *Uniform Crime Reports* show that, in 1970, 16.9% of all arrests for Type I offenses were women, and in 1987, 21.6% of all the arrests for serious offenses were women. In other words, the percentage of women arrested for serious offenses has increased, but the rate at which they have been sentenced to state prisons has remained relatively stable.

Table 2 goes back to 1925 and examines rates of incarcerations by gender. Between 1925 and 1979, the aggregate female incarceration rate ranged from 5 to 10 per 100,000 female population compared to the male range of 149 to 264 per 100,000 male population. From 1979 to 1985, there was an increase in the incarceration rates of both men and women, but the increase for men was substantially greater. From 1980 to 1985, the male rate increased from 274 per 100,000 to 394 per 100,000, while the female rate increased from 11 per 100,000 to 17 per 100,000.

Table 3 shows the types of institutions to which men and women are committed at the federal and state levels. Note that three times as many men as women have been committed to maximum and closed institutions at the federal level and twice as many at the state level.

In 1988, among the women assigned to maximum security prisons, 15% were on death row. Between 1981 and 1988, the percentage of women on death row ranged from 8% in 1981 to a high of 17% in 1987.

By and large, however, the types of prisons to which men and women are sent reflect the type of offenses for which they were committed. As the data in Tables 4 through 6 show, the absolute number of women sentenced to prison for homicide usually has been less than 100 per year in three of the most populous states: California, New York, and Pennsylvania. For every year, the data across all three states show that for each type of offense for which they are found guilty, men are more likely than women to be sentenced to prison (see California Dept. of Justice 1988; New York State Division of Criminal Justice Services 1988; Pennsylvania Commission on Crime and Delinquency 1987).

Note also that within each state, the ordering of the types of crimes for which defendants are most likely to receive a prison sentence does not differ noticeably between men and women. The two most likely offenses are homicide and robbery. In Pennsylvania and California, they are followed by burglary; in New York, drug violation is the third most frequent offense for which men and women are most likely to be sentenced to prison. In California, there is no difference in the rank ordering for all six types of offenses between men and women. The differences that occur in Pennsylvania and New York are slight and cover offenses involving assault, burglary, theft, fraud, and drugs.

Table 7 compares the offenses for which men and women were sentenced to all state prisons in 1979 and 1986. In 1986, women represented a smaller percentage of the violent offenders than they did in 1979 (40.7% as opposed to 48.9%). For the violent offenses, murder and robbery are most frequently cited for both men and women. Among the property offenses, women are more likely to be committed for fraud and theft than they are for burglary, whereas men are most likely to be committed for burglary.

Table 8 shows the age and education of inmates of federal and state correctional institutions from 1960 to 1980 as recorded in the decennial U.S. Census report. Most notable is the increased educational levels of all inmates under custody. By 1980, approximately 27% of all male inmates and 22% of all females under federal custody had some college education compared to 1960 when only 9% of the males and 5% of the females had attended college. State inmates show a similar pattern. In 1960, 4% of the males and 5% of the females had some college education. These percentages jumped to 18% of the men and 19% of the women in 1980. Approximately one-third of all federal and state inmates had a high school education by 1980. In 1960, over 50% of the men and women had an elementary school education. In 1980, that percentage dropped to 22% for the men and 20% for the women.

The age distribution of inmates has not changed much over the years, save perhaps for a slight shift from a smaller percentage of male and female inmates in the 30 to 39 age range and a larger percentage in the 20 to 24 age range.

Table 9 examines the occupational backgrounds of men and women under federal and state custody. We see that the number of incarcerated women who reported never having worked increased over the years, but with the high percentage of "absence of information" about work histories, it is difficult to make too much of that trend. We also see that among women for whom there are occupational data, the number reporting a white-collar occupation, especially in the professional, technical, and administrative categories, increased, while the percentage reporting a blue-collar occupation declined. Although this trend seems reversed for the men, again we cannot be certain because of the number not reporting their occupational category.

Table 1
Females as a Percentage of All Sentenced Prisoners by Type of Institution: 1971–1987

	Number of Sentenced Prisoners in All Institutions	Percentage Female	Percentage Female in Federal Institutions	Percentage Female in State Institutions
1971	198,061	3.2	3.7	4.7
1972	196,183	3.2	3.7	3.1
1973	204,349	3.3	4.1	3.1
1974	229,721	3.5	4.4	3.2
1975	253,816	3.8	4.6	3.4
1976	262,833	3.8	5.4	3.8
1977	300,024	4.1	5.9	3.7
1978	306,602	4.2	6.2	3.9
1979	314,006	4.2	5.9	3.9
1980	328,695	4.1	5.8	4.0
1981	368,772	4.2	5.6	3.9
1982	414,362	4.3	5.5	4.2
1983	437,238	4.4	5.5	4.3
1984	462,442	4.5	5.8	4.4
1985	503,601	4.6	6.0	4.5
1986	546,659	4.9	6.4	4.7
1987	581,609	5.0	6.3	4.8

Source: U.S. Department of Justice, *Prisoners in State and Federal Institutions* (Washington, DC: Bureau of Justice Statistics), annual.

Note: Figures include all inmates sentenced for more than one year.

Table 2

Prisoners in State and Federal Institutions: Aggregate Incarceration Rates: 1925–1983

Year	Males	Rate	Females	Rate	Year	Males	Rate	Females	Rate
1925[a]	88,231	149	3,438	6	1956	182,190	218	7,375	9
1926	94,287	157	3,704	6	1957	188,113	221	7,301	8
1927	104,983	173	4,363	7	1958	198,208	229	7,435	8
1928	111,836	182	4,554	8	1959	200,469	228	7,636	8
1929	115,876	187	4,620	8	1960	205,625	230	7,688	8
1930	124,785	200	4,668	8	1961	212,268	234	7,881	8
1931	132,638	211	4,444	7	1962	210,823	229	8,007	8
1932	133,573	211	4,424	7	1963	209,538	225	7,745	8
1933	132,520	209	4,290	7	1964	206,632	219	7,704	8
1934	133,769	209	4,547	7	1965	203,327	213	7,568	8
1935	139,278	217	4,902	8	1966	192,703	201	6,951	7
1936	139,990	217	5,048	8	1967	188,661	195	6,235	6
1937	147,375	227	5,366	8	1968	182,102	187	5,812	6
1938	154,826	236	5,459	8	1969	189,413	192	6,594	6
1939	173,143	263	6,675	10	1970	190,794	191	5,625	5
1940[b]	167,345	252	6,361	10	1971[c]	191,732	189	6,329	6

Year	Males	Rate	Females	Rate	Year	Males	Rate	Females	Rate
1941	159,228	239	6,211	9	1972	189,823	185	6,269	6
1942	144,167	217	6,217	9	1973	197,523	191	6,004	6
1943	131,054	202	6,166	9	1974	211,077	202	7,389	7
1944	126,350	200	6,106	9	1975	231,918	220	8,675	8
1945	127,609	193	6,040	9	1976	252,794	238	10,039	9
1946	134,075	191	6,004	8	1977[d]	267,097	249	11,044	10
1947	144,739	202	6,343	9	1977	274,244	255	11,212	10
1948	149,739	205	6,238	8	1978	282,813	261	11,583	10
1949	157,663	211	6,086	8	1979	289,465	264	12,005	10
1950	160,309	211	5,814	8	1980	303,643	274	12,331	11
1951	159,610	208	6,070	8	1981	339,375	303	14,298	12
1952	161,994	208	6,239	8	1982	379,075	335	16,441	14
1953	166,909	211	6,670	8	1983	401,870	352	17,476	14
1954	175,907	218	6,994	8	1984	426,713	370	19,395	16
1955	178,655	217	7,125	8	1985	460,210	394	21,406	17

Source Bureau of Justice Statistics, *State and Federal Prisoners, 1925–1985* (Washington, DC: U.S. Department of Justice, 1986.)

Note: Incarceration rates are the number of prisoners per 100,000 residential population.

a Data for 1925 to 1939 include sentenced prisoners in state and federal prisons and reformatories whether committed for felonies or misdemeanors.

b Data for 1940 to 1970 include all adult felons serving sentences in state and federal institutions.

c Data for 1971 to present include all adults and youthful offenders sentenced to state or federal correctional institutions whose maximum sentence was more than a year.

d Before 1977, only prisoners in the custody of state and federal correctional systems were counted. After 1977, all prisoners under the jurisdiction of state and federal correctional systems were counted. Figures for both custody and jurisdiction are shown for 1977 to facilitate comparisons.

Table 3

Adult Inmate Population by Security Level and Sex: June 30, 1988

	Federal Prisons		State Prisons	
	Men	Women	Men	Women
Maximum security				
Number	600	10	98,364	2,173
Percentage	1.5	0.4	19.4	9.3
Close security				
Number	9,712	233	48,213	1,565
Percentage	24.0	8.4	9.5	6.7
Medium security				
Number	11,012	698	195,178	11,117
Percentage	27.2	25.1	38.5	47.4
Minimum security				
Number	14,213	1,613	131,741	7,013
Percentage	35.1	58.0	26.0	29.9
Trusty				
Number	0	0	10,263	524
Percentage	0.0	0.0	2.0	2.2
Other				
Number	4,994	228	22,906	1,049
Percentage	12.3	8.2	4.5	4.5
Total				
Number	40,531	2,782	506,665	23,441
Percentage	100.0	100.0	100.0	100.0

Source: American Correctional Association, *1989 Directory* (Laurel, MD, p. xxv).

Note: Numbers exclude inmates incarcerated in Washington, DC (men = 8,292; women = 462) and in Cook County, Illinois (men = 5,696; women = 308). Percentages may not add up exactly to 100% due to rounding.

Table 4

California: Persons Convicted in Superior Courts and Sentenced to Prison by Type of Offense and Sex: 1982–1987

	1982		1983		1984		1985		1986		1987	
	Number Convicted	% Sentenced to Prison	Number Convicted	% Sentenced to Prison	Number Convicted	% Sentenced to Prison	Number Convicted	% Sentenced to Prison	Number Convicted	% Sentenced to Prison	Number Convicted	% Sentenced to Prison
Homicide[a]												
Female	97	71.1	87	64.4	86	67.4	101	75.2	100	75.0	100	73.0
Male	1,035	83.2	858	86.7	854	88.8	833	89.9	966	92.3	927	92.3
Robbery												
Female	241	41.1	254	44.5	216	45.8	231	51.9	272	52.2	262	55.7
Male	4,447	64.4	4,135	70.7	3,820	69.9	4,589	70.4	4,451	69.8	4,150	71.3
Burglary												
Female	397	29.5	428	32.2	543	35.7	613	37.8	651	37.5	658	39.7
Male	9,641	41.2	9,181	46.0	9.213	475	9,900	49.4	9,963	50.2	9,350	50.7
Assault												
Female	329	17.6	314	18.8	358	21.2	356	19.7	408	14.0	354	22.6
Male	3,750	29.5	3,475	33.3	3,635	34.6	4,071	36.2	4,342	37.5	4,013	38.9
Theft												
Female	1,635	9.8	1,879	13.6	2,200	12.7	2,622	14.8	2,426	19.8	2,206	18.4
Male	6,313	22.3	6,394	25.7	6,638	27.7	7,418	29.4	7,366	31.1	7,270	32.0
Drug law violations												
Female	1,132	7.6	1,417	10.5	1,675	11.2	2,392	10.0	3,115	13.2	3,883	12.5
Male	7,322	14.6	9,074	16.4	11,224	17.2	17,371	17.5	22,995	21.3	26,702	23.3
Total												
Female	3,831	15.4	4,379	17.6	5,078	17.6	6,315	17.8	6,972	20.2	7,463	19.5
Male	32,508	34.7	33,117	36.8	35,384	36.3	44,182	35.2	50,083	35.6	52,412	35.6

Source: California Department of Justice, Division of Law Enforcement, Bureau of Criminal Statistics, unpublished data.

a For Homicide, "Percentage sentenced to prison" includes persons sentenced to death.

Table 5

New York: Persons Convicted in Upper Courts and Sentenced to Prison by Type of Offenses and Sex: 1982–1987

	1982		1983		1984		1985		1986		1987	
	Number Convicted	% Sentenced to Prison	Number Convicted	% Sentenced to Prison	Number Convicted	% Sentenced to Prison	Number Convicted	% Sentenced to Prison	Number Convicted	% Sentenced to Prison	Number Convicted	% Sentenced to Prison
Homicide												
Female	121	52.9	122	63.9	96	59.4	124	66.1	126	62.7	54	48.1
Male	1,716	78.7	1,650	80.6	1,544	79.5	1,430	78.7	1,387	81.5	778	76.9
Robbery												
Female	279	31.5	349	35.8	340	29.7	311	30.9	415	41.7	417	36.5
Male	6,392	60.5	8,149	60.2	7,378	58.9	6,768	58.8	7,497	59.7	6,900	62.3
Burglary												
Female	208	12.0	212	15.6	217	24.4	174	17.2	205	17.1	203	27.6
Male	6,124	34.7	6,928	39.4	6,009	40.0	5,961	39.7	6,220	42.7	5,854	43.7
Assault												
Female	155	16.8	139	20.1	158	17.7	192	19.3	176	18.2	127	18.1
Male	1,522	30.4	1,522	30.1	1,795	29.8	1,833	31.9	1,740	34.1	1,265	31.6
Larceny												
Female	437	11.4	600	9.5	545	14.7	567	16.6	619	13.1	453	12.1
Male	2,060	23.3	2,310	23.6	2,500	26.8	2,995	27.1	3,147	30.2	2,314	30.8
Drug law violations												
Female	503	16.9	624	19.6	686	19.7	966	21.3	1,440	24.1	1,787	20.6
Male	4,651	37.6	4,823	38.0	5,655	42.7	6,760	41.7	11,219	43.0	12,026	38.1
Total												
Female	1,703	19.8	2,046	21.7	2,042	22.2	2,334	23.4	2,981	25.1	3,041	22.4
Male	22,465	44.7	25,382	46.5	24,881	46.6	25,747	45.4	31,210	46.9	29,137	45.2

Source: New York State Division of Criminal Justice Services, Bureau of Statistical Services, unpublished data.

Table 6

Pennsylvania: Persons Convicted in All Courts and Sentenced to Incarceration by Type of Offense and Sex: 1981–1986

	1981		1982		1983		1984		1985		1986	
	Number Convicted	% Incarcerated	Number Convicted	% Incarcerated	Number Convicted	% Incarcerated	Number Convicted	% Incarcerated	Number Convicted	% Incarcerated	Number Convicted	% Incarcerated
Murder												
Female	56	53.6	54	48.1	64	71.9	74	85.1	45	82.2	45	86.7
Male	428	75.9	469	81.9	499	87.6	522	85.1	398	89.7	371	90.0
Robbery												
Female	60	43.3	105	52.4	120	56.7	98	65.3	66	68.2	85	68.2
Male	1,941	74.4	2,456	73.7	2,173	80.1	2,460	83.6	1,608	84.6	1,648	87.0
Burglary												
Female	89	34.8	172	42.4	131	46.6	129	47.3	110	40.0	84	52.4
Male	3,058	62.2	4,486	60.3	4,394	68.9	4,207	73.5	3,212	77.0	2,945	78.1
Aggravated assault												
Female	184	23.4	209	22.0	196	33.7	181	39.2	155	38.1	149	37.6
Male	1,609	40.5	1,725	43.4	1,494	56.0	1,552	60.4	1,231	61.3	1,224	67.3
Other assault												
Female	260	15.4	304	21.1	329	21.0	358	24.9	335	26.3	314	23.2
Male	2,682	29.0	3,077	32.1	3,593	36.7	3,576	38.7	3,227	39.8	3,377	39.7
Theft												
Female	539	18.7	2,947	11.7	2,195	20.0	2,048	21.5	1,822	25.9	1,673	27.2
Male	4,832	35.4	7,243	32.5	6,813	42.5	6,441	44.2	5,599	45.4	5,269	44.5

	1981		1982		1983		1984		1985		1986	
	Number Convicted	% Incarcerated	Number Convicted	% Incarcerated	Number Convicted	% Incarcerated	Number Convicted	% Incarcerated	Number Convicted	% Incarcerated	Number Convicted	% Incarcerated
Forgery												
Female	238	27.7	229	32.8	206	35.4	246	41.1	233	44.6	281	38.1
Male	652	50.9	587	49.9	691	59.8	694	65.4	617	66.1	690	64.5
Fraud												
Female	388	19.8	225	20.0	289	28.4	295	33.6	411	31.1	393	26.2
Male	935	31.3	676	35.5	1,018	38.1	1,123	42.9	1,013	41.9	1,164	41.9
Drug law violations												
Female	455	17.4	517	22.2	649	24.8	669	24.8	619	31.2	634	33.1
Male	3,108	28.3	3,121	31.3	3,606	37.5	3,791	38.6	3,686	40.7	4,133	46.6

Source: Pennsylvania Commission on Crime and Delinquency, unpublished data.

Table 7
Offense Distribution of State Prison Inmates by Sex: 1979 and 1986

	Percentage of Prison Inmates[a]			
	1979		1986	
	Male	Female	Male	Female
Violent offenses				
Murder	12.2	15.5	11.2	13.0
Negligent manslaughter	3.8	9.8	3.0	6.8
Kidnapping	2.2	1.4	1.7	0.9
Rape	4.5	0.4	4.4	0.2
Other sexual assault	2.0	0.3	4.7	0.9
Robbery	25.6	13.6	21.3	10.6
Assault	7.7	7.6	8.1	7.1
Other violent offenses	0.3	0.4	0.8	1.2
Total	53.3	49.0	55.2	40.7
Property offenses				
Burglary	18.6	5.3	17.0	5.9
Larceny-theft	4.5	11.2	5.6	14.7
Motor vehicle theft	1.5	0.5	1.4	0.5
Arson	0.6	1.2	0.7	1.2
Fraud	3.8	17.3	3.2	17.0
Stolen property	1.3	0.9	2.0	1.6
Other property offenses	0.8	0.4	0.5	0.4
Total	31.2	36.8	30.4	41.3
Drug offenses				
Possession	1.5	2.7	2.9	4.0
Trafficking	4.3	7.1	5.3	7.3
Other drug offenses	0.4	0.7	0.2	0.7
Total	6.2	10.5	8.4	12.0

Source: Adapted from Bureau of Justice Statistics, *Profile of State Prison Inmates* (Washington, DC: U.S. Department of Justice, 1986).

[a] Figures do not add up to 100% because two offense categories ("Public order offenses" and "Other offenses") were excluded from the table.

Table 8

Age and Education of Inmates in Federal and State Correctional Institutions: 1960, 1970, 1980

	1960				1970				1980			
	Federal		State		Federal		State		Federal		State	
	% Male	% Female	% Male	% Female	% Male	% Female	% Male	% Female	% Male	% Female	% Male	% Female
Age (years)												
< 15	0.0	0.6	0.1	0.1	0.0	0.6	0.3	0.5	0.3	0.3	0.3	0.4
15–19	8.0	7.8	8.6	10.1	3.7	3.8	8.4	11.6	7.6	5.1	7.9	6.1
20–24	20.7	16.0	19.6	17.0	25.4	27.7	26.2	22.8	22.8	21.4	29.9	23.6
25–29	18.5	20.5	18.2	17.7	19.8	23.5	20.3	18.5	22.4	17.4	24.9	25.9
30–39	31.7	31.6	28.5	32.4	27.2	24.0	24.1	24.8	28.3	25.0	24.7	25.8
40–49	13.5	17.1	15.0	14.2	15.3	17.2	13.4	15.4	11.3	9.0	7.9	9.2
50–64	6.9	6.3	8.7	7.5	7.6	3.3	6.2	4.5	6.3	4.6	3.9	5.7
65 +	0.7	0.0	1.4	0.9	1.0	0.0	1.0	1.9	1.0	17.2	0.5	3.3
Education (years)												
Elementary												
0–4	10.4	10.1	16.6	14.2	6.3	6.4	7.9	5.8	3.7	4.6	3.9	4.8
5–8	39.4	46.7	41.8	39.8	30.9	24.9	33.8	29.6	14.5	18.7	17.7	15.1
High school												
1–3	26.8	25.0	27.2	28.9	33.9	38.6	34.3	37.4	22.2	25.6	30.1	29.1
4	14.8	13.8	10.6	12.3	20.3	21.8	18.6	20.1	32.6	29.1	29.9	31.8
College												
1–3	7.0	3.3	3.1	3.8	6.1	6.0	4.6	5.6	18.3	14.6	15.1	15.5
4+	1.7	1.2	0.8	1.0	2.4	2.3	0.8	1.5	8.7	7.3	3.3	3.7

Source: U.S. Bureau of the Census, 1960 Decennial Census, *Characteristics of Persons under Custody in Correctional Institutions*, Tables 4 and 25; 1970 Decennial Census, *Persons in Institutions and Other Group Quarters*, Tables 3 and 24, 1980 Decennial Census, *Persons in Institutional and Other Group Quarters*, Table 14..

	1960				1970				1980			
	Federal		State		Federal		State		Federal		State	
	% Male	% Female	% Male	% Female	% Male	% Female	% Male	% Female	% Male	% Female	% Male	% Female
Service[f]	9.5	36.0	8.3	49.7	10.4	39.6	12.7	41.7	14.7	28.2	15.1	32.9
Farming, forestry, or fishing[g]	6.2	2.5	6.5	2.6	5.2	1.2	4.1	3.3	7.3	5.5	7.3	3.6
Total	69.5	62.3	67.0	71.3	76.0	54.8	86.6	72.1	80.2	55.5	85.7	61.8
No occupation reported	11.9	8.8	24.2	11.4	—	—	—	—	—	—	—	—

Source: U.S. Bureau of the Census, 1960 Decennial Census, *Characteristics of Persons under Custody in Correctional Institutions,* Table 25; 1970 Decennial Census, *Persons in Institutions and Other Group Quarters*, Table 24; 1980 Decennial Census, *Persons in Institutional and Other Group Quarters*, Table 14.

a Figures are not strictly comparable across years due to changes in occupational categorizations.

b For 1960 and 1970, totals include inmates 14 years and older, but for 1980, totals include inmates 16 years and older.

c For 1960, figures indicate the number of inmates who reported last working in 1950 or later; for 1970, 1960 or later; and for 1980, 1975 or later.

d Included in this category are inmates who last worked in 1959 or earlier and those who did not report the last year that they worked.

e Includes all nonfarm laborers and operatives. For 1980, figures include inmates who had been employed in the armed services.

f Includes private household workers.

g Includes all farm-related occupations, including farm owners and managers as well as laborers.

Table 9

Occupational Status of Inmates in Federal and State Correctional Institutions: 1960, 1970, 1980[a]

	1960				1970				1980			
	Federal		State		Federal		State		Federal		State	
	% Male	% Female	% Male	% Female	% Male	% Female	% Male	% Female	% Male	% Female	% Male	% Female
Total with Occupation[a, b, c]	75.0	56.5	61.4	44.8	72.1	57.3	67.6	65.8	72.5	54.8	66.2	61.1
Never worked	4.5	11.5	3.9	12.9	7.1	9.0	7.3	18.6	8.5	21.9	11.8	20.1
No occupational information[d]	20.6	31.9	34.7	42.3	20.8	33.6	25.0	15.6	19.0	23.2	22.0	18.8
Occupation type												
White collar												
Professional, technical, or administrative	9.1	6.0	3.8	4.4	12.8	17.9	5.8	5.3	9.2	13.2	6.2	11.4
Clerical	4.8	14.8	2.7	10.0	4.7	21.9	5.1	18.5	4.9	7.1	3.8	8.8
Sales	4.8	8.1	2.3	2.9	6.4	5.4	2.5	4.1	5.6	24.1	4.4	18.0
Total	18.7	28.9	8.8	17.3	24.0	45.2	13.4	27.9	19.7	44.4	14.4	38.2
Blue Collar												
Craft	18.7	3.8	12.9	0.4	18.9	0.0	21.3	2.9	20.6	6.5	22.8	3.7
Operatives/labors[e]	35.1	20.0	39.3	18.6	41.5	14.0	48.5	24.2	37.6	15.3	40.5	21.6

Inside Women's Prisons

The American prison system has been a target of the equal rights movement because, by and large, it continues to provide separate facilities for men and women. Separate prisons were established for women beginning in the 1880s as a reform intended to give them the benefit of rehabilitation then being sought for young men and boys in new reformatories.

Advocates of the Equal Rights Amendment (ERA) who directed their interests at the female offender claimed that the same reasoning that was persuasive to the Supreme Court in *Brown* v. *the Board of Education* (that segregation by itself denies to blacks equal opportunities and equality in their educational experiences) should apply to women because of the maintenance of a separate prison system. Schools that segregate by race and prisons that segregate by sex are basically discriminatory.

The authors of a note in the May 1973 *Yale Law Journal* claimed that although the Supreme Court had as yet not made the same determination concerning segregation on the basis of sex that it made for segregation on the basis of color (separate, by its nature, cannot be equal) the passage of the ERA would compel such a result (Arditi, Goldberg, Hartle, Peters, & Phelps 1973). As of 1989, there were 19 coed prisons in 11 states in the state system and 7 coed institutions in the federal system.

The fact that women prisoners comprise only 5% of all prisoners continues to influence the conditions of their incarceration in many important ways. Indeed, the effect begins from the moment a woman is sentenced. Because there are fewer female institutions, a woman is likely to be sent much farther from her community than is her male counterpart. Few states operate more than one female penal institution. Women inmates thus experience greater difficulty in keeping track of their families and their possessions. The superintendent at the California Institution for Women characterized the situation as follows:

> Almost all the women who come to prison have husbands and children. If a man goes to prison, the wife stays home and he usually has his family to return to and the household is there when he gets out. But women generally don't have family support from the outside. Very few men are going to sit around and take care of the children and be there when she gets back. So—to send a woman to prison means you are virtually going to disrupt her family. She knows that when she gets out she probably won't have a husband waiting for her. It will really mean starting her life over again.

It is also more difficult for her to communicate with her lawyer and to gain access to her parole board.

The size of the female prison population also affects the heterogeneity of the populations within women's prisons. Women's prisons contain a more heterogeneous population than do prisons for men. They include a wider range of ages than do the male prisons, and there is less differentiation by types of offenders. All but five states have more than one institution for male offenders, and the decision about which type of institution to use is based on age and type of offense.

But not all of the differences between men's and women's institutions that derive from the principle of sexual segregation result in women experiencing more negative treatment. The stereotypes that are held of women in the larger society provide some advantages to the female inmates. Burkhart (1973) pointed out the following:

> Women just weren't considered as dangerous or as violent as men. So—rather than the mass penitentiary housing used for men—women's prisons were designed as a domestic model—with each woman having a "room" of her own. Often no more than stretches of open fields or wire fences separate women prisoners and the "free world"—armed guards are rarely visible. Just like women outside, a woman prisoner would be confined to "the home."
>
> "The home" planned for women was a cottage that was built to house 20 to 30 women—who would cook their own food in a "cottage kitchen." The cottages in most states were built to contain a living room, a dining room, and 1 or 2 small reading rooms. (367)

Physically, then, female institutions are usually more attractive and more pleasant than the security-oriented institutions for men. They tend to be located in more pastoral settings, and they tend not to have the gun towers, the concrete walls, and the barbed wire that so often characterize the male institutions. Women inmates usually have more privacy than men; they tend to have single rooms; they may wear street clothes rather than prison uniforms; they may decorate their rooms with bedspreads and curtains provided by the prison. Toilet and shower facilities also reflect a greater concern for women's privacy. Because women prisoners are perceived as less dangerous and less escape prone than men, most states also allow them more trips outside the prison than they do their male counterparts.

Considering the statistics which estimate that between 56% and 75% of incarcerated women have young children, the number of institutions accommodating the special needs of mothers with children are disproportionately low (Baunach 1979; Feinman 1986; McGowan & Blumenthal 1978). Based on a 1989 survey the author conducted of women's prisons, only 35% (13) of the institutions reported having either "rooms with cribs, high chairs, or other 'baby equipment," or "rooms to talk privately, read, listen to music with older children," and only 50% (19) of the responding institutions reported having "rooms with toys and other facilities for children up to 6 years of age." Even fewer, 30% (11), reported having "places to prepare food for children" (Simon & Landis 1991:97).

Not surprisingly then, we find also a great disparity among the institutions in the amount of time allowed for mother-child visitation. Seven of the 37 institutions responding allowed visitation 7 days a week. These institutions, representing five state correctional systems, include Bedford Hills Correctional Facility in New York, Albion Correctional Facility in New York, Huron Valley Women's Facility in Missouri, Florence Crane Women's Facility in Missouri, Oregon Women's Correctional Facility, Pennsylvania State Correctional Institution, and the Wyoming Women's Center. Eleven of the facilities permit visitation once a week (with the number of hours allowed during this visit ranging anywhere from 1 hour to 10 hours), 3 permit it 2 times a month, and another 2 permit visitations only once a month.

At least half (19) of the institutions responding reported that they had a furlough program whereby mothers may visit their children at home or in halfway houses. Most often, however, these programs have stringent eligibility requirements and are available only to those offenders on work release, those convicted of relatively minor crimes, or those within sight of their release dates.

As of the summer of 1989, the Federal Bureau of Prisons reported housing a total of 3,629 women in 12 federal facilities and in five state facilities that contract to accept female inmates from the federal system. Of the 12 federal facilities housing women, five accept only women while the other seven accept both women and men. Together, the five federal facilities that accept only women house approximately 73.3% of all incarcerated female federal prisoners. These facilities include two federal correctional institutions, one located in Alderson, West Virginia, and another in Lexington, Kentucky, which together house approximately 59.1% of all women incarcerated in the federal system. The other exclusively female facilities include three federal prison camps located in Danbury, Connecticut; Marianna, Florida; and Phoenix, Arizona. These institutions collectively house approximately 14.2% of federal women prisoners.

Child visitation is somewhat more problematic in the federal system than it is in the state system because there are only a small number of facilities to serve the population of federal female offenders. While there may be only one facility within a state that houses female offenders, women adjudicated under the federal system are more likely to be incarcerated outside of their home states. Once in the federal system, an inmate may be housed in any federal facility throughout the country. This situation has obvious negative implications for the continuity of family life, for both men and women. It is particularly salient for women when one recalls that a large majority of all the women incarcerated in the federal system reside in just two institutions—Alderson and Lexington. Thus, we must keep this geographic reality in mind to qualify our examination of the child-care facilities provided by the federal women's institutions.

All of the facilities provide rooms with toys and other conveniences for children up to 6 years of age. Alderson and Lexington appear to have the more uniform and comprehensive provisions—in terms of both facilities and time—for child visitation than do the prison camps, albeit they may have larger numbers of inmates whose families cannot take advantage of such provisions. All of the federal facilities have furlough programs for eligible mothers, and the surveys suggest that they are somewhat more liberal than those offered at the state level. In at least two of the facilities, an inmate may become eligible within 2 years of release, and at least 1 other allows eligibility within 1 year of release.

Concluding Remarks

To conclude, we note again that women comprise about 6% of all inmates in federal prisons and about 5% of all inmates in state institutions. These figures have remained relatively stable over the past 20 years. We also see that, while the female incarceration rate has risen in the 1980s, it has not increased nearly as much as the male incarceration rate. Women are much more likely than men to be assigned to medium- and minimum-security institutions at both the federal and state levels. The types of offenses for which women are most likely to receive prison sentences are fraud, larceny, homicide, robbery, and drug violations. A big improvement has occurred over the past 15 years in the facilities that are available for contacts and visits with female inmates' children.

References

American Correctional Association (1989). *Directory*. Laurel, MD: Author.

Arditi, R.R.F., Goldberg, Jr., Hartle, M.M., Peters, J.H., & Phelps, W.R. (1973). The sexual segregation of American prisons: Notes. *Yale Law Journal* 82: 1229–1273.

Baunach, P.J. (1979). Mothering, from behind the prison walls. Paper presented at the American Society of Criminology annual meeting.

Burkhart, K.W. (1973). *Women in prison*. New York: Doubleday.

California Department of Justice, Division of Law Enforcement, Bureau of Criminal Statistics (1988). Unpublished data, Sacramento.

Feinman, C. (1986). *Women in the criminal justice system.* New York: Praeger.

McGowan, B., & Blumenthal, K. (1978). *Why people punish the children: A study of children of women prisoners.* Hackensack, NJ: NCCD.

New York State Division of Criminal Justice Services, Bureau of Statistical Services (1988). Unpublished data, Albany.

Pennsylvania Commission on Crime and Delinquency (1987). Unpublished data, Harrisburg.

Simon, R.J., & Landis, J. (1991). *The crimes women commit, the punishments they receive.* Lexington, MA: Lexington Books.

U.S. Bureau of the Census (1960). *Characteristics of persons under custody in correctional institutions.* Washington, DC: U.S. Government Printing Office

——— (1970). *Persons in institutions and other group quarters.* Washington, DC: U.S. Government Printing Office.

——— (1980). *Persons in institutions and other group quarters.* Washington, DC: U.S. Government Printing Office.

U.S. Department of Justice (1971–1987, annually). *Prisoners in state and federal institutions.* Washington, DC: U.S. Government Printing Office.

U.S. Department of Justice (1986). *Profile of state prison inmates.* Washington, DC: U.S. Government Printing Office.

——— (1986). *State and federal prisoners, 1925–1985.* Washington, DC: U.S. Government Printing Office.

Females Behind Prison Bars

Concetta C. Culliver
Murray State University

The female in prison has been one of the most understudied areas relevant to the American system of criminal justice. However, this is not to say that there has been a scarcity of female criminals, for throughout the history of mankind, women have always engaged in their share of criminal activity. In the fourteenth century, for example, females were convicted of petty theft (stealing), pickpocketing, and prostitution.

In their 1986 publication, *The Imprisonment of Women*, Dobash, Dobash, and Gutteridge suggested that many of the early imprisoned women were committed to prison cells for theft, begging, and prostitution, even if the crime entailed family survival. Also, revealing facts concerning female criminality are illustrated in Jones' book of 1980, *Women Who Kill*. In this case, Jones discussed female criminals who murdered their lovers or husbands in defiance of the male patriarchal society.

Early criminologists, mainly men, traditionally felt it important to devote little time to the study of female criminals, in or out of prisons, since crime committed by women was miniscule and not as serious as that of their male counterparts. In fact, at one time, the female criminal was portrayed as a peculiar being—an oddity—and any attention directed toward her, even though scant, portrayed her to be physically, emotionally, or psychologically aberrated. Pioneer criminologist Cesare Lombroso (1894) rationalized the criminal activity of women in terms of physiobiological differences, believing that women were prone to be passive, less violent, and more law abiding. Those women who did commit criminal acts were perceived to be very masculine, with demeanors that resembled the male criminal or even the noncriminal man. Later, the female criminal was depicted as a sexually controlling deviant who relished manipulating men for profit or even being manipulated by them.

Today, women continue to fill the ranks among the criminal offender population in American society. While the female offender population is not as enormous as that of the male offender population, women appear to be catching up with their male criminal counterparts, committing more serious property offenses, such as larceny, forgery, fraud, embezzlement, and drug offenses (Allen & Simonsen 1986; U.S. Department of Justice 1988). In a 1988 report by the FBI, a rapid increase was noted for female offenders for such crimes as robbery, burglary, and the illegal use and possession of weapons. In fact, the increase shown was even higher than that reported for male offenders committing the same crimes. Even violent crime among women is on the increase; the figure is higher than the figure for men (Pollock-Byrne 1990). Goetting and Howser (1983) found more women are being incarcerated for drug offenses (cocaine and heroin) and indicated that drug involvement appears to be higher for female offenders than for male offenders. Meanwhile, Glick and Neto (1977) examined the criminal records of female offenders (misdemeanants, felons) and found female offenders serving one year or less had been convicted in the following proportions: 41% for property crimes (shoplifting, forgery, fraud, etc.); 20% for drug offenses; and 11% for violent crimes (assault, battery, armed robbery). Female felony offenders with one or more years were convicted as follows: 43% for violent crimes (murder, armed robbery); 29% for property crimes (forgery, fraud, larceny); and 22% for drug offenses.

Currently, there are 47 state correctional institutions and 13 federal prisons in the United States housing female offenders, who most often are young, poor, nonwhite, unmarried mothers and are high school dropouts who have drug-related problems (cocaine, alcohol, heroin) (Glick & Neto 1977). McDonough et al. (1981) lamented that the majority of imprisoned women were unemployed at the time of their incarceration; however, even when they were employed, the work was of an unskilled nature. McDonough et al. (1981) also showed female offenders to be without male companionship at the onset of their incarceration. The idea of punishing women by placing them behind prison bars is not a recent phenomenon; the imprisonment of women can be traced to the bridewells (sixteenth-century prisons) of England. In bridewells, they were exposed to deplorable conditions: disease was rampant; no attempt was made to segregate them by age, sex, or even type of offense; they were forced to work long hours; and they were exposed to corrupted guards and violent offenders. Also, when they were sentenced to bridewells, they were sentenced for substantially longer periods than were male criminals (Fox 1984). Once incarcerated, however, they did not forfeit their feminine "duties." In bridewells, female criminals were expected to cook, clean, and operate spinning wheels. Being perceived as sexual commodities, they were expected to engage in sexual activity with male convicts for the purpose of maintaining harmony and preventing unrest among the male convict population (Dobash et al. 1986). At times, they were permitted to engage in prostitution for their own well-being and to satisfy the sexual desires of corrupted guards (Fox 1984). Little attention was shown for the safety and health of female offenders.

Female Criminals in Colonial America

The treatment of female criminals incarcerated in Colonial America was not that different from treatment received in bridewells. In fact, many ideas used with criminals, male or female, were brought into the American colonies by settlers from England. In addition, many of England's corrupt criminals, including women, were transported to America. Women were incarcerated in large rooms along with men and children, and the strong preyed upon the weak. Still, female offenders were used as sexual objects, satisfying the sexual urges of hostile, angry, and frustrated guards and wardens. Female prisoners were exposed to the same harsh physical punishment, hard labor, and hangings as were male prisoners. They, in fact, were treated more harshly because they had become lawbreakers.

Female Criminals in the Penitentiary System

After the enactment of the Penitentiary Act of 1779, which called for secure and sanitary holding places championed by William Penn and his Quaker followers, penitentiaries, better known today as correctional institutions, were established. The first known such institution was the Walnut Street Penitentiary in Philadelphia, Pennsylvania. For the first time, female offenders were segregated from male convicts. However, treatment was only marginally better. These institutions were overcrowded and filthy (Freedman 1974). The women were subject to floggings, harsh physical punishment, forced prostitution by male wardens and guards, sadistic beatings, rape, and illegitimate births. Prison officials believed women, in general, to be pious, pure, and good law-abiding citizens, and when they became criminals, they were beyond reformation. Using this perception, they rationalized the harsh punitive tactics used against female offenders.

Even the more modern prison institutions, such as the Auburn State Penitentiary in New York, failed to improve conditions for female criminals. At Auburn, the women were housed together in one large antiquated room and left unattended for long periods of time. Windows were sealed to prevent communication with male offenders. Male convicts, however, had their own separate cells. One scandalous situation occurred at the Auburn Prison when a female offender became pregnant during her imprisonment and was flogged brutally by a prison guard (possibly the one who impregnated her), and she died shortly after giving birth. Although this case had no strong impact on the court system, it did have a strong influence on the public and led to the appointment of a matron in 1832 to supervise the women's quarters, replacing male guards (Freedman 1981). Generally speaking, female offenders in prison institutions throughout the United States received inferior treatment to that of their male counterparts (Rafter 1985).

Female Criminals During the Reform Movement

During the latter part of the nineteenth century, the perception of female criminals changed. Their criminal activity was viewed as a reflection of their environment, such as poverty, an inadequate home life, and/or interaction with an evil male (Freedman 1974). With this perception, reformers such as Dorothea Dix and Elizabeth Fry (known as the mother of female prison reform) championed the need for better conditions for imprisoned women. It was during this period that attempts were made to "feminize" the prison surroundings of the incarcerated woman. For example, in one institution, it was noted that women were permitted to decorate their rooms with curtains and flowers; they were provided with a piano, educational classes, and readings (Feinman 1984; Freedman 1981). Of greater interest is the fact that female matrons were hired to operate and manage prison institutions for women (Freedman 1974; Rafter 1985). Later, separate institutions were established for women with the premise that the care and supervision of female criminals could best be handled by female wardens and guards of which Freedman (1974) made the following comment:

> Male prejudices, male exploitation, and male-dominated institutions, the reformers believed, denied justice to female criminals. Thus, they reasoned, if male influence were removed by placing the female criminal solely in the hands of her sisters, virtue might be restored. Female officers would provide the salutary influences of education, religion, and love to redeem the female criminal class. (86)

More specifically, these institutions for women prisoners operated with a tone of benevolence and compassion. Training included housework, sewing, knitting, cooking, laundering, gardening, and farming.

According to Rafter (1985), women's prisons during the reform movement were categorized into two distinct types: the reformatory and the custodial institution. Women imprisoned in reformatories were not considered hardened criminals; most were under the age of 25, white, native born, unmarried, and were incarcerated for drunkenness, prostitution, and/or sexual misconduct (adultery). Women committed to custodial institutions were between the ages of 31 and 50, white, and imprisoned for more serious offenses. Women incarcerated under reformatory conditions were carefully chosen. Blacks were excluded (Rafter 1985) from the reformatory system. Despite this, they comprised approximately 70% of the women incarcerated from 1860 to 1887; by 1900, they comprised 90% of the female prison population. For the period 1926–1934, the figure declined to 65%, and it was during this time that reformatories first opened their doors to black female offenders, where they were segregated from white female offenders.

In the South and the West, prison facilities for women entailed makeshift arrangements, which prevailed well into the 1900s. Alternative methods were used with female criminals who had committed less-serious felony acts. Females considered serious felon offenders and blacks were subject to prison farm labor or housework (Rafter 1985). Moreover, in the South, farm labor was designated for black female criminals, while sewing and gardening were reserved for white female criminals.

The Imprisonment of Women: 1930s–1970s

Until the 1930s, the early reformatory model still prevailed, primarily serving young white misdemeanants (Pollack-Byrne 1990). Women imprisoned in these institutions continued to be protected against sexual abuse, physical abuse, and hard labor. Still, with the reformatory concept, women were not spared the pains of imprisonment. They had sexual needs that remained unmet, and they were exposed to overcrowded conditions. Yet, the philosophy surrounding the imprisonment of women in reformatories emphasized preparation for "womanhood." Consequently, female offenders continued to be exposed to work that exemplified "gender roles." For the female prisoner, this meant cooking, housework, sewing, knitting, laundering, gardening, farming, and caring for children.

With the 1930s came changes for the reformatory system. One major change was that felons were imprisoned in reformatories rather than in custodial institutions as they once were. This change evolved when the states found it to be more feasible to shut down all custodial units that were specifically used to imprison the more hardened female criminals and blacks. Nonetheless, institutions to incarcerate female criminals continued to be constructed during the early and mid-1900s, mainly in rural areas.

Lekkerkerker's (1931) description of female prison institutions denotes a "country club" living arrangement:

> The farm certainly has charms: the buildings, scattered wide apart, form an attractive whole with the romantic lake, the wood and thicket, the rolling hills and green pasture, which offer the women abundant opportunity for healthy outdoor sports such as hiking, swimming, fishing, sleighing, and skating in winter, picking berries, chopping wood, etc. which, in fact, is often done by them. (121)

This style of prison life for women existed well into the 1970s.

In spite of this, female criminals during the 1970s, were treated as "dependent children." Visiting numerous prisons for women, Burkhardt (1979) described the conditions as dismal: guards teased and harassed female offenders; there was a lack of meaningful activities (social, academic, vocational) for the women; and homosexual relationships became the escape hatch to compensate for their feelings of despair and sense of hopelessness. Even the programs that were available (tailoring, cosmetology, nurse's aides, typing, food services, etc.) were obsolete and sex stereotyped.

Female Prisons of the 1980s

Currently, the 60 or so correctional institutions, both federal and state, that house female offenders in the United States are smaller and most often classified as medium- or minimum-security facilities. A large majority of women are housed in co-correctional facilities managed and supervised by male wardens or superintendents. Moreover, males are increasingly employed to serve as correctional officers in female prisons.

Contemporary programs for female prisoners are a missing element. The few programs that exist tend to build on sexual stereotypes or on the aspect of "feminine role" or "womanhood," still alluding to early prison reform philosophy. With a domestic and family orientation, such programs include cosmetology, food services, housekeeping, nurse's aide work, and, on a small scale, clerical skills development. Educational programs for women stop at the secondary level, whereas for male offenders, these programs proceed to the college level.

Medical, nutritional, and recreational services in women's prisons are lacking; of particular importance is the need for adequate medical care. The use of psychotropic drugs is 10 times higher in female prisons than in male prisons. Today, most female prisons share physicians and hospital facilities with male prisons.

Of greater importance to female offenders who are mothers is the continuance of their relationships with their children. Researchers have shown that the majority of women behind prison bars are mothers; some even give birth to children shortly after being imprisoned, and separation from their children is a major concern (Baunach 1982; Glick & Neto 1977; Stanton 1980).

Legal Rights and Issues of Female Prisoners (1960s–1980s)

Until the 1960s, females in prison basically had no rights; upon conviction, it was a civil death for them, and they, in fact, had no more rights than slaves (*Ruffin* v. *Commonwealth* 1871). What few rights they had were those provided through statutory law or correctional policy.

Later, with the reversal of the *Ruffin* v. *Commonwealth* case, the courts ruled that prisoners did have civil rights protection; but when it came to matters concerning the rights of prisoners, the courts operated using a hands-off approach, believing that correctional officials, with their expertise, were capable of handling correctional affairs. However, it was the *Cooper* v. *Pate* (1964) case that opened the doors for increased court intervention relevant to prisoner rights.

Voicing their concern for the lack of adequate treatment programs (academic, vocational, medical, psychological), female prisoners found support for improved programs and services. In the 1979 case of *Glover* v. *Johnson*, for example, female offenders of the Detroit House of Correction claimed that the educational and vocational programs were inferior when compared to those provided male prisoners. In this instance, the courts ruled that prison officials were obligated to improve educational and vocational services for female offenders. This decision supported the decision in a prior court case, *Barefield* v. *Leach* (1974), in which the courts advised the state of New Mexico to operate prisons for women using constitutional standards and guidelines.

Furthermore, the lack of medical services for female offenders has been found to be unconstitutional, especially if it meets the courts' test of "deliberate indifference." In the *Estelle* v. *Gamble* (1976) case, the Supreme Court declared that "cruel and unusual punishment is when medical care is deliberately denied inmates, causing needless pain and suffering."

In a similar vein, a class action suit was filed by female offenders at the Bedford Hills Correctional Facility in New York (former home of Jean Harris, convicted killer of the Scarsdale Diet physician), in which female offenders contested inadequate medical care. Upon finding numerous medical flaws (delayed health screening, a defective chest X-ray machine, and poor gynecological care), the court mandated improved nurse screenings, prompt access to a doctor during sick call, improved follow-up care, better access to medical care, and periodic self-audits (Pollock-Byrne 1990).

Overall, prenatal care and services for incarcerated female offenders are almost nonexistent. Nutritional services for pregnant prisoners are often inadequate, and this may lead to low birth-weight babies, prenatal mortality, birth defects, and mental retardation (Bershad 1985).

Abortion is another major problem that plagues the minds of imprisoned women. In a report by the National Prison Project of the

American Civil Liberties Union, it was revealed that oftentimes these women are coerced by prison officials into aborting their fetuses. Even with abortions, female offenders are still denied adequate medical treatment (*Morales* v. *Turman* 1974).

Contrary to this, if female prisoners willingly submit to having abortions performed, prison officials may decline these requests because of their refusal to bear the costs involved. Nonetheless, it was through the *Lett* v. *Withworth* (1976) case that one female prisoner challenged her right to an abortion. In this instance, the court did rule that the offender's constitutional rights had been violated. Yet, the matter of abortions for women behind prison bars remains unresolved, primarily because the courts feel that imprisoned women should shoulder full financial responsibility for their own abortions (Bershad 1985).

Women giving birth to babies during their imprisonment have not met with much success in their attempts to keep their newborns in prison with them. Female offenders have to be transported to nearby hospitals to give birth, and shortly afterward, they are immediately ushered back to prison, leaving their newborns at the mercy of others. The courts, in general, have maintained a hands-off approach, delegating any such decision to correctional officials. Prison officials, most often are in favor of mother and child separation, and when imprisoned mothers have sued to keep their newborns with them inside prison walls, they lost (*Cardell* v. *Enomoto* 1976). Some states, however, have readjusted their procedures to allow mothers to remain with their newborns by enacting legislation to grant women immediate parole upon birth. Other states have instituted laws whereby female prisoners and their babies can reside in community correctional facilities. Decisions of this nature take into consideration several factors, including seriousness of offense and prior criminal history.

Maintaining ties with children left to be cared for by relatives or friends or even the state is a major concern of female prisoners. Upon incarceration, these women (mainly single) were the sole providers of care to their children, and though ties are severed because of imprisonment, these mothers live with pain and guilt from lack of interaction with their children. At times, many imprisoned women are pressured to place their children up for adoption. In these cases, the courts operate with the premise that the needs of children take precedence over parental rights.

Whether or not imprisoned women can support their children upon their release from prison strongly influences states' decisions to release children back to them. So, if women are not provided with vocational training programs, it becomes even more difficult for them to reunite with their children.

Protection against out-of-state transfers is a right guaranteed to female offenders by the Constitution. A case of this nature, *Park* v. *Thomson* (1976), was challenged in court. The court ruled that this type of transfer would create a hardship for the offender.

No adequate classification system exists for female prisoners; the current system is more congruent to the needs of male prisoners. Without a proper system for females, the less serious female offenders are housed with more serious felony offenders. Rippon and Hassell (1981) suggested this to be "unintentional punishment." In the absence of an appropriate classification system for women, the court ruled it unconstitutional to treat female offenders more harshly than male prisoners by imprisoning the less serious offenders with hardened female offenders (*Commonwealth* v. *Stauffer* 1969).

Privacy rights for imprisoned women is a matter in which court intervention was necessary. Women at the Bedford Hills Prison claimed an invasion of privacy with the presence of guards near showers and cells, especially during evening hours. The lower court deemed it important to uphold the privacy rights of female prisoners and restricted the assignment of male correctional officers to certain areas within the prison. Later, a portion of this decision was reversed by the Second Circuit Court of Appeals when the court argued that women should be afforded more privacy during sleep hours by issuing them pajamas (protection against nightgowns becoming disarranged during sleeptime), by installing frosted glass showers, and by using more-suitable procedures to afford female prisoners more privacy with the presence of male correctional officers working in female prisons (*Forts* v. *Ward* 1980).

Female offenders have challenged the differential punishment strategies to which they are subject on the basis of gender discrimination. Upon hearing the *Canterino* v. *Wilson* (1982) case, the court held that the system (Kentucky) used discriminatory procedures that were in direct violation of the constitutional rights of female offenders in that they were punished differently from their male counterparts, even if the offense was of a minor nature. More specifically, the court noted a system influenced by "gender" without meaningful goals or direction.

Female prisoners have better access to the courts through law books and law clerks (other offenders) resulting from the *Bounds* v. *Smith* (1977) case. Because female prisoners were not provided legal services and programs (law books, inmate lawyers), the court, through *Glover* v. *Johnson* (1979), mandated that Michigan provide paralegal training for female prisoners, thereby facilitating access to the courts. In a similar vein, the Kentucky court system ruled, based on equal protection, that legal services and programs (law libraries, books, etc.) for female prisoners be restructured to make them equivalent to those provided male prisoners (*Canterino* v. *Wilson*, 1982).

Policy Implications and Recommendations

Crime among women, though not as astronomical as that of men, has changed considerably since the early bridewell days. Today's female offender is not only committing crimes of a sexual nature—prostitution—she is also committing more serious type of offenses: larceny, fraud, embezzlement, forgery, drug offenses (possession, use, trafficking), aggravated assault, and murder.

The treatment (disciplinary, training, services) of women in prison since the old bridewell days, when they were cast into the old dark hulks with their male counterparts, has changed significantly. Today, women are not as subject to the harsh physical and sexual abuse of yesterday. This is not to say, however, that these practices still do not exist; since the 1960s, women have sought to keep these practices in check by seeking redress through the courts.

However, training programs for the imprisoned woman, with the exception of a few minor changes, have remained somewhat stagnant. Imprisoned women continue to be provided with vocational training skills (laundry work, sewing, cooking, cosmetology, clerical) that revolve around the theme "womanhood" or "gender role," perhaps in an attempt to mold them into wives, mothers, and homemakers. Female prisoners of today are far removed from this ideal.

The characteristics of imprisoned women today are quite different from those of yesterday: they are the primary caretakers of their children; they are welfare recipients; many are illiterate with no marketable skills; and many are addicted to drugs (cocaine, heroin, alcohol). As more women enter the prison system, these problems will become greater; therefore, it is of paramount importance that specific recommendations be made relevant to the treatment of women using the following recommendations:

1. Institute training programs that would enable imprisoned women to become literate.
2. Provide female offenders with programs that do not center on traditional gender roles—programs that will lead to more economic independence and self-sufficiency.
3. Establish programs that would engender more positive self-esteem for imprisoned women and enhance their assertiveness and communication and interpersonal skills.
4. Establish more programs that would allow imprisoned mothers to interact more with their children and assist them in overcoming feelings of guilt and shame for having deserted their children. In addition, visitation areas for mothers and children should be altered to minimize the effect of a prison-type environment.
5. An alternative to mother-and-child interaction behind prison bars would be to allow imprisoned mothers to spend more time with their children outside of the prison.
6. Provide imprisoned mothers with training to improve parenting skills.

7. Establish more programs to treat drug-addicted female offenders. Moreover, once departing prison, these women should have adequate follow-up care/treatment.
8. Establish a community partnership program to provide imprisoned women with employment opportunities.
9. Establish a better classification system for incarcerated women—one that would not permit the less-hardened offender to be juxtaposed with the hardened female offender.
10. Provide in-service training (sensitivity awareness) to assist staff members (wardens, correctional officers) in understanding the nature and needs of incarcerated women.

References

Allen, H., & Simonsen, C. (1986). *Corrections in America.* New York: Macmillan.

Barefield v. *Leach*, 10282 (D.N.M., 1974).

Baunach, P. (1982). You can't be a mother and be in prison. . . can you? Impacts of the mother-child separation. In B.R. Price & N. Sokoloff (Eds.), *The criminal justice system and women* (pp. 64–65). New York: Clark Boardman.

Bershad, L. (1985). Discriminatory treatment of the female offender in the criminal justice system. *Boston College Law Review* 26(2): 389–438.

Bounds v. *Smith*, 430, U.S. 817 (1977).

Burkhardt, K. (1979). *Women in prison.* Garden City, NY: Doubleday.

Canterino v. *Wilson*, 546 F. Supp. 174 (W.D. Ky. 1982).

Cardell v. *Enomoto*, 701-094 (Sup. ct. Calif. San Francisco Co. 1976).

Commonwealth v. *Stauffer*, 214 (Pa. Super. 113, 241 A. 2d 718, 1969).

Cooper v. *Pate*, 378, U.S. 546 (1964).

Dobash, R., Dobash, R., & Gutteridge, S. (1986). *The imprisonment of women.* New York: Basil Blackwell.

Estelle v. *Gamble*, 429, U.S. 97 (1976).

Feinman, C. (1984). An historical overview of the treatment of treatment of incarcerated women: Myths and realities of rehabilitation. *Prison Journal* 63(2): 12–26.

Forts v. *Ward*, 434 F. Supp. 946 (S.D.N.Y.) rev'd and remanded, 566 F. 2d 849 (2d Cir. 1977), 471 F. Supp. 1095 (S.D.N.Y. 1979), affd in part and rev'd in part, 621 F. 2d 1210 (2d Cir. 1980).

Fox, J. (1984). Women's prison policy, prisoner activism, and the impact of the contemporary feminist movement. *Prison Journal* 64(2): 15–36.

Freedman, E. (1974). Their sister's keepers: A historical perspective of female correctional institutions in the U.S. *Feminist Studies* 2: 77–95.

——— (1981). *Their sister's keepers: Women's prison reform in America, 1830–1930.* Ann Arbor: University of Michigan Press.

Glick, R., & Neto, V. (1977). *National study of women's correctional programs.* Washington, DC: U.S. Department of Justice.

Glover v. *Johnson*, 478 F. Supp. 1075 (E.D. Mich. 1979).

Goetting, A., & Howser, M. (1983). Women in prison: A profile. *Prison Journal* 63: 27–46.

Jones, A. (1980). *Women who kill.* New York: Fawcett Book Group.

Lekkerkerker, E.C. (1931). *Reformatories for women in the United States.* Gronigen, the Netherlands: J. B. Wolters.

Lett v. *Withworth*, C-1-77-246 (S.D. Oh. 1976).

Lombroso, C. (1894). *The female offender.* New York: Appleton.

McDonough, J., Iglehart, A., Sarri, R., & Williams, T. (1981). *Females in prison in Michigan, 1968–1978.* Ann Arbor: University of Michigan, Institute of Social Research.

Morales v. *Turman*, 383 F. Supp. 53 (E.D. Tex. 1974).

Park v. *Thomson*, 356 F. Supp. 783 (D. Hawaii 1976).

Pollock-Byrne, J. (1990). *Women, prison, & crime.* Pacific Grove, CA: Brooks/Cole.

Rafter, N. (1985). *Partial justice: State prisons and their inmates, 1800–1935,* Boston, MA: Northeastern University Press.

Rippon, M., & Hassell, R. (1981). Women, prison and the Eighth Amendment. *North Carolina Central Law Journal* 12: 434–460.

Ruffin v. *Commonwealth*, 62 Va. 790 (1871).

Stanton, A. (1980). *When mothers go to jail.* Lexington, MA: Lexington Books.

U.S. Department of Justice (1988). *Report to the nation on crime and justice.* Washington, DC: U.S. Government Printing Office.

Intimate Abuse Within an Incarcerated Female Population: Rates, Levels, Criminality, a Continuum, and Some Lessons about Self-Identification

William R. Blount
University of South Florida

Joseph B. Kuhns III
Florida Mental Health Institute

Ira J. Silverman
University of South Florida

Acknowledgments

The authors wish to acknowledge the gracious cooperation of the Florida Department of Corrections; Richard L. Dugger, Secretary; with particular recognition to Marta Villacorta, Superintendent of Broward Correctional Institution; James E. Curington, Jr., Superintendent of Florida Correctional Institution; his administrative secretary, Rene Smith; and Robert P. Kriegner, FDOC's Research and Statistics Administrator. Marie Apsey, Hillsborough County Victims Assistance Program Coordinator; and Magdalene Deutsch and Dr. Manuel Vega, Department of Criminology, University of South Florida also deserve special thanks. Finally, we are heavily indebted to the many women who agreed to participate and to those individuals who helped us record their stories: Carrie Scholz, Susan E. Dalton, Debra VanAusdale, Lynn Conner, Girlesa Cadavid, Tabatha Burns, Verndina Moore, Cecilia Troutman, Greta Snitkin, Doreen Phillips, Sonia Clarke, Roy Heinz, Candace Christensen, Brenda Wood, Kendra Smith, and Conrad Zamka.

This research was supported in part by research grants CO180, CO223, and CO242 from the Florida Department of Corrections.

Address correspondence to William R. Blount, Department of Criminology-SOC 107, University of South Florida, 4202 E. Fowler Avenue, Tampa, FL 33620–8100.

Abstract

Using a definition of Less Severe abuse (pushing/shoving/ slapping) and a random sample of 178 Florida female inmates, a full two-thirds qualified. With a definition of More Severe abuse (broken bones/beating), one-third qualified. That abuse at any level is characterized by an accompanying array of other controlling and intimidating behaviors, in addition to those of physical battery, is documented and discussed. The commonalities across levels become a continuum, and abuse is shown to be a continuum of control and intimidation, one wherein physical attacks are but one means to an end.

No difference in the rate of severe abuse among Florida's incarcerated women was noted over a four-year period even though major changes have taken place in Florida's female prison population (a marked decrease in the proportion of women incarcerated for violent offenses occasioned by a 36% increase in the female inmate population, most of whom were women incarcerated for drug offenses).

Overall, 32% of the women felt they had been mistreated; 3% met neither definition, 21% were in the Less Severe group, and 71% were in the More Severe group. The impact of socialization on the one hand and the difficulties of ownership on the other are discussed as contributing factors to this critical decision.

While this population did not appear to be atypical of women in general, that the rates of abuse were so very much higher (6 to 10 times even by conservative estimates) indicated that abuse and criminality occur together and, like substance abuse, are part of that subculture.

We would suggest an addiction model be used to understand the dynamics of abuse, such that the controlling and intimidating behaviors (including the physical attacks), once a means to an end, become an end in themselves. Such a model at once allows for movement from states of little or no abuse to states of continuous and brutal abuse, yet also accounts for relationships where the nature and severity of abuse (or lack thereof) remain constant.

Introduction

The young woman known as Gayle (not her real name) is a 29-year-old black high school graduate who has not attended college. She has five sisters, two brothers, and one child. During the three and a half hours the authors spent with her, Gayle reported that, during her most recent intimate relationship, her boyfriend pushed her, shoved her, forcibly poked her in the chest or arm, slapped her, beat her, forced her to have sex after he beat her, threatened to hurt her physically, controlled who she associated with, read her mail, laughed at her when she was angry, referred to her in the third person, humiliated her by making her beg, screamed or shouted in her face, and checked up on her to make sure she was doing what she said she would be doing.

The woman known as Lisa (not her real name) is a white 48-year-old with a GED who was trained both as a nurse's aide and an optical lab technician. She has four sisters. Lisa and her husband have two children (now in their 20s), and she has three from a previous marriage. She reported that her husband had given her a black eye, given her bruises, punched her, grabbed her hard enough to bruise, beat her, threw her down, twisted her arm, tore her clothing, backhanded her, slapped her, and hit her with an object. He also made her feel bad about herself, blamed her for the lack of money, threatened to keep the kids if she left him, threatened to leave her without money, slammed doors and cupboards, and pounded his fists on the table.

These are not atypical stories of battered women. Similar accounts may be found in Prizzey (1974), Martin (1976), Browne (1987), and Walker (1979) to name only a few. What may be atypical, however, is that both Gayle and Lisa are in prison; Gayle for punching a law enforcement officer in the face when the officer arrested her for stealing a car, and Lisa for forgery. Even though both have criminal records, this is their first experience in prison. How Gayle and Lisa compare with other women in prison, those who have abuse histories and those who do not, and what they can teach us about the nature of abuse, is the subject of this essay.

Walker (1984) had asserted that many women currently in prison in this country have been battered. She further indicated that up to one-half of these women are in prison for offenses they committed to avoid further battering, including check forgery to pay bills, theft of food or other items that were denied by the batterer, selling drugs to maintain the batterer's source of supply, and hurting another person so the batterer would not hurt her. Assertions of this kind are quite common, and while they may be true, they are questionable because they lack a concrete empirical base.

Perhaps such assertions are a function of the many studies that deal with women who kill their partners and the role of abuse in those homicides (i.e., Biggers 1979; Browne 1987; Mann 1988; Walker 1984, 1989; Weisheit 1984). In fact, only one known study, conducted by Crawford (n.d.), other than that by Blount, Vega, and Silverman (1988), focused on examining abuse within the relationships experienced by the larger population of women in prison.

Crawford (n.d.) surveyed a representative sample of 1,880 adult female offenders incarcerated in state correctional facilities and 214 juvenile offenders held in long-term juvenile state facilities. She found that 20.8% of the adults and 4% of the juveniles reported being physically abused by a husband. Abuse by boyfriends was reported by 23.4% and 12.3%, respectively. Fourteen percent reported that such abuse occurred one to two times, 40% reported that it happened three to ten times, and 46% reported that it occurred 11 times or more. Further, 5.85% of the adults indicated they were sexually abused by their husbands, while no juveniles reported this type of abuse. Finally, 1.6% of the adults and 1.1% of the juveniles indicated that they had committed the offense for which they were incarcerated "to escape abuse."

The present authors (Blount, Vega, and Silverman 1988) collected data from the records of 1,076 women incarcerated in Florida during August 1985, a sample that included all women incarcerated for murder and that represented 90% of all women incarcerated in the state's prisons during that month. There were sufficient data in the files to make a decision relative to severe physical abuse in 46.1% of the cases (n = 496). Data from these cases revealed that 25.4% had been involved in intimate relationships in which they were battered. Of the women incarcerated for homicide, half had been battered by intimates, and in three-quarters of the cases, those same women killed their abusers.

While the information in the inmate files maintained by the Florida Department of Corrections is excellent as far as it goes, its purpose is not to document interpersonal relationships. Much of that type of information is contained in the presentence/postsentence investigation reports, documents often incomplete or missing altogether from inmate records. Even after almost a year of effort devoted to tracking documents across the state, we were only able to find sufficient information to feel comfortable coding battery or the lack thereof for half the population. While confident regarding these data, verification was sought on the abuse rate and thus inquiries were expanded to include face-to-face interviewing. Some of the results of those interviews are reported here.

By describing the women who participated in the study, it is hoped that a contribution to the literature on female offenders could be made and that these women could provide a perspective that might help the reader better understand the overall dynamics of spouse abuse. Accordingly, the data were approached in four ways: (a) to examine rates of physical abuse, (b) to examine the constellation of other behaviors associated with levels of physical abuse, (c) to examine how levels of abuse might be associated with demographic and criminal variables, and (d) to learn what these women might teach about the more general issue of assimilating abusive experiences.

Definitions

The phrase, "abuse between intimates" (or "intimate abuse") is preferred to that of spouse abuse. Although both appear in these pages and are used synonymously, "intimate" is the more accurate. The area of interest here, which is also common throughout the abuse/domestic violence literature, was with intimate couples regardless of marital status. Accordingly, the women were questioned about intimate relationships, not about relationships between spouses. There are, therefore, relationships included in these data in which the two principals were not married. Further, since the study's orientation concerned relationships, relationships were also reported where the two principals were of the same gender. While the former situation (not married) would not make these data unique, the presence of the latter might. The exact number of lesbian relationships is unknown (although it is not large) and they were not separated in this manner, but the reader is advised that they exist.

"Abuse," too, has been defined in various ways. While a full exploration of the many definitional issues is beyond the scope of this essay, two definitions were selected for the present purpose. The use of more than one definition allowed the authors (a) to appeal directly to more than one opinion about the specific behaviors that constitute abuse; (b) to note if those specific behaviors are associated with other variables differentially; (c) to be cautious when making generalizations about the typical abused woman, a temptation too easily acceded to when only a single view is employed; and (d) to address a broader spectrum of behaviors.

To this end, the definitions were selected with some care, and do reflect what is common in the literature. These choices also provide an insight into at least one of the debates currently in progress, that is, when abuse is synonymous with battery (Weis 1989).

The first definition, modeled after Straus (1990), consisted of most of the items used in the Conflict Tactic Scales defined as "minor" violence. This was the more general of the two definitions and contained the more "benign" behaviors (pushing, shoving, grabbing). This definition tended to classify individuals as abused more liberally than did the second but, like the second, spoke specifically to physical abuse.

The second definition was taken from the authors' earlier work (Blount, Vega, & Silverman 1988; Blount et al.) and was meant to be a fairly restrictive definition of abuse/battery. This definition required an injury sufficient to require hospitalization, whether or not hospitalization occurred. It involved such things as burning with a cigarette, scalding, breaking bones, beatings, physically attacking the sexual parts of the body, or combinations of other types of physical punishment. Table 1 presents the items for both definitions. In order not to give false impressions about the severity of the abuse to which these women were subject, the names of the categories are those of "Less Severe" and "More Severe."

Table 1
Defitional Elements

Less Severe		More Severe
As Used by Strauss[1]	As Used Here	
Pushing	Pushing/shoving	Broke bones in body
Shoving		Beating
Grabbing	Grabbing hard enough to bruise	Burn with a cigarette, hot water, burner, etc.
Slapping	Slapping/Backhand	Cut nipples with a knife
Throwing things	No equivalent	Cause to bleed during sex
No equivalent	Forcefully poking chest or arm	Give a black eye *and* give bruises *and* punch; *and* kick

1 E.g., 1990.

Both definitions include only physical acts and may be legally characterized as battery and aggravated battery. Many other definitions were possible, including those that contained a broader range of behaviors that could include psychological and economic factors such as those mentioned by both Gayle and Lisa. However, it is the descriptions of physical acts, specifically those of severe physical mistreatment, which are most widely recognized in the abuse literature and are the only factors that bring intervention by the criminal justice system (when they are recognized in that context at all).

Moreover, the physical acts are merely symptomatic of a constellation of behaviors designed to intimidate and control (Blount, Vega, & Silverman 1988; Pence & Peymor 1986). Therefore, if selected strictly on the basis of these clearly defined physical items, the larger and often less well-defined array of behaviors that accompany them should be identified. Once documented, the term "abuse" could be used in its broadest sense.

Participants

Gayle's and Lisa's histories of abuse immediately both sets them apart from some of the women in prison and aligns them with others, just as their criminal record differentiates them from "free" women and, at the same time, unites them with their fellow inmates. They are 2 of 178 women in Florida's prisons randomly selected in September 1989 who consented to participate in this study. The subjects were drawn from Broward Correctional Institution and Florida Correctional Institution, the two primary facilities for women in Florida at the time of the study. The data reported here were part of a larger effort that involved three groups of subjects: two in prison and one in the "free" world. The other prison group consisted of the women who were incarcerated for homicide and who had not been selected for the random sample, while the nonprison sample was drawn from four shelters for battered women from around the state. In all, 311 interviews were completed, 178 comprising the main and random sample.

After their initial orientation and training, the first five or six interviews by each interviewer were closely monitored and reviewed, and the interviewer was thoroughly debriefed. Further, as each interview was finished, the questionnaire was immediately reviewed for obvious omissions or unclear responses. Each interview took from two to four and a half hours. Data collection took place between October 1989 and February 1990.

Because of work assignments, court dates, medical visits, and transfers, it was often necessary to make several attempts to see a particular inmate. In 16 cases, inmates who were initially identified as being housed in one prison were eventually interviewed in the other.

Inmates were given every consideration by our all-female interview team, were assured they could refuse to answer any individual question with which they felt uncomfortable, and could also choose to terminate the interview at any time. Only two chose to do so once we saw them face to face. There were another 20 of the originally selected 200 we were unable to interview in spite of all our efforts. It is possible that at least a few of these simply made themselves unavailable.

Data Collection Instrument

In addition to basic demographic information and a section dealing with childhood experiences, the major portions of the interview schedule examined relationships and the dynamics associated with those relationships. One portion included a list of 134 different behaviors that could be considered abusive. Referred to as "The Behavior Checklist," the items appear here as the appendix. The checklist included 29 physical behaviors, 16 sexual behaviors, 32 verbal behaviors, 46 nonverbal behaviors, and 11 behaviors involving children. The frequency of each (never, rarely, sometimes, often) was also recorded. These items were drawn from the literature and the personal experiences of abuse counselors.

It is important to note that the words "abuse" or "abusive" never appeared in the questions, *nor were they ever used during the interviews*.

The remaining sections of the interview schedule examined issues that might have resulted in arguments, attempts to get help, the reactions of others to their situations, and examined whether the respondents felt they had ever been mistreated. In addition to the main schedule of some 250 items, separate questions were prepared for specific groups. If an individual was involved in a homicide, questions probed the participation of the subject's intimate in the offense. If the individual was involved in the homicide of an intimate, separate questions were prepared for that circumstance as well. Additional information for the incarcerated subjects examined the instant offense, sentencing information, and prior arrests.

Because of the relatively small number of women involved in the random sample (approximately 12% of the women then incarcerated), we were interested in the extent to which this sample accurately reflected the prison population as a whole. An earlier study (Lanza-Kaduce et al. 1990) provided a series of variables for all women incarcerated in Florida as of June 30, 1989. Table 2 provides a comparison of those selected demographic and criminal variables for which similar measures were available. With the possible exception of our sample being slightly younger, the sample is characteristic of the population of women incarcerated throughout Florida at that time.

Rates of Abuse

The random sample was divided into three groups: those who met the definition of Less Severe abuse, those who met the definition of More Severe abuse, and those who met the Neither definition.

The 178 women were found to be divided almost equally: 33.1% in the Neither category ($n = 59$), 34.3% in the Less Severe category ($n = 61$); and 32.6% in the More Severe category ($n = 58$). These data are at the top of Table 3 on page 427.

We were immediately struck by three facts. First, the population had divided so evenly. Consistent with our earlier findings, we had expected approximately 25% of the population to fall within the More Severe category but were completely unprepared for such an even division. Second, the rate of battery as defined by our More Severe criteria had increased from 25% to 33%. Some increase in rate was likely simply because we had conducted personal interviews rather than having relied only on information in the prison records, but we were

Table 2

A Comparison of the Random Sample to the Total Female Prison Population

Background Variable	1989 Population[1] (n = 1,444)	Random Sample[2] (n = 178)
Age		
< 26	30.4	36.0
26–30	30.5	20.8
> 30	39.1	43.3
Race		
White	43.5	44.4
Nonwhite	56.5	55.6
Offense		
Homicide/ manslaughter	16.6	14.6
Other violent	14.8	16.9
Property	21.9	24.7
Drug	38.5	41.0
Other	7.8	2.8
Sentence length		
0–4 years	58.6	53.9
5 or more years	41.4	46.1

1 As of June 1989.

2 As of September 1989.

surprised by the small magnitude of that change. One obvious conclusion is that our earlier procedures and the data available produced excellent approximations to those figures obtainable by direct interview. Aside from this important methodological point, we had confirmed over four years with two samples and two methodologies that 25% to 33% of the female prison population have been severely battered at the hands of an intimate.

Third and finally, we also were provided with evidence that how one defines abuse radically affects the rate estimates. Using the Less Severe criteria, one-third of this population qualified as physically abused. The combination of this criteria with those of the More Severe criteria resulted in an overall proportion of 67% of the population reporting physical abuse. This proportion far exceeds the 44% reported by Crawford (n.d.) (21% suffered at the hands of husbands plus 23% suffered at the hands of boyfriends) but certainly adds credence to the assertion by Walker (1984) and others that the majority of women in prison have suffered some form of physical abuse. No support was found for the notion that the women were coerced into their criminal behavior by abusers.

Given that most of the women in our sample reported battery, and 25% to 33% reported severe battery, we wanted to gauge just how different these rates were from other groups of women. Straus and Gelles (1988) report 16 studies (including data from their 1975 and 1985 National Family Violence Surveys) that used the Conflict Tactics Scales on populations ranging from large probability samples to samples of dating couples to samples of couples in therapy. The definition we used for "Less Severe" is quite close to that used for "any violence" by Straus and Gelles. Rates reported for "any violence" by the husband on the wife (excluding couples in therapy) ranged from 108 per 1,000 to 355 per 1,000, with Straus and Gelles arguing that their rate of 116 per 1,000 is the most accurate. Not included in this list was a study by Teske and Parker (1983), who used a probability sample of all women living in Texas who were over 18 and held a valid Texas driver's license. The 1,210 respondents reported a rate of 62 per 1,000 for physical abuse within the last 12 months and 225 per 1,000 over their lifetimes.

Independent of which rate or rates truly reflect the general population, all pale in comparison to the 669 per 1,000 found here. This rate is more than six times that of the lowest, almost six times greater than that of Straus and Gelles and almost twice that of the higher rate. Only the rate reported by couples in therapy for marital conflict (740 per 1,000) comes close, and we would expect that rate to approach 100%.

Reporting on seven studies of "severe violence" by the husband (also including data from the 1975 and 1985 National Family Violence Surveys), Straus and Gelles note rates ranging from 8 per 1,000 to 102 per 1,000 and again suggest their rate of 34 per 1,000 is most accurate. The present definition of "More Severe" is virtually identical to "severe violence" as used by Straus and Gelles. As was true for any violence, the rates for our earlier incarcerated sample and the current one of 254 to 326 per 1,000 far exceeded those reported for the various samples from the "free" world. We are 32 to 40 times higher than that reported by Straus and Gelles, and 2 to 3 times higher than the most extreme rate reported.

In the face of these data, to conclude that incarcerated women suffer physical abuse to a greater extent than other women would seem the grandest of understatements. Their rate is many times that of women in the general population—conservatively 6 to 10 times as great.

Discussion of Similarities and Differences Between the Groups Generated by the Definitions

It is important to discuss the "Neither" group, the women who were either not abused at all or at least were not subject to the extent of abuse experienced by the women in the other two groups. While that was precisely the case as we shall presently demonstrate, this should not be interpreted to mean that none of the 59 women in this group experienced behaviors which, particularly if taken together, could be considered abusive. A careful examination of the individuals in this group revealed that at least 14% were in very tightly controlled situations, even though no incident of physical attack was reported.

For example, the 8 women comprising this 14% included individuals who selected 26 or more of the 134 items; one who selected 35 items; and, in the most extreme case, one who selected 42 (31% of 134 items). While there was great diversity among these eight individuals, the items selected included such things as control associates, control dress, read mail, ignore, laugh at when angry, play mind games, interrupt, insult family and friends, put you on a budget and then remove the money while constantly questioning you about spending habits and blaming you for the lack of money, restrain from leaving a room, control where you are, and control where you go.

Given this caveat, several procedures tested the assumption that the women included in the Neither group could be characterized as having a history of little or no abuse, that the individuals in the Less Severe group could be characterized as having a history of abuse more than the Neither group but less than the More Severe group, and that the More Severe group contained those women with the most severe abuse histories. One such set of analyses is presented in Table 3.

As Table 3 indicates, each of the analyses produced differences in the expected direction, confirming the premise that the experiences of the women in each of these groups were significantly different in intensity (the number of behaviors reported and the frequency with which they occurred). With respect to the average number of behaviors RARELY occurring, the Neither group reported the lowest mean at 4.86, significantly smaller than the Less Severe group mean of 9.03, which was also significantly smaller than the More Severe group mean of 15.22. For those events that were reported to have occurred SOMETIMES, the means were arranged in precisely the same way; the Neither group reported an average of 3.73, the Less Severe group reported 8.93, and the More Severe group reported an average of 17.24 behaviors. For those behaviors reported to have occurred OFTEN, the Neither group and the Less Severe group were not significantly different (averages of 1.93 and 4.03, respectively), but both reported significantly fewer behaviors than the 20.50 reported by the More Severe group.

Table 3

Average Number of Items Identified on the Behavior Checklist by Frequency of Occurrence by Level of Abuse[1]

Variable (n)	Neither (59) (33.1%)	Less Severe (61) (34.3%)	More Severe (58) (32.6%)	F	*p*	# of pairs significant
# RARELY occurring	4.86	9.03	15.22	22.05	<.0001	all
# SOMETIMES occurring	3.73	8.93	17.24	39.44	<.0001	all
# OFTEN occurring	1.93	4.03	20.50	29.88	<.0001	2
TOTAL behaviors indicated	10.52	21.95	53.40	73.24	<.0001	all
Median # occurring	8	18	50			
Range	0–42	2–73	3–123			
Average % reported[2]	8%	16%	40%			
Sumtot[3]	18.12	39.00	111.21	58.64	<.0001	all

1 Twelve individuals reported none of the behaviors had ever occurred in their most recent intimate relationship, and four reported only one. All 16 were in the Neither group.

2 Computed by dividing the average reported for TOTAL by 134.

3 A measure incorporating the frequency with which each behavior occurred; such that each behavior which occurred RARELY was weighted "1," each which occurred SOMETIMES was weighted "2," and each OFTEN was weighted "3," and the weights were summed.

Predictably, the TOTAL reported behaviors followed the established pattern with the Neither group's average of 10.52 being significantly lower than the Less Severe group's average of 21.95 and that being smaller than the More Severe group's 53.40. Moreover, while the ranges provide insight into the variety of behaviors reported (the "accompanying arrays of behaviors"), they, along with the medians and average percentage reported, also followed the now familiar pattern. "Sumtot," a measure incorporating the frequency with which behaviors occurred, also followed the pattern (18, 39, 111) and should be interpreted similarly, that is, more behaviors more often.

Noting how the frequencies lie within each group was also revealing. For example, of 53.40 total behaviors reported by the women in the More Severe group, most occurred OFTEN (20.50), fewer occurred SOMETIMES (17.24), and the fewest occurred RARELY (15.22). This progression was reversed for the other two groups (most occurring RARELY and the fewest occurring OFTEN). Further, the 20.50 behaviors by the More Severe group reported to have occurred OFTEN represented 40% of all behaviors reported. This was in contrast to the 1.93 (Neither) and 4.03 (Less Severe), which represented less than 20% of the behaviors reported.

Given that the quantity of behaviors and the frequency with which they occurred were obviously different, the specific behaviors themselves were scrutinized to determine if those most often reported by each group were also different. Table 4 indicates both differences and similarities and clearly documents the array of behaviors that accompany physical abuse.

Similar

Beginning with the group for which physical abuse was absent, the top five items reported by the Neither group were (a) tell you he knows what you are thinking (45.8%); (b) laugh at you when you are angry (39.0%); (c) control who you associate with (35.6%); (d) slams doors and cupboards (32.2%); and (e) tell you you're crazy (29.3%). Each of these five behaviors was also reported by at least one-third of the Less Severe group and four were reported by more than one-half.

Further, each of these five behaviors were also reported by more than 60% of the women in the More Severe group, and four were reported by 70% or better. In addition, six of the Neither group's "Top 10" were among the "Top 10" for the Less Severe group, and three were among the "Top 10" of the More Severe group (represented by the quote marks on Table 4). In fact, all of the Neither group's "Top 10" were also reported by the other two groups and all typically at much higher percentages.

These results suggest a commonality of experiences as one scans from a nonabusive situation to a severely abusive one and from a relationship devoid of physical violence and pain to one where that is a consistent theme. The remainder of Table 4 amplifies these phenomena. Notice, for example, that only two physical items appear in the Less Severe "Top 10," one in the top third (pushing/shoving, 60.7%) and one in the bottom third (slapping, 48.3%). In the More Severe "Top 10," however, the four most commonly reported behaviors are all physical, and the reporting rates have jumped to 80%.

Notice too that the array of behaviors accompanying the physical items also increase in the frequency with which they are reported as do the physical items themselves when they appear. It is the accompanying behaviors, the "arrays" to which we referred earlier, which allow us now to use the term "abuse" in its broader sense, that is, to represent a constellation of behaviors with a broader purpose. Only some of those behaviors might be physical.

Internally Consistent

We also are struck by the internal consistency of each group. The women in each group quite clearly agreed on the most common behaviors, particularly the top five. The extent to which these behaviors are common increases dramatically with each successive level—from approximately 30% in the Neither group through 50% in the Less Severe group to 80% agreement in the More Severe group.

Table 4

Behaviors Most Frequently Reported[1,2]

Neither Top 10	Neither %	Less Severe %	More Severe %
1. Tells you he knows what you're thinking	**45.8**	54.1"	59.6
2. Laughs at you when you're angry	**39.0**	47.5'	77.6"
3. Controls who you associate with	**35.6**	45.9	77.6"
4. Slams doors, cupboards	**32.5**	31.1	69.0
5. Tells you you're crazy	**29.3**	52.5"	75.9'
6. Reminds you he's the man of the family	**28.8**	50.0'	74.1
6. He makes all the "big" decisions	**28.8**	68.3"	62.1
8. Interrupts you when you're trying to express yourself	**27.1**	44.3	70.7
8. He watches pornographic films	**27.1**	33.3	41.4
10. Checks up on you to make sure you're doing what you told him	**25.4**	62.3"	70.7
Less Severe Top 10			
1. He makes all the "big" decisions	28.8'	**68.3**	62.1
2. Checks up on you to make sure you're doing what you told him	25.4'	**62.3**	70.7
3. Pushing/shoving you	-0-	**60.7**	79.3
4. Tells you he knows what you're thinking	45.8"	**54.1**	59.6
5. Tells you you're crazy	29.3"	**52.5**	75.9'
6. Restrains you from leaving a room	11.9	**50.0**	75.9'
7. Reminds you he's the man of the family	28.8'	**50.0**	74.1

8. Slapping you	-0-	**48.3**	82.4"
9. Laughs at you when you're angry	39.0"	**47.5**	77.6"
9. Screams or shouts in your face	18.6	**47.5**	75.9
More Severe Top 10			
1. Slapping you	-0-	48.3	**82.4**
2. Gave you bruises	-0-	18.0	**80.4**
3. Pushing/shoving you	-0-	60.7"	**79.3**
4. Beating you	-0-	-0-	**78.9**
5. Controls where you go	23.7	46.7	**77.6**
5. Controls who you associate with	35.6"	45.9	**77.6**
5. Laughs at you when you are angry	39.0"	47.5"	**77.6**
8. Talking in loud tones	23.7	42.6	**77.6**
9. Restrains you from leaving a room	11.9	50.0'	**75.9**
9. Tells you you're crazy	29.3"	52.5"	**75.9**
9. Screams or shouts in your face	18.6	47.5'	**75.9**

1 As reflected by the proportion of women in each group who indicated that the behavior had occurred at least once in their most recent intimate relationship.

2 A double quote (") indicates the item ranks in the top 5 of another group; single quote (') indicates the item is one of the last 5 of another group.

While it may be a coincidence, we also noticed that the behavior reported most often in the Neither group (tell you he knows what you are thinking, 45.8%) was less frequently reported than the lowest behavior reported for the Less Severe group (scream or shout in your face, 47.5%), a pattern which also appeared when comparing the behavior reported most often in the Less Severe group (he makes all the "big" decisions, 68.3%) with the least commonly reported behavior of the More Severe group (scream or shout in your face, 75.9%).

Yet Different

While there were commonalities across groups, there were differences as well not only in terms of the frequency with which women identified those behaviors as having occurred but also in terms of the specific behaviors that were reported. We can particularly see the infusion of control/intimidation behaviors that do not involve physical contact; at first, only a few are reported and then more are commonly reported—subtle differences perhaps, yet present nonetheless. Specifically, the Neither group reported three such behaviors (two controlling and one intimidating): control who you associate with (ranked third at 36%), check up on you (ranked tenth at 25%), and the intimidator of slamming doors and cupboards (ranked fourth at 33%), and these were reported by fewer than half of the women in the group. The Less Severe group also reported two controlling and one intimidating behaviors, but these behaviors were not only reported by more members of this group, they could be characterized as restricting and intrusive: check up on you (now ranked second at 60%), restrain you from leaving a room (ranked sixth at 50%), and the intimidating scream and shout in your face (ranked ninth at 48%). These accompany the two physical items of pushing/shoving (ranked third at 61%) and slapping (ranked eighth at 48%).

At the More Severe level, there are five behaviors (three controlling and two intimidating), each of which is quite common. The three control behaviors are control where you go (ranked fifth at 78%), control who you associate with (also ranked fifth at 78%), and restrain you from leaving a room (ranked ninth at 76%), while the two intimidating behaviors are talk in loud tones (ranked eighth at 78%) and scream and shout in your face (ranked ninth at 76%). These are combined with four physical items (slapping, 82%; bruises, 80%; pushing/shoving, 79%; and beating, 79%), which ranked one through four, respectively.

While the three groups, therefore, represent three different types of environments, they would also appear to represent three different levels: each more restrictive, controlling, and intrusive. The first (Neither), where negative interactions are infrequent and verbal; the next (Less Severe), where negative interactions are more frequent and not only involve more restrictive and intrusive behaviors but involve battery as well; and the most extreme (More Severe), where the nonbattering behaviors are most intense and intrusive, and battery is common. The proportions also clearly demonstrate, moreover, that the behaviors identified by the women at the lower level were also experienced by the women in the other two. Those behaviors experienced at the middle level were not so common in the first and were quite common in the last. Our commonality has become a continuum of control and intimidation, one wherein the physical attacks are one of several means to an end.

Whether one moves from one level to another was beyond the design of the current study, but the suggestion is easily made. Women in the Neither group were in much better circumstances and in better relationships than were women in the other two groups, and it seems at least arguable that women in the Less Severe group were in better relationships than were women in the More Severe group. The Neither group then represents women who experienced few behaviors of an abusive nature. Whether or not these behaviors provide a foundation for moving from this level to those behaviors experienced by the Less Severe group (the addition of more intrusive and intense elements) and then on to those behaviors experienced by the More Severe group with the most intrusive, intense, and physically damaging elements is a worthy working hypothesis.

Demographics and Criminality

Demographic Characteristics

Having documented the levels represented by the three groups, it was of interest to see whether or not the differences in abuse histories were associated with demographics. These analyses are presented in Table 5.

The Less Severe group was younger by approximately 4 years than the other two groups and contained proportionately more nonwhite women. Straus and Gelles (1988) state that blacks are a population at high risk for violence, and since the black women in Smith's (1986) study were more likely to leave the relationship before it became repeatedly assaultive, we would have expected to find fewer and fewer nonwhite women as the level of abuse increased. That was not the case. Starke and Flitcraft (1988) indicate that the data on race are inconclusive. On the one hand, they cite evidence that abuse is two to three times greater among blacks than whites (not the case here), while on the other, they also indicate that among groups with similar incomes, blacks are less likely than whites to experience spousal violence. As there were no differences in weekly income among the current sample, we could expect greater proportions of whites in our more abusive groups. That, too, was not the case. These data suggest that race is *not* an issue, at least among incarcerated populations.

Women in the Neither group were better educated, showing a significantly greater proportion with degrees, in general, and advanced degrees, in particular. Half of the advanced degree holders (six) in the Neither group had AA degrees (compared to one in each of the other groups), one had a bachelor's degree (compared to one in the Less Severe group and three in the More Severe group), and five held post–high school technical degrees (compared to three in the Less Severe group and one in the More Severe group). Women in the Less Severe group were the least well educated.

Table 5
Demographic Characteristics by Abuse Group[1]

Variable	(n)	Neither (59)	Less Severe (61)	More Severe (58)	Total (178)	Signif. income level
Age in years		32.6	27.0	31.0	30.1	.001
Race						
White		55.9	32.8	44.8	44.4	
Nonwhite		44.1	67.2	55.2	55.6	.04
Degrees earned						
No degree		23.7	51.7	39.7	38.4	
High school		55.9	40.0	51.7	49.2	.007
AA, BA, other		20.4	8.3	8.6	12.4	
Years in school		11.5	10.8	10.7	11.0	ns
Weekly income[2]						
Less than $200		28.8	31.1	24.1	28.1	
$200 to $399		35.6	26.2	25.9	29.2	
$400 or more		35.6	42.6	50.0	42.7	ns
Employment[3]						
Noncriminal		72.4	53.4	55.2	60.3	
Criminal		27.6	46.6	44.8	39.7	.07
Parents married						
Yes		89.7	67.8	86.0	81.0	
No		10.3	32.2	14.0	19.0	.005
Changes in living arrangements						
None		62.3	39.2	60.0	54.1	
One or more		37.7	60.8	40.0	45.9	.03
Number of siblings		3.8	3.9	4.0	3.9	ns
Church attendance						
Regularly		52.8	52.0	39.6	48.1	
Not regularly		47.2	48.0	60.4	51.9	ns
Importance of religion						
Not		2.0	11.8	15.4	9.7	
Somewhat		23.5	17.6	15.4	18.8	
Very		74.5	70.6	69.2	7.4	ns

1 Percentages are reported except for age, years in school, and number of siblings.

2 The categories for weekly income were chosen because of the large amounts of money listed by women engaged in criminal activity (drug sales, forgery, prostitution) which greatly skewed absolute dollar figures.

3 Ninety-eight percent of the women were employed. The four unemployed women (one in the Neither group, and three in the Less Severe group) were dropped from the analysis.

While there were nonsignificant differences in the level of weekly income, the Neither group tended to earn their money through noncriminal means as opposed to the other two groups. The Less Severe group showed a significantly smaller proportion of their parents being married (67.8) and likewise a greater proportion of changes in living arrangements (60.8). There were no differences in the rate of church attendance or in the importance of religion.

Other than the Less Severe group being younger, containing a larger proportion of nonwhite women with fewer of their parents married, having experienced more living arrangement changes, and being the most poorly educated, and the Neither group appearing to be better educated than the other two, these data suggest that women within a prison population who suffer abuse are not demographically distinguishable from other female inmates.

Factors Relating to Criminality

We now turn our attention to factors relating to criminality. These are, after all, unique to this sample and one of the reasons we chose this population for study. Table 6 indicates that, like the demographic characteristics, there was little to distinguish these groups. If anything, there were fewer distinctions between the abuse groups considering their criminality than there were demographically.

The proportion of women incarcerated by offense category was not significantly different: roughly 15% being incarcerated for murder, 17% for other violent offenses, 25% for theft-related offenses, and the majority (42%) being incarcerated for drug-related offenses. This breakdown differs from that found 4 years earlier (Blount et al. 1991) in which 32% of the population was incarcerated for murder, 33% for other violent offenses, 25% for property offenses, and only 10% were in prison for drug and other offenses. It is apparent that the "war on drugs" has altered significantly the characteristics of the population of women in Florida's prisons in only 4 years (September 1985 to September 1989). It is also notable that one half of the women convicted of murder were in the More Severe abuse group in both samples.

Table 6
Factors Relating to Criminality[1]

Variable	(n)	Neither (59)	Less Severe (61)	More Severe (58)	Total (178)	Signif. income Level
Offense						
Murder		12.3	11.7	21.4	15.0	
Misc. violence		12.3	18.3	21.4	17.3	
Theft-related		28.1	30.0	17.9	25.4	
Drug offenses		47.4	40.0	39.3	42.2	ns
Co-defendants						
None		72.9	79.2	72.0	74.7	
Intimate		12.5	4.2	2.0	6.2	
Other		14.6	16.7	26.0	19.2	ns
Under the influence						
No		82.6	69.0	71.4	74.6	
Yes		17.4	31.0	28.6	25.4	ns
Sentence length in years		7.4	6.1	10.1	7.8	.06
Mandatory sentence						
No		77.6	88.5	84.2	83.5	
Yes		22.4	11.5	15.8	16.5	ns
If yes, average length:		11.1	8.1	17.9	12.5	ns
Prior adult offense						
No		44.4	45.5	40.7	43.6	
Yes		55.6	54.5	59.3	56.4	ns
If yes, average number:		11.4	5.1	5.1	7.1	.03

[1] Percentages are reported except for sentence length, average mandatory sentence length, and number of priors.

Three-quarters of the sample had no co-defendants, and when one was involved, it was someone other than the intimate. In addition, the majority of the women were not under the influence of alcohol or drugs at the time the crime was committed.

There was some distinction as a function of sentence length and number of prior adult offenses. Women in the More Severe group tended to have longer sentences, perhaps because of the larger number of individuals convicted of murder in this group. Even though just over one-half of each group indicated that a prior adult offense did exist, the Neither group reported twice as many as the other two groups, indicating that those offenses might have been of a less serious nature. The vast majority of the group (83.5%) did not have mandatory sentences of any kind, and if one existed, it tended to average 12.5 years. Such data provide no support for the suggestion that women were motivated to commit their criminal acts because of fear of abuse. Thus, with the exception of the More Severe group tending toward longer sentences and the Neither group's having significantly more prior adult offenses than those in the other two groups, those women who experienced little or no abuse (Neither) were again virtually indistinguishable from those women who had experienced abusive relationships. The notion that the Neither group might be less "criminal" (smaller proportion deriving income from criminal sources) seems obviated by the higher number of prior offenses among the repeat offenders in this group.

Comparison of the 1985 Prison Population and the 1989 Prison Population

As noted before, the proportion of women in prison by offense category changed dramatically over this period. The proportion of women incarcerated for theft-related offenses remained at 25%. For the other categories, both murder and other violent offenses declined by half—murder from 32% to 15% and other violent offenses from 33% to 17%. This amazing turnaround was occasioned by the sharp increase in women incarcerated for drug offenses which shifted the population in this category from a mere 10% four years ago to the current 42%.

This change in instant offense apparently brought with it several others. The proportion of women with prior offenses decreased from 68% to 56%, and the average number of prior arrests went from five to seven, indicating that the individuals convicted of drug offenses were coming to prison with longer arrest histories than the individuals already there who had been convicted of more violent offenses. In addition, we saw a dramatic reduction in the proportion of women under the influence of alcohol or drugs at the time of the arrest from 55% to 25%, which is particularly surprising given the huge increase in the proportion of women incarcerated for drug offenses. Other things remained relatively stable. The racial balance was identical. The use of co-defendants increased only slightly from 25% to 31%, and the number of years of reported education went up by 1, to 11. Overall, the female prison population increased by 36% during these same four years.

Reactions to Historical Precedent and Its Aftermath

Having thus far described three groups of women, each having experienced different levels of abusive relationships and having been unable to distinguish the groups by either the demographic or criminal variables available to us, we turned our attention to the reactions of these women to the nature of their most recent intimate relationships.

There are many descriptions of the roles historically assigned to women, and while there have been brief periods of enlightenment, the majority of that history is one of subjugation. Dobash and Dobash (1978) provide an excellent account of this legacy, including the Laws of Chastisement, which consolidated authority in the husband as the sole head of the household. Under these laws, a husband could physically punish his wife for various offenses, real or imagined. This tradition was embellished years later under English Common Law, which established the infamous "Rule of Thumb," allowing a husband to beat his wife with a rod or switch, provided the circumference was no greater than the girth at the base of his right thumb (Dobash & Dobash 1978).

On the secular side, a woman was viewed as the rightful property of her husband, and since he could be held responsible for her actions, it was deemed necessary that he be able to discipline her. For its part, organized religion reinforced and encouraged such subjugation not only by supporting the right of the husband to discipline (the Bible has often been quoted as a source and justification for male domination) but also by restricting her participation in the liturgy or excluding her entirely.

Although the U.S. Constitution was originally drawn up omitting the Laws of Chastisement, they were quickly reinstated through state and case law (Dobash & Dobash 1979). Without belaboring the point, women have not fared well in the courts since that time (e.g., Browne 1987; Okun 1986). Louisiana jurisprudence, for example, currently provides for the severe restriction or outright prohibition of expert testimony regarding the battered woman syndrome (Hudsmith 1987), and Edwards (1985) describes how the gender-role stereotypes have become codified in both civil and criminal remedies resulting in distinct differences in terms of the way the sexes are treated by the judiciary. In reviewing the laws of rape, Pagelow and Pagelow (1984) note that these statutes perpetuate the tradition of male dominance within the family not only in terms of the conditions under which prosecution will proceed but also in terms of the penalties.

Today, it is unlawful in every jurisdiction in the United States for a man to strike his wife. Attacks on spouses are covered by various assault and battery statutes, depending upon the jurisdiction (Frieze & Browne 1989; Goolkasian 1986). Even so, law enforcement both in this country (e.g., Kuhl & Saltzman 1985) and abroad (Edwards 1989) have traditionally treated incidents of spouse battery as private matters rather than matters for arrest. More recently, the Florida Supreme Court's (1990) Gender Bias Committee not only noted the shortcomings within the criminal justice system as it responds to women subjected to violence at the hands of men but also documented the more subtle forms of discrimination that permeate the system.

While women are no longer legal property of men, the combination of religious ideology and centuries of law expressly espousing, allowing, and encouraging violence against women has established a cultural mindset that continues to encourage women to be perceived as subservient to men. This mindset is manifested in families, in communities, and in neighborhoods.

For their part, women have either internalized or struggled against this identification. Victims of abuse by an intimate normalize, rationalize, or justify their partners' behaviors, typically citing stress, illness, drugs or alcohol, or that they probably deserved what they got for acting in a particular manner, or that men do after all have the right to hit their wives (Bograd 1988). Ferrer (1983) identified six techniques of rationalization used by battered women to neutralize their abuse. These include appeal to the salvation ethic, denial of the injury, denial of victimizer, denial of victimization, denial of options, and the appeal to higher loyalties.

Women have, therefore, been socialized not only to accept male dominance and control, but to expect and welcome it, perhaps even being uncomfortable without it. One would predict then, that these influences would also be a likely part of the life experiences of the women in our sample.

Evidence of Impact: Ownership and Denial

As noted previously, the word "abuse" or "abused" never appeared on the interview schedule, nor was it used by the interviewer at any time. There was, however, one question that provided insight into the woman's attitude toward her relationship. That question occurred after a section dealing with issues the couple may have had disagreements or arguments over and a section allowing the respondent to tell us how she felt about her partner when they first met and then again after she had come to know him well. The question was simply, "Did he ever mistreat you in any way?"

Before proceeding, we acknowledge that as benign and as value neutral as this question was meant to be, and even though it came often after an hour or more of conversation in a positive atmosphere, we recognize that "mistreatment" or "mistreated" is a value judgment. Thus, for a person to label themselves in this way requires the recognition that someone has done something to them that is bad or wrong. This is quite a different thing than applying such a label to someone else. It is a quantum leap.

Women have, after all, been socialized to accept many of the behaviors on the checklist as appropriate and normal within intimate relationships. Even if they suspected those behaviors were excessive, they may not have wished to admit that they were happening to them. Korbin (1986), for example, reports that she discovered a blatant history of abuse among two of the women she interviewed, yet neither had previously indicated any abuse. Upon questioning, Korbin reveals that the women did not report it, one because, from her perspective of growing up in a violent environment, her physical and sexual abuse was "normal" ("it happened to everyone"), and the other was ashamed.

Such conflicts have been apparent to those in the helping professions for some time, and there is much literature available describing the difficulties women face as they struggle to become aware of themselves as valuable and valued individuals. Part of this struggle involves accepting equal roles within the family and in a society that continually reinforces male domination as not only appropriate but expected. Sanford and Donovan (1984), for example, provide an excellent discussion of how women are socialized to be less assertive and less combative than men and the crippling impact of that socialization as they attempt to achieve individuality and parity. Walker (1979) also discusses the difficulty women have in classifying themselves as "battered." Many begin by describing "a friend" and are unclear regarding the behaviors that might fit the definition.

More recently, Kelly (1988) noted the lack of words available to describe these experiences adequately. The terms "battered woman" or "spouse abuse" did not exist until recently, and the cultural responses and pressures associated with those terms, where they do exist, have served to make it ever more difficult for women to apply these terms to themselves. "I don't understand," "I don't know," "No one ever told me" are most common.

Besides, as the cycle of violence so aptly points out (e.g., Walker 1979, 1984), there is always a state of reconciliation after an abusive incident in which the abuser is contrite, apologetic, loving, and a model companion. This, along with the fact the abuser does not behave that way "all the time," may serve to cloud feelings of "mistreatment."

Finally, to admit that one had been mistreated would be to admit that one was involved in a relationship with a mistreator. The shame of such bad judgment or such lack of control over how one is treated makes a person reluctant to make such an acknowledgment. It is easier by far to say "I am not mistreated" because "he does not mistreat me."

The woman we identified as Gayle chose this option. Even though she was in the More Severe group and later described beatings in detail, when given the opportunity to describe her mate, she indicated that he was attentive, handsome, gentle, wonderful, comforting, warm, and exciting; cared for others; and allowed her to be herself. Unlike Gayle, Lisa felt that she was mistreated and described her husband as dominating, strong, self-centered, suspicious, cold, possessive, and controlling, although she also indicated that he was gentle, wonderful, and exciting.

Gayle continued in her relationship, while Lisa left. Lisa indicated that she stayed in the relationship as long as she did because of the children, finally leaving because of "the severity of the beatings, the way he treated the kids, and his involvement with other women."

Are Gayle and Lisa typical? Table 7 suggests they are and confirms what history and an appreciation of the cultural mindset of "man as dominant by right" would lead us to believe, that is, there were women in each group who felt they had *not* been mistreated, in spite of some very clear evidence to the contrary. In response to that evidence, there were also women in each group who felt they *had* been mistreated. It was encouraging to note that the proportion of women who felt they had been mistreated increased significantly with the level of abuse, that is, almost none of the women in the Neither group felt mistreated (3.4%; $n = 2$), approximately one-fifth of the Less Severe group did (21.3%; $n = 13$), and over two-thirds of the More Severe group did (70.7%; $n = 41$). That 80% of the Less Severe group did not feel mistreated while 70% of the More Severe group did may be the most revealing aspect about the effects of socialization, what we expect, and what we are willing to tolerate in our intimate relationships.

Table 7
"Did He Ever Mistreat You" Responses by Abuse Group

	Neither	Less Severe	More Severe	Total
Mistreated?				
Yes (n)	2	13	41	56
(%)	3.4	21.3	70.7	31.5
No (n)	57	48	17	122
(%)	96.6	78.7	29.3	68.5
Total (n)	59	61	58	178
(%)	33.1	34.3	32.6	100.0

Note: Chi square (2) = 65.87, $p < .001$

What Lets Them Know?

We wondered why one woman would apply the mistreated label to herself while another with similar experiences would not. Since there were only two cases in the Neither group, we first examined their responses before restricting our analyses to the women in the other two groups.

Neither

Both of the women who labeled themselves as mistreated in this group identified more behaviors from the checklist than the group average of 11+, although only 1 was among the highest 14% of this group discussed earlier. This subject, who had separated from her intimate, reported a constellation of 29 behaviors on the checklist, 12 of which occurred rarely, 8 of which occurred sometimes, and 9 of which occurred often.

In addition to the 12 behaviors reported to have occurred rarely, those behaviors reported to have occurred sometimes included control where you go, keep the car keys, make you ask for money, lock you out of the house, and have sex with the older girls. Those behaviors that occurred often included control associates, make you dependent upon him for transportation, use visitation for harassment, check up on you, said his needs were first, said the property was his, made all the big decisions, reminded her he was the man of the house, and his moods controlled the family moods.

It is not difficult to comprehend why this woman felt mistreated. Not only were there a great variety of negative behaviors (including incest), but many of them occurred regularly. What is less obvious and yet demonstrates the important role of socialization is that eight other women within this group who reported similar constellations of behaviors did not report feeling mistreated.

The other subject who accepted the mistreated label reported roughly half as many behaviors (15), 14 of which occurred rarely and 1 (his moods controlled the family) occurred sometimes. Those events which occurred rarely included putting her down in front of others, insulting family and friends, making the children her responsibility, laughing when she was angry, said the property was his, and reminding her he was the man of the house. Perhaps it was the number of behaviors that convinced this individual to accept the label, or perhaps her self-image was stronger than others in her situation. Whatever the explanation, she was unique in this group.

Given that half the group reported eight or fewer behaviors of this type, all of which occurred only rarely, it is understandable that most of the women in this group would not feel mistreated, arguing that these behaviors were typical of most intimate relationships, and the fact that they occurred so infrequently was evidence that the relationship was by and large positive and solid. We do feel, however, that the quantity and the frequency of the behaviors reported by 14% of this group makes the 97% figure for *not* feeling mistreated higher than expected.

Less Severe/More Severe

There being too few cases in the Neither group, we restricted our analyses to those women in the Less Severe and the More Severe groups in order to gain some insight concerning the dynamics of the decision/recognition of mistreatment. Again, we focused on the number and types of behaviors reported by these women as the most promising areas of investigation.

Recalling that the More Severe group consistently reported significantly more behaviors than the Less Severe group (see Table 3), Table 8 presents information on the number of behaviors that were reported to have occurred rarely, sometimes, and often, and the total number of behaviors reported by women in both abuse groups broken down by their self-evaluation of mistreatment.

With the exception of those behaviors occurring rarely, the women in the More Severe group who believed they had been mistreated consistently reported more behaviors occurring in their most recent intimate relationship than did the women in the other three groups. For example, under the category "Occurring SOMETIMES," Table 8 indicates that the women in the More Severe group who acknowledged mistreatment reported an average of 19.76 separate behaviors. This number was not only significantly larger than the number reported by the similarly abused women in the More Severe group who did not feel they were mistreated (11.18) but was also significantly larger than the numbers reported by the women in the Less Severe group regardless of how they felt about being mistreated (8.92 mistreated; 8.94 not mistreated).

This pattern repeated itself for those behaviors occurring OFTEN and for the TOTAL number of behaviors indicated. It is also important to note that overall (TOTAL), both the mistreated *and* not mistreated women in the More Severe group chose more behaviors than did their counterparts in the Less Severe group.

More Severe

At the More Severe level, women who felt they had been mistreated consistently selected more behaviors that had occurred than did those women who did not feel they had been mistreated, recording twice as many behaviors occurring SOMETIMES, and four times the number occurring OFTEN, a total of 62 separate behaviors occurring with at least some regularity in the relationship. This is twice the number reported by those women in that same group who did not feel they had been mistreated.

It is plausible that the sheer volume and variety of behaviors directed at them made it impossible for them to continue to deny the recognition of their mistreatment. What is also plausible is that such recognition "opened the flood gates" of behaviors denied or repressed. Following that logic, we would expect some inflation of counts (the number of behaviors identified) by those women who acknowledged mistreatment (recognition bringing acknowledgment), since we did, after all, ask the mistreatment question before we presented the checklist. As attractive as the "flood gates" hypothesis might be, it is insufficient. While it may account for some inflation, it is also likely that women who felt mistreated did indeed experience not only more behaviors, but behaviors which occurred more often, eventually overwhelming them. Such an explanation is not applicable, however, to the women in the Less Severe group.

Less Severe

What is particularly striking from Table 8 is that, for those women classified as Less Severe, there were simply no instances in which the number of behaviors reported were different for those women who felt they had been mistreated compared to those women who did not feel they had been mistreated. Overall, this group reported an average of 9 behaviors occurring rarely, 9 sometimes, and 4 often, for a total of 22. Indeed, something else besides the volume and variety of negative behaviors was responsible for the mistreated decision.

We turned our attention, therefore, to the specific behaviors reported by these women to see whether or not there might be differences in the behaviors themselves, which could account for the

Table 8

Average Frequency of Behaviors by Level of Abuse and Whether the Woman Felt She Had Been Mistreated[1,2]

	Less Severe	More Severe	Total	Less Severe	More Severe	Total
	Occurring RARELY			Occuring SOMETIMES		
Mistreated?						
Yes	11.00	15.07	14.09	8.92	19.76	17.15
				**		*
No	8.50	15.59	10.35	8.94	11.18	9.52
				F (3, 115) = 11.51, $p < .001$		
	Occurring OFTEN			TOTAL INDICATED		
Yes	4.46	26.15	20.93	24.38	61.59	52.63
	**		*	**		*
	3.92	6.88	4.69	21.29	33.65	24.52
	F (3,115) = 15.99, $p < .001$			F (3,115) = 28.20, $p < .001$		

1 Cell sizes were Less Severe/yes = 13; Less Severe/no = 48; More Severe/yes = 41; and More Severe/no = 17.

2 Although not specifically indicated on this table, differences between the Less Severe and More Severe groups were significant (see Table 3).

* Mistreat vs. not is significant.

** Interaction is significant.

fact that some women felt mistreated and others did not, given that the raw number of behaviors reported was identical. Table 9 gives some insights.

While the majority of individual behaviors did not show significant differences between women who felt mistreated and those who did not, there were a few behaviors that did differentiate. These fell into two categories: (a) those where the behavior itself was reported to have occurred at any time (the first five on Table 9) and (b) those where the behavior occurred more frequently among those who felt mistreated (the last two on Table 9). Women who felt mistreated reported that the partners in their most intimate relationships insulted their family and friends, decided what both would buy, held their hands behind their backs, put down their abilities, and put down women's "lib" significantly more often than those who did not feel mistreated. These women also reported experiencing being pushed and shoved and told they were crazy more often than did those who did not feel mistreated.

These results were surprising, not only because the physical variables failed to differentiate between the groups (although pushing/shoving and hold your hands behind your back did), but also because only pushing/shoving you and telling you you are crazy appeared among the Top 10 behaviors identified by this group overall (see Table 4). Eight of the Top 10 behaviors were common to both those who felt mistreated and those who did not. The message seems to be that occasional battery (slapping was reported by 48% of these women) was considered acceptable (tolerable?), and that occasionally being screamed at, laughed at, reminded he is the man of the house, being restrained from leaving a room, being told he knows what you are thinking, being checked up on, and having someone else make the "big" decisions (among other things) in addition to being slapped was insufficient to view oneself as mistreated.

Other variables also failed to provide obvious clues. For example, the number of friends each group had was the same (2), as was the age at which they left home (17), the age difference between themselves and their most recent intimate (5 years), the length of the relationship (4.4 years), and the number of children (1.5).

Table 9
Behaviors Cited Differently by Those in the Less Severe Group: Mistreated vs. Not

Behavior	Mistreated? Yes	No	*p*
	Differences in occurrence (% Yes)		
Insults your family and/or friends	53.8	18.7	.04
Decides what both of you buy	53.8	10.4	.01
Holds your hands behind your back	30.8	12.5	.03
Puts down your abilities	30.8	10.6	.05
Puts down women's lib	23.1	12.5	.05
	Differences in frequency		
	Sometimes	Rarely	
Pushing/Shoving	46.2	45.8	.02
	Often	Sometimes	
Tells you you are crazy	30.8	27.1	.05

During the course of the interview, and immediately after the administration of the Behavior Checklist, a series of questions were asked which referred to the type of behaviors that they had just described. The second of these failed to provide any insight, although the first did. The second of these questions asked if their fathers had "done these things" to their mothers. There were nc significant differences; 60% of both those who felt mistreated and those who did not said no, 20% said they were not sure or did not know, and 20% said yes.

The first of these questions wanted to know whether they had been involved in any other relationship in which their partner had done "these types of things" to them. A trend ($p < .10$) indicated that approximately one-half (46%) of the women who felt mistreated had been in similar relationships at least once before, while this was the first such relationship for over 70% of the women who did not feel mistreated. Even though this trend was not significant, occasioned by the small number of women who felt mistreated (20% of the overall group, n = 13), this result at least provides a lead. Some of these women may have left previous relationships for precisely the reasons they were feeling mistreated in their current one.

An additional clue was gained from the data on arguments. Those who felt mistreated reported nine things argued about with the most common being his jealousy and money. Those who did not feel mistreated named many more items (20), and none appeared to dominate.

Whether these few items were sufficient to create a critical mass which influenced women in the Less Severe group to believe they were mistreated is, on the one hand, an interesting hypothesis, and on the other, mere speculation. As mentioned earlier, "mistreated" is a value judgment, hinged on subtle pressures, outside influences, and personal feelings of self-worth. It is a condition most easily applied to someone else. Overcoming the resistance to accept the label for oneself is a personal, sensitive, and far different and graver matter. Additional work needs to be done in this area.

More Severe

In contrast to the women in the Less Severe group, women in the More Severe group who felt mistreated and those who did not clearly differentiated themselves. Table 10 shows this dramatic difference. Each of the "Top 10" behaviors reported in Table 4 was significant, as were many others. While all women reported that the Table 10 behaviors occurred, those who felt mistreated consistently reported higher frequencies. For example, at least 25% of those women who felt mistreated indicated that *each* of these 10 behaviors occurred often, compared to 0% (2 behaviors), 6% (6 behaviors), or 12% (3 behaviors) of the women who did not feel mistreated.

Table 10

Behaviors Cited Differently by Those in the More Severe Group: Mistreated vs. Not*

Behavior	Mistreated?	% Often	% Sometimes	% Rarely	% Never	*p*
Slaps you	yes	33.3	35.9*	15.4	15.4	
	no		29.4	47.1*	23.5	.01
Gives you bruises	yes	23.1	35.9*	33.3	7.7	
	no		5.9	47.1*	47.1*	.001
Pushing/Shoving you	yes	26.8	56.1*	7.3	9.8	
	no	5.9	23.5	23.5	47.1*	.001
Beats you	yes	32.5*	32.5*	17.5	17.5	
	no	5.9	17.6	47.1*	29.4	.03
Controls where you go	yes	48.8*	24.4	12.2	14.6	
	no	11.8	17.6	29.4	41.2*	.01
Controls who you associate with	yes	48.8*	24.4	12.2	14.6	
	no	11.8	11.8	35.3	41.2*	.01

Laughs when you are angry	yes	46.3*	22.0	17.1	14.6	
	no	5.9	29.4	23.5	41.2*	.02
Talks in loud tones	yes	53.7*	12.2	12.2	22.0	
	no	5.9	64.7*	5.9	23.5	.001
Restrains you from leaving a room	yes	36.6*	29.3	17.1	17.1	
	no	5.9	23.5	29.4	41.2*	.05
Tells you you are crazy	yes	36.6*	22.0	24.4	17.1	
	no	5.9	11.8	41.2*	41.2*	.03
Screams or shouts in your face	yes	48.8*	26.8	7.3	17.1	
	no	11.8	17.6	29.4	41.2*	.01

* Most common response.

Those women who felt mistreated also indicated 18 separate issues argued about ("we argue about almost everything"), while those who did not feel mistreated listed significantly fewer at 13 issues commonly argued about.

There were similarities, however; if nothing else again fortifies our belief that, even under conditions of severe mistreatment, applying such a label to yourself is a step not eagerly or easily taken.

Their number of friends averaged two, the age at which they left home was 17, the age difference between themselves and their respective spouses was just over 4 years, while the length of the current intimate relationship was 4.6 years, and the number of children was 2. The number of similar relationships in which the women had been involved previously also showed no significant differences; 65% of both groups indicated they had never before been in a relationship quite like this one. When asked whether they were aware if their father had done similar things to their mother, half said no, one-fifth said they weren't sure or didn't know, and one-third said yes.

Observations, Conclusions, and Parting Thoughts

Abuse as a Universal Phenomenon

The lack of demographic/criminal differences among the groups immediately suggests that abuse is a universal phenomenon among couples. If abuse was somehow a function of criminality or demographics, we should have seen differences at least in terms of the presence or absence of abuse, if not also in terms of the levels of abuse. Neither of these was true within our incarcerated population. The only distinguishing characteristic, also common among "free world" women, was that women in the Neither group were better educated (more college graduates) than were women in the other two groups.

There are other dynamics here as well. For the abuser's part, it also appears that there is a line which, once crossed, permits almost any kind of behavior. The object of the attack becomes less than human. Perhaps this is bound up with the physical act of striking. Our culture does, after all, teach and reinforce a "might makes right" philosophy.

Adults as well as children resort to violence to obtain their ends if persuasion and intimidation do not work (as do nations, as the recent Gulf War attests). Males are particularly infused with these notions.

Still, to be a bully is unacceptable. We are also taught that violence is an inappropriate way to gain one's ends, and specifically that "boys are not to hit girls." Perhaps, once this taboo has been overcome, we have the necessary permission to take whatever steps we choose for our immediate gratification. The horrors we can inflict on our intimate are limited only by our imaginations. Besides, we discipline our children and our pets first through persuasion, then intimidation, and then physical attack. It is not surprising that we treat our fellow humans in this fashion and and not surprising that we use these same patterns with our intimates.

Abuse and Criminality

While we have evidence to conclude that abuse is a universal phenomenon among couples, the much higher rate at which abuse occurred to the women in our study (conservatively 6 to 10 times that of other groups of women) is evidence that domestic violence is associated with criminality. It is characteristic of individuals involved in criminal behavior (at least among those women who are eventually incarcerated for their participation in crime). The two appear associated in the same way in which substance abuse is related to criminality; that is, they occur in the same environment. Such an explanation fits all the data. While there is little of a demographic or criminal nature to differentiate those women who suffered abuse in their intimate relationships from those women who did not, the fact that the women were in environments where criminal activity occurred also increased the probability that they would suffer abuse from their intimates.

This is a phenomenon reminiscent of the drug/crime connection highly debated in the 1980s (see, e.g., Blount 1982a, 1982b; Inciardi 1981). The end result of that debate was the simple recognition that individuals who are involved in criminal activities are often also involved with drugs, and individuals who use drugs often become involved in criminal activity. The two co-exist; one does not necessarily create the other. Thus, women involved in criminal activity are not only more likely to use and abuse substances, they are also more likely to be abused by their intimates.

Battery and Abuse

We were particularly pleased to be able to demonstrate (convincingly we think) that abuse as a phenomenon is a collection of behaviors, a constellation or "array" if you will, of which battery is but one. We also believe we were able to suggest, at least, that abuse can exist without battery being present at all (the top 14% of the Neither group). What we do not know is the extent to which such "battery free" constellations exist. Put another way, just how many abusive relationships exist where battery is entirely absent? Is the percentage more or less than that for incarcerated women? Would the abuse rates be higher in the general population if we dealt more openly with controlling and intimidating behaviors (e.g., laugh at you when angry, interrupt you, check up on you, control your associates, slam doors and cupboards, scream or shout in your face) in addition to or instead of the slapping and beating we commonly use?

To do that could radically change our conception of what constitutes an abusive relationship; although beyond the common theme of physical attacks of one nature or another, what constitutes an abusive relationship is anything but consistent in the literature. Perhaps this uncertainty among professionals is reflected by the uncertainty among our sample regarding their own mistreatment.

Wherever this line of thought takes us, it is abundantly clear that when acts of battery are used to define abusive relationships, those relationships are at once also characterized by a host of other behaviors and can, therefore, be properly defined as abusive in a broader sense, that sense being associated with an environment of intimidation and control.

Self-Identification

That women subjected to many different kinds of controlling and intimidating behaviors (including physical attacks), some with a good deal of frequency, would not consider themselves mistreated, while other women in identical circumstances would, argues strongly for the effects of socialization. Precisely what behaviors in what frequency are required to overcome the denial and/or force the recognition that one's relationship is abusive is unknown. What we do know is that women in the Less Severe group did not feel mistreated while women in the More Severe group did, and each group made its decision in overwhelming numbers. Thus, while we may not be able to distinguish between those behaviors that constitute mistreatment and those that do not at each level, it is clear there are distinct differences among levels. Somewhere there may exist a "magic line," and it is possible that once that line has been crossed the attitudes shift dramatically.

Such a decision hinges on subtle pressures, personal experiences, outside influences, and feelings of self-worth. We acknowledge that this is a complex series of issues. We also acknowledge the inability of the present questionnaire to be sensitive to these complex subtleties and consider this an important issue to be examined in subsequent research.

We suspect, however, that it will be more fruitful to search for a "critical mass" than for a specific behavior. One should not ignore the haystack when searching for the needle. It may well be that the needle is not particularly distinctive, but merely one part of what goes into making up the haystack itself. One also needs to be cognizant of the regularity with which the behaviors occur.

Abuse as a Continuum

When discussing the three groups, we have argued for a continuum of intimidation/control which, at the low end, is reflected by fairly benign behaviors occurring at low frequencies and at the high end includes extreme physical punishment and intimidation at very high frequencies. This leaves the middle of the distribution with the introduction of physical behaviors, stronger intimidation measures, and more intense psychological pressures at higher frequencies than at the lower end, and yet not as high or intense as those at the high end of the continuum.

Admittedly, this continuum may be somewhat contrived since the Less Severe group was defined as those women who had suffered certain physical behaviors, and the More Severe group was defined as those women who had received severe physical punishment. What was not contrived, however, and what argues strongly in favor of a continuum was the frequency and intensity with which those behaviors were reported by the women in each group. What was also not contrived was the constellation of factors, the array of behaviors that accompanied those physical items which were used to define the groups. We are more convinced than ever that the physical items are simply symptomatic, merely more easily identified behaviors that can be used as benchmarks on a continuum of abuse.

We would also stress that a continuum has two ends, one where the behavior does not exist at all and one where the behavior exists for all. The present data do, we believe, support this contention. Three themes pervade this continuum: persuasion, intimidation, and physical attack.

Abuse as Addiction

We are reminded of the addiction model when confronted with the three groups and their distinct differences on the one hand and the commonalities of escalating physical violence and other intimidating and controlling behaviors (which identify them as points along a larger continuum) on the other.

There would appear to be separate "states" or stages that may be long-lasting or permanent either through the adaption of the partners, fear of change, acceptance of the situation, or all of these. An addiction model would accept such an explanation. At the same time, there is also the distinct possibility for escalation and movement from a situation of no control to one of control without physical intervention and with infrequent reinforcement, to one where some physical violence is present and then on to one where severe physical violence is commonplace. That too would fit an addiction model.

Such a model would suggest that controlling and intimidating behaviors, including the physical attacks, were once a means to an end, much like alcohol and drugs were once used for escape or self-aggrandizement. After prolonged use, however, more of the substance is required, and a greater number of controlling and inhibiting behaviors are applied until behaviors that were once a means to an end become an end in themselves.

Just as the drinking husband blames his alcoholic state for his brutal attacks on his spouse yet continues those brutal attacks after he stops drinking, the abuser uses his intimate to provoke and excuse his own behavior. The bewilderment of abused women who are at an absolute loss to agree upon what "sets him off" fits such a model quite well. It is not unlikely that many abusers are individuals who enjoy, indeed relish and feel inadequate without the control, the intimidation, and the cowering present within their intimate relationships. Such would be the "drug of choice."

Thus, an addiction model has much to recommend it. We are not suggesting that abusers are "addicts" necessarily, although we can certainly argue that point for at least a portion of them, but rather that such a model is convenient for understanding the dynamics of abuse between intimates: it fits the data.

References

Biggers, T.A. (1979). Death by murder: A study of women murderers. *Death Education* 3: 1–9.

Blount, W.R. (Ed.) (1982a). Alcohol, drugs and crime: Part I (special issue). *Journal of Drug Issues* 12(2).

——— (Ed.) (1982b). Alcohol, drugs and crime: Part II (special issue). *Journal of Drug Issues* 12(3).

Blount, W.R., Vega, M., & Silverman, I. J. (1988). Spouse abuse and homicide in Florida's incarcerated women. Paper presented at the Academy of Criminal Justice Sciences annual meeting, San Francisco.

Blount, W.R., Danner, T.A., Vega, M., & Silverman, I.J. (1991). The influences of substance abuse among adult female inmates. *Journal of Drug Issues* 21: 449–467.

Bograd, M. (1988). How battered women and abusive men account for domestic violence: Excuses, justifications, or explanations? In G.T. Hotaling, D. Finkelhor, J.T. Kirkpatrick, & M.A. Straus (eds.), *Coping with family violence* (pp. 60–77). Newbury Park, CA: Sage.

Brown, C. (1985). Expert testimony on battered woman syndrome: Its admissibility in spousal homicide cases. *Suffolk University Law Review* 19: 877–905.

Browne, A. (1987). *When battered women kill*. New York: Free Press.

Crawford, J. (n.d.). *Tabulation of a nationwide Survey of State Correctional Facilities for Adult and Juvenile Female Offenders*. College Park, MD: American Correctional Association.

Daniel, A.E., & Kashani, J.H. (1983). Women who commit crimes of violence. *Psychiatric Annals* 13: 697–713.

Dobash, R.E., & Dobash, R.P. (1978). Wives: The appropriate victims of marital violence. *Victimology* 2: 426–442.

——— (1979). *Violence against wives: A case against the patriarchy*. New York: The Free Press.

Edwards, S.S.M. (1985). Socio-legal evaluation of gender ideologies in domestic violence: Assault and spousal homicides. *Victimology* 10: 186–205.

——— (1989). Police role: using discretion? In S.S.M. Edwards (Ed.), *Policing "domestic" violence: Women, the law and the state* (pp. 81–110). Newbury Park, CA: Sage.

Ferrer, K.J. (1983). Rationalizing violence: How battered women stay. *Victimology* 8: 203–212.

Florida Supreme Court (1990). *Report of the Florida Supreme Court Gender Bias Study Commission*. Tallahassee: Florida Supreme Court.

Frieze, I.H., & Browne, A. (1989). Violence in marriage. In L. Ohlin & M. Tonry (eds.), *Family violence* (pp. 163–218). Chicago: University of Chicago Press.

Goolkasian, G.A. (1986). *Confronting domestic violence: The role of criminal court judges*. Washington, DC: U.S. Department of Justice, National Institute of Justice.

Hudsmith, R. (1987). Admissible of expert testimony on battered woman syndrome in battered women's self-defense cases in Louisiana. *Louisiana Law Review* 47: 979–992.

Inciardi, J.A. (1981). *The drugs crime connection.* Beverly Hills, CA: Sage.

Kelly, L. (1988). How women define their experience of violence. In K. Yllo & M. Bograd (Eds.), *Feminists' perspective on wife abuse* (pp. 114–132). Newbury Park, CA: Sage.

Korbin, J. (1986). Childhood histories of women imprisoned for fatal child maltreatment. *Child Abuse & Neglect* 10: 331–338.

Kuhl, A., & Saltzman, L.T. (1985). Battered women and the criminal justice system. In I.L. Moyer (Ed.), *Changing roles of women in criminal justice system: Offenders, victims, and professionals* (pp. 180–196). Prospect Heights, IL: Waveland Press.

Lanza-Kaduce, L., Blount, W.R., Holten, N.G., Terry, W.C., Garten, P., Boulnois-Manning, S., Mahan, S., Frank, H., Dundes, L., Kuhns, J. B. III, Taylor, D.W., & Godshall, B.C. (1990). *Prison utilization study: Risk assessment techniques and Florida's inmates.* Volume I: *Application to males and females.* Tallahassee, FL: Division of Economic and Demographic Research, Joint Legislative Management Committee.

Mann, C.R. (1988). Getting even? Women who kill in domestic encounters. *Justice Quarterly* 5: 31–51.

Martin, D. (1976). *Battered wives.* San Francisco, CA: Glide.

Okun, L. (1986). *Woman abuse: Facts replacing myths.* Albany, NY: State University Press.

Pagelow, M.D., & Pagelow, L.W. (1984). *Family violence.* New York: Praeger.

Pence, E., & Paymor, M. (1986). *Power and control: Tactics of men who batter, an educational curriculum.* Duluth: Minnesota Program Development, Inc.

Prizzey, E. (1974). *Scream quietly or the neighbors will hear.* Short Hills, England: Ridley Enslow.

Sanford, L.T., & Donovan, M. (1984). *Women and self-esteem.* New York: Anchor Press/Doubleday.

Smith, S.L. (1986). Why white women stay and black women don't: Toward a theory of black domestic violence. Unpublished master's thesis. Southern Illinois University, Carbondale.

Starke, E., & Flitcraft, A. (1988). Violence and intimacy. In V.G. Van Hasselt, R.L. Morrison, A.S. Bellack, & M. Hersen (eds.), *Handbook of family violence* (pp. 293–317). New York: Plenum Press.

Straus, M.A. (1990). The national family violence surveys. In M.A. Straus & R. J. Gelles (Eds.), *Physical violence in American families* (pp. 3–21). New Brunswick, NJ: Transaction Publishers.

———, & Gelles,. R.J. (1988). How violent are American families? Estimates from the National Family Violence Resurvey and other studies. In G.T. Hotaling, D. Finkelhor, J.T. Kirkpatrick, & M. A. Straus (Eds.), *Family abuse and its consequences: New directions in research*. (pp. 110–189). Newbury Park, CA: Sage.

Teske, R.H.C., Jr., & Parker, M.L. (1983). *Spouse abuse in Texas: A study of women's attitudes and experiences*. Huntsville, TX: Sam Houston State University, Criminal Justice Center, Survey Research Program.

Walker, L.E. (1979). *The battered woman*. New York: Harper & Row.

——— (1984). *The battered woman syndrome*. New York: Springer.

——— (1989). *Terrifying love: Why battered women kill and how society responds*. New York: Harper & Row.

Weis, J.G. (1989). Family violence research methodology and design. In L. Ohlin & M. Tonry (Eds.), *Family violence,* Volume 11: *Crime and Justice: A review of research* (pp. 117–162). Chicago: University of Chicago Press.

Weisheit, R.A. (1984). Female homicide offenders: Trends over time in institutionalized population. *Justice Quarterly* 1: 471–489.

Appendix A
The Behavior Checklist

Now I am going to read some behaviors that occur in some relationships. As I read each one, I need you to tell me if any of these apply to your partner towards you. If these things have happened, please tell me if they happened rarely, sometimes, or often.
(Interviewer: If respondent indicates an item is not applicable [E.G., no children], write "N/A" to the left of the 1 in that row.)

	Behavior	Never	Rarely	Sometimes	Often
		1	2	3	4
1.	pushing/shoving you	1	2	3	4
2.	forcefully poking your chest or arm	1	2	3	4
3.	burn you with a cigarette, hot water, burner, etc.	1	2	3	4
4.	backhand you	1	2	3	4
5.	tie you up	1	2	3	4
6.	broke bones in your body	1	2	3	4
7.	gave you a black eye	1	2	3	4
8.	gave you bruises	1	2	3	4
9.	hold your hands behind your back	1	2	3	4
10.	hold your head under water	1	2	3	4
11.	slapping you	1	2	3	4
12.	hit you with object	1	2	3	4
13.	choking you	1	2	3	4
14.	pulling your hair	1	2	3	4
15.	punching you	1	2	3	4
16.	kicking you	1	2	3	4
17.	grabbing you hard enough to bruise you	1	2	3	4

	Behavior	Never	Rarely	Sometimes	Often
18.	beating you	1	2	3	4
19.	throwing you down	1	2	3	4
20.	twisting your arm	1	2	3	4
21.	tripping you	1	2	3	4
22.	biting you	1	2	3	4
23.	holding you down	1	2	3	4
24.	tearing your clothing	1	2	3	4
25.	using a knife to threaten or hurt you	1	2	3	4
26.	using a gun to threaten or hurt you	1	2	3	4
27.	holding his hand over your mouth	1	2	3	4
28.	chasing you in a car, try to run you down	1	2	3	4
29.	take off when you're trying to get in the car	1	2	3	4
30.	restrain you from leaving a room	1	2	3	4
31.	control where you are	1	2	3	4
32.	control where you go	1	2	3	4
33.	control every movement you make (i.e., walking, talking, chewing)	1	2	3	4
34.	control how you dress	1	2	3	4
35.	keep the car keys from you	1	2	3	4
36.	do not allow you to have a phone	1	2	3	4
37.	tear the phone out of the wall	1	2	3	4
38.	control who you associate with	1	2	3	4
39.	move you far away from family & friends	1	2	3	4
40.	ignoring you for long periods of time	1	2	3	4
41.	monitor your phone calls	1	2	3	4
42.	read your mail	1	2	3	4
43.	making you dependent on him for transportation	1	2	3	4

	Behavior	Never	Rarely	Sometimes	Often
44.	making the children your responsibility (they're your kids)	1	2	3	4
45.	does not allow you to use any birth control	1	2	3	4
46.	putting you down in front of others	1	2	3	4
47.	insult your family and/or friends	1	2	3	4
48.	laugh at you when you're angry	1	2	3	4
49.	hardly ever refer to you by name (i.e., my old lady, my wife)	1	2	3	4
50.	making you feel bad about yourself	1	2	3	4
51.	putting down your abilities (i.e., to be a mother, a lover, a friend)	1	2	3	4
52.	tell you you're crazy	1	2	3	4
53.	play mind games	1	2	3	4
54.	interrupt you when you're trying to express yourself	1	2	3	4
55.	humiliate you by making you beg	1	2	3	4
56.	keep you from getting a job	1	2	3	4
57.	requesting you quit your job	1	2	3	4
58.	making you lose your job	1	2	3	4
59.	make you ask him for money	1	2	3	4
60.	give you an allowance	1	2	3	4
61.	only let you take care of the checkbook	1	2	3	4
62.	take your money	1	2	3	4
63.	constantly question your spending (even when you hardly spend)	1	2	3	4
64.	blame you for no money	1	2	3	4
65.	he decides what both of you buy	1	2	3	4
66.	physically attack the sexual parts of your body	1	2	3	4
67.	force you to be a prostitute	1	2	3	4
68.	blame you for his sexual failures	1	2	3	4

	Behavior	Never	Rarely	Sometimes	Often
69.	urinate or defecate on you	1	2	3	4
70.	force you to ingest urine or feces	1	2	3	4
71.	insert foreign objects in your vagina or anus	1	2	3	4
72.	force you to have vaginal sex	1	2	3	4
73.	force you to perform oral sex	1	2	3	4
74.	force you to have anal sex	1	2	3	4
75.	tie you up during sex	1	2	3	4
76.	make you have sex after beating you	1	2	3	4
77.	make you have sex with animals	1	2	3	4
78.	make you have sex with other(s)	1	2	3	4
79.	make you watch while he has sex with animals	1	2	3	4
80.	make you watch while he has sex with other(s)	1	2	3	4
81.	cut your nipples with a knife	1	2	3	4
82.	cause you to bleed during sex	1	2	3	4
83.	he reads pornographic magazines	1	2	3	4
84.	he watches pornographic films	1	2	3	4
85.	he makes you perform acts that he's seen in pornography	1	2	3	4
86.	he has sexual relationships with the older girls	1	2	3	4
87.	require the children to participate in sex with both of you	1	2	3	4
88.	tell the children that their mother is crazy	1	2	3	4
89.	physically mistreat the children	1	2	3	4
90.	sexually mistreat the children	1	2	3	4
91.	tell the children that he doesn't know who their father is	1	2	3	4
92.	use the children to give you messages	1	2	3	4

	Behavior	Never	Rarely	Sometimes	Often
93.	using visitation as a way to harass you	1	2	3	4
94.	tell you if you leave him, he'll take the kids from you	1	2	3	4
95.	tell you that if you divorce or separate, that he will kill anyone you may want to have a relationship with	1	2	3	4
96.	threaten to commit suicide	1	2	3	4
97.	threaten to kill you	1	2	3	4
98.	threaten to report you to welfare	1	2	3	4
99.	threaten to hurt you physically	1	2	3	4
100.	threaten to hurt or kill your loved ones	1	2	3	4
101.	threaten to hurt or kill the children	1	2	3	4
102.	threaten to hurt or kill pets	1	2	3	4
103.	threaten to rape you	1	2	3	4
104.	threaten to tell others how awful you are	1	2	3	4
105.	threaten to leave you with no money	1	2	3	4
106.	driving recklessly to scare you	1	2	3	4
107.	take the kids for visitation and not return for days to scare you	1	2	3	4
108.	force you to commit a crime for money	1	2	3	4
109.	treat you like a servant	1	2	3	4
110.	tell you that women are all alike	1	2	3	4
111.	tell you that a woman is the weaker sex	1	2	3	4
112.	tell you that your place is to be at home and taking care of him, the children and the housework	1	2	3	4
113.	tell you that his needs are first	1	2	3	4
114.	referring to all of your property as his	1	2	3	4

	Behavior	Never	Rarely	Sometimes	Often
115.	his moods control the entire family's moods	1	2	3	4
116.	he makes all the "big" decisions	1	2	3	4
117.	remind you that he's the man of the family	1	2	3	4
118.	he puts down women's lib	1	2	3	4
119.	put you in fear by using looks, actions, or gestures as if to say "you'll be sorry for that"	1	2	3	4
120.	scream or shout in your face	1	2	3	4
121.	tell you he knows what you're thinking	1	2	3	4
122.	check up on you to make sure you're doing what you told him	1	2	3	4
123.	require you to sit still for long periods of time	1	2	3	4
124.	perform strange rituals involving you, or making you watch	1	2	3	4
125.	talking in loud tones	1	2	3	4
126.	destroying property	1	2	3	4
127.	destroy something you like	1	2	3	4
128.	make you destroy something you like	1	2	3	4
129.	squeeze your hands hard, in public, as a warning to behave yourself	1	2	3	4
130.	slams doors, cupboards	1	2	3	4
131.	pounding fist on the table	1	2	3	4
132.	lock you out of the house	1	2	3	4
133.	walk around like he's ready to blow up	1	2	3	4
134.	treat you like a child	1	2	3	4

Little Girls Grown Up: The Perils of Institutionalization

Clemens Bartollas
University of Northern Iowa

The woman in prison has been called the "forgotten offender" (Simon 1975). Several reasons explain the lack of interest in the woman prisoner. Women prisoners have been ignored because women's prisons are much less forbidding and physically oppressive than the fortresslike male dungeons that offend prison reformers. Women prisoners also have received limited attention because they are few in number compared to male prisoners. Of approximately 771,000 state and federal prisoners, only about 40,000 are women (U.S. Department of Justice 1991). Furthermore, women prisoners have tended to be content to do their time and not to call attention to themselves.

Researchers have also neglected the incarcerated woman. The few studies reported prior to 1960 found that women prisoners coped with institutionalization by developing a pseudo-family system. Attracted to the micro-society of a small group, rather than the total inmate subculture, women inmates became involved in varying degrees of lesbian alliances. The interracial aspects of the courtship process received further attention: White inmates played the female roles and black inmates played the male roles in the pseudo-family structure that was established.

During the 1960s and early 1970s, researchers investigated other aspects of the pseudo-family life in women's prisons. More than a dozen journal articles and several books were published depicting the coping and adjustment patterns of the confined woman prisoner. Ward and Kassebaum's (1965) *Women's Prison: Sex and Social Structure*,

Giallombardo's (1966) *Society of Women: A Study of Women's Prisons*, and Heffernan's (1972) *Making It in Prison: The Square, the Cool and the Life* are the most important of these studies. Although these books do an excellent job describing the substitute world established by women prisoners, which resembles life outside of the prison, they fail to describe alternative adaptations that women make to prison life.

Studies in the mid- and late 1970s added other dimensions to the adjustment that women prisoners make. Burkhart (1976) found that women prisoners were becoming more aggressive and less compliant to prison life. She argued that women were no longer content to do laundry, mend clothes, and scrub floors. Riots in several women's prisons in the mid-1970s indicated that women could respond in a collective way to prison conditions. In the late 1970s, it also became clear that women were beginning to develop a legalistic response to prison life, as they began to file civil suits protesting prison conditions.

In the 1980s, Freedman (1981) and Rafter (1985) published books on the history of women's prisons. Most recently, Pollock-Byrne's (1990) study of women's prisons shows that aspects of the prisoner subculture other than homosexuality must be explored to understand the woman prisoner's adaptation to confinement.

The Female Adolescent Prisoner

Until 1960, the number of studies concerning the female adolescent confined in training school equaled those about the incarcerated adult woman. These early studies also found that female adolescent inmates became involved in varying degrees of lesbian alliances and pseudo-family relationships. But only two major studies have been found in the past 20 years on the female adolescent's adjustment to training school: Giallombardo's (1974) *The Social World of Imprisoned Girls* and Propper's (1976) dissertation (later revised and published in 1981), "Importation and Deprivation Perspectives on Homosexuality in Correctional Institutions: An Empirical Test of Their Relative Efficacy."

Giallombardo (1974), in examining three training schools in various parts of the United States, found a kinship, but varied, system that existed, in each of the training schools. She further found that the social organization of female adolescents in training schools mirrored the sex-role structure in the larger society. But Propper (1976/1981) found little evidence supporting Giallombardo's contention that female adolescents playing husband and wife roles were more likely than other adult women inmates to engage in homosexual activities. In other words, according to Propper, family roles and homosexual activity may be mutually exclusive events.

In sum, studies on confined female adolescents, even more than studies on adult women prisoners, lack the rigor characteristic of studies on juvenile and adult male prisoners. They have typically found that female adolescents adhere strongly to small clusters of inmates, in which the needs for intimacy and personal security are satisfied. In addition, most researchers have focused upon the pseudo-family relationships found in training schools. Yet many areas of institutional adjustment and impact have been ignored, such as female adolescents' involvement in victimization of other inmates, patterns of aggression directed toward staff and inmates, attempts to cope with confinement by manipulating peers and staff members, and the effect of coeducational and privately operated institutions upon confined female adolescents.

Methodology

The purpose of this study was to examine the coping behavior and attitudes of two samples of female adolescents confined in juvenile institutional placements. The settings for this research were a state juvenile correctional system located in the Southeast and a private residential facility in the Midwest. Six of the state's seven coeducational facilities and two of the private facility's three coeducational campuses served as sites for data collection. The state sample consisted of 160 female adolescent residents representing 29% of the total institutional population, and the private sample was made up of 40 female adolescent residents representing 44% of the total placement population.

Data were collected from the respondents in the state coeducational facilities by self-administered questionnaires. Matched questionnaires were completed by dormitory staff members for each respondent. The residents were asked to indicate how they felt regarding their own behaviors and attitudes as well as the behaviors and attitudes of both residents and staff with the Likert scale questions. Six summated scales were constructed from 31 Likert scale statements. Placed into six logically defined and categorized groups and summed, the scales were then cut in half based on the description of cases. The scales were given the following titles: (a) straight time, (b) victimization by peers, (c) acceptance of institutional life, (d) adherence to the inmate subculture, (e) manipulation of others, and (f) cons and games directed toward staff (Sieverdes & Bartollas 1980).

Data were collected from the sample in the private facility from self-administered questionnaires and interviews. The self-administered questionnaires given to residents consisted of 50 Likert questions (adapted from Shichor & Bartollas' (1990) Silverlake study and from Sieverdes and Bartollas' (1980) study of coeducational training schools in the Southeast). The staff questionnaire consisted of 22 Likert questions (adapted from Shichor & Bartollas' and Sieverdes & Bartollas' studies). In order to receive a larger number of answers, strongly agree and agree answers were combined as well as disagree and strongly disagree answers. Staff members also were asked an open-ended question at the end of the questionnaire: "What changes are needed in the facility?" This examination of the attitudes of female adolescents and of the staff who worked with them is part of a larger study that compared the institutional impact of this private facility with the state training school for boys.

In addition to questionnaires, one-half of the female adolescents and two staff members in each of their cottages were interviewed. Staff interviews averaged 30 minutes, while residents' interviews averaged 20 minutes. Residents were asked what their previous placements were, how long they had been there, what they liked and disliked about their placements, whether they had been abused, whether they felt that the houseparents were concerned about them, and whether this placement was helpful or harmful to them. In addition, residents were encouraged to discuss anything they wanted concerning cottage life. Houseparents were questioned about the length of time they had worked in the cottage, the cottage treatment emphasis, what they liked and disliked about their jobs, their particular philosophy of working with adolescents, and how they were able to maintain job interest and avoid burnout considering the 4-day on and 4-day off schedules they worked.

The state sample of 160 female adolescents was 61% black. The modal age of females in this sample was 15; the range was 7 through 17 years. The private sample of 40 female adolescents was 100% white. The modal age of females in this sample was also 15; the range was 13 through 17 years.

In the state sample, 70% of the female adolescents were placed in a training school as a result of a status offense. Although juveniles in this state cannot be referred directly to a correctional facility for committing a status offense, they can be placed on probation for a status offense. Subsequent status or delinquent offenses are defined as a violation of probation, which makes it possible for the juvenile judge to adjudicate them to training school. Only 11% of the female adolescents in the state sample have never been on probation prior to their current confinement. In the private sample, 50% of the female adolescents were placed at this facility for status offenses, especially runaway behaviors, and the other 50% for minor stealing and shoplifting-related offenses.

What is striking about the two samples is the difference in the seriousness of prior delinquent behaviors between female and male institutional placements. For the male adolescents, almost without exception, they had committed delinquent acts for several years, had been to juvenile court at least twice, had been referred to one or more private programs, had long histories of drug use, and were regarded as the end-of-the-line delinquents in this state. In contrast, female adolescents as a group appeared to have started socially unacceptable behaviors later, were more frequently referred to the juvenile court for family-related problems, had committed minor offenses, and had less drug use or addiction than male residents in their backgrounds. Furthermore, nearly all of the female adolescents, especially in the private sample, had experienced abuse or neglect. Sexual abuse in their family backgrounds was particularly evident. For example, all 10 of the female residents in one private cottage had been sexually abused, and the majority of females in other private cottages had some history of sexual abuse.

Findings

The data in the state study of coeducational training schools reveal that most female adolescents do not find institutionalization as bad as they thought it would be, but neither do they find it a pleasant or a positive experience. To begin with, they state that they do not trust staff members. Indeed, two-thirds of the female adolescents indicate that they trust peers more than they trust staff members. The majority (58%) do acknowledge that the best way to make it in the institution is to agree with everything the staff said and to comply with whatever the staff expected (Sieverdes & Bartollas 1980). Thus, the relationships between residents and staff are characterized by manipulation and impression management.

Institutionalized female adolescents in this study may trust peers more than staff, but they still experience victimization by other residents or must endure the threat of victimization by others. Significantly, over half of the female residents score on the high end of the victimization index. A majority of the female residents claim that other residents are always trying to "break me down" and 60% agree with the comment that other residents take advantage of them. Moreover, 57% of the female residents, regardless of race, express anxiety and concern about the possibility of institutional victimization.

A disturbing incident took place in one of the coeducational institutions during the process of data collection that dramatically highlights the possibility of institutional victimization. A female adolescent who had arrived at a cottage only the night before was confronted by a peer early the next day. When she responded in what was interpreted as an unacceptable way, it was decided that she needed an attitude adjustment. That night, when staff were not around, she was attacked sexually by several peers and was penetrated with a broomstick.

Regardless of the possibility of victimization, females are still more favorable toward confinement than males in state coeducational institutions. Over 75% state that institutional life is not as bad as they had anticipated. Moreover, 65% find "doing time" easy. While 55% of the females score on the high-agreement end of the scales measuring satisfaction with the training school, white female adolescents have a more positive view of confinement than black residents.

According to these data, these female adolescents adhere strongly to the inmate subculture norm against informing on peers. Sixty-one percent underscore their solidarity by agreeing with the statement, "I would never rat on a friend here." Approximately 75% of the female residents also believe that they have to live with the continual risk of some other resident informing on them.

Interestingly, while these female residents are reluctant to inform on peers and distrusted staff, they associate in small cliques consisting of "good friends" for protection and security from other residents. In this regard, no single female adolescent group exists that has the allegiance of all residents within the cottage or institution. Furthermore, both blacks and whites are drawn into peer groupings and cliques with equal intensity.

Finally, female adolescents in the coeducational training schools are far less likely to manipulate staff than are male residents because they find staff more difficult to con or manipulate. Moreover, female residents are less likely to harass staff than male residents; only about 25% of the female residents actively harass staff. Less than a quarter of the female respondents state that they are considered troublemakers by staff. Black female adolescents, in this regard, push and harass staff members and are labeled as troublemakers by the staff more often than are white females.

Female adolescents in the private placement, like those in state placements, are more positive about their confinements than are male adolescents in the private facility and much more positive than are the male adolescents confined in the state's training school. The female adolescents in the private placement, as a group, do not want to be confined, but they generally feel that the experience has some positive outcomes.

In terms of their responses to self-administered questionnaires, females are more likely than male residents in private placements to agree that "youths in the institution are pretty much like those on the outside," that "this facility really prepares residents for the outside world," and that "most of the rules around here are strictly enforced." Similarly, these female adolescents are more likely than male residents to disagree that "treatment here is a waste of time," that "this place usually seems more concerned about keeping residents under control than with helping them with their problems," and that "most residents here are interested in just getting by."

Interviewed female adolescents in the private placement offer considerably more positive evaluations about the efficacy of treatment and their rapport with cottage staff than do the male adolescents. Several female adolescents noted:

> Ok, I wished I wasn't here, but I guess I have to be. It helps you through your problems. You don't have as many as when you first came in.
>
> . . . .
>
> I would rather be at home, but if I were still at home, I would still be doing the same stuff. We're like a family. If we have a problem, the rest of the cottage helps you through it. I like Mrs. Jones, the houseparent on the other shift. I feel I can talk with her about my problems.
>
> . . . .
>
> Sometimes I like it and sometimes it gets me down. I know I am helping myself now. I write my problems down in a journal, and it helps me. I know houseparents are generally concerned.
>
> . . . .
>
> It has been a good experience. I get along with my houseparents. They're real fun to joke around with, too. They teach you a lot of things here like responsibility. I've a better relationship with my parents.

However, there were female adolescents who strongly objected to their placements at this private facility as they questioned whether they were receiving any benefit from their stay. One of the most negative stated:

> You don't have treatment here. Nobody wants to be here. I hate being told what to do. All my life I've been my own boss. When they first came here, they wanted me to be a kid. I've never been a kid before. It is not an easy place to adjust to with all their rules. You have no freedom. You can't even go to the bathroom without permission. When you compare my runaway problem with what others have here, I don't think that CHINAs [children in need of assistance] should be mixed with delinquents. Staff also aren't fair to me. I am not a brown-nose. I don't kiss butt.

Significantly, while this respondent was probably the most negative among female residents, her response was fairly typical among male residents. Males also objected much more strongly than female interviewees to the rigid structure and unyielding rules of the private placement. Males also more frequently questioned whether the houseparents cared about them. Furthermore, more male than female residents had developed intensely negative relationships with certain houseparents.

Discussion

According to this investigation of male and female adolescents in a private program and in six state training schools, females have an easier time adjusting to institutionalization than do males. Females do not experience as much victimization from peers as do males, nor do females feel as alienated from staff as males. Females also tend to feel that the institutional experience is not as negative as do males. Furthermore, soft-end females in the private facility have an easier time with institutionalization than do hard-end females in state training schools. Indeed, some females in the private facility view several advantages to their confinement, that is, learning to accept responsibility, learning to communicate with an adult (houseparent), learning to accept limits on behavior, and learning to work through problems.

However, one disturbing factor about both samples is that all of the confined female adolescents have been committed to institutional care for minor offenses. Although Cernkovich, Giordano, and Pugh (1985) found a number of chronic female delinquents who had committed violent, serious property and drug offenses in an Ohio training school for girls, no serious offenses were identified in the delinquent backgrounds of these two samples. Instead, runaway behavior, sexual misconduct, incorrigibility at home, and shoplifting made up the criminal repertoire of these female adolescents.

Even more disquieting is the fact that one or two female adolescents in each privately administered cottage had committed absolutely no offenses. They came from multiple problem-oriented families and were typically victims of abuse and neglect. Yet, even with those female adolescents who had committed minor delinquent offenses as stealing, some evidence of sexual abuse was found in most of their backgrounds. Victimized at home by fathers, stepfathers, uncles, or other relatives, they continue to be victims as they are committed to long-term institutional placements. The female adolescents in these two samples clearly have some adjustment problems in society, but it seems oppressive to confine them at all, much less place them with delinquents and status offenders during confinement.

Perhaps most disturbing of all is the racist implications of this study. While the state sample of 160 female adolescents is 61% black, the private sample of 40 female adolescents is 100% white. When it is remembered that the state sample is made up of 70% status offenders, it is clear that black female adolescents commit status offenses the same as do whites. Why, then, in the midwestern states are there no black female status offenders? Black female adolescents also are heavily involved in minor stealing and shoplifting. Why are none of these youth found in this highly regarded private operation?

Both male and female adolescents in the private placement stay a time and a half as long as female adolescents confined in the coeducational state training school and twice as long as male adolescents confined to the training school for boys. It can be claimed, of course, that this additional time is necessary because residents receive needed treatment services that require them to stay longer. But there are several reasons why the efficacy of treatment is open to question at this private placement.

First, the high turnover among staff at this private facility results in continual instability in the cottage environment with the uncertainty of the new houseparent's attitude and rule enforcement pattern. The great variation among enforcement of the rules with staff increases the importance of how much slack the new staff member allows. Instability in a cottage is not usually conducive to a therapeutic milieu.

Second, the exhausting work schedule at the private placement tends to result in losing good staff members. The average day begins at 5:30 A.M. and lasts at least until 11:00 P.M. If this daily schedule is not sufficient to burn out the best intended and motivated staff member, the policy of working 4 days on and 4 days off usually completes the task. Interestingly, younger staff members, who tend to relate much better with residents, have higher turnover rates than older staff members. Older staff members, frequently retired farmers and their wives, are generally more concerned about following the rules than relating to residents or helping them have a positive institutional experience.

Third, other than what appears to be a positive experience in a sexual abuse group conducted by a social worker, which female adolescents in her cottage attended, there are almost no traditional means of treatment technologies conducted at any of the three campuses. Instead, the philosophy of treatment intervention seems to revolve around making certain that the residents follow the cottage and institutional rules. This results in the most rigid and structured environment that this author has ever seen in a juvenile correctional facility. Male residents strongly react to what they consider to be an oppressive environment; it is interesting that the reaction is not stronger among female residents.

Fourth, two or three male residents in each cottage have jobs in the local communities. They are more positive about the freedoms and responsibilities they have, but for most residents (females even more than males) boredom is a constant feature of institutional life. In the summers, especially, the absence of programming means that too many residents spend too much time within the cottage.

Finally, juvenile privatization is praised these days because it provides a more normalizing experience for youth. Indeed, private operations are supposedly structured to offer advantages over state training schools, such as residents are able to attend school in the community, to enjoy off-campus shopping and entertainment trips, and to participate in regularly scheduled home visits. The fact is that female adolescents from this private facility, regardless of the campus to which they are assigned, are stigmatized in the school experience. None of the interviewed male or female adolescents ever mentions the school experience in a positive light. Apparently, as one male youth noted, unless a youth from the private facility has athletic skill and can participate on the football or basketball teams, he or she will not be accepted.

Conclusions

This study does little to reject the frequent finding that female adolescents have been treated more harshly than male adolescents since the founding of the juvenile court at the turn of the century (Schlossman & Wallach 1978). Female adolescents in this study stay as long or longer than males even though males have been charged with much more serious crimes. This study also suggests that the fear of female adolescents' sexual activity has resulted in their discriminatory treatment by the juvenile justice system. Clearly, female adolescents' runaway behavior remains one activity that society will not tolerate, because of the likelihood of sexual activity.

The protection that the Juvenile Justice and Delinquency Prevention Act (JJDPA) is supposed to provide status offenders becomes more problematic when the issue of adolescent female sexual activity enters the picture. The overriding concern is to find a means to justify the institutionalization of female adolescents so that society can protect them against their acting-out tendencies. Juvenile court systems can place these female adolescents on probation for status offenses and then, as does the state in this one sample, reclassify them as delinquents when they violate probation with another status offense. Or even better, as juvenile jurisdictions across the nation are doing at the present time, female adolescents can be sent to private placements.

The danger is that the not-for-profit private placements will be more concerned about "making money from kids" than they are in providing therapeutic services for residents. What is known is that private operations usually keep residents longer than they would be confined in state facilities. These facilities also may not meet state standards in the services they deliver to residents. Moreover, as Shichor and Bartollas (1990) found in a comparison of private and public juvenile placements in southern California, private vendors do not always provide the services they promise to provide or have the staff on duty they claim to have. Furthermore, the JJDPA requiring separation of delinquents from status offenders seems to be violated more in private than in state placements. Shichor and Bartollas found that this problem arises because privately operated programs tend to admit all categories of offenders, which usually contradicts the supposed selectiveness of their intake policies. As a result, the runaway female adolescent may have frequent contact with the male adolescent gang member, robber, or drug pusher.

In sum, the process of growing up as a female adolescent may result in her involvement in socially unacceptable behavior. She is far better off to commit delinquent offenses than status offenses, especially those that threaten society's attempt to place a moral chastity belt around female adolescents. Reformers have effected many positive changes in institutionalization for male delinquents. Unfortunately, as this and other studies document, there is still a long way to go for female adolescents. Being vigilant with this population is particularly important because it is politically powerless, socially rejected, and easily exploited.

References

Burkhart, K.W. (1976). *Women in prison.* Lexington, MA: D.C. Heath/Lexington Books.

Cernkovich, S.A., Giordano, P.C., & Pugh, M.D. (1985). Chronic offenders: The missing cases in self-report delinquency research. *Journal of Criminal Law and Criminology* 76: 705–732.

Freedman, E. (1981). *Their sisters' keepers: Women's prison reforms in America, 1830–1930.* Ann Arbor: University of Michigan.

Giallombardo, R. (1966). *Society of women: A study of a women's prison.* New York: Wiley.

——— (1974). *The social world of imprisoned girls.* New York: Wiley.

Heffernan, E. (1972). *Making it in prison: The square, the cool and the life.* New York: Wiley.

Pollock-Byrne, J.M. (1990). *Women, prison and crime.* Pacific Grove, CA: Brooks/Cole.

Propper, A.M.L. (1976). *Importation and deprivation perspectives on homosexuality in correctional institutions: An empirical test of their relative efficacy.* Unpublished doctoral dissertation, University of Washington, Seattle. *Dissertation Abstracts International.* Later published in a revised form as A. Propper (1981). *Prison homosexuality: Myth and reality.* Lexington, MA: D.C. Heath.

Rafter, N. (1985). *Partial justice: State prisons and their inmates, 1800–1935.* Boston, MA: Northeastern University Press.

Schlossman, S., & Wallach, S. (1978). The crime of precocious sexuality: Female juvenile delinquency in the Progressive era. *Harvard Educational Review* 48: 65.

Shichor, D. (1970). A typological study of juvenile correctional organizations. Unpublished doctoral dissertation, University of Southern California.

Shichor, D., & Bartollas, C. (1990). Private and public juvenile placements: Is there a difference? *Crime and Delinquency* 36: 286-299.

Sieverdes, C.M., & Bartollas, C. (1980). Institutional adjustment among female delinquents. In A.W. Cohn & B. Ward (Eds.), *Improving management in criminal justice* (pp. 91–103). Beverly Hills, CA: Sage.

Simon, R.J. (1975). *Women and crime.* Lexington, MA: D.C.Heath/Lexington Books.

U.S. Department of Justice (1991). *Prisoners in 1990.* Washington, DC: Bureau of Justice Statistics.

Ward, D., & Kassebaum, G. (1965). *Women's prison: Sex and social structure.* Chicago: Aldine.

Criminalizing of Pregnant Women Drug Abusers

Renée Goldsmith Kasinsky
University of Massachusetts, Lowell

The social control and the attempt to regulate women's behavior during pregnancy has become a major social issue. The popular press has focused on the crack kid or the baby with fetal alcohol syndrome to the neglect of the pregnant women who are their mothers. While these children do raise serious problems for our society, one of those least discussed is the subordination of these mothers' problems and rights to the supreme interests of their fetuses. In the late 1980s and 1990s the subjugation of a woman's right to privacy, bodily integrity, and autonomy to that of her fetus is no longer a fictitious future as described in the *Handmaid's Tale* (Atwood 1986). Their reproductive functions are subject to the scrutiny and monitoring of the patriarchal state. It raises questions for all women regarding the encroachment of the state's coercive powers over their lives.

I will focus on society's treatment of these pregnant mothers with addiction problems who are buffeted by contradictory public policies and inadequate social programs. Questions of equity and the adequacy of our health system in serving poor women and women of color on the fringes of society are real concerns that need to be addressed. An analysis of recent legal and medical attempts to socially control pregnant drug abusers will show the impact of these social forces on both their lives and ours.

Who is the pregnant drug user? What is her world like? What decisions does she face? A hypothetical example will give us some clues.

A young 25-year-old Hispanic woman, Maria, finds she is pregnant. The pregnancy may have been unwanted in the first place, either because of abuse or pressure from her partner (Karmen 1982). Maybe she is a crack addict and had sex in exchange for drugs ("Some Inner City Women" 1989). Or perhaps the pressure she felt to become pregnant came from a more subtle source: lack of any hope for employment or other personal fulfillment may have led her to seek self-worth in motherhood (Austin 1989). If she did receive birth control counseling, she may have been directly advised to be sterilized[1] or forced, by lack of alternatives, to make sure she had no further pregnancies. However, it is even more likely that she did not receive any counseling. Once pregnant, Maria may have wanted to terminate her pregnancy but did not know where to get information about abortion and could not afford one anyway.[2] Perhaps she really wanted a baby, but knows she would be solely responsible for its care and can not afford to raise a child on her own.[3] If Maria decides to keep the baby, it is likely that poor nutrition, stress, and unsafe housing have already put her pregnancy at risk (Nsiah-Jefferson 1989). She cannot afford to go to a private doctor for prenatal care because she lacks insurance, and there may not be any public prenatal clinic in her community[4] (McNulty 1988). If she is a drug addict, she has virtually no chance of getting treatment for her drug problem or health care for her pregnancy (Brotman, Hutson, & Suffet 1984; McNulty 1988). As a yet unknown addict, if she managed to attend a publicly supported clinic or hospital she was probably subjected to mandatory drug screening or urine testing for drugs (Moss 1990). It is likely that the results of this testing were given to the Department of Social Welfare, who, in turn, may have shared the information with the local police in her jurisdiction. If she lives in a jurisdiction where the district attorney has announced a policy to prosecute pregnant drug addicts, he/she will use this information in a possible indictment of Maria for the crime of distributing cocaine to a person under 18, on grounds that she allegedly ingested cocaine while pregnant with her baby. Maria may make the decision to stay away from any available care to avoid this kind of detection. Faced with the threat of jail, she may try to abort the fetus.

Once the baby is born, the state may attempt to legally take the baby away from her and place it in foster care.

Drug use generally and cocaine use in particular are more pervasive among women arrested for other serious crimes (National Institute of Justice 1991). In 13 of the 21 Drug Use Forecasting Cities, the proportion of women testing positive for any drug is higher than it is for men. Furthermore, the trend data show that the proportion of women testing positive for cocaine has been higher than that of men over the past few years (National Institute of Justice 1990). According to James Inciardi, most of these women are crack users.

Some researchers such as Patricia Erickson and Glenn Murray (1989) have focused their attention on the emphasis and assumptions that lie behind these official statistics. They argue that there is a double standard being applied to women's use of cocaine. These authors suggest that women who use cocaine are subject to more negative stereotyping and social repercussions than are men who have engaged in the same drug use and negative behavior.

In addition to a gender interpretation, there is also an important class phenomenon operating in the visibility and treatment of drug abusers. Cocaine use is by no means restricted to the institutions off lower-class street life. Middle-class and upper-class women are also involved in drug use, though they have been more invisible. According to the latest household study on drug abuse, reflecting middle-class usage, almost one in every ten American women have tried cocaine (National Institute of Drug Abuse 1992). However it is the lower-class crack users who have been consistently singled out by our institutions for punishment.

Media reports have emphasized the use of crack among mothers especially among ethnic and racial minorities in inner city street life settings. Drug experts such as Inciardi have focused on the "sex-for-crack" phenomenon among poor women in crack houses (Inciardi, Lockwood, & Pottieger 1993). The prosecution of mothers who use drugs by the criminal justice system has been of the predominantly poor, Third World-emigrant women who have given birth to drug-exposed babies. According to the Center for Reproductive Law and Policy, since 1987 at least 165 women in 26 states have been arrested on criminal charges because of their drug behavior during pregnancy (cited in Paltrow, Fox, & Goetz 1992). Tens of thousands more women have had their children removed from them and taken into custody by welfare agencies.

There appear to be two very different approaches to what is being defined as the problem of illicit drug use by pregnant women and drug-exposed newborns. In one approach, drug addiction is perceived as a criminal matter, and in another approach the issue is perceived and treated as a medical matter. The former approach sees the prosecution of these women as a way to stop them from using illegal drugs. The medical and health and social welfare approaches suggest that addiction can be more accurately viewed as a symptom of a complex series of health issues. However, the focus is still on the victim and barely deals with the larger issues of inequality in the social system.

The pregnant drug users who have been identified and subjected to either social welfare or criminal actions have been, for the most part, poor women who have been prosecuted by a largely white social welfare establishment and/or prosecuted by white male district attorneys representing the state's interests. More than half of all the recent prosecutions of pregnant women are women of color (Paltrow 1990). Let us look now at the legal history of cases involving fetal abuse.

Legal Cases and Fetal Endangerment

Between 1925 and 1942 the United States Supreme Court recognized for the first time that addiction is a disease, not a moral weakness.[5] The next three decades of constitutional litigation brought significant advances in the recognition of the rights of women, poor people, and people of color. The treatment of drug- and alcohol-addicted pregnant women is a throwback to the Progressive era, when government willingness to control the most private of individual choices was unabashed, and racial and economic justifications for government coercion were more socially acceptable.

What are some of the major legal and constitutional issues involving these recent fetal rights cases and issues surrounding drug testing of women and newborns as the basis for civil and criminal proceedings? Prosecutors have attempted to apply existing laws concerning drug trafficking or child abuse in wholly unprecedented ways to criminalize the behavior of women during their pregnancies. Recent examples of district attorneys' various actions can be seen through the following cases.

In 1985 Pamela Rae Stewart was criminally charged under a California child support statute for failing to follow her doctor's instructions while pregnant (*People* v. *Pamela Rae Stewart* 1987). Stewart had given birth to a severely brain damaged son who died approximately 6 weeks after birth. The national media focused on the allegation that she had used illegal drugs during her pregnancy. Her prosecution was triggered, at least partially, by a positive test for amphetamines in the urine of her newborn son. Although the San Diego Municipal Court dismissed the case in 1987 on the grounds that the statute did not cover the conduct alleged, the case remains important as one of the first times that prosecutors utilized a statute designed to protect children to prosecute the mother because of her behavior during pregnancy.

The first woman successfully prosecuted on charges stemming from her addiction during pregnancy was Jennifer C. Johnson, a 23-year-old African-American woman (*Jennifer Johnson* v. *State of Florida* 1989). She gave birth to two infants who both tested positive for cocaine. The prosecution was initiated by hospital officials who turned over the test results to county attorneys. Jennifer Johnson was convicted of delivery of an illegal substance to a minor. She was convicted in Florida under a drug pushing statute of two counts of delivery of a controlled substance to a minor, and received a sentence of 15 years: 1 year to be served on "community control"[6] followed by 14 years of probation. As conditions of her sentence, Johnson must participate in a drug rehabilitation program and obtain a high school equivalency diploma. She cannot possess controlled substances, consume alcohol, associate with individuals who possess drugs, or enter a bar without the permission of her probation officer. Johnson must also perform 200 hours of community service and remain employed. If she becomes pregnant, she must enter a judicially approved prenatal care program (*Jennifer Johnson* v. *State of Florida* 1989).

The *Commonwealth* v. *Josephine Pellegrini* (1990) case in Massachusetts has been seen by some attorneys as a possible precedent for other jurisdictions. The defense focused on the rights of the mother, while the state treated the case as one of child abuse. On July 2, 1989, Pellegrini, a 24-year-old mother of 3 children gave birth to Nathan in Brockton, Massachusetts. Tests showed that the baby was born with cocaine metabolites—the product of the drug after the body has broken it down—in his urine. There was no evidence that the child was harmed, and he was released to his mother. About 6 weeks later, Nathan was found to have burn injuries on his feet due to a lit cigarette or lighter. After this incident, prosecution was initiated under the law which prohibits the distribution of class B substances to persons under 18 years old (*Commonwealth* v. *Josephine Pellegrini* 1990).

Judge Suzanne Del Vecchio, a superior court judge, dismissed the case on October 15, 1990. She ruled that this state statute does not encompass an *in utero* transfer, and even if it did, prosecuting a woman for it would be an unconstitutional violation of her privacy rights. The judge in her 16-page decision noted that a court's intrusion into "her most private areas, her inner body" quoted from the defendant's brief must be justified by a compelling state's interest. While the court has a valid interest in the health of a viable fetus, "there is no showing in this case that the infant suffered an injury as a result of the traces of cocaine found in his urine and, therefore, the state's interest in this case is not shown to be compelling." The judge suggested that protection of a fetus can be achieved by less restrictive means, "such as education and making available medical care and drug treatment centers for pregnant women" (*Commonwealth* v. *Josephine Pellegrini* 1990:6, 8).

Health and Welfare Approaches

Prosecutors in two South Carolina cities, Greenville and Charleston, have joined together with individuals at local public hospitals to establish a procedure for prosecuting pregnant women who test positive for the presence of illicit substances. In Charleston, women who come into the public hospital for prenatal care or delivery are selectively tested for drugs; those who test positive have their names turned over to the police. The police then go to the hospital. The women, who are still recovering from the delivery, are handcuffed and taken to jail and stay there until they can make bail (Paltrow 1990b).

The impetus for criminal prosecutions is a drug test given either to the mother during pregnancy, immediately prior to delivery, or to the infant at the time of birth. These tests raise the issues of discrimination, consent, and confidentiality. They often target women who cannot afford prenatal care or can afford only to go to public hospitals or clinics. These women are labeled "high risk" and are tested routinely without their consent. Yet, those who can afford private care remain effectively insulated from state intrusion (Robin-Vergeer 1990).

Child abuse statutes adopted since 1960 have most recently been applied against pregnant mothers who abuse drugs. These state statutes require that mandated reporters, including physicians and medical personnel, make a report whenever they know or reasonably suspect that a child has been abused. Definitions of abuse vary, but usually include physical abuse, sexual abuse, and some forms of neglect. The laws grant immunity to those who make mandated reports—and impose serious consequences, including both criminal and civil liability, on those who fail to do so. Most child abuse reporting laws incorporate the concept of "reasonable suspicion" for mandated reporters (English 1990:4).

The new reporting requirements imposed in some states in cases of prenatal drug use remove the element of professional judgment by making drug exposure alone, and sometimes a positive drug test alone, the basis of a mandatory report. Oklahoma, Florida, Utah, and Massachusetts have adopted an addictive model, requiring reports in cases of drug dependence or physical addiction of an infant (English

1990). For example, the formal policy of the Massachusetts Department of Social Services (DSS) is that infants who are born with a positive toxicology trigger an automatic referral to DSS and are handled within the current framework as a child abuse case. If warranted, an investigation will be conducted and one likely outcome of this investigation is the involvement of the police and the district attorney's office.

In civil neglect proceedings, social service agencies have also begun to use child abuse laws that were never intended to apply to a mother's prenatal behavior to take custody of infants born with positive toxicologies. "Parental fitness," is the prevailing legal standard that must be met before a court may find neglect. In the 1989 case of the *Department of Social Services* v. *Felicia B.*, state social service workers alleged that the respondent's use of cocaine while pregnant, detected by a test on her newborn, constituted neglect. The court relied on the common law rule that one may be liable for the later consequences of one's earlier actions as support for the proposition that potential harm could constitute neglect.

In these cases, social services workers are making a major assumption that the evidence of drug use indicates neglect. Yet this is a problematic assumption because a positive toxicology test alone does not provide substantive information about the impairment of mother or child. According to Kary Moss, an attorney with the ACLU's Women's Rights Project in Nassau County, an extremely conservative, heavily anti-abortion area of New York State, "a positive toxicology test can mean that a newborn is taken away and court proceedings are then initiated to deprive the mother of custody of the child." "But," Moss added, "in other areas, like New York County, they undertake an investigation of the family before they initiate a proceeding to remove the child." She takes the position that "the ability of the drug-using woman to parent should be assessed independently in determining what action is in the best interests of the child" (qtd. in Bader 1990:8).

State deprivation of a parent's custodial rights solely on the basis of prenatal substance abuse presumes parental unfitness, when the parent may not be unfit. The new requirements that explicitly mandate reporting of drug exposure or positive toxicology screens are not necessary if existing child abuse reporting laws are adequate to trigger reports in appropriate cases. Without the explicit mandate, medical professionals caring for newborn infants would determine whether or not to make a report of abuse or neglect based upon the same standard that they use in all cases. For example, in California, prior to the decision in *Troy D.*, a report showing evidence of "fetal abuse" would not be triggered by a toxicology screen alone but would have to be based on other facts indicating that the infant was a victim of abuse or neglect. In those cases where the mother was able to provide a level of care that was appropriate to the child's needs, hospital personnel would not be required to file a report (English 1990).

Experts have suggested that, taken to its logical extreme, a reporting obligation applicable to prenatal activities that can have an adverse effect on a fetus, and thus on a newborn child, would have far-reaching implications. A wide variety of acts or conditions on the part of a pregnant woman that could pose some threat to her fetus include the following: failing to eat well; using nonprescription, prescription, or illegal drugs; engaging in sexual intercourse; exercising; not exercising; suffering physical harm due to accident or disease; working or living near possibly toxic substances; smoking; drinking alcohol; and even ingesting something as common as caffeine.

The above criminal prosecutions and civil proceedings have drastically altered and distorted the meaning and context of child abuse proceedings. In the *Stewart* case, the prosecutor attempted to apply to a fetus a state law that was designed to protect children. In the parallel civil case of *Felicia B.,* the child abuse laws were extended to the actions of the mother herself, rather than the usual case of seeking to protect the interests of the mother and child against a third party. In the *Johnson* and the *Pellegrini* cases, the drug statutes were utilized. None of the women in the above cases has been arrested for the crime of illegal drug use or possession. Instead, they are being arrested and prosecuted for a new crime: becoming pregnant while addicted to drugs. The biological event of conception transforms the woman from drug user into a drug trafficker or child abuser, with significantly greater penalties than mere possession or use both for herself and her child.

While the behavior of pregnant women is subjected to governmental scrutiny and punishment, men are spared exposure to criminal sanctions for behavior which is equally or more harmful to the fetus, such as intravenous drug use. In the *People* v. *Pamela Rae Stewart* (1987) case, prosecutors targeted a woman, but not her male companion, despite the fact that one of the woman's allegedly harmful actions toward the fetus was to engage in sexual intercourse. Males who have used physical violence against their pregnant partners and who have thereby inflicted injuries to the fetus have also not been targeted for action.

Inadequate Health and Drug Treatment for Women

Pregnant women who use drugs find themselves in a paradoxical situation. One possible option to avoid prosecution or imprisonment may be an abortion. In Washington, D.C., a woman mysteriously miscarried days before a hearing which had been scheduled by a judge who had threatened to put her in jail because he believed she was using drugs while pregnant (English 1990).

Ironically, this same woman was probably denied early information preventing her from making an informed choice regarding abortion. Recent Supreme Court rulings allow states to make it impossible for an indigent woman to obtain an abortion (at least a safe one) by foreclosing both government reimbursement for private abortions and the use of public hospitals and clinics. Furthermore, the Court, by approving a policy of "encouraging childbirth" by providing funds for that option alone, has permitted the government to use financial coercion to influence women's reproductive decisions.[7] According to the *New York Times*, basic medical information about abortion will now be withheld from the nearly 4 million women being served in the 4,500 public clinics throughout the country (Greenhouse 1991). These government regulations are a clear violation of a woman's right to control her pregnancy without interference from the government. This ruling clearly discriminates against poor women who cannot afford privately funded health care and denies them the choice to terminate their pregnancy. Poor Third World-emigrant women of color will figure prominently in these statistics ("Some Inner-City Women" 1989).

Some questions of ethics and responsibility are raised by health care policies concerning these pregnant women. The purpose of consent and confidentiality laws, in large measure, is to encourage patients to seek necessary medical care and to be candid with the health care professionals providing treatment. And yet there is some suggestive evidence that the use of these laws is forcing women to retreat rather than to seek care. For example, following Pamela Rae Stewart's arrest, a San Diego health care worker reported that some pregnant women were not obtaining prenatal care because of fear of prosecution for drug use. Many medical experts believe that mandatory reporting laws not only frightens pregnant mothers away from prenatal services but away from drug treatment programs as well (Lerner 1990; Moss 1990). In Minnesota the reporting statute imposes no criminal sanction and is designed only to get more women into drug treatment programs. Yet, Minnesota doctors fear the law is having the opposite effect, as pregnant drug users avoid treatment and withold information from their doctors in order to avoid being reported (Lerner 1990).

The collision between these protections and the child abuse reporting requirements may have adverse consequences for children. For example, toxicology testing of infants may be used for diagnostic purposes in appropriate cases. However, physicians who have no reason to suspect abuse or neglect based on other available information may be reluctant to order such tests if they will automatically trigger a mandatory obligation to report. These new laws represent a departure from the established framework of the reporting statutes. In conclusion, we have seen that a negative consequence of this social policy is that these tests may become the basis of child abuse reports, child welfare investigations, and even removal of the child from the mother's custody.

Although prosecutors say their main motive in these cases is to provide an incentive for women to stop using drugs, drug treatment is largely unavailable to pregnant women, even if they are motivated to receive it. Their pregnancy, compounded by poverty, often acts as a disqualifying factor. As Representative George Miller concluded after congressional research and hearings on the subject, "Women who seek help for drug addiction during pregnancy cannot get it." Two-thirds of the hospitals surveyed by the House Select Committee reported that they had no drug treatment programs to which their pregnant patients could be referred; none reported the availability of special programs geared to providing comprehensive drug treatment and prenatal care to this population ("Born Hooked" 1989). Likewise, in a survey of drug abuse treatment programs in New York City, Dr. Wendy Chavkin (1989), of the Columbia University School of Public Health, surveyed 78 drug treatment programs in New York City (95% of the city's programs). She found that 54% of the city's drug programs categorically excluded pregnant women; 67% denied treatment to pregnant addicts on Medicaid; 87% denied treatment to pregnant women on Medicaid who are specifically addicted to crack. Fewer than half (44%) simultaneously provided prenatal care (Chavkin 1989). National estimates indicate that half of the addicted mothers who are not in drug treatment programs lose child custody by the time their children are one year of age (Tittle & St. Claire 1989).

Phyllis Savage (cited in Malaspine 1989), the Family Director at Odyssey House, New York City's only drug treatment program where mothers and small children can live together, explained that the lives of the 21 women in the program "have never been anything but hellish. . . . All they know is rage and anger and abuse. . . . This is the first place that many of our women have been where they can't get hit . . ." (Malaspina 1989:20). Research has shown that 80% to 90% of female drug addicts and alcoholics have been victims of rape or incest, or other kinds of violent abuse. This link between alcohol and violence against women has been made only in recent years (Coakley 1989; Kaufman, Straus, & Straus 1987; Leff 1990; Morgan 1989; Room 1990).

Alternative Responses to Infant Addiction

There is no logical stopping point for efforts to police maternal behavior during pregnancy (McNulty 1988). While the bulk of recent public attention has been focused upon illegal drug use by women during pregnancy, other legal substances, including tobacco and alcohol, have also been demonstrated to have the potential to injure the fetus. At least two states have recently enacted legislation authorizing state intervention upon the birth of a child afflicted with fetal alcohol syndrome.[8] The *Angela Carder* case barring a forced caesarean raises the question of whether pregnant women can be held responsible for refusing to undergo less dangerous or invasive procedures in the interest of fetal health. Kaminer (1990) suggests that fetal rights theories that impose affirmative obligations on women might impose similar obligations on the state. She raises some critical questions. "What is the state's duty to care for its new fetal citizenry? Does it extend beyond a grant of discretionary power to punish pregnant women? What affirmative demands for health care and nutrition might an enfranchised fetus make on its government?" (p. 17). Even more to the point: What affirmative actions should mothers demand and see as part of their rights for living on this planet?

A broad cross section of organizations and individuals have united to point out the dangers of prosecuting women for drug or alcohol use. Included among these are the American Medical Association, the American College of Obstetrics and Gynecology, the National Council on Alcoholism, the National Women's Health Network, and the American Civil Liberties Union. These groups point out that real solutions would include making available reproductive health services, including abortion, sex, and parenting education, as well as prenatal and other health care[9] (Lazarus & West 1987). Affirmative legal and legislative remedies may be a first step in a more positive direction.

In December 1989, the American Civil Liberty Union's Women's Rights Project filed the first in a series of lawsuits on behalf of pregnant crack addicts and alcoholics against four private alcohol and drug treatment programs in New York City. Two of the plaintiffs, both crack addicts, had sought treatment from defendant programs and were told they could not be admitted because they were pregnant. As a result of their drug use, both women were later deprived of custody of their children at birth, and only one of the women has since regained custody. They sought damages and injunctive relief declaring the policy unlawful and ordering the programs to cease discriminating against pregnant women. Two of the cases have been settled. The issue of whether hospitals can use "reasonable medical judgment" to exclude pregnant mothers is still on appeal before the court. Forcing alcohol and drug treatment programs to admit pregnant women will allow women who seek help for their addiction to receive it (Moss 1990; Moss, personal communication August 1991; *Elaine W.* v. *North General Hospital* 1991).

State legislatures can create laws that aid both the mother who uses drugs and her fetus without forcing women to flee the health care system. Such laws may provide early treatment, intervention, and child care services for parents while they undergo alcohol or drug treatment. Legislatures could also provide increased funding of prenatal services for poor women (Moss 1990). Each of these measures could go a long way toward improving the chances that pregnant addicts would conquer their addictions and obtain the health care they need, while taking the child's needs into account as well. For example, Rhode Island has amended its 1989 Maternal and Child Health Services law to provide outpatient alcohol and drug treatment services, as well as childbirth and parenting preparation programs for pregnant women who meet certain financial requirements.[10] Florida passed a law in 1986 providing that "no parent of a (drug exposed) newborn infant shall be subject to criminal investigation solely on the basis of such infant's drug dependency."[11]

Comprehensive nonpunitive care that will meet the needs of the pregnant substance abuser must be provided by both the state and the private sector. Nonsexist and nondiscriminatory policies must be adopted and enforced in existing drug treatment programs, and more funds, including the money that is presently being used to arrest women and place their children in foster care, must be made available for drug treatment and education. Finally, prosecutors and lawmakers must stop pretending that the criminal prosecution of pregnant women is a quick fix for the problems of drug addiction when we have known for years that drug abuse, like most other causes of infant mortality and morbidity, requires long-term solutions involving significant societal commitments to rehabilitation, treatment, and education of individuals, as well as the elimination of poverty, race, and gender discrimination (Chasnoff1989).[12]

In conclusion, the current fetal rights movement casts pregnant addicted mothers in the role of child abusers and attempts to speak on behalf of their unborn fetuses. Though it has been documented that the phenomenon of maternal drug use can be found across class and race lines, society has attempted to control socially those primarily young, poor Third World-emigrant mothers who, due to lack of resources, have received little prenatal care or drug treatment of any kind. These mothers have been given few options and support for their pregnancy and have been discriminated against by a society that utilizes its public welfare and criminal justice institutions to actively prosecute the poor. Because these women have violated traditional female expectations and roles as mothers, they have been subject to extra harsh punishment. At the same time, men are spared exposure to criminal sanctions for behavior that is equally or more harmful to the fetus.[13] There are better ways to address the problems facing children who were exposed to drugs *in utero* than by criminally punishing mothers and abrogating mothers' parental rights. Mothers' and children's rights need not be at odds. The overall health care and nutrition of both the mother and the child should be of equal importance to a society that has an interest in producing future generations of healthy people.

Notes

1. Poor women of color have been subjected to sterilization for decades. This abuse may take the form of blatant coercion or more subtle influences on women's decisions to be sterilized. Nsiah-Jefferson, "Reproductive Laws, Women of Color, and Low-Income Women," in *Reproductive Laws for the 1990s: A Briefing Handbook* (N. Taub & S. Cohen, Eds., 1988) points out that sterilization services are provided by states under the Medicaid program, while

information about and access to other contraceptive techniques may not be available.

2. Federal regulations prohibit abortion counseling and referral by family planning clinics that receive funds under Title X of the Public Health Service Act. In May 1991 the Supreme Court case *Rust* v. *Sullivan* supported these federal regulations. This decision means that poor women who use Title X–funded clinics are unable to obtain information from the clinics about both abortions and where abortion information can be obtained. Furthermore, the limits on federal and state Medicaid funding for abortions make it impossible for many indigent women to obtain abortions.

3. In 1984, 52% of black female-headed families lived in poverty. See G. Jaynes and R. Williams (1989) *A Common Destiny: Blacks and American Society*.

4. Many poor women of color cannot afford prenatal care. In recent years, access to prenatal care has actually declined among poor and African-American women, resulting in high rates of infant mortality and low birth weight.

5. The *Linder* v. *U.S.1* (1925) case recognized that forced sterilization is an unconstitutional exercise of state power.

6. Community control means a form of intensive, supervised custody in the community, including surveillance on weekends and holidays, administered by officers with restricted case loads. Community control is an individualized program in which the freedom of an offender is restricted within the community, home, or noninstitutional residential placement and specific sanctions are imposed and enforced.

7. In May 1991 the Supreme Court in *Rust* v. *Sullivan* supported federal sanctions that bars employees of federally financed family planning clinics from all discussion of abortions with their clients. Chief Justice William Rehnquist delivering the majority decision argued that it was a simple matter of government regulating the programs it pays for.

8. Ind Code Ann & 31-6-4-3-1 (Burns 1987) provides that a child born with fetal alcohol syndrome may be considered a "child in need of services" for purposes of removal from its natural parent(s). In Utah, medical personnel must report the birth of any child with fetal alcohol syndrome to the Division of Family Services (Utah Code Ann & 62A-4-504[1989]). Willful failure to report such birth is a misdemeanor in the state. (Utah Code Ann 62A-4-511 [1989]).

9. "National estimates show that one out of every five women of childbearing age has no maternity care coverage, either through government programs or private health insurance" (W. Lazarus and K. West, *Back to Basics,* pp. 23–24).

10. 1989 Rhode Island Public Laws 252.

11. Florida Stat. Ann 415.503(8) (a) 2 1986 & Supp., p. 2, 1989.

12. The infant mortality rate in the U.S. is the worst among the eighteen industrialized nations. The National Commission to Prevent Infant Mortality called for "universal access" to early maternity and pediatric care for all mothers and infants (Chasnoff 1989).

13. Male partners of pregnant battered women have not been targeted by prosecutors for their infliction of injuries to the fetus in the course of physically abusing the women.

References

Alters, D. (1989, November 1). Women and crack: Equal addiction, unequal care. *Boston Globe*, 14.

Atwood, M. (1986). *The Handmaid's Tale.*

Austin, R. (1989). Sapphire bound. *Wisconsin Law Review* 3: 558–559.

Bader, E. (1990). Pregnant drug users face jail. *New Directions for Women* (March/April): 8.

Bibvoglia, A. (1987). The ordeal of Pamela Rae Stewart. *Ms* (July–August): 92.

Born hooked: Confronting the impact of perinatal substance abuse: Hearing before the Select Committee on Children, Youth and Families (1990, April 27). 101st Congress, 1st Session, George Miller, Chairman.

Brotman, R., Hutson, D., & Suffet (Eds.) (1984). *Pregnant addicts and their children: A comprehensive care approach.*

Chasnoff (1989). *Women and health* 15(3): 1–3.

Chavkin, W. (1989, July 13). Help, don't jail addicted mothers. *New York Times*, A21.

Coakley (1989, August 23). Suspect is said to be battered, frightened. *Boston Globe*, 22.

Commonwealth v. *Josephine Pellegrini*, Crim. Action No. 87970 (Plymouth Sup. Ct. 1990, 6, 8).

Department of Social Services v. *Felicia B.*, 144 Misc., 2nd 169, 543 (N.Y.S. 2nd 637, Family Ct. 1989).

Drug use Forecasting (1990, 1991). (Annual Report) Washington, DC: National Institute of Justice.

Elaine W. v. *North General Hospital*, No. 6230/90 (N.Y. Supreme Court App. Div. 1991): Brief of Plaintiff-Respondent.

English, A. (1990). Prenatal drug exposure: Grounds for mandatory child abuse reports? *Youth Law News* 2: 6–8.

Erickson, P., & Murray, G. (1989). Sex differences in cocaine use and experience. *American Journal of Drug and Alcohol Abuse* 15: 135–152.

Fink, J.R. (1990). Effects of crack and cocaine upon infants: A brief review of the literature. *N.Y. Legal Aid Society*, 1–10.

Florida Stat Ann. 415.503(8) (1986).

Geller, A. (1991). The effects of drug use during pregnancy. In Paula Roth (Ed.), *Alcohol and drugs are women's issues* (pp. 101–106). Metuchen, NJ: Women's Action Alliance and Scarecrow Press.

Greenhouse, L. (1991, May 24). 5 Justices uphold U.S. rule curbing abortion advice. *New York Times*, A1.

Inciardi, J., Lockwood, D., & Poettieger, A. (1983). *Women and crack-cocaine.* New York: Macmillan.

Ind. Code Ann. 31-6-4-3-1 (1987).

Jaynes, G., & Williams, R. (1989). *A common destiny: Blacks and American society.* Washington, DC: National Academy Press.

Jennifer Johnson v. *State of Florida.* No. 89-1765 (Fla. Dist. Ct. of App., 1989).

Kaminer, W. (1990). Penalizing pregnancy?: The fetal rights controversy. *Radcliffe Quarterly.*

Karmen, A. (1982). Introduction to Part II: Women victims of crime. In B.R. Price & N.J. Sokoloff (Eds.),*The criminal justice system and women.*

Kaufman, K., Straus, G., & Straus, M. (1987). The "drunken bum" theory of wife beating. *Social Problems* 34: 213–230.

Klemestrud, J. (1974, August 26). A hard look at drugs and the middle-class woman. *New York Times.*

Kolata, G. (1989, August 11). On streets ruled by crack, families die. *New York Times*, 1.

LaCroix, S. (1989, May 1). Birth of a bad idea: Jailing mothers for drug abuse. *The Nation*, 585.

Lazarus, W., & West, K. (1987). Back to basics: Improving the health of California's next generation. *Southern California Child Network* 23–24.

Leff, L. (1990, March 5). Treating drug addiction with the women in mind. *The Washington Post*, E1, E4.

Lerner, M. (1990, January 15). Law requiring reporting of pregnant drug users is backfiring, critics say. *Star Tribune*, 1.

Linder v. *U.S.1*, 268 U.S. 5 (1925), accord *Robinson* v. *California*, 370 U.S. 660.

McNulty, M. (1988). Pregnancy police: The health policy and legal implications of punishing pregnant women for harm to their fetuses. *N.Y.U. Rev. Law & Social Change* 16: 277, 319.

Malaspina (1989, November 5). Clean living. *Globe Magazine*, 20.

Matchan, L. (1990). Middle-class drug use in pregnancy seen. *Boston Globe*, 1, 81.

Moss, K. (1990a). Legal issues: Drug testing of post partum women and newborns as the basis for civil and criminal proceedings. *Clearinghouse Review* (March): 1406–1414.

——— (1990b). Substance abuse drug pregnancy. *Harvard Women's Law Journal* 13: 278–299.

National household survey on drug abuse: Population estimates 1991 (1992). Rockville, MD: National Institute on Drug Abuse, 31.

Nsiah-Jefferson (1989). Reproductive laws, women of color and low-income women. *Women's Rights Law Reporter* 11(1) (Spring): 14–39.

Paltrow, L. (1989, October 29). State by state case summary of criminal prosecutions against pregnant women. American Civil Liberties Union Reproductive Freedom Project Memorandum

——— (1990). When becoming pregnant is a crime. *Criminal Justice Ethics* (Winter/Spring): 41–50.

People v. *Pamela Rae Stewart*, No. M 508197 (San Diego Mun. Ct. 1987).

Robin-Vergeer, B.I. (1990). The problem of the drug exposed newborn: A return to principled intervention. *Stanford Law Review* 745, 759–760.

Room, R. (1990). Alcohol as an instrument of intimate domination. Paper presented to the Study of Social Problems annual meeting.

Rust v. *Sullivan*, S. Ct. (May 1991).

Some inner-city women addicted to crack trade sex for drugs or turn to prostitution to support their addiction (1989, August 11). *New York Times*, 1.

Tittle & St. Claire (1989). Promoting the health and development of drug-exposed infants through a comprehensive clinical model. *Zero to Three: Bulletin of the National Center for Clinical Infant Programs* 9: 18–20.

Utah Code Ann. 62A-4-504 (1989).

Utah Code Ann. 62A-4-511 (1989).

A Radical Analysis of a Treatment Program for Cocaine-Abusing Mothers*

Sue Mahan
Della Alice Prestwood
University of Central Florida at Daytona Beach**

Introduction

This analysis is based on critical conceptions of crime and criminology and raises questions about conventional presumptions toward cocaine-abusing mothers. The outline was taken from Quinney's (1970) ideas about the social reality of crime. Quinney noted that what is defined to be crime reinforces the interests of the wealthy and powerful. Since crime is defined to serve the interests of the ruling order, it is possible to note the ways in which various specific criminal definitions reinforce the status quo. In this instance, the focus is on cocaine-abusing pregnant women. Yet, this very focus is biased by the presumptions about cocaine mothers that are prevalent. The controversy over policy and legal procedure to handle the problem has been addressed toward "fetal endangerment" in its most narrow sense. Since the focus has been on pregnant cocaine abusers, the broader nature of the problem for children and society may be ignored.

---

* Revised from a presentation for the Academy of Criminal Justice Sciences, Nashville, Tennessee.
** Maurie Karsham and Nellie Allen were instrumental in preparing this report.

At the same time, law enforcement and criminal justice systems devise programs that are also narrowly focused. Within that narrow focus, conflict arises from attempts to criminalize and punish cocaine-addicted mothers. With the focus of the problem strictly limited to issues arising from pregnancy, women are rightfully concerned. Important issues of women's rights to privacy and autonomy are at stake.

However, as long as debates about fetal endangerment are so strictly focused on the pregnant addict, many more significant problems are not being considered. Issues of class, race, and sex bias are fundamental to social reality and fundamental to public conceptions about crime. Each of these fundamental issues is also basic to ideas about cocaine moms and efforts to treat them.

While public attention is directed toward cocaine moms and their resulting problems, there will be little notice of mothers addicted to alcohol, prescription medications, and other toxic substances whose behaviors are not the subject of public campaigns. Nor will there be interest in fathers or other family members who will not be held accountable for the problems of children. Moreover, as long as the public is concerned about poor, black, pregnant, cocaine addicts, who will be concerned about medical, environmental, governmental, or occupational fetal endangerment at its most devastating?

Cocaine Mothers in the Literature

There are at least 375,000 babies born each year affected by their mothers' cocaine use according to conservative estimates (Fallon, 1990). Putting the problem of pregnant cocaine users in perspective, it is significant that over 5 million women of childbearing age use an illicit drug. Almost 1 million use cocaine, an estimated 3 million use marijuana, almost 6 million are alcoholic, and almost 24% smoke cigarettes. In a survey of pregnant women published in 1990, 15% tested positive for substance abuse according to the U.S. House of Representatives (U.S. House of Representatives 1990).

Studies show that mothers using cocaine or marijuana had babies with smaller neonatal head circumferences and impaired fetal growth (Chasnoff et al. 1989). Use of cigarettes and alcohol add to the amount of impairment. Any interventions aimed at improving infant mortality must include a comprehensive approach to substance abuse (Zuckerman et al. 1989).

Women became more heavily involved with cocaine and narcotics in the 1980s. Women have also become more likely to be arrested for sale of drugs than before. Women drug users usually started between 14 and 15 years of age, having begun shoplifting or other criminal activities prior to their involvement with chemical substances (Inciardi & Pottieger 1986).

The number of cases of cocaine mothers being handled by the courts is increasing rapidly. By February 1990, at least 44 women had been prosecuted for fetal abuse from cocaine use during pregnancy ("Many Disagree with Punitive Approach to Stemming Drug Abuse During Pregnancy" 1990). Until now, the majority of criminal actions against cocaine mothers originated in Florida and South Carolina, two politically conservative states ("Critics Call Crackdown" 1990).

The estimated cost for infants born with problems due to cocaine in Florida is about $8,179 per baby. Of the total budget allocated by the state, 11.8% goes to prevention, compared to 82.2% spent on after-birth medical care. The Florida State Health and Rehabilitative Services response to the increasing problem of cocaine mothers is to develop better methods for tracking cocaine babies and the use of intervention specialists to get the mothers in for treatment and prenatal care (Florida Department of HRS 1989).

The narrow focus on cocaine mothers has begun to shift slightly in recent months. Researchers at Yale have discovered that cocaine use is related to subfertility and low sperm counts (Bracken et al. 1990). Others have found that fathers who take two or more alcoholic drinks a day have smaller than average infants (Blakeslee 1991). The importance of the fathers' contribution to cocaine babies needs to be given much more study. In the meantime, real solutions to drug problems must address jobs, housing, education, counseling, coaching, child care, health care, skill training, and food all at the same time (C. Johnson 1990).

A Case Study

This report concerns a program that was initially directed toward problems faced by cocaine-abusing mothers. The process of development has been divided into four phases from suggestions about the social reality of crime provided by Quinney (1970). His four phases are interactive and repetitive. In Phase One, criminal definitions are formulated. Phase Two includes the application of those criminal definitions. Phase Three involves the construction of conceptions about criminals, and Phase Four considers the development of behavior patterns in relation to the criminal definitions.

Methods of Study

Observation was one of the most important tools in this case study. Regular weekly sessions made it possible to keep track of ongoing developments in a treatment program for cocaine mothers from an insider's point of view. The parenting program being examined was implemented in a gradual way, and regular weekly meetings were essential for keeping the program going.

At the same time, information was also gathered from the popular press, professional journals, and government documents. Researchers also attended seminars, parenting classes, and other public forums held in 1989 and 1990. All relevant materials addressing the problems arising from fetal endangerment in Florida were considered in the study.

Each of the researchers was responsible for a different aspect of the study. Mahan, as principal investigator, was in charge of organizing and executing the study, and also carried out the weekly observations. Prestwood covered literature, background, and library research and investigated the resources of local organizations. Allen was one of the founders of the program for cocaine moms and provided support and expertise throughout the study. Karsham contributed background and materials about parental education, observations from other parenting courses, and assisted with the weekly parenting sessions.

Phase One

Definitions of crime. In the fall of 1989, Hope House was opened, for "cocaine moms" and their children. Although the program was particularly designated for pregnant cocaine-abusing women it also included other women with children who had abused cocaine. It was located in one of the oldest public housing projects in Daytona Beach, Florida. From an economic perspective, the environment was bleak. From a social perspective, drug abuse was a common problem in the neighborhood. From the perspective of the criminal justice system, police activity was high in the area. The impetus for Hope House came from leaders in the health and rehabilitation field in the community and the director of the city's housing authority. A large apartment was set aside for a residential treatment center for "cocaine moms." Furnishings and supplies were largely donated. The center was operated with the support of a black women's social sorority and largely through the efforts of one of its leading members. The home was to provide temporary shelter for mothers with drug treatment problems. The program was meant for pregnant women who had serious drug abuse problems, particularly cocaine. Women were not eligible for residence until they had spent at least 30 days under close supervision for detoxification. In its earliest phase, Hope House was meant to hold approximately six women and one or two of their children. It soon became obvious that many of the residents had more than two children in the custody of relatives or foster parents.

During the first phase, there was no telephone in the house, nor was there a staff member present on a regular basis. A peer counselor was designated to be in charge in the absence of a staff member. This resident-in-charge was the subject of many complaints from the other residents, and she was also implicated when crack use in Hope House was documented. The first program lasted for only a few months. It was closed after a local television station broadcast a news report showing residents dealing in crack cocaine through the windows of Hope House.

During the first phase of the program, there were five women involved. Four of the women were pregnant, three of whom delivered cocaine-free babies. It was not possible to assess directly the extent of prenatal harm done by cocaine; however, one of the babies had extensive birth defects. A fourth pregnant mother left the program shortly before her baby was due.

The failure of Phase One for Hope House showed that treatment for cocaine abuse is complex and difficult. Frequent relapses are common. Despite the bad publicity, there was still support for the program, but Hope House was to undergo a drastic change with reorganization.

Adviser. During the authors' first few visits to Hope House in October 1989, the role of researcher was the most important one. Private interviews were held with four women in residence and with members of the staff and cooperating agencies. After the preliminary visits, one researcher agreed to return to Hope House weekly for parental advising with any of the residents who wanted to meet with her.

For the next two months, parenting sessions were held on a one-to-one basis. Residents were assigned by staff members and volunteered to talk to the researcher about problems with children and family. Regular weekly sessions were informal, personal, and had no particular agenda.

Gaining confidence. During the earliest phase of the parenting program, parental advising sessions and interviews provided a basic, informal needs assessment. These personal one-to-one sessions were the source for topics covered in the parenting classes that followed.

At the same time, during the earliest phase of the program, informal conversations with residents and others involved with Hope House helped the researcher to become more familiar with the environment. Early visits provided a better understanding of the social world of substance-abusing parents through observations and experiences.

In addition, the early phase of parental advising at Hope House served to build some personal relationships. During Phase One, the researcher also had to build a positive reputation and trust. The early relationships laid a foundation on which the parenting program could be built.

Phase Two

Authorities enforce crime. When Hope House was reopened two months later in February 1990, it was located in the same bleak environment, but it was larger and the walls had been painted. More importantly, Hope House had become a part of a network of drug rehabilitative services called the Anti-Recidivist Effort. A small budget was set aside. The focus was still on cocaine mothers, but the organization was a well-established, broader effort to address other substance-abuse problems.

At the same time, greater control was established. A full-time staff position was assigned. A disciplinary regime was clearly posted and enforced. After reorganization, there was increased supervision, surveillance, and structure.

During Phase Two, treatment and training were organized to involve other programs. The increased interaction between programs led to a broader spectrum of parenting problems among the participants. However, it was still considered a "women's program." All of the mothers were substance abusers, and most were addicted to cocaine.

Group leader. After Hope House was reorganized and reopened in February 1990, a more formal series of parenting classes grew out of the preliminary advising sessions. A plan was developed to include 10 of the topics that had been the subjects of many of the preliminary advisory sessions. Materials from many sources were rewritten and adapted to make them meaningful for the parents who were part of the program at Hope House.

During Phase Two, there were as many as 15 women in attendance at the parenting classes. In addition to the residents at Hope House, women from other drug treatment programs were referred to parenting classes by their counselors. Some were ordered to attend parenting classes by the juvenile court judge in hearings over custody of their children.

Classes lasted for an hour once a week. The discussions were often intense and dynamic. In some cases, the mothers felt they were being forced to attend the classes against their will, and resistance or hostility was the result. At times, mothers were understandably angry. Overcoming their initial resistance to change and resentment toward interference were the most important and difficult aspects of the parenting classes.

Routinizing. The second phase of the parenting program was important because, during that time, a routine was established and the parenting program became formalized. In order to standardize the classes, a syllabus was developed. The preliminary materials for the course draw heavily from two sources: Systematic Training in Effective Parenting (STEP) and Glasser's Reality Therapy.

The STEP program includes 10 lessons; for full participation, a parent was expected to complete all ten classes. With the support of the University of Central Florida, a certificate of participation was created. They were awarded to students at their tenth class meeting.

Course completion was useful to participants when they were involved with juvenile court hearings about their children. In some cases, parenting classes were required as a part of a treatment program. In many cases, although the parents came "voluntarily," it was obvious they did not want to be there. Attending parenting classes was held contingent upon other benefits, along with parental rights and custody of children. During Phase Two, the question of a policy of state coercion forcing parents to attend classes became a significant one. It is not a clear-cut issue and is far too complex to be addressed adequately here. However, participants were given as much freedom of choice as possible within the limits that were laid down by the court or by their commitments to substance-abuse treatment programs. Despite initial resistance, many participants expressed appreciation for what they had learned in the classes.

Phase Three

Conceptions about the crime arise. Phase Three of the program involved implementing and maintaining interest in the parenting classes and lasted until the end of 1990. Since students did not always attend consecutive classes, flexibility had to be built into the course so that, with each class, students could be exposed to some basic parenting concepts without being confused or forced to repeat the same lessons again and again. The initial outline was expanded, and the development of a curriculum was under way. The parenting course was built on suggestions from local professionals in all aspects of substance-abuse rehabilitation. Interviews not only solicited their expertise but also served to increase their knowledge and understanding about the parenting classes.

Parenting class instructor. By the closing weeks of 1990, the parenting classes at Hope House had become well established. Fifteen participants had been given certificates for attending at least 10 sessions. Another volunteer got involved in developing materials and acting as discussion director for the classes that were still being held regularly on a weekly basis. In December 1990, the first male parent completed the program. He was court ordered to attend parenting classes in order to retain custody of his daughter, and he chose to attend the classes at Hope House. He brought his daughter with him to one of the sessions.

Community efforts to support the parenting classes were sought. The researchers contacted and interviewed numerous social and judicial professionals whose input was important for the parenting program.

Change and revision. During Phase Three, the parenting classes became even more routinized. "Graduations" were celebrated almost every week. There was a high dropout rate among participants but there was also a high return rate because many students came back again. Some participants attended 10 consecutive weeks; others completed 10 classes over a course of more than 10 weeks.

In order to accommodate the classes to the irregular attendance of the participants, materials had to be changed and revised constantly. Many sources of materials were found. Information from a local child abuse prevention program and a public school parenting program, for example, were adapted for the course. During Phase Three, it was also important to build a broad base of community support for the program. In the course of time, a view of the larger perspective developed. The narrower focus on "cocaine mothers" was broadened to include caregivers, whatever their relationship to children.

Phase Four

Behavior patterns develop from criminal associations. Phase Four involved a reorientation for the parenting program at Hope House in January 1991. The classes expanded to meet the needs of substance-abusing parents and potential parents—mothers and fathers as well as grandparents and other caregivers.

Phase Four is not the final phase, nor is it complete. It is a phase from which radical implications may be drawn. During Phase Four, the responsibility for parenting was placed in a wider context, and the attention on "cocaine moms" was shifted to include "dads" and "families."

Parenting program facilitator. In the early weeks of 1991 a reorientation of the parenting classes took place. Rather than parental advice for cocaine mothers, which had been the goal at the outset, the program had grown into a parenting course for substance-abusing parents. In time, the focus of the research changed from the problem of cocaine moms to the problems in substance abusing families. The curriculum remained flexible, and new materials were sought constantly.

Attendance was bad during the first two weeks of 1991, so redirection was sought. After the successful completion of the program by one substance-abusing father, other males asked to participate. Sessions in late January and February included as many fathers in attendance as mothers. Other family members also came to class from time to time. In one family, both a grandmother and a mother who cared for the same children participated together in the parenting program.

Revitalizing. At the beginning of Phase Four, it became clear that the parenting classes needed revitalization and reorganization.

Attendance and interest had fallen off. At this time, another need for the program arose. Substance-abusing fathers who were committed to The Anti-Recidivist Effort drug treatment program in the same neighborhood as Hope House were included. The day of the class was changed, announcements were printed, and the classes were off to a new start with the beginning of 1991.

At the same time, additional materials were added to the curriculum for the program. Other lessons about responsible parenting were added from numerous sources. As the program developed, materials were divided into 10 sections corresponding with the 10 weeks required for participation. As much variety and flexibility as possible is built into each subject so that it is possible for the participating parents to attend many different classes on the same subject without repetition. Also, different approaches supporting and expanding the ideas of STEP and Glasser's Reality Therapy were added to reinforce important lessons.

Another part of Phase Four of the parenting program involved seeking additional resources. This time all efforts were volunteered, without outside sources of funding. New efforts began to garner other monies to develop the program further. Initially, an application was filed for a local grant for $500 for more information and illustrations to expand the supply of parenting class materials.

This program is merely a beginning. It only begins to address the cogent issues important for parenting in substance-abusing families. In its present low-budget format, the course is only a small part of a parenting program. Class discussion is only a preliminary step. To be really meaningful, parenting courses must also provide learning sessions including parents with children present. Present facilities are inadequate for activities involving parents and children together.

The present classes do not provide adequate meaningful follow-up for the majority of the participants. Future plans, if funds become available, include regular supper sessions for "graduates" and their children to provide support for participants after they complete the class.

Discussion

At the outset of this study, there was a simple focus for our efforts. Some prosecutors had defined being pregnant and addicted to cocaine as a crime and prosecuted women for fetal endangerment. It was significant because it was addressed as a crime only women can commit. Clearly, that is a very limited perspective on the problems that arise for children when their caretakers abuse drugs.

Hope House is a community-based treatment program for cocaine-addicted mothers and their babies. The parenting classes for substance abusers being developed here address the larger issues for families and caregivers. It is an admittedly small step in redirecting the resources and redefining the issues surrounding fetal endangerment away from a narrow focus on cocaine moms. The subjects of future studies will continue to expand to include significant issues for the prevention and treatment of substance-abusing parents.

References

Blakeslee, S. (1991, January 1). Research on birth defects shifts from moms to dads. *The Daytona Beach News Journal*, 2A.

Bracken, M.B., et al. (1990, February). Association of cocaine use with sperm concentration, motility, and morphology. *Fertility and Sterility: Official Journal of the American Fertility Society* , 315–322.

California State Attorney General (1988). *Child abuse prevention handbook.* Sacramento, CA: Crime Prevention Center.

Chasnoff, I., et al. (1989, March 24). Temporal patterns of cocaine use in pregnancy: Perinatal outcome. *Journal of the AMA* , 71.

Congressional Research Service (1990, March 18). *Birth, life and death: Fundamental life decisions and the right to privacy*. Washington, DC: Library of Congress, 4–7.

Critics call crackdown on cocaine moms a bad idea (1990, January 29). *The Orlando Sentinel*, B4.

Curriden, M. (1990). Holding mom accountable. *ABA Journal* (March): 50–53.

Fallon, S.A. (1990). Drug abuse claims babies of addicts. *State Government News* (June): 9–10.

Gest, T. (1989, February 6). The pregnancy police on patrol. *U.S. News and World Report*: 50.

Inciardi, J.A., & Pottieger, A.E. (1986). Drug use and crime among two cohorts of women narcotic users. *The Journal of Drug Issues* (Winter): 91–106.

Johnson, C. (1990, April 23). Testimony of Charlene Johnson to the Select Committee on Children, Youth and Families. In *Reach, Inc.* (pp. 1–4). Washington, DC: U.S. House of Representatives.

Johnson, P. E. (1990). The ACLU philosophy and the right to abuse the unborn. *Criminal Justice Ethics* 9(1): 48–51.

Kantrowitz, B. (1989, October 2). Cocaine babies: The littlest victims. *Newsweek* , 55.

Logli, P.A. (1990). Drugs in the womb. *Criminal Justice Ethics* 9(1): 23–29.

Many disagree with punitive approach to stemming drug abuse during pregnancy (1990). *American Council on Obstetrics and Gynecology* (ACOG) *Newsletter* 35: 5.

Mariner, W.K., Glantz, L., & Annas, G.J. (1990). Pregnancy, drugs and perils of prosecution. *Criminal Justice Ethics* 9(1): 30–40.

Mills, C.E., & Bishop, L. (1990, June). Should pregnant women be held criminally liable for substance abuse? *State Government News*, 22–23, 29.

Nelson, L.J., & Milliken, N. (1988, February 19). Compelled medical treatment of pregnant women. *The Journal of the AMA*: 1060–1066.

New York State Senate (1989, December). *Crack babies: The shame of New York.* Albany, NY: Senate Committee on Investigations, Taxation and Government Operations.

Nolan, K. (1990). Protecting fetuses from prenatal hazards. *Criminal Justice Ethics* 9(1): 13–22.

Paltrow, L. (1990). When becoming pregnant is a crime. *Criminal Justice Ethics* 9(1): 41–47.

Quinney, R. (1970). *The social reality of crime.* Boston: Little, Brown.

U.S. House of Representatives Select Committee on Chi dren, Youth and Families (1990, April 19). *Fact sheet: Women addiction and perinatal substance abuse* .

Zuckerman, B., et al. (1989, March 23). Effects on maternal marijuana and cocaine use on fetal growth. *The New England Journal of Medicine*, 762–768.

Organizational Barriers: Conducting Evaluation Research in Female Correctional Institutions

Phyllis A. Gray
Melvin C. Ray
Mississippi State University

Abstract

The present essay highlights organizational barriers encountered while conducting an evaluation study of rehabilitation programs in a midwestern state's correctional institution for women. Four subgroups (i.e., inmates, prison staff, parole officers, and parolees) were included in the study. Some of the problems encountered by the researchers were a function of characteristics of complex organizations such as miscommunication, formalization, and centralization. This essay gives a detailed account of the strategies employed by the researchers to overcome the barriers encountered. Moreover, the authors recommend strategies to minimize the difficulties associated with correctional research. The major recommendations for future research focus on design strategies and marketing techniques.

Introduction

Over the last 50 years, sociologists have been on the periphery in terms of conducting policy-oriented research in the area of corrections/penology. Moreover, social scientists in general have only recently been recognized by corrections officials as research resources.

Given that most departments of corrections do not have the resources and personnel to conduct policy-related research, they will increasingly solicit the assistance of sociologists and other social scientists.

The American Corrections Association, the primary standards and accreditation governing body for departments of corrections, has urged them to "open their doors" to more outside analysts. In particular, there is a need for research focusing on diverse topics including recidivism, social climate, organizational efficiency, and a variety of evaluation studies. External social researchers are preferred to internal analysts because of their supposedly greater objectivity.

The objective of the present essay is twofold. First, it offers a brief description and discussion of a dichotomous taxonomy of departments of corrections. These ideal types of correctional organizations have implications for social science research projects. Second, this essay presents a qualitative analysis of the barriers encountered by the researchers in their attempts to conduct an evaluation study of rehabilitation programs in a correctional institution for women. The focus of the analyses is on correctional subsystems and processes that are important to social researchers involved in studies related to women in departments of corrections.

The state of women in departments of corrections has been elevated to a legitimate area of study in recent years. The impetus for this change stems from the fact that the female prison population has been increasing annually, women are serving longer sentences, and approximately one-third of all women released from state prisons recidivate (De Constanzo & Scholes 1988). Yet, there is a dearth of studies that have focused solely on the plight of female inmates. One possible explanation for the neglect of women prisoners in the literature is that, in the past, women were imprisoned for less-serious offenses and the size of the population did not lend itself to high-powered quantitative analyses.

Research on women in departments of corrections is still in its formulative years as a scientific body of literature. To augment the development of such a body of knowledge, this study includes the results of a qualitative analysis of correctional subsystems. The observations and accounts were gleaned from a study of women prisoners that was conducted by the researchers.

The focal concerns of the present essay are the organizational types, structures, and subsystems that exist in women's correctional institutions. It is important to note that, because the study was designed to determine the perceived effectiveness of rehabilitation programs in a women's correctional institution, the research design included four correctional subsytems. Each posed unique problems for the researchers.

Typology of Women's Correctional Institutions

Complex organizations became subject to sociological inquiries as a result of Weber's (1947) seminal work *The Theory of Social and Economic Organizations*. He noted that complex organizations, whether they are large, small, private, or public, have similar structures and characteristics that increase their effectiveness or productivity. Weber proposed that specific characteristics (i.e., formalization, centralization, communications) functioned to enhance the efficiency and effectiveness of organizational operations and goal attainment.

Correctional institutions are viewed as complex organizations because they require high levels of coordination and control to obtain their goals. In fact, most of the early prison studies embellished the classical approach to organizations; they focused on the division of labor and superordinate-subordinate relationships among the personnel and inmates (Berk 1977; Cressey 1977; Irwin 1980; Snarr & Wolford 1985).

Treatment vs. Custody Goals

Correctional institutions are not only categorized on the basis of security levels but also in terms of their goal orientation, treatment, or custody. Berk (1977) and Cressey (1977) distinguished between organizational characteristics in treatment- and custody-oriented penal institutions. In treatment institutions, communication networks are open, and for the most part, a complementary mixture of both vertical and horizontal communication patterns exist. As a result, inmates perceive that they are involved in a caring relationship and therapist-client scheme rather than a superordinate-subordinate interaction scheme.

In custody-oriented institutions, according to Leger and Stratton (1977), communication structures are vertical and unilateral. The nondirective information flows upward, while nonexplanatory directives flow downward to the subordinates or front line staff. In these types of organizations, staff members do not enjoy any discretion or decision-making opportunities in terms of dealing with the inmate population. Consequently, there is a strict subordinate vs. superordinate, inmate-staff relationship style.

Based on the aforementioned characteristics of treatment and custody institutions, the facility in this study is categorized as a treatment-oriented correctional institution. Staff and inmates openly communicated; moreover, the women published a monthly newsletter that addressed some of their concerns.

Patterns of Authority (Formalization)

Formalization refers to the rules and procedures that are designed to sustain productivity and goal attainment of the organization. In terms of the rules and procedures that are inherent in complex organizations, Hall (1982) noted that there are two major types: formal and informal. The former refers to written rules and guidelines that are posted in open areas, whereas the latter refers to rules that are derivatives of informal social interactions between the staff and inmates. Formal rules and procedures dominate both custody- and treatment-oriented penal institutions. However, unwritten or informal rules and regulations are more prevalent in treatment-oriented institutions and can, in some cases, be as equally binding as formal rules or regulations.

The degree of formalization varies by goal orientation. That is, rules and procedures are generally more restrictive and punitive in custody institutions than those in treatment-oriented prisons. These differences in formalization influence the social climate in correctional institutions. Personnel in treatment institutions have greater discretionary powers, which aid in the treatment of inmates on an individual level.

Centralization

Centralization refers to the extent and degree to which power is distributed within an organization. The distribution of power is essentially a function of the type or nature of the organization. An organization is said to have a centralized power structure when most decisions are made hierarchically. In contrast, decentralized power structures are described as a system in which major sources of power can be delegated by lower-level decision makers to subordinate personnel. Thus, in highly centralized organizations lower-level personnel are not allowed to make important decisions, and in situations in which they appear to have the authority to do so, the procedures that they follow are programmed by a centralized power structure (Hall 1982).

In custody-oriented institutions, centralization dominates. Centralization of power in custody-oriented institutions is required to ensure strict and unwavering rule enforcement. However, decentralized power structures are most evident in treatment-oriented institutions because decentralized power structures allow for greater flexibility in terms of implementing needed rules and procedures as new situations arise.

Therefore, at the organizational level, social scientists should fiı st identify the goals of the department of corrections in which the study will take place. The goals of penal institutions are not always made explicit in terms of stated objectives and policies; thus, some background information on the institution should be examined before designing the study. Researchers should identify all of the correctional subsystems that will be affected by their studies and identify formal and informal rules and procedural barriers that are likely to present themselves during the course of the study. These barriers can then be addressed prior to the research process, thereby alleviating time delays and aborting key aspects of the study.

The remainder of this essay addresses issues related to an evaluation study of rehabilitation programs in a midwestern state's correctional institution for women. The design of the study provided for the inclusion of responses from the range of correctional subsystems that may be focal concerns of social scientists in the corrections area. Thus, the essay illustrates the sequence of events and procedures that led to the successful completion of the study, in spite of the unique barriers that each subsystem presented to the research team.

This study was the product of a number of factors. First, one of the authors worked as an intern for a midwestern department of corrections' institution for women. It was the only institution for women except for the classification center that housed the maximum security unit for women in the state. During the intern's tenure with the department of corrections, she worked closely with the inmates, staff, and administrative personnel. She was privileged to administrative communications that dealt with inmates, security staff, and treatment staff concerns, procedures, and rules. Moreover, she participated in some of the rules and procedure changes that occurred while she was there. In sum, she acquired some valuable insights into the formal and informal structures and processes that exist in a women's penal institution.

Recidivism had been identified as a salient concern for both inmates and the staff; in the authors' opinion, this information set the stage for the administration's favorable reaction to the study. In addition to the inside information gleaned as an intern, the media had also focused attention on the problem of female recidivism in the state. Thus, the problem was not perceived as an internal problem but as a public concern.

As a result, the study was designed to compare the perceptions of four correctional subsystems in terms of the effectiveness of specific rehabilitation programs on female recidivism in the state. Questionnaires were administered to inmates, prison staff, parole officers, and parolees.

Inmate Organization

Inmate organization refers to the formal and informal structures and processes that characterize inmate relations and behavior patterns. Previous prison studies have identified several components of inmate organization that could serve as barriers in attempts to conduct an evaluation study of rehabilitation programs. Berk (1977) found that inmates' attitudes toward their institutions, staff, and programs, in part, were a function of the type of orientation reflected in the facility, treatment or custody. Inmates in custody-oriented institutions tend to express less-favorable attitudes toward the administration, staff, and programs.

Moreover, inmates in custody-oriented facilities tend to create antagonistic subcultures, thus creating serious problems for the administration and outsiders in terms of obtaining their input on prison issues (Irwin 1980; Irwin & Cressey 1963). Irwin and Cressey reported that inmates develop a convict code in their attempts to adapt to their confinement. The codes include informal rules such as "do not inform," "do not openly interact or cooperate with guards or the administration," and "do your own time."

The prison codes or guidelines posed serious problems to the researchers. For instance, "do not inform"—this rule goes directly against the essence of sociological inquiry, especially inquiries concerning the structures and processes extant in correctional institutions. Inmates who adhere to this rule for fear of being subject to inmate sanctions are reluctant to participate in any external projects.

However, the most pronounced barrier encountered was a function of the code "do not openly interact or cooperate with guards or the administration." Because of the shared interest in determining the perceived relative importance of the various treatment programs on recidivism, the superintendent, acting in her superordinate role, decided that the inmates would be more willing to participate in the study if she were to send them a memo and "ask" for their participation. Because the initial announcement concerning the recidivism study was associated with the superintendent and the department of corrections, the inmates failed to respond because their inclusion in the study would have them violating the most enforced prison code "do not openly interact or cooperate with guards or the administration."

In terms of the initial contact with the inmates about the study, there was some miscommunication between the superintendent and the principal investigator concerning what information would be given to this sample. However, after being informed of the request and the low response rate, the researchers sent each inmate who was eligible to be included in the study a letter explaining that the study was being conducted by a member of the sociology department of a midwestern university and that the researchers were not employees of the department of corrections. Moreover, the inmates were made aware of the objectives of the study, confidentiality measures, and that their participation would be on a voluntary basis.

Upon receiving the memo from the researchers, approximately one-third of the inmates who had initially refused to be included in the study changed their minds and asked to participate. Surprisingly, they (n = 12) were not allowed to participate in the study because of their initial refusal of the superintendent's solicitation. Nevertheless, the inmate sample (n = 54) included 66% of the eligible inmates.

Another barrier that was encountered by the research team in terms of the recidivist inmate population was the relatively low literacy rate. Those inmates who could not read or write had to be interviewed, with someone reading the items to them and soliciting their responses orally. This aspect of the research created an unanticipated barrier in terms of time delays.

Prison Staff Organization

The correctional officers' subsystem has been the focus of several inquiries in general (Crouch 1980; Marquart 1986; Webb & Morris 1978). Other prison studies have focused on specific characteristics of staff and inmates such as race (Hawkins 1976; Kinsell & Sheldon 1981), gender (Alpert 1984; Cullen et al. 1985; Horne 1985; Jurik 1985; Stinchcomb 1986; Zimmer 1986), and educational levels (Cullen et al. 1985; Poole & Regoli 1980).

Gaining rapport with line staff officers and middle management personnel can be difficult due to the degree of formalization within the organization. For example, several studies have found a positive relationship between formalization and alienation existing in complex organizations (Bonjean & Grimes 1970; Dewar & Werbel 1979). In addition, low morale among employees has been found in highly formalized organizations (Cohen 1965; Crozier 1964).

Research focusing on the extent and degree of alienation existing among correctional officers shows that it is often reflected in terms of the guards' perceptions of powerlessness, isolation, and self-estrangement. Overall, alienation has been associated with negative prejudices toward co-workers, inmates, and the administration (Poole & Regoli 1981; Toch & Klofas 1982). Hence, alienation among correctional officers should work to facilitate and perpetuate a sort of subculture, similar to the inmates', among correctional officers. As a result, a correctional officer's code, "do not cooperate with the administration," may exist in both treatment- and custody-oriented facilities. An additional code may also exist: "Do not openly help inmates."

In terms of the focal study, information concerning the research was forwarded to the prison staff members; a letter ensuring confidentiality was also attached to the questionnaire. The package was then placed in each staff member's mailbox. The first wave of the survey was disappointing because only approximately one-fifth of the staff population returned the questionnaire.

Again, similar to the situation with the inmate population, the superintendent had requested or solicited the participation of the staff. After they were ensured that their responses would not affect their job tenure and, more importantly, their identities would not be revealed, some decided to fill out the questionnaires. After the last wave of questionnaires arrived, approximately 50% (n = 32) of the staff members were included in the study.

Parole Officers' Organization

> A parole officer can be seen going off to his/her appointed rounds with Freud in one hand and a .38 Smith and Wesson in the other hand. It is by no means clear that Freud is as helpful as the .38 in most areas where parole officers venture. . . . Is Freud backup to the .38? Or is the .38 carried to support Freud? (Fogel, cited in McCleary 1978:10–11)

The third subsystem to be approached by the researchers was the parole or community corrections organization. Given the focus of this essay, only a brief discussion of the organization's characteristics will be presented; instead the focus of this section is on the factors that acted as barriers to completing the recidivism study.

There is some disparity in terms of parole programs existing in this country; nevertheless, the general structure follows one of three forms (Reid 1987). First, the institutional, which is mainly found in juvenile institutions. In these parole-granting organizations, the correctional staff makes the parole decision. The second organizational form is the independent authority model. The salient characteristic of this model is that it is not integrated with the correctional institution. The other, the "consolidated model," is characterized by the parole-granting authority being in the department of corrections and yet having independent jurisdiction.

Role typologies of parole officers received some attention in previous studies (Czajkoski 1973; Erickson 1977; Glaser 1969; Klockars 1972; Ohlin, Piven, & Pappenfort 1956). As a result, perceptions of the activities and attitudes of parole officers should be taken into consideration when designing a study that calls for their assistance. For example, Ohlin, Piven, and Pappenfort (1956) reported that parole officers develop behavioral styles that influence their attitudes toward co-workers, parolees, and administration. First, the punitive style officer is more of a disciplinarian and is more concerned about molding the parolee according to middle-class values and norms. Punitive officers tend to use coercion in the form of threats and punishment; moreover, he/she is overly suspicious of parolees. But protective and welfare officers are more client oriented; they attempt to assist parolees in any way possible to keep them from returning to prison.

Thus, in terms of the parole officers' subsystem, those officers who could be classified as employing a protective or welfare style were more amenable to helping the researchers conduct their study. In contrast, the punitive officers thought of the study as another way the parolees could attract more bleeding hearts and eventually beat the system.

Similarly, at the managerial level of the parole organization, the researchers were astonished by the litany of miscommunications that took place in terms of the information about the study being filtered down to the line staff. This barrier was a function of "work role constraint" (or its opposite, autonomy) that was privately held by middle management. Payne and Pugh (1976) defined "work role constraint" as the extent and amount of activities personnel could be involved in without authorization from their superordinates. Thus, the concept is somewhat similar to Hall's (1963) "Hierarchy of Authority." In addition, hierarchial communication barriers were also apparent, in terms of the amount of direct supervision or surveillance of subordinates.

The research design called for all parole officers who supervised female parolees to be included in the study. Therefore, the deputy director of community corrections was contacted and asked to cooperate with the research team by informing her managerial and line staff members about the study and to solicit their cooperation. The managerial staff consisted of executive directors who supervised districts across the state. It was at this level that communication problems were the most pronounced.

First, some of the executive directors failed to comply with the deputy director's directives to inform their line staff about the study. Therefore, when some of the parole officers received a packet from the researchers informing them about the study, instructing them to provide their parolees with a questionnaire, and requesting that the parole officers themselves also fill out a survey, they were reluctant because they had not been given authority to do so by their superordinates. This lack of communication caused a time delay and a low response rate for the parole officers and parolees.

Second, one executive director, after being contacted by the deputy director, decided that he needed additional information from the researchers before his district would comply. Thus, role constraint was not enforced severely in the organization, thereby allowing middle management personnel some discretion in terms of responding to directives from their superordinates. Eventually, due to the endless request for additional information and approval forms, neither parole officers nor parolees in that district were included in the study.

Parolees' Organization

Parole officers were also asked to help the research team generate a sample of ex-inmates who had been paroled for at least a year without any parole violation or new sentences. Formalization of rules and procedures prohibited some of the parole officers from assisting in this aspect of the study. However, one executive director, operating within the constraints of the organization's parameters, did generate a computer listing that contained the names, district of residence, phone numbers, and parole officer's name for each parolee who met the criteria. Parolees' addresses could not be released.

As a result, this subgroup had to be interviewed via telephone. However, there was still another hindrance; the phone listing did not include area codes. In the end, only 11 out of 41 of the women who were eligible for the study were interviewed.

Some of the problems encountered with this subgroup were inevitable. First, parolees are transient, thus making it extremely difficult to contact them. Second, some of the parolees harbor some resentments toward the department of corrections, so they refused to assist the researchers in any way, even though they were told that the research was not being conducted by the department of corrections. In that respect, some of the parolees decided to participate voluntarily in the study. Other ex-inmates did not participate in the study due to death or their return to a penal institution.

Discussion of Recommendations

As stated earlier, the American Corrections Association has encouraged departments of corrections to open their doors to outside researchers so that a diverse pool of experts can address the problems inherent in their organizations. Therefore, it is imperative that sociologists become sensitive to the structures and processes that permeate departments of corrections. Background information about an organization's social climate, formalization, centralization, and communication structures will help researchers avoid devastating time delays and nonresponses.

Additionally, future researchers should also use the following recommendations as a guide for conducting policy-oriented research for departments of corrections and research in correctional institutions for women. First, social scientists, in the conceptual stage of their research problems, should familiarize themselves with the organizational structure of the unit of analysis. In this present example, the unit of analysis was both the department of corrections and its subsystems. This is readily accomplished by drawing an organizational diagram. These illustrations provide observers with the likely flow of commands and information.

Second, the researcher should establish rapport with key personnel in the organization. Criminal justice agencies are extremely suspicious of outsiders, especially free-style, liberal academicians. Principal researchers should go to great lengths to have someone on their team who has some experience in corrections. The presence of such an individual will increase the researchers' credibility from the department of corrections perspective.

Third, the conceptualization of the problem and design should be done in cooperation with the department of corrections. This is not to say that the department of corrections should define the problems, rather it should have an opportunity to help clarify the problems from its perspective, so that the researcher is not in direct conflict with the goals of the department.

The design stage of corrections research is one that should be approached with caution and perseverance. Caution is advised because of the legal barriers that are inherent in criminal justice studies; perseverance is advised because of the maze of bureaucratic structures that are encountered before the research is started.

After the research has been approved by the authority-granting components of the organization, the researchers should examine the subsystems that will be contacted and asked to participate in the study. In other words the researchers should study the structures and processes that are likely to exist in various subsystems of interest. Failure to consider such factors is likely to lead to unnecessary delays and modifications.

Fourth, staff and administration's behavioral patterns are generally influenced by the goal of the organization, whether custody or treatment oriented. Administration and staff personnel in custody-oriented institutions tend to stress security concerns and vices of the inmate population. Their obsession with security and routinization conflicts directly with most prison research. Therefore, researchers should design studies that are amenable to highly structured routines and time schedules. However, staff and administrators in treatment-oriented institutions are more open to changes in schedules and routines, and they are relatively more client oriented than are custody personnel.

Fifth, inmates have a distinct organization; it is comprised of both formal and informal rules and procedures. Prison codes vary by type of correctional orientation. Custody-oriented institutions are likely to foster restrictive codes discouraging inmate-staff interaction and cooperation. Thus, in custody-oriented institutions, researchers should analyze the inmate hierarchy and the social climate. The results of these inquiries will alert the researcher to potential barriers.

Characteristically, treatment orientations tend to lessen the saliency of lines of demarcation between staff and inmates. Moreover, the therapist-client interaction scheme weakens the social structures that tend to emerge in custody institutions. Overall, treatment and/or minimum security units are more amenable to prison research than are long-term, maximum security institutions.

Sixth, parole officers are in somewhat of a dubious position. Their job requires them to play several, almost conflicting roles:

punitive versus treatment officers. As stated earlier, parole officers' role styles influence their attitudes toward inmates, administrators, and outsiders. Moreover, their caseloads tend to be overbearing, thus causing them to be overworked and hesitant about taking on any additional responsibilities.

The most effective strategy in working with parole officers is to market the study in terms of its potential to help alleviate some of their caseload problems; that argument will undoubtedly be attractive to parole officers and management personnel. This approach requires the researchers to examine the target parole agency for a short period of time to acquaint themselves with the attitudes and caseloads. In sum, design the study so that it will require the least amount of time and effort of the parole officers.

Finally, the most difficult population to study in terms of recidivism research are parolees. As noted earlier, this is the most transient group. As a result, their whereabouts are generally questionable; addresses and employment status are constantly changing. In addition, telephone numbers are incorrect due to delinquent bills or efforts to avoid contact by their parole officers.

Thus, researchers should allocate considerable time allotments to contacting this sample. It is imperative that rapport is established with the community corrections department and parole officers, because their assistance in providing the necessary information to make contact with parolees is essential.

The approach to employ in soliciting parolees' assistance in the study is similar to the strategy used for inmates. Remember that parolees were once imprisoned and might still adhere to some of the convict codes. Therefore, researchers, in their initial contact with the parolees, should make it perfectly clear that they are in no way employed or associated with the department of corrections. Moreover, parolees are likely to refuse to cooperate for fear of their identity being revealed, thus causing their parole to be revoked. In any event, extreme caution should be given toward confidentiality measures, and they should be explained early in the initial contact.

In conclusion, criminal justice agencies are increasingly looking for scientists to conduct policy-oriented research. The success or failure of these research efforts will depend, to a large extent, on the research design of the study. Moreover, the successful studies in the area of corrections will have taken into consideration characteristics of the organization such as their structures and processes and the organizations of the subsystems of interest to the proposed study.

References

Alpert, G.P. (1984). The needs of the judiciary and misapplication of social research: The case of the female guards in men's prisons. *Criminology* 22: 441–456.

Berk, B. (1977). Organizations, goals and inmate organization. In R. Leger & J. Stratton (Eds.), *The sociology of corrections: A book of readings* (pp. 276–300). New York: Wiley.

Bonjean, C.M., & Grimes, M.D. (1970). Bureaucracy and alienation: A dimensional approach. *Social Forces* 48: 365–373.

Clemmer, D. (1940). *The prison community*. New York: Rinehart and Co.

Cohen, H. (1965). *The demonics of bureaucracy*. Ames: Iowa State University Press.

Cressey, D. (1977). Prison organizations. In R.G. Leger & J.R. Stratton (eds.), *The sociology of corrections: A book of readings* (pp. 20–33). New York: Wiley.

Crouch, B. (1980). The book vs. the boot: Two styles of guarding in a southern prison. In B. Crouch (Ed.), *The keepers* (pp. 207–224). Springfield, IL: Charles Thomas.

Crozier, M. (1964). *The bureaucratic phenomenon*. Chicago, IL: University of Chicago Press.

Cullen, F., Link, B., Wolfe, N., & Frank, J. (1985). The social dimensions of correctional officer stress. *Justice Quarterly* 4: 505–533.

Czajkoski, E.H. (1973). Exposing the quasi-judicial role of the probation officer. *Federal Probation* 37: 9–13.

De Constanzo, E., & Scholes, H. (1988). Women behind bars. *Corrections Today* (June): 104–108.

Dewar, R., & Werbel, J. (1979). Universalistic and contingency predictions of employee satisfaction and conflict. *Administrative Science Quarterly* 24: 426–448.

Erickson, C.L. (1977). Faking it: Principles of expediency as applied to probation. *Federal Probation* 41: 36–39.

Etzioni, A. (1977). Power, goals and organizational compliance structures. In R. Leger & J. Stratton (Eds.), *The sociology of corrections: A book of readings* (pp. 7–20). New York: Wiley .

Fayol, H. (1949). *General and industrial management.* London: Pitman and Sons.

Giallombardo, R. (1966). *Society of women: A study of a women's prison.* New York: Wiley.

Glaser, D. (1969). *The effectiveness of a prison and parole system.* Indian–apolis, IN: Bobbs-Merrill.

Hall, R. (1963). The concept of bureaucarcy. *American Journal of Sociology* 69: 32–40.

——— (1982). *Organizations: Structure and process* (3rd ed.). Englewood Cliffs, NJ: Prentice-Hall.

Hawkins, G. (1976). *The prison: Policy and practice.* Chicago: University of Chicago Press.

Horne, P. (1985). Female correctional officers: A status report. *Federal Probation* 69: 46–54.

Irwin, J. (1980). *Prisons in turmoil.* Boston, MA: Little, Brown.

Irwin, J., & Cressey, D. (1963). Thieves, convicts and the inmate culture. *Social Problems* 10: 142–155.

Jurik, N.C. (1985). An officer and a lady: Organizational barriers to women working as correctional officers in men's prisons. *Social Problems* 32: 375–388.

Kinsell, L.W., & Sheldon, R.G. (1981). A survey of correctional officers at a medium security prison. *Corrections Today* 43: 40–51.

Klockars, C.B. (1972). A theory of probation supervision. *Journal of Criminal Law, Criminology and Police Science* 63: 550–557.

Leger, R.G., & Stratton, J.R. (1977). *The sociology of corrections: A book of readings.* New York: Wiley.

McCleary, R. (1978). *Dangerous men: The sociology of parole.* Beverly Hills, CA: Sage.

Marquart, J. (1986). Doing research in prison: The strengths and weaknesses of full participation as a guard. *Justice Quarterly* 3: 15–32.

Ohlin, L.E., Piven, H., & Pappenfort, D.M. (1956). Major dilemmas of the social worker in probation and parole. *National Probation and Parole Association Journal* 2: 21–25.

Payne, R.L., & Pugh, D.S. (1976). Organizational structure and climate. In M.D. Dunnette, (Ed.), *Handbook of industrial and organizational psychology* (pp. 1125–1174). Chicago: Rand McNally.

Poole, E.D., & Regoli, R.M. (1980). Role stress, custody orientation and disciplinary actions: A study of prison guards. *Criminology* 18: 215–226.

——— (1981). Alienation in prison: An examination of the work relations of prison guards. *Criminology* 19: 251–270.

Reid, S.T. (1987). *Criminal justice: Procedures and issues*. St. Paul, MN: West Publishing.

Smith, R., Milan, M., Wood, L., & McKee, J. (1976). The correctional officer as a behavioral technician. *Criminal Justice and Behavior* 4: 345–360.

Snarr, R.W., & Wolford, B. (1985). *Introduction to corrections*. Dubuque, IA: Wm. C. Brown.

Stinchcomb, J.B. (1986). Correctional officer stress: Looking at the causes, you may be the cure. Paper presented at annual meeting, Academy of Criminal Justice Sciences, Orlando, FL.

Toch, H., & Klofas, J. (1982). Alienation and desire for job enrichment among correction officers. *Federal Probation* 46: 35–44.

Webb, G.L., & Morris, D.G. (1978). *Prison guards: The culture and perspective of an occupational group*. Austin: Coker Books.

Weber, M. (1947). *The theory of social and economic organizations* (Ed. by T. Parsons, trans. by A.M. Henderson & T. Parsons). New York: Oxford University Press.

Zey-Ferrell, M. (1979). *Dimensions of organizations: Environment, context, structure, process, and performance*. Santa Monica, CA: Goodyear Publishing Company.

Zimmer, L. (1986). *Women guarding men*. Chicago: University of Chicago Press.

Epilogue

Predicting what the female offender will be like by the year 2000 is an excellent strategy for ending this publication. Some contend that we now have the so-called "new female criminal." However, the question arises: Does the new female criminal really exist?

That the female criminal today is much different from what she was yesterday considering the types of crimes that she is now engaging in, by the year 2000 we will continue to see a "changed female criminal." Such changes involving female criminality will be greatly influenced by social and economic (domestic, international) forces. Nevertheless, for the three major sections covered in this text, I make the following predictions.

Prevalence, Crime Typology

In some aspects, the incidence rate for female crime will increase, especially, for property offenses—larceny-theft, fraud, illegal drug involvement (sales, usage), and embezzlement. The gender inequality experienced in the workplace by women will strongly influence female criminality. For example, as more women continue to occupy low-paying jobs while confronted with social and economic pressures, they will be more prone to crimes such as embezzlement, fraud, and forgery.

The "War on Drugs" will continue to contribute significantly to the number of women entering jails and prisons. More women will become chemically dependent either on drugs (cocaine, crack) or alcohol. Consequently, correctional officials will continue their quests for better treatment programs to assist female offenders with drug addiction problems.

To some, considering female criminality today, chivalry may indeed seem dead, particularly in the criminal justice system. It still exists, however. But as more women are arrested for crimes that increasingly resemble those of their male counterparts, we can expect to see a decrease in chivalry from police officers, prosecutors, and judges.

Moreover, it is expected that, as women commit more-serious crimes, there will be an even greater need for equalization in punishment, bringing it in line with crimes traditionally in the male domain. Women will receive more-severe sentences for the more-serious crimes. In fact, we can expect to see an increase in violent crime among female offenders (aggravated assault, homicide, child abuse).

Due to current socioeconomic conditions regarding women, more delinquency will occur among girls reared in lower-class households, as well as father-dominated households—that is, households that stress domesticity for girls. Therefore, female juvenille delinquency will be increasingly similar to male juvenile delinquency.

Research and Programmatic Treatment Needs

Because of the lack in research necessary for understanding more about female criminals, the following are suggestions for further research germane to the topic of female criminality:

1. Further studies are necessary relevant to the dynamics of female criminality and how criminal justice officials (police, court officials, probation officers, prosecuting attorneys, and judges) react to female criminals.
2. More research is needed to ascertain how the female offender differs from her male counterpart on the basis of offense type.
3. Chivalric treatment of female criminals should be systematically researched using crime typology, education, and socioeconomic status to determine which female criminals inspire the most chivalry.

4. More research studies should explore black female criminality at all stages of the criminal justice system.
5. Additional research is vitally important to understanding the causes of female juvenile status offending and especially the role of parents in the detention of female status offenders. Even family structure should be studied in relation to its impact on juvenile female criminality.
6. Studies should be conducted to examine the impact of drugs (alcohol, crack, cocaine, heroin, etc.) on female criminal activity.
7. Evaluation research should be done on an ongoing basis to assess the effectiveness of current programs (academic, vocational, social, psychological) operating within female prisons and female juvenile detention centers as well as in community correctional programs.

Program/Treatment Needs of Female Offenders

At the correctional level, the following programs are recommended:

1. Implement more programs that will combat the illiteracy problems among female offenders, enabling more women to become eligible for vocational and academic training.
2. Establish appropriate drug counseling programs to assist female offenders with problems of drug addiction.
3. Establish programs that, whenever feasible, would permit female criminals to work in private industry, i.e., as bookkeeper, keypuncher, receptionist, etc.
4. Establish a "volunteer buddy system" that will enable female offenders to interact with successful noncriminal women from the community.
5. Provide female criminals with parent training programs that will enable them to develop more effective parent training skills. In addition, expand the parent and child visitation programs in female institutions.

6. Provide training for female offenders that would assist them with self-esteem enhancement.
7. Establish more programs to protect young females from sexual and physical attack in the home.
8. Implement peer programs using noncriminal peers for juvenile female offenders.
9. Establish programs that address the needs of the small number of older female offenders (geriatric services).
10. Establish programs for handicapped female offenders.

Biographical Sketches

JAY ALBANESE is Professor and Chair of the Department of Political Science and Criminal Justice at Niagara University. He was Visiting Professor at the School of Criminology at Simon Fraser University in British Columbia, Canada, in 1988. Dr. Albanese received his B.A. degree from Niagara University and M.A. and Ph.D. from the School of Criminal Justice at Rutgers University. He is the author of eight books on issues of crime and justice, including *Organized Crime in America* (2nd ed.) (Anderson, 1989), *Myths & Realities of Crime and Justice* (3rd ed.) (Apocalypse, 1990), *Crime: A Dozen of America's Existing and Emerging Problems* (with Robert Pursley) (Prentice Hall, 1993), and *Dealing with Delinquency* (2nd ed.) (Nelson-Hall, 1993). Dr. Albanese was recipient of the Teaching Excellence and Campus Leadership Award from the Sears Foundation for 1989–1990 and is Past President of the Northeastern Association of Criminal Justice Sciences.

CLEMENS BARTOLLAS is Professor of Sociology, University of Northern Iowa, Cedar Falls. His educational background includes a B.D. in Theology from the Princeton Theological Seminary. His publications involve correctional administration, correctional treatment program, and juvenile delinquency.

WILLIAM R. BLOUNT, Ph.D., is Professor and Chair of the Department of Criminology at the University of South Florida in Tampa. Dr. Blount has a long-standing interest in female criminality, having participated in the generation of several large databases focusing on women and crime. His interest in domestic violence/spouse abuse originated from his involvement with alcohol addiction research and treatment programs, since aggression is characteristic in households with addicts. His most recent research includes a study of the impact of the legal lottery on illegal numbers games, a risk assessment study of both male and female inmates in Florida, an evaluation of a project designed to improve processing of injunctions for protection against domestic violence, and a survey of law enforcement officers' attitudes concerning arrests for spousal violence.

DEAN J. CHAMPION received his Ph.D .from Purdue University in 1965. He taught at the University of Tennessee until 1990, when he joined the Criminal Justice faculty at the California State University, Long Beach. His publications include 14 texts, an edited work, and numerous articles. Some of his more recent books are *Corrections in the United States* (Prentice-Hall), *The Juvenile Justice System* (Macmillan), *Criminal Justice in the United States* and *Probation and Parole in the United States* (both Merrill/Macmillan), and *Felony Probation* and *The U.S. Sentencing Guidelines* (both Praeger Publishers). Forthcoming are *Research Methods for Criminal Justice and Criminology* (Prentice Hall), *Predicting Dangerousness and Risk* (Greenwood Press), and *Police-Community Relations* (Prentice Hall, co-author George E. Rush). His articles have appeared in the *Journal of Criminal Justice*, *Crime and Justice*, *Journal of Contemporary Criminal Justice*, *American Journal of Criminal Justice*, *Crime and Delinquency*, and *Criminal Justice Review*. His professional interests include judicial and prosecutorial decision making, juvenile rights, and jailhouse lawyers/correctional law.

NOREEN L. CHANNELS is a Professor in the Department of Sociology at Trinity College, and an Adjunct Professor at the University of Connecticut Law School. She has a master's degree in Social Work from the University of Connecticut and a Ph.D. in Sociology from Michigan State University. Her professional work is in the uses of social science methods and information in nonacademic contexts, especially legal settings; she has published a volume entitled *Social Science Methods in the Legal Process*. In research related to that reported in this volume, Channels and Sharon Herzberger recently published "Criminal-Justice Processing of Violent and Nonviolent Offenders: The Effects of Familial Relationships to the Victim" in *Abused and Battered*, edited by Dean Knudsen and JoAnn Miller.

CONCETTA C. CULLIVER, editor, is an Assistant Professor and Director of Criminal Justice at Murray State University. She has worked in correctional administration with adult and juvenile offenders (male, female) and has served as a consultant to several criminal justice agencies in the U.S. Virgin Islands and several eastern Caribbean islands. She has evaluated and planned literacy training programs for female offenders and was named at the request of the Governor of the Virgin Islands to serve on the Correctional Task Force Commission, and by the Governor of Maryland to serve on the Juvenile Delinquency Task Force Commission. She has written and published a variety of articles involving criminal justice.

THOMAS DURANT, JR., Ph.D., is currently Associate Professor of Sociology, Louisiana State University, Baton Rouge. His teaching and research concerns criminology, gerontology, and international development. He earned the doctorate in sociology at the University of Wisconsin, Madison. He has published extensively in the areas of socioeconomic development in developing countries in Africa, social gerontology, and ethnic minorities and has done extensive international travel in connection with his research. His most current research involves factors influencing technology transferral from research agencies to resource-poor farmers in Uganda and factors influencing alienation among the elderly. He has received a number of professional and community service awards. Among his professional service awards are the Urban League of Greater New Orleans Research Award, the International Service Award, and the U.S. Peace Corps Beyond War Award.

CRAIG J. FORSYTH is an Associate Professor of Sociology at the University of Southwestern Louisiana. His current research interests include deviant lifesytles, maritime law, and the sociology of family and work.

JAMES ALAN FOX is a Professor and Interim Dean of the College of Criminal Justice at Northeastern University in Boston. His publications include 8 books, 30 articles, and 20 columns, primarily in the areas of criminal statistics and mass/serial murders. Also, Dr. Fox is the founder and Editor-in-Chief of the *Journal of Quantitative Criminology.* As a nationally recognized authority on homicide, Dr. Fox has appeared on hundreds of television and radio programs around the country. Finally, Professor Fox frequently gives lectures and expert testimony, including three appearances before the U.S. Congress.

ROBERT GRAMLING is Professor of Sociology at the University of Southwestern Louisiana. His research interests lie in the areas of social impacts of economic activity, particularly on the family and crime and microscopic social theory.

PHYLLIS A. GRAY is an Assistant Professor of Sociology and a Research Sociologist at Mississippi State University. She is a 1982 graduate of South Carolina State College and received her master's (1984) and Ph.D. (1987) from Iowa State University. She is a specialist in criminology and race relations, and her research has focused on female offenders, juvenile detention, blacks on white campuses, and black youth. Her research has appeared in the *Journal of Research in Crime and Delinquency*, *Explorations in Ethnic Studies*, and *Youth and Society*.

SHARON D. HERZBERGER is Professor and Chairperson of the Department of Psychology at Trinity College. She earned her master's and doctoral degrees from the University of Illinois. Her research focuses on child abuse and aggression within the family. Among her publications is a recent article in *American Behavioral Scientist* (1990) entitled "The Cyclical Pattern of Child Abuse: A Study of Research Methodology."

FRANK H. JULIAN received his law degree from West Virginia University. After a stint as a practicing attorney, he turned his energies to higher education teaching and administration. After serving nearly 20 years as a dean or vice president, he became a full-time faculty member (Associate Professor of Legal Studies) at Murray State University. He is the author of dozens of published articles on a wide range of topics. His research and publication record over the past half-dozen years reflects his interest in various legal issues, management practices, leadership development, and outcomes assessment. He also has served for several years as the editor of a quarterly higher education newsletter distributed throughout the South.

RENÉE GOLDSMITH KASINSKY is Associate Professor of Criminal Justice at the University of Massachusetts at Lowell. She edited *Crime Oppression and Inequality,* Ginn Press, subsidiary of Simon & Schuster (1991), which explores issues of class, race, gender, and age in relation to crime. She also has an interest in international refugees and law. Her earlier book, *Refugees from Militarism: Draft-Age Americans in Canada,* nominated for the Sorokin Award, was published by Transaction, Rutgers State University Press (1976). Her current writings focus on gender in relation to both white-collar and common crime. She is the editor of the series, "Feminism and the Social Sciences" for Peter Lang Publishers.

JOSEPH B. KUHNS III, M.A., a Senior Statistician for the University of South Florida Foster Child Study Project, a grant held by the Department of Epidemiology and Policy Analysis, Florida Mental Health Institute, University of South Florida. He completed his M.A. in Criminology in August 1990 at the University of South Florida and is pursuing a doctorate in Research and Measurement. He is currently managing a research project that is attempting to measure the effects of an intensive wraparound intervention program for foster children in Tampa, based on educational achievement, emotional/behavioral development, and familial reintegration. He has participated in research in the areas of substance abuse, prostitution and AIDS knowledge.

JACK LEVIN received an M.S. in Communication Research in 1965 and a Ph.D. in Sociology in 1968, both from Boston University. He is a Professor of Sociology at Northeastern University in Boston. His publications include 12 books (including *Mass Murder: America's Growing Menace,* with James A. Fox) and approximately 90 articles and columns in professional journals, popular magazines, and newspapers. His works in progress include *The Gainesville Campus Murders* (with J. Fox) to be published by Avon Books and *Hate Crimes: Prejudice and Violence in America* (with J. McDevitt) to be published by Plenum Press. He has appeared frequently on national television and is often cited by the national press. He was CASE Professor of the Year in Massachusetts for 1991.

JOAN MCCORD, Ph.D., is Professor of Criminology at Temple University. Her research has included studies of the etiology and prevention of various forms of deviant behavior. Past President of the American Society of Criminology and former Chair of the Crime, Law, and Deviance Section of the American Sociological Association, she is Vice Chair of the National Research Council's Committee on Law and Justice.

SUE MAHAN is an Associate Professor and Coordinator of the Criminal Justice Program for the University of Central Florida at Daytona Beach. She is a co-author with Ralph Weisheit of *Women Crime and Criminal Justice* published by Anderson Press in 1988. She has written papers and articles about female offenders, co-ed prisons, and prison violence, among other subjects. She was named a Kellogg Fellow for 1992–1993 for her work in international development.

CHRIS E. MARSHALL is an Assistant Professor in the Department of Criminal Justice at the University of Nebraska at Omaha. He received his Ph.D. in Sociology from Iowa State University. His theoretical interests include the interplay of social control and power. He is currently working on a theoretical reconceptualization of techniques of social control used in modern society. Other research interests include fear of crime, self-protective measures utilized by citizens, and the use of weapons by crime victims in self-defense.

INEKE HAEN MARSHALL is a Professor in the Department of Criminal Justice at the University of Nebraska at Omaha. She grew up in the Netherlands, is a Dutch citizen, and maintains personal and professional ties with the Netherlands. She received her graduate training both in the Netherlands (Catholic University, Brabant) and the United States (College of William and Mary and Bowling Green State University). She has published several articles on Dutch crime and crime control, and she is in the process of co-editing a book on drugs and drug policy in the Netherlands. She is currently involved in an international self-report study of youthful misbehavior funded by the National Science Foundation. Additional areas of interest include comparative criminology, women and the law, and criminal careers.

MARTIN MILKMAN is an Assistant Professor in the Department of Economics and Finance at Murray State University. Dr. Milkman received his B.A. from Brandeis University in 1982, where he graduated with honors in Economics. He received his M.S. in 1986 and his Ph.D. in 1989 from the Department of Economics at the University of Oregon. Dr. Milkman's major research interests are labor economics and the economics of education. In addition to his position at Murray State University, he has served as an economist at the United States Department of Energy and as a Visiting Professor at Gonzaga University and the University College of Belize. Some of his recent publications appear in the *Journal of Education for Business*, the *Journal of Research and Development in Education*, the *Social Science Perspectives Journal*, and the *National Social Sciences Journal.*

DELLA ALICE PRESTWOOD is a Substance Abuse Counselor for the Reality House treatment program in Volusia County, Florida. Her interest in the criminalization of pregnancy developed from her senior research project while she was an undergraduate student at the University of Central Florida. She graduated with honors in 1990 and is currently working on a master's degree at the University of Florida in Gainesville.

POLLY F. RADOSH is an Associate Professor of Sociology at Western Illinois University. Dr. Radosh received her Ph.D. in 1983 from Southern Illinois University-Carbondale. She taught at the University of Minnesota-Morris for one year and has been teaching at Western Illinois University since 1984. She has published articles primarily on topics related to women's social status and women's crime. She has published in *Humanity and Society*, *Sociological Spectrum*, the *Journal of Crime and Justice, Population Research and Policy Review*, and *Sociology Analysis*.

MELVIN C. RAY is an Assistant Professor of Sociology and Corrections Coordinator at Mississippi State University. He received his doctorate from Iowa State University. His recent works have appeared in *The Journal of Social Psychology*, *Youth and Society*, and *Sociological Spectrum*. He is currently conducting research in the areas of drug control program evaluation, juvenile detention, criminal justice policies and minorities, youth gangs, and labeling theory.

CORAMAE RICHEY MANN, Professor of Criminal Justice at Indiana University, Bloomington, received undergraduate and graduate degrees in clinical psychology from Roosevelt University in Chicago and her Ph.D. in sociology (criminology) from the University of Illinois, Chicago. Her research has been directed toward those oppressed by the juvenile and criminal justice systems: youth, women, and racial/ethnic minorities. The author of numerous scholarly articles and book chapters on these topics and a book, *Female Crime and Delinquency*, Dr. Mann just completed *Unequal Justice: A Question of Color* and is currently writing *Women Murderers: Deadliest of the Species?* As a Ford Foundation Research Fellow, Dr. Mann studied the processing of women in felony courts; her current research on women murderers was inspired by that fellowship challenge. Dr. Mann's teaching interests include minorities and crime, juvenile justice, females and crime, homicide, career criminals, the ecology of crime, and victimless (vice) crimes.

SHELLEY B. ROBERTS is Project Director of the Retired Seniors Volunteer Program in Lafayette, Louisiana. She received her B.A. in Sociology from the University of Southwestern Louisiana.

RUTH SEYDLITZ is an Assistant Professor at the University of New Orleans. Her research interests include delinquency, racial and ethnic relations on college campuses, media communications, and environmental issues. She has published articles on male and female delinquency and the effects of media reports of hazard events on the public's responses. She has presented research on male and female delinquency and on the effect of oil industry development on social disorganization, long-term human capital, and the economics of health in Louisiana communities.

IRA J. SILVERMAN, Ph.D., is a Professor of Criminology at the University of South Florida. He has published widely on a variety of criminal justice topics with much of his research centering on female criminality. Currently, he is involved in a 10-year follow-up study of patterns of female crime at two Florida correctional institutions and a study of spouse abuse. He has published several books, including *The Nature of Crime* (Saunders 1978) and *Crime and Criminology* (Harper & Row 1986) and is currently working on a text in Corrections under contract to West Publishing Company.

RITA J. SIMON received her Ph.D. from the University of Chicago. She is a University Professor of Law and Public Affairs at The American University. Among her recent publications are *The Crimes Women Commit, The Punishments They Receive* and *Women's Movements in America: Their Successes, Disappointments, and Aspirations.* She has served as Editor of *The American Sociological Review* (1978–1990) and the *Justice Quarterly* (1983–1985).

DARRELL STEFFENSMEIER is a Professor of Sociology at the Pennsylvania State University, University Park. His research interests include the sociology of law, organized crime, and structural covariates of crime (including race, gender, and age). His recent book, *The Fence: In the Shadow of Two Worlds*, was the recipient of the 1987 Award of Outstanding Scholarship of the Society for the Study of Social Problems. During 1990–1991 he served as Project Director and Principal Writer of *1990 Report—Organized Crime in Pennsylvania: A Decade of Change.*

CATHY STREIFEL is a recent Ph.D. of Pennsylvania State University (1989) and now is Assistant Professor of Sociology at Purdue University. She has co-authored articles on gender and crime and age and crime that have appeared in major criminology and sociology journals. Her current research interests include gender and crime deviance, judicial decision making, and homelessness.

SARAH TINKLER is an Associate Professor in the Department of Economics at Weber State University. Dr. Tinkler received her B.A. from Cambridge University in England, where she graduated with honors. She then attended the University of Oregon, where she received her M.S. in Economics in 1987, and her Ph.D. in Economics in 1989. Dr. Tinkler's research interests include economic education and labor economics. Dr. Tinkler's recent research has focused on the effectiveness of Writing Across the Curriculum (WAC) programs.

NANCI KOSER WILSON is Associate Professor of Criminology at Indiana University of Pennsylvania, where she is also a member of the Women's Studies faculty. Her research has focused on feminist criminology and, more recently, environmental crime. Recent publications include "Gendered Interaction in Criminal Homicide," in Anna F. Kuhl (Ed.), *The Dynamics of the Victim-Offender Interaction* (forthcoming from Anderson Press) and "Feminist Pedagogy in Criminology," in the *Journal of Criminal Justice Education* 2(1), (Spring 1991).

BENJAMIN S. WRIGHT received his Ph.D. in Criminology from Florida State University and is currently an Assistant Professor in the Department of Criminal Justice at the University of Baltimore. His past research interests have included an investigation into the use of psychological tests as predictors of recruit police performance, race and gender influences in field training officer program evaluations, federal sentencing guidelines and recidivism, and the link between police productivity and the crime clearance rate. At this time, he is involved in the project that explores patterns of racial disparity observed in the arrest rate. His current research interests involve understanding how race, ethnicity, and gender influence how individual suspects are processed at each state in the criminal justice process.